CHEYENNES AND
HORSE SOLDIERS

CHEYENNES AND HORSE SOLDIERS

THE 1857 EXPEDITION
AND THE BATTLE OF SOLOMON'S FORK

By

William Y. Chalfant

Foreword by Robert M. Utley

Illustrations by Roy Grinnell

University of Oklahoma Press : Norman and London

Dedication

This book is dedicated to my children, David and Kristin, who encouraged me to write it, to my dear wife, Martha, without whose help, encouragement, and support it could not have been written, and to those men of the old First Cavalry and of the Cheyenne Tribe whose story it is.

Library of Congress Catalogue Card Number: 89-32203
ISBN: 0-8061-2194-7

The paper in this book meets the guidelines for permanence and durability of the Committee on Production Guidelines for Book Longevity of the Council on Library Resources, Inc.∞

CONTENTS

Part Two
The Expedition's March to the South Platte

Part Three
A Rendezvous with Destiny

Part Four
The Pursuit

Part Five
The Finale

Illustrations

Sketches

Photographs

Maps

Foreword
By Robert M. Utley

The struggle between Indian and white for possession of the North American continent continues to captivate the public. The interest is understandable, for the story is a significant and dramatic theme in the history of the United States.

In popular perceptions, the two decades following the Civil War, the period that features Custer's Last Stand and the final surrender of Geronimo, overshadow all that went before. But much that went before is also dramatic and significant, sometimes more significant.

Such are the events treated in this book. For sheer drama, the clash between cavalry and Cheyennes on Solomon's Fork can hardly be surpassed in the history of Indian conflict. In significance, it is a pivotal event in the origins of a quarter century of warfare between the U.S. Army and the tribes of the Great Plains.

With this book, William Y. Chalfant has plugged one of the large gaps in the history of Indian hostilities between the Mexican War and the Civil War. Reflecting popular preoccupation with later events, historians have slighted this period. Until now, no satisfactory account of the scope of this book has treated the first major collision between whites and Cheyennes on the southern plains.

Of many virtues, this book boasts two that deserve highlighting. First, although an attorney by profession, Chalfant has mastered the skills of both indoor and outdoor research. He has dug deeply into official records, private papers and diaries, Indian accounts, and other original sources. No known shred of paper bearing on the subject has been left unstudied. Also, paper in hand, he has stood on and pondered virtually every square foot of landscape on which the events of his story took place. Both his text and his specially commissioned maps reflect this careful attention to terrain. This combination of indoor and outdoor research, first celebrated by Francis Parkman but all too rare in recent years, has resulted in the first comprehensive, truly authoritative telling of this stirring chapter in the history of the Great Plains.

A second virtue is a sharp focus on both sides of the battle lines. His narrative shifts back and forth in order to show the movements of both adversaries. More important, he has penetrated the culture of each to probe the motives, attitudes, and ways of thinking and behaving that gave direction and meaning to the movements. This is the story not solely of two peoples in conflict, but of human beings caught up in historical forces beyond their comprehension.

Here is history that will stand the test of time.

Acknowledgments

A book is the culmination of the efforts of many people, a history probably more than most, and the author is merely the one among them who drew together on the written page the knowledge gleaned from their joint efforts. It is therefore appropriate to take a moment to give credit to those whose unstinting efforts enabled a story to be told.

The Bibliography at the end of the book reveals a part of my debt, but only a part. The essential hours of research were provided by staff members in libraries, state historical societies, national historic sites, the National Archives, and many others. To name them all would, of course, be impossible, but all have earned my deep gratitude. Especially worthy of note are the contributions of a few. Sara Judge, Bob Knecht, and Don Rowlison of the Kansas State Historical Society were ever ready to lend their time and efforts, as were others in the historial societies of Kansas, Nebraska, Colorado, Wyoming, Virginia, and Missouri.

Ready assistance was likewise given by staff members of the Library of Congress; the National Archives; the American Antiquarian Society of Worcester, Massachusetts; the Henry E. Huntington Library, San Marino, California; the United States Military Academy Library, West Point, New York; and the Spencer Research Library of the University of Kansas. Terry Van Meter, curator of the United States Cavalry Museum, Fort Riley, Kansas, supplied invaluable information. John Metcalf of Hill City, Kansas, was kind enough to share with me his prodigious knowledge of the battle site and what took place there in 1857 and since.

Special thanks must go to George F. McCleary of the University of Kansas School of Cartography, Department of Geography-Meteorology, who along with his son John B. McCleary, and former students Nancy M. Fightmaster, Karen Lee Tucker, Dennis R. Albers, Jefferson S. Rogers, and Michael D. Kempainen, developed the maps used to illustrate the narative. The journal of Lt. Eli Long was found by Richard J. Sommers, Ph.D., Archivist-Historian at the U.S. Army Military History Institute at Carlisle Barracks, Pennsylvania. To him I am most indebted. For her review of the letters and diary of 1st Lt. J. E. B. Stuart, I also owe special thanks to my young friend Mary (Molly) Carey, of Richmond, Virginia.

Research is only one facet of the help a writer needs. Carolyn McGovern, a cousin by marriage, tried to impress upon me the importance and need for careful editing. I appreciate her help. This aided the yeoman efforts of my wife, Martha, who used up many hours and days in trying to keep my words flowing in an intelligible and grammatical form, and who otherwise endured with stoicism the life of a widow while her husband wrote. Without her constant assistance, patience, encouragement, and devotion, it would not have been done.

One to whom I am especially grateful is a scholar who more than any other living white man knows and understands the Cheyennes and their culture. Father Peter J. Powell of Chicago, Illinois freely offered his assistance and advice to enable me to write about the expedition from the perspective of the Cheyennes. I am equally indebted to another. Robert M. Utley of Santa Fe, New Mexico shared his wisdom and vast experience with me by reviewing, critiquing and making suggestions to improve the end product. Another Santa Fean, Roy C. Grinnell, an accomplished artist and a distant relative of George Bird Grinnell, the early authority on the Cheyenne Indians, contributed the careful illustrations used to bring to life important parts of the story.

Last but not least, are those who made the greatest contribution, but to whom it is impossible to do more than give recognition. These include the late John G. Neihardt, a man I greatly admire for his brilliant prose and poetry. With the kind consent of his daughter, Hilda Neihardt Petri, the trustee of his trust, I have quoted from his *Song of the Indian Wars* at the beginning of each chapter.* Necessarily included are George Dashiell Bayard, who had the foresight to write letters home during the expedition; David S. Stanley, who committed his memory of the expedition to paper in his memoirs; J. E. B. Stuart, whose diary and letters add a broad dimension to the story; and Robert M. Peck, a journalist who in later life reconstructed the expedition from his diary and notes to create a remarkable series of articles in his Washington, D.C., newspaper. Greatest of all was the assistance rendered by Eli Long, whose careful journal recounted each day as he experienced it on the march. Within the limits of his knowledge of the country, he was a careful and astute observer and a man of great and gentle humor. I should like to have known him.

To all of the above, and to others who rendered their help, I give my heartfelt thanks. I hope I shall not have wasted their efforts.

WILLIAM Y. CHALFANT

Hutchinson, Kansas

The Song of the Indian Wars is still in print and available from the University of Nebraska Press, Lincoln, Nebraska. It is now included in the *Twilight of the Sioux*, volume 2 of *The Cycle of the West*.

Prologue

The story that follows is true. It recalls events that took place near the end of the sixth decade of the nineteenth century, at a time when Plains Indians still lived their free, traditional life and roamed over the vast territories they inhabited like the great herds of buffalo they hunted across the seemingly limitless expanse of grassland. White culture, advancing inexorably westward, like a rising tide lapped hungrily at the eastern borders of the Indian country, as if seeking the right excuse to engulf it and make the land its own. In the East, forces were at work that would delay but not deter the process, for the question of states' rights was about to be settled over the issue of slavery. In the West, the fate of the Plains Indians was already in the balance, with white travelers and immigrants moving over the Santa Fe and Oregon-California trails in ever-increasing numbers, slaughtering the great herds of buffalo and other wildlife as they passed and depriving the Indians of the food supply nature had given them.

Against this background, long ago, in the valley of a small stream flowing through the high plains of what is now northwestern Kansas, occurred an event of the sort from which legends are born. Somehow the story fell into obscurity. Yet for a brief moment the Cheyenne Expedition of 1857 brought together on the stage of history men whose names would within the next two decades become familiar to people across the nation. Theirs was a story filled with real heroes and events born of the struggle between them. For this remote contest there was, unfortunately, no chronicler. Later events involving most of its participants, Indians and whites alike, during the period of the War Between the States and the Indian wars, overshadowed the drama played out in this distant and then unknown part of the Great Plains. However, it involved an equally dramatic and significant confrontation between the people of two cultures, a page in the continuing tragedy of the Plains Indians. It is this story, from the perspective of both sides, that follows.

For a reader to comprehend the events that climaxed in the battle at Solomon's Fork, it is necessary to understand the people and circumstances of a different day and the mores and attitudes that influenced their thinking. One must try to imagine a time before roads and towns, before buildings, trees, and cultivated fields, before any physical evidence of European culture on the Great Plains. The arena for this drama was a great ocean of grass, broken here and there by some surprising range of hills or buttes or by the sparse and scattered stands of cottonwoods rising above the banks of the shallow streams that meandered through the emptiness.

Across the immense wilderness of the plains roamed herds of bison and antelope in numbers so great as to defy an accurate count by the first awestruck white intruders. Deer, bear, elk, prairie wolves, coyotes, and other forms of wildlife—winged and four-legged—also were there in profusion. This vast preserve served as hunting ground and larder for various tribes of nomadic Plains Indians. Living a life in harmony with nature, they were intelligent, proud, independent, warlike, and protective of the lands which they believed had been given them by the Creator, and which they needed to sustain their people.

By the beginning of the nineteenth century pale-faced strangers from the East began to enter this country. First they came slowly, a few at a time, bewildered at the wonders they observed. Then a hunger for land seized them. They lived by the plow, not by the hunt, and their way of life required exclusive possession of the soil. To the Indians the land belonged to God, was made for His children's use, and was no more susceptible of individual ownership than the air. Whites reasoned that the West could be put to a better use than merely as habitat for nomadic Indians and wildlife. Representing "civilization," they thought they should put the new land to that better use. And so they took it.

The Cheyenne Expedition was a microcosm of the unfolding

story of the greater tragedy, a single episode in the ongoing struggle for possession of Indian lands. When that struggle ended, most survivors among the native American peoples were confined in abject poverty to the meanest portions of lands once theirs. As the stories of their valiant struggle for survival tell us, however, they were fewer in number but not a lesser people. Their bravery and determination in the face of insurmountable odds constitute an important part of the legacy they left their progeny; even now we wonder at the richness of that heritage.

The story of the Cheyenne Expedition is found today only in surviving records of the military and the Bureau of Indian Affairs, in contemporary news reports, and in a few letters and diaries and later writings by some of the participants. From the perspective of the Cheyennes, the expedition was noted by only one or two early white scholars who recorded some of the oral stories and traditions of survivors or their descendants. Even so, taken from their respective repositories, these combine to paint a fascinating picture of native life in the waning days of their freedom and independence, of the conditions that led the army to make war against the Cheyennes, of the trials and ordeals of the soldiers sent to subdue them, and of the unusual events occurring at the confrontation on the Solomon. The pages which follow draw upon these sources to recount the actual events as they were experienced by those involved. Occasionally, where both possible and useful, statements or observations of participants, gleaned from their writings or those of other members of the command, have been used to tell part of the story. Who, after all, can tell it better than they?

Although it was only one of the more than 140 days the expedition spent in the field, in a real sense the climax occurred on July 29, 1857, on the south fork of the Solomon River. The irony and significance of what happened that day can be truly understood only if the reader is familiar with the Cheyenne Indians and their way of life, and with the nature of cavalry operations across the plains in the mid-1850s. For those lacking such a background it may be helpful to read the sketches found in Appendices A and B before starting the narrative.

To appreciate the happenings on Solomon's Fork it is first necessary to learn something of the events leading to the conflict and the motivations of each of the adversaries. Therefore, allow your mind's eye to take you back to a distant time and to places far different in appearance from what they now are. Give flesh and blood to those long dead, and feel with them the winds that caressed them on their journeys, the searing heat that stalked them across the plains, and the thrill and excitement of the dangers they faced, red man and white man alike. It is a song no longer heard.

Part One

The Prelude to War

1

The Seeds of Conflict

> *And now Arapahoe*
> *The word was; now Dakota; now Cheyenne;*
> *But still one word: "Let grass be green again*
> *Upon the trails of war and hatred cease,*
> *For many presents and the pipe of peace*
> *Are waiting yonder at the Soldier's Town!"*
> *And there were some who heard it with a*
>   *frown*
> *And said, remembering the White Man's guile:*
> *"Make yet more arrows when the foemen smile."*
> *And others, wise with many winters, said:*
> *"Life narrows, and the better days are dead.*
> *Make war upon the sunset! Will it stay?"*
> *And some who counselled with a dream would*
>   *say:*
> *"Great Spirit made all peoples, White and Red,*
> *And pitched one big blue teepee overhead*
> *That men might live as brothers side by side.*
> *Behold! Is not our country very wide,*
> *With room enough for all?" And there were*
>   *some*
> *Who answered scornfully: "Not so they come;*
> *Their medicine is strong, their hearts are bad;*
> *A little part of what our fathers had*
> *They give us now, tomorrow come and take.*
> *Great Spirit also made the rattlesnake*
> *And over him the big blue teepee set!"**

*The Song of the Indian Wars by John G. Neihardt (New York: The Macmillan Company, 1925), 28–29. Excerpts from this work appear at the beginning of each chapter.

A Clash of Cultures

Hostilities between people of the United States and Indians of the western plains began almost as soon as there was significant contact between them. From the time European settlers first came to North America, their relationship with native inhabitants had been troubled. Initially friendly, Indians of the eastern United States grew antagonistic as they began to understand the Europeans' intention of making the land and its natural resources theirs. As the primarily Anglo-Saxon society established in the East expanded, with it grew the vexing problem of what to do about the Indians.

In the end Thomas Jefferson contrived the policy deemed most appropriate to prevent continuing bloodshed between the parties. The policy was removal. Indians residing in areas occupied or desired by white men in the East were to be removed to lands beyond the ninety-fifth meridian, lands not then a part of any state nor occupied by whites. There Indians would live in perpetuity, free to adopt or reject European style civilization as they chose, in lands from which white habitation and exploitation were forever barred.[1] The government established a Permanent Indian Frontier along the ninety-fifth meridian and to guard it constructed a series of forts along a line extending from Minnesota to Louisiana. In theory these forts protected Indians from whites as much as whites from Indians. One was Fort Leavenworth, the principal guardian fortress of the southern plains.[2]

Presidential administrations following Jefferson's pursued Indian removal with great vigor. They cajoled or coerced more than fifty thousand eastern Indians into surrendering more than 100 million acres of their original homelands in exchange for approximately 32 million acres in the West, together with the pledge of annual annuities. In the end, no longer possessed of the power or will to resist white encroachment and exploitation, most accepted the new homes.[3]

The vast area lying beyond the ninety-fifth meridian, extending west to the Spanish and the British possessions, was then known as the Indian Territory. Lands provided to immigrant Indians consisted of tribal reservations carved from this territory and, for the most part, located along the eastern borders of what later became Nebraska, Kansas, and Oklahoma. The extent and boundaries of the reservations were arbitrarily determined, without much regard

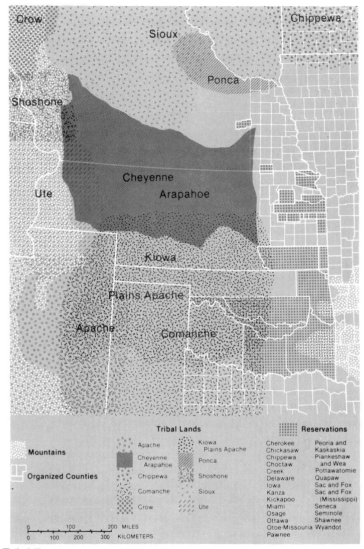

Tribal Territories on the Great Plains

Tribal Lands   ▦ Reservations

Mountains

Organized Counties

Apache   Kiowa Plains Apache

Cheyenne Arapahoe   Ponca

Chippewa   Shoshone

Comanche   Sioux

Crow   Ute

Cherokee   Peoria and Kaskaskia
Chickasaw
Chippewa   Piankeshaw and Wea
Choctaw
Creek   Pottawatomie
Delaware   Quapaw
Iowa   Sac and Fox
Kanza   Sac and Fox (Mississippi)
Kickapoo
Miami   Seneca
Osage   Seminole
Ottawa   Shawnee
Otoe-Missouria   Wyandot
Pawnee

0   100   200 MILES
0   100   200   300 KILOMETERS

for the size of the population to be supported. On them were placed
Iowas, Otoes, Missouris, Kansas, Osages, Sacs and Foxes, Kicka-
poos, Delawares, Wyandottes, Shawnees, Chippewas, Ottawas,
Peorias, Kaskaskias, Weas, Piankashaws, Potawatomis, Miamis,
Cherokees, Quapaws, Creeks, Choctaws, Chickasaws, Seminoles,
and other tribes.[4]

West of the new line of reservations lay largely unexplored lands
inhabited by the powerful and warlike nomadic tribes of the Great
Plains. Comanches, Kiowas, and Plains Apaches roamed the territory south of the Arkansas River. Largest of these tribes were the
Comanches, a Shoshonean people, who had moved onto the plains
many generations earlier. Their country extended south from the
Arkansas nearly to the junction of the Pecos River with the Rio
Grande and the Balcones Escarpment. On the east they claimed
and freely roamed the territory reaching to the Cross Timbers,
about ninety-seven degrees longitude, and on the west from Bent's
Old Fort southward along the Purgatoire River to the foothills of
the Rocky Mountains and beyond to the Pecos. Known to the Spanish as Comanchería, this range measured approximately four hundred miles from east to west and six hundred miles from north to
south. By the 1850s there were seven principal bands of Comanches, of whom the Yamparika, Kotsoteka, and Nokoni generally
stayed to the north and regularly frequented valleys and tributaries
of the Arkansas, Cimarron, and Canadian rivers. Comanches were
great warriors and hunters and had very large herds of horses. Reputedly they were among the finest horsemen in the world.[5]

The Kiowas, though less numerous than the Comanches, were
also fine horsemen and able warriors. With them generally moved
a small Athapascan-speaking band known to history as the Gat-
tackas or Kiowa-Apache. The usual range of the Kiowas was
through the northern part of the territory they claimed in common
with the Comanches, generally between the Arkansas and the Red
River. Though tending to stay farther west, various bands of Plains
Apaches occupied the same country. The Plains Apaches, while
formidable by white standards, were never the able horsemen or
warriors that their Comanche and Kiowa neighbors were.[6]

North of the Arkansas, in territory bounded on the west by the
foothills of the Rocky Mountains, on the east by a line drawn
roughly at ninety-eight degrees longitude (about where the Santa

Fe Trail crossed the Little Arkansas River), and on the north by
the Platte, roamed the southern bands of the Cheyenne and Arapahoe tribes. Of these the Cheyennes were decidedly more warlike,
better horsemen, and, by 1857, more numerous. Arapahoes preferred to stay near the Arkansas or the South Platte. Each of the
many bands of Cheyennes had its own favorite territory within the
larger range.

The Permanent Indian Frontier, designed to assure both immigrant and native Indians their own separate homelands forever,
lasted only from 1817 to the late 1840s. Conquest of New Mexico
by General Kearny's Army of the West, acquisition of Oregon Territory from Great Britain, and discovery of gold in California in
1849 conspired to give it a rapid burial. In its place came the
organization of nearly all lands west of the Missouri River into
states and territories—Texas, California, and Oregon as states,
and New Mexico, Kansas, Utah, Nebraska, and Washington as
territories. Public lands thus were opened for white ownership and
settlement, requiring termination of Indian claims. These devel-
opments opened yet another chapter in the long story of broken
promises and treaties. Lands guaranteed to Indians in perpetuity—
for so long as grass grew, streams flowed, and winds blew—were
once more demanded by whites. Such a seemingly insatiable thirst
in turn required a new series of treaties defining Indian lands and
rights.[7]

The eastern immigrant Indians were too weak to resist white
demands. Beyond the Cottonwood River on the Santa Fe Trail, and
the Little Blue River to the north, however, other people proved
less pliant. Here, in short-grass country, home of the buffalo,
ranged the southern Plains Indians. Before the 1850s their contact
with white people had been limited to encounters (occasionally unfriendly) with travelers on the Santa Fe and Oregon-California
trails and dealings with trappers, traders, and hide hunters. After
the discovery of gold in California, however, relations with whites
deteriorated. The enormous increase in traffic over the two trails
converted these Indians into implacable foes of white intrusion
onto the plains. Increasing the friction, white settlers began to
flood into Kansas and Nebraska in 1854, sending new pressures
west into the domain of the Plains tribes.

The 1850s marked the beginning of a period of warfare that con-

Crossing the plains on the Santa Fe Trail on the south, or the Oregon-California Trail on the north, carried with it the ever-present danger of attack by Plains Indians, who bitterly resented the intrusions of whites into their country.

tinued until the early 1890s. In the end the western tribes, too, would lose, but only after a long and tragic fight in which they lost most of what had once been theirs.

Trails, Traders, and Soldier Towns

Humans appeared on the Great Plains thousands of years ago, yet except for occasional exploration, European white men did not become a significant presence until the early nineteenth century. Small bands of trappers and traders—Spanish, French, and American—established themselves, seasonally if not permanently, in the mountains and along some of the streams across the plains. Most whites, however, were travelers, traders, and merchants using the two great trails. These were the Santa Fe Trail, which led from Independence, Missouri, to the capital of New Mexico, and the Oregon-California Trail, which led from Independence north and west across the Plains and the Rocky Mountains to Utah, Oregon, and California.

By far the oldest trail across the plains was the one to Santa Fe. Much of it followed old Indian trails. Commencing with Coronado in 1541, more than twenty known expeditions by Europeans or Americans had traveled along all or part of its length before 1821. In September of that year Capt. William Becknell led a small party of American traders to Santa Fe, the first to reach that city following Mexico's independence from Spain. They followed the Arkansas to the Purgatoire River, thence southwest up the Purgatoire and beyond, probably crossing the mountains at Trinchera Pass. On their return they essentially followed what became the original Santa Fe Trail, later known as the Cimarron route or cutoff. Becknell's example resulted in a rush of hardy adventurers and traders eager to exploit the potential of commerce with Santa Fe, and in only a few years the number of people who traveled the trail grew rapidly from a trickle to a torrent. In time the Santa Fe road became a great highway for traders, soldiers, explorers, immigrants, and fortune seekers, some traveling as far as California, some no farther than Indian trading posts scattered along its length.

The sudden upsurge in commerce with Santa Fe stimulated other interests, and explorers and mountain men flooded into the region. The increase in traffic and hazards of travel through Plains Indian country led the government to survey and mark the trail in 1825.

Completed by Joseph C. Brown under the supervision of three government commissioners, the survey resulted in the Santa Fe Trail becoming the first national highway in the West.[8]

The volume of traffic using the Santa Fe Trail and the wide variety of merchandise carried by the wagon trains, created both uneasiness and temptation for Cheyennes and other Plains tribes. One result was that the tribes frequenting the Arkansas began to raid caravans almost as soon as the trail was used.

The earliest Indian raids along the Santa Fe Trail were mainly harassing, but 1828 witnessed such devastating attacks and heavy losses that by 1829 trade had been cut to one-fourth that of the previous year. Following loud outcries by traders, military escorts were ordered for trading caravans through Indian country to the Mexican border in 1829, 1833, 1834, 1843, and 1845. There was usually but one escorted caravan each year, the round trip taking approximately four to six months.[9] In each, the troops were charged with defending the caravan from marauding Indians or raiders from Texas, but not with patrolling the trail itself. Travelers who dared to brave its course independent of the caravans did so at their own peril.[10]

Traffic along the Santa Fe Trail and ensuing hostilities with the Plains Indians did not deter the fur trappers and traders who did business with them. In 1833 Charles Bent, William Bent, and Ceran St. Vrain, doing business as "Bent, St. Vrain, and Company," commenced construction of their famous adobe trading post on the north bank of the Arkansas River adjacent to the trail to the mountains. Named "Fort William" for its resident proprietor, William Bent, it was popularly referred to as "Bent's Fort," and later as "Bent's Old Fort." For some sixteen years it ruled a trading empire that encompassed much of the southern plains and extended into the mountains of modern Colorado and New Mexico. During the period of its existence, William Bent exercised considerable influence over the Indians of the region and did much to maintain a tenuous peace between the natives and the European intruders.[11]

In the summer of 1846, following the U.S. declaration of war with Mexico, Gen. Stephen W. Kearny led his Army of the West across the trail to capture New Mexico. Leaving the original Santa Fe Trail, which turned south at Chouteau's Island, he moved along the old trail used by trappers and traders on the north bank of the

Arkansas to Bent's Old Fort, then south into Mexican territory along Timpas Creek to the Purgatoire River, whose valley he followed to Raton Pass, from there crossing into present New Mexico. He probably established this route to avoid the area of the old trail patrolled by Mexican cavalry, to take advantage of relatively abundant water, and to bypass the lands of the Comanches and Kiowas. Ultimately known as the Mountain or Bent's Fort branch of the Santa Fe Trail, it was little used until the War Between the States.[12]

What in the beginning had been a mere trickle of goods carried by a few caravans each season became a stream of men, animals, and wagons with the onset of the Mexican War. Then, in 1849, discovery of gold in California started a veritable flood of migration. This rapid growth in movement along western trails prompted a new phase in relations with Indians of the plains. Periodic escorts for trading caravans were no longer sufficient to protect commerce and the stream of people now moving westward in ever-increasing numbers.

As Plains Indians began to recognize the threat to their traditional way of life, raids to obtain material goods became a war to save their homeland and tribal existence. Faced with open hostilities, the army realized that a series of military stations would be required to provide security along the trail. Fort Leavenworth, constructed near the eastern end of the Santa Fe Trail in 1827, and Fort Marcy, built in the city of Santa Fe in 1846, were too far distant from the trouble spots to assist effectively. The army's quartermaster department, therefore, established a small adobe-and-log fort two miles west of present-day Dodge City during the spring of 1847. Called Fort Mann, it was not originally intended as a combat military post, but rather as a station where wagons could be repaired and travelers and animals might find a safe haven in the heart of Plains Indian country. Although enlarged to serve as a military post early in 1848, it was almost constantly surrounded by hostile bands of Comanches, Kiowas, Cheyennes, and Arapahoes, and proved ineffective for its intended purposes. It was abandoned during September 1848.[13]

Need for protection along the trail continued, the result of heavy losses to Indian raiders, and in September 1850 the First Dragoons established a new post about three-quarters of a mile above the ruins of old Fort Mann. At first called Fort Mackey for Col. Aeneas Mackey, then Fort Sumner for its builder, Lt. Col. E. V. Sumner,

In 1847 a small post named Fort Mann was built next to the Arkansas River between the lower and middle crossings. The first military installation on the Santa Fe Trail in Plains Indian country, it was remote and difficult to supply. Since it was not an effective deterrent to the Indian raiding and harassment of commerce along the trail, it was abandoned in September 1848.

on June 25, 1851, it was officially designated Fort Atkinson in
honor of Col. Henry Atkinson.* Primarily a base for patrolling the
trail, it served also as the principal point for the government to
hold councils with the southern Plains Indians and distribute treaty
goods, and for traders and Indians to meet and bargain. The abandonment of Bent's Old Fort in 1849 enhanced Fort Atkinson's value
for these purposes because, during its entire existence, it was the
only military installation in hostile Plains Indian country along or
near the Santa Fe Trail. There, on June 19, 1851, in a major council, the government sought to persuade the Comanches, Kiowas,
Cheyennes, Arapahoes, and Plains Apaches to attend the Great
Council to be held at Fort Laramie. The Cheyennes and Arapahoes
accepted and, in September, signed the 1851 Treaty of Fort Laramie (Horse Creek). The other tribes declined, but on June 26,
1853, they signed the Treaty of Fort Atkinson, the southern version
of the Fort Laramie treaty.[14]

The sites for both Fort Mann and Fort Atkinson were selected
because they were above the point where the Dry Route and the
Wet Route of the Santa Fe Trail converged, and below the Middle
(Cimarron) Crossing and the Upper Crossing of the Arkansas, which
meant that nearly all eastbound and westbound traffic passed the
little installations.† As with Fort Mann a few years earlier, Fort

---

*Construction of the outer walls of Fort Atkinson was of heavy buffalo-grass sod,
probably stripped from the hills above the site, and reinforced by wood posts. Its
length was approximately 355 feet north and south, and it was approximately 150
feet wide at the north end, tapering to 60 feet at the south end. The buildings
within were built against the outer walls of the fort, with barracks and quarters
along the north wall and the north half of the west wall, and wagon or wheelwright
and blacksmith shops at the middle of the west wall and near the northeast corner.
It had storage for commissary and quartermaster supplies, a military magazine, a
sutler's store, an Indian trading post, and a mail station. The entrance gate was
at the southeast corner where the south wall extended approximately 20 feet to
the east to screen the entrance or exit of wagons or personnel. The buildings were
built of sod and adobe brick, with roofs formed of poles laid over with brush, sod,
and canvas. Colonel Sumner recommended permanent one-story stone buildings
for the post, but it was abandoned before any were constructed. See Louise Barry,
Beginning of the West, 802–803, 854, 856, 860, 873, 965–68, 1117; LeRoy R.
Hafen, *Broken Hand*, 245, 280; *KHC*, 4:363–66, *KHQ*, 15:329–30.
†The Middle Crossing was not known as the Cimarron Crossing until the 1860s.
It is denoted "Middle Crossing" herein to distinguish it from the Upper Crossing
and the Lower Crossing. There were several variations in the Middle Crossing,
and it was that in primary use after 1853 which was actually known as the Cimar-

Atkinson proved too remote and difficult to defend and supply. On September 22, 1853, the post was officially abandoned and its walls and buildings destroyed, leaving heaps of sod and adobe marking the site.[15]

The road to Santa Fe is much older than that leading to Oregon and California, but the latter played an equally important part in the history of the West. Explorers, military expeditions, missionaries, and trappers had been moving along the Platte River since at least 1812, when Robert Stuart and six other trappers traveled the river's length from South Pass to the Missouri. Its real beginning as an established road, however, was in 1841 when the Bidwell-Bartleson immigrant party, the first bound for Oregon, followed its path from Westport Landing (in present Kansas City, Missouri) to their destination. In 1842, Lt. John C. Frémont led an exploring and mapping expedition along its length from the mouth of the Kansas River to Fort Laramie and beyond to South Pass.[16] The first large migration along the Platte River Road occurred in 1843, when nearly a thousand people traveled the trail to Oregon to assist in acquiring that territory from Great Britain by populating it with pro-American citizenry, a cause successfully completed in 1846.[17]

The Oregon-California Trail (also known as the Oregon Trail, California Trail, Overland Trail, and Great Platte River Road— among other variants) followed the south bank of the Platte to its forks, crossed the South Platte to the west of the forks and headed to the south bank of the North Platte at Ash Hollow, then continued along the south bank to Fort Laramie and beyond. From south of the Platte four primary starting points converged at different locations below the second Fort Kearny, Nebraska. The first and most famous was from Independence, Missouri, where the trail crossed into Indian Territory along with the Santa Fe Trail, breaking off from the latter west of present Gardner, Kansas, and moving northwest until it reached the valley of the Platte approximately seventeen miles east of Fort Kearny. Other important roads joined the original route, including those from Fort Leavenworth (primarily a military road), from St. Joseph, Missouri, and from the first Fort Kearny (later Nebraska City, Nebraska).[18]

---

ron Crossing. See Louise Barry, "The Ranch at Cimarron Crossing," *KHQ*, 39:345–66.

Located about three-quarters of a mile above the ruins of Fort Mann, Fort Atkinson was established in 1850 by Col. E. V. Sumner and a detachment of the First Dragoons. Garrisoned by one company of the Sixth Infantry, during the travel season it was also occupied by a company of Dragoons sent from Fort Leavenworth to patrol the trail. Like Fort Mann, its remote location, the difficulty of supply, and the frequent presence of large bodies of hostile Plains Indians made it untenable, and it was abandoned in 1853.

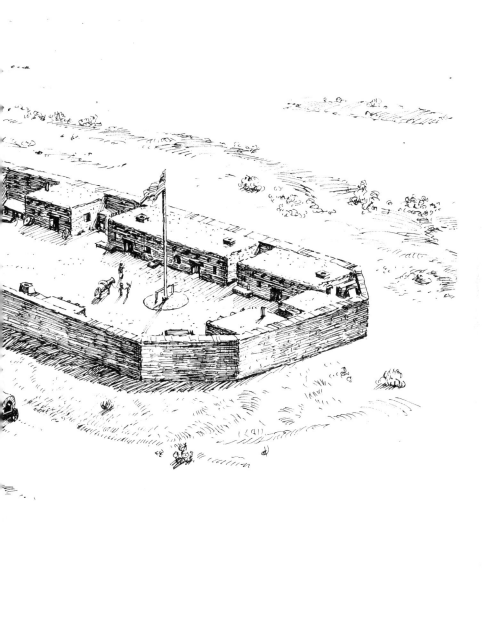

The same forces requiring military intervention and protection along the Santa Fe Trail were at work along the vast length of the Oregon-California Trail. Where the Santa Fe road traversed the southern extremities of Cheyenne and Arapahoe country and then went southward into Comanche, Kiowa, and Plains Apache territory, the trail along the Platte marked the northern limits of southern bands of Cheyennes and Arapahoes. North of the South Platte and Platte lay the country of the northern bands of Cheyennes and Arapahoes and Teton Lakota Sioux. The Teton Lakota were a large and powerful tribe, and of their people the southern Brulé, Oglalla, and Miniconjou regularly camped along the trail. The great upsurge in traffic following acquisition of Oregon and discovery of gold in California brought all these native inhabitants into increasingly frequent, often violent contact with whites. As a result, the 1844 report of the Secretary of War recommended establishing a chain of military posts from the Missouri River to the Rocky Mountains. In 1847, Indian Agent Thomas Fitzpatrick suggested that Forts Laramie and Hall be acquired by the military to protect travelers and commerce.[19]

The first post along the Platte River, Fort Kearny, was established in the fall of 1847 two or three miles above the head of Grand Island and seventeen miles above the intersection of the main trail from Independence with that from old Fort Kearny. By the mid-1850s the fort consisted of a scattering of sod and wooden structures, the more important ones grouped around a parade ground in whose center was a tall flagpole.* Unlike Forts Mann and Atkinson along the Santa Fe Trail to the south, Fort Kearny

---

*By May 1849, the new Fort Kearny had approximately ten buildings, including a sutler's store. The building material for all the original buildings was sod cut from the plains in blocks two or three feet square and laid up in courses with the grass side down. The first wooden building, completed by the middle of 1849, was the post hospital. By 1850, Fort Kearny consisted of a large storehouse with a lead roof and numerous small buildings to house officers and men, all built with sod walls. There were two frame structures, a double two-story officers' quarters, and the post hospital. Construction activity continued and by the end of the year a frame guardhouse had been added and two more frame buildings started—a two-story barracks and quarters for the post commander. In 1852 a third frame officers' quarters was built, and in 1855 and 1856 an adjutant's office, laundress's quarters, bakery, powder magazine, and more stables were added, along with a second frame barracks for the enlisted personnel. See Merrill J. Mattes, *The Great Platte River Road*, 172–91, 194–97, 202–203, 208–13.

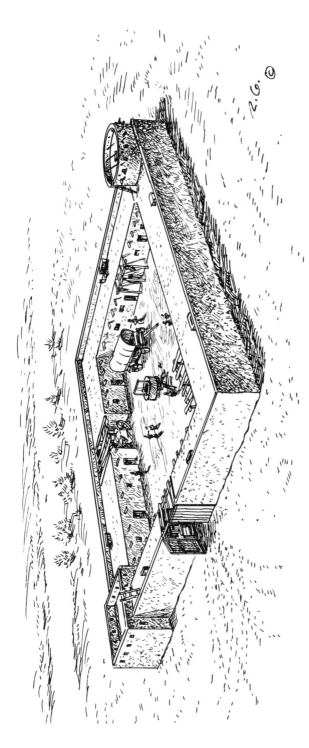

Along the Trappers' Trail from Taos to Fort Laramie, where it ran parallel with and along the east bank of the South Platte River, were four early trading posts, three of which were built of adobe. The southernmost was Fort Lupton, built in 1837.

had no wall or palisade, making it far more typical of a military post on the plains.[20]

Fort Laramie, the second military post founded on the trail along the Platte, appropriated the site and adobe structure of the famous trading post established by William L. Sublette on the Laramie River near its confluence with the North Platte. Its location, at the western edge of the plains and the beginning of the mountain west, was a strategic point for fur trappers and Indian traders and for councils with Indians of the mountains and northern plains. There, too, the Trapper's Trail (or Taos Trail), running north from Taos, joined the old Indian trail used by travelers along the Platte. The army purchased the trading post from the American Fur Company on June 26, 1849, and immediately commenced new military construction. Within five or six years Fort Laramie had taken on the appearance of a mature military post on the plains, its principal buildings clustered around the parade ground and the old adobe trading post on the southwest side. Like Fort Kearny, Fort Laramie never had a walled enclosure.[21]

On September 17, 1851, the government signed a treaty with most of the Plains tribes at Horse Creek, near Fort Laramie. Engineered by Thomas Fitzpatrick, agent for the Indians of the upper Platte, upper Kansas, and upper Arkansas rivers, this was one of the largest and most colorful assemblages of Plains Indians ever seen upon the continent. Present were various divisions of Teton Lakota Sioux, northern and southern bands of Cheyennes and Arapahoes, Shoshonis, Crows, and delegations from the Gros Ventres, Assiniboines, Minnitarees, and Arikaras—more than ten thousand in all. The treaty was intended to bring peace between whites and Indians and between the tribes of the plains, but its practical effect was short-lived.[22]

The Santa Fe Trail and the Oregon-California Trail, along with their military posts, represented the most significant intrusion of European peoples onto the plains. However, the old Indian trail following the Arkansas to the mountains, used by white trappers, traders, and explorers from early in the nineteenth century, experienced a substantial increase in traffic following construction of Bent's Old Fort in 1833, and a great intensification during the 1849 California Gold Rush, when the trail west from the Upper Crossing of the Santa Fe road became known as the California Trail. While some gold seekers went to California by way of Santa Fe, most using the southern route bypassed the crossing of the Arkansas and continued along the north side of the Arkansas to the mouth of Fountain Creek. There they intersected the old Trappers Trail from the south, which they followed north along the east banks of Fountain Creek and Jimmy Camp Creek, thence proceeding overland to the headwaters of the east fork of Cherry Creek. They followed Cherry Creek to the South Platte, which they crossed either at the mouth of Cherry Creek or farther northeast at the site of old Fort St. Vrain. From there the forty-niners moved to the northwest and an intersection with the Oregon-California Trail. The Trappers Trail itself continued northward to Fort Laramie.[23]

Long before the war with Mexico and the gold rush of 1849, four small trading posts were constructed along the South Platte. In 1835, Louis Vasquez and Andrew Sublette built an adobe post called Fort Vasquez along the old Trappers Trail on the east bank of the South Platte River, about one mile south of present Platteville, Colorado. In 1837, three new posts were built in quick succession. First was Fort Lupton (or Fort Lancaster), an adobe fort built by Lancaster P. Lupton about one mile north of present Fort Lupton, Colorado; second was Fort Jackson, built by the American Fur Company one and one-half miles south of Fort Vasquez; and third was Fort St. Vrain (also called Fort Lookout or Fort George), built by Bent, St. Vrain, and Company approximately seven miles north of Fort Vasquez to protect the northern reaches of their trading empire from unwelcome competition.[24]

By 1838 the intense rivalry caused the American Fur Company to close Fort Jackson. They sold out to Bent, St. Vrain, and Company and demolished the fort. Fort Vasquez capitulated in 1842. It was abandoned and gradually fell into ruin. Lancaster Lupton withstood the competition better than the others, but in 1844 he too gave in and abandoned his post. Their objective accomplished, the Bents closed Fort St. Vrain, and by 1846 it was in ruins.[25]

The homeland and hunting grounds of the southern bands of Cheyenne and Arapahoe were now surrounded—on the north by traffic along the Oregon-California Trail, on the south by the Santa Fe Trail, and on the west by the Trappers Trail. Eastward lay reservations of immigrant tribes, and beyond them, like pressure building behind a dam, the rapidly growing white population. The "Soldier Towns," as Indians called military posts, were in some respects an even greater irritant than the trails and the travelers

North of Fort Lupton was Fort Vasquez, built in 1835, the oldest of the adobe trading posts located along the east bank of the South Platte River

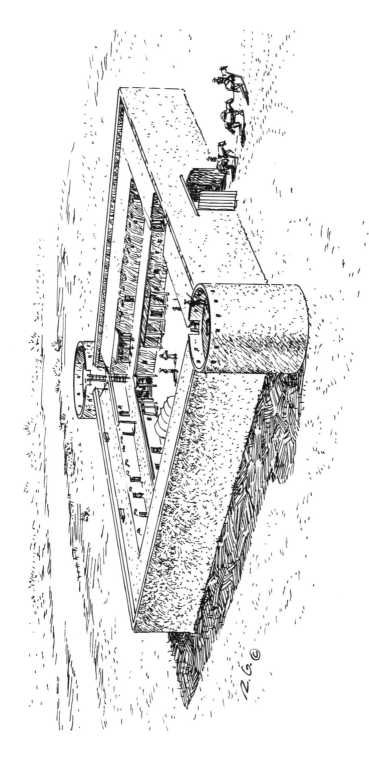

Farthest north of the adobe trading posts along the South Platte was Fort St. Vrain, built in 1837 by Bent, St. Vrain and Company.

who destroyed their food supply. Indians had been told the forts were built to protect them from whites, but what soon became apparent was that the only actions taken by soldiers were against Indians.

By 1853 the only permanent white presence on the plains consisted of Forts Kearny and Laramie along the Oregon-California Trail, a few trading houses along the Arkansas and Platte rivers, and Fort Atkinson (then in its last days) on the road to Santa Fe. Apart from these the region was devoid of European culture and civilization. It was still Indian country, a wilderness untouched by civilization and as the Creator had made it.

2

The Cheyenne Troubles

So the Cadmian breed,
The wedders of the vision and the deed,
Went forth to sow the dragon-seed again.
But there were those—and they were also men—
Who saw the end of sacred things and dear
In all this wild beginning; saw with fear
Ancestral pastures gutted by the plow,
The bison harried ceaselessly, and how
They dwindled moon by moon; with pious
      dread
Beheld the holy places of their dead
The mock of aliens.
                    Sioux, Arapahoe,
Cheyenne, Commanche, Kiowa and Crow
In many a council pondered what befell
The prairie world.   *(21)*

1853–1855: First Blood

The Fort Laramie Treaty of 1851 had given hope to both Indians and whites that their mutual problems with travel along the trails were finally resolved. In 1852, despite increased migration and travel, things went smoothly. During the winter, hoping once again to develop a profitable trade with Indians, William Bent set stone-cutters to work cutting and curing stone for use in the erection of a new trading post to be located on the Arkansas near the western end of the Big Timbers, about thirty-seven miles east of Bent's Old

Fort.* Bent's New Fort, as it became known, was sufficiently complete to be stocked with merchandise by the summer of 1853. Soon
thereafter, trading with the Indians was renewed.[1]

The Indian trade at Bent's New Fort never rose to the levels
experienced at Bent's Old Fort in the 1830s and 1840s. Increased
use of the Santa Fe Trail and the California Trail had a profound
impact upon buffalo herds and other wildlife, bringing hunger to
Indian camps and apprehension for their future. Slaughter of buffalo and withdrawal of herds from the trail cut deeply into the trade
in hides. Other signs of trouble began to appear. In 1853, Congress
authorized a survey of possible routes for transcontinental railroads, and Capt. John W. Gunnison was appointed to survey a
route near the thirty-eighth and thirty-ninth parallels—directly
through the lands of Cheyennes and Arapahoes.[2]

Among whites as well as Indians, the summer of 1853 brought
anxiety along the trail up the Arkansas. Fort Atkinson, on the
verge of abandonment, was nearly always surrounded by one or
more large camps of Comanches, Kiowas, Cheyennes, or Arapahoes. Following attacks on wagon trains and threats against the
garrison, the army sent Company B of the First Dragoons under
Maj. Robert H. Chilton to relieve the fort and patrol the trail.
Cheyennes were constantly having disputes with immigrants and
traders, and the commanding officer of the fort had his hands full
trying to prevent an explosion.[3]

Restlessness and fear are infectious. Along the Oregon-California
Trail the 1853 season started quietly enough, and for a while it
promised to pass as peaceably as that of 1852. However, heavy
migration and consequent depletion of game, along with the con-

*The new structure, built in a rectangle, measured approximately 95 feet east to
west and 188 feet north to south. Its limestone walls were 16 feet in height and
had parapets running around the walls for defense. There were gates in the east
and north walls, and above the ladder at the north gate was a stone lookout post.
Within were twelve rooms built against the walls in the fashion of Bent's Old Fort,
with walls 10 feet high, ceiling joists of one-foot-thick cottonwood logs, and dirt
floors. The rooms inside included quarters for Bent and his employees, a 55-foot-
long warehouse and other support facilities. See George E. Hyde, *Life of George
Bent*, 65; David Lavender, *Bent's Fort*, 324; Eli Long, "Journal of the Cheyenne
Expedition of 1857," entry for June 17, 1857; Nolie Mumey, *Old Forts and Trading Posts of the West, Bent's Old Fort and New Fort*, 126–28; Robert M. Peck,
"Rough Riding on the Plains," *The National Tribune*, March 14, 1901, 1.

tinuing problem of cholera and other European diseases, made bands frequenting the Platte as sullen and hostile as those along the Arkansas. By mid-June they were harassing immigrants. The first open conflict involving the military occurred on June 15. Some young men from a village of eighty to one hundred lodges of Miniconjou Sioux on the north bank of the North Platte, across from the mouth of the Laramie River, had seized a ferry on the North Platte when the operator refused to take them across the river. A sergeant from the fort retook the boat, prompting a young Sioux to fire his old musket at him. The angry sergeant reported the incident, and 1st Lt. Richard B. Garnett, post commander, ordered 2d Lt. Hugh B. Fleming to take twenty-three men and an interpreter to the village and arrest the man who had fired the shot. If the Indians refused to deliver him, Fleming was to seize two or three prisoners to compel compliance. When he arrived and made his demand, the frightened Miniconjous ran to a nearby ravine, shooting their guns and bows and arrows as they went. Fleming ordered a charge, and in the ensuing melee three Indians were killed and two taken prisoner. The seeds of war were sown.[4]

The following year, 1854, first showed promise for peace. In the south, along the Santa Fe Trail, there were a number of minor incidents. In early May, forty Cheyenne warriors stopped and surrounded the eastbound mail party along the Arkansas, demanded food, and attempted to run off the mules.[5] There were other angry encounters, but for the most part southern bands of Cheyennes, along with their allies—Arapahoes, Comanches, Kiowas, Plains Apaches, and Osages—were preoccupied with preparations for a war of vengeance on the Pawnees.[6]

Of greater portent for relations between whites and the Indians of the plains were two events that took place far away in Washington, D.C. First, on February 7, Thomas Fitzpatrick, the only white agent the Indians had ever trusted, died of pneumonia in the Brown Hotel while on business with the Indian Bureau. He was replaced in April by John W. Whitfield, previously agent for the Potawatomies and the Kansas.[7] Second, on May 30, President Franklin Pierce signed the Kansas-Nebraska Act, creating and opening for white settlement the new territories of Kansas and Nebraska.[8] The western boundaries of both extended to the crest of the Rocky Mountains and included all the country of the northern and south-

ern bands of Cheyennes and Arapahoes, and a significant portion
of the lands of the Teton Lakota Sioux, the Comanches, the Kiowas, and the Plains Apaches.[9]

Along the Oregon-California Trail, 1854 had also begun peacefully. Though still resentful, aside from minor harassment the
Sioux did not interfere with the free movement of immigrants. To
reduce the cost of protecting the road, early in the year the army
had withdrawn two companies of the Mounted Riflemen stationed
at Fort Laramie, leaving one company of the Sixth Infantry as the
only garrison.[10] On May 18, Lieutenant Garnett was transferred
from Fort Laramie, leaving young and inexperienced Lieutenant
Fleming in temporary command. It was a weak and ineffectual
military post that was charged with protection of the trail as the
last of the year's immigrant trains passed and the Sioux gathered
for the annual distribution of treaty goods.[11]

In early August a small party of Cheyennes from one of the
northern bands ran off some cattle grazing within two miles of the
fort.[12] On August 18 a wagon train of Mormon converts from Den-
mark passed a camp of Brulé Sioux near the trading post of James
Bordeaux, about eight miles below the fort. As they moved slowly
past, a lame cow that had fallen behind took fright and ran into the
Indian camp. The Mormon train moved on without trying to retrieve
the cow, presumably because they feared the Indians. Thinking the
cow abandoned, High Forehead, a Miniconjou temporarily camping with the Brulés, killed it, and it was cooked and eaten.

The incident of the cow was reported to Lieutenant Fleming first
by the Mormon party and shortly after by the chief of the Brulé
Sioux, Martoh-Ioway (Bear That Scatters His Enemies), known to
the whites as "Conquering Bear," or simply "Bear." According to
the Fort Laramie Treaty, a signatory tribe whose members had
taken property from whites had to compensate the victims before it
could receive its annual annuities. Because of this, Bear went to
the fort and related the circumstances to Lieutenant Fleming, advising that the cow had been killed by a Miniconjou, not a Brulé,
and offering to give him over as a prisoner.[13] At first Lieutenant
Fleming did not seem to take the matter seriously, preferring to let
Agent Whitfield resolve it when he arrived; but a new officer at the
post, Bvt. 2d Lt. John L. Grattan, persuaded him that it should be
dealt with immediately and firmly to discourage similar incidents.
Grattan was well known as brave and ambitious, but he also was

hotheaded and contemptuous of the Indians. He had repeatedly stated that with ten men he could defeat the entire Cheyenne nation and with thirty could rout all the Indians on the plains.[14]

Ordered to arrest and return the guilty Miniconjou, on August 19, Grattan took twenty-nine volunteers, the Indian-hating post interpreter Auguste Lucien, and two twelve-pounder howitzers.[15] When the detachment arrived at the Brulé camp, the howitzers were unlimbered and all weapons loaded. A forty-five-minute conference with the Bear and other Brulé chiefs followed, and Lucien, apparently drunk, gave them to understand that if the Miniconjou was not delivered, the soldiers would "eat their hearts raw." Whatever was said, the soldiers rose suddenly and started to bring their howitzers to bear on the Miniconjou lodges. Shots rang out, and the Bear fell mortally wounded. At the same time, the howitzers were fired, but the shot struck only the tops of lodgepoles. Nervous soldiers then started to flee toward the fort while angry Brulés attacked with bows, arrows, and tomahawks. In a few minutes the fight was over, leaving Grattan, Lucien, and all of the soldiers dead except one so badly wounded that he died shortly thereafter.[16]

Following the fight, frenzied Brulé braves seized supplies and treaty annuities stored at Bordeaux's trading post and at the American Fur Company post three miles upriver, then pillaged the farm operated by the fort before moving north to the Niobrara River.[17] The Grattan Massacre, as the white press later called it, left the fort manned by only forty-two men. At Fleming's request, two companies of infantry under Maj. (Bvt. Lt. Col.) William Hoffman were sent as relief, arriving on November 12, at which time Hoffman took command.

When word of what had happened reached the East, neither the army nor the press would believe that Lieutenant Grattan was at fault or that he had, in fact, attacked the Indians. Even reports to that effect from Lieutenant Fleming, Major Hoffman, and the new agent, John Whitfield, were dismissed as uncorroborated. The Grattan fight raised a great furor both in Congress and in the press, precipitating demands for vengeance.[18]

Retribution came in the form of Col. (Bvt. Brig. Gen.) William S. Harney, a methodical and implacable soldier who believed in giving no quarter to the enemy. An expedition was ordered against the Sioux to seek vengeance for the deaths of Lieutenant Grattan and the others, and Harney was appointed its commander. He arrived at St. Louis on April 1, 1855, and began preparations for the campaign. On July 18 he moved to Fort Leavenworth, the expedition's headquarters, where he assembled some six hundred infantry, light artillery, and cavalry, the last to be led by Lt. Col. Philip St. George Cooke, a veteran Indian fighter. The expedition departed Fort Leavenworth on August 4, following the Oregon-California Trail to Fort Kearny and beyond in search of the Sioux.[19]

While the army was preparing its campaign of revenge, relations between Plains Indians and whites had deteriorated. Northern bands of Cheyennes and Arapahoes, who had been camping near Fort Laramie at the time of the Grattan fight and knew what had happened, waited only long enough to collect their treaty goods from Agent Whitfield. Before departing, they demanded that the trail be abandoned and that their treaty goods thereafter include weapons and ammunition as partial compensation for wrongs done to them. The goods distributed, they quickly moved away. Whitfield reported them to be the "sauciest" he had met and in need of a severe lesson to make them behave.[20]

On November 13 a small war party of Brulés attacked a mail stage twenty-two miles below Fort Laramie, killed three employees, wounded and robbed a passenger, and carried off $10,000 in gold. To the north, Brulés and other Sioux spent the winter of 1854–55 preparing for war. On February 13, 1855, a party of Miniconjou raiders drove off some sixty-five horses and mules from the trading post of Ward and Guerrier seven miles northwest of Fort Laramie. Up and down the trail more such raids took place.[21]

Early in the summer of 1855, the Upper Platte Agency was split from that of the upper Arkansas and upper Kansas. Thomas S. Twiss, appointed agent for the upper Platte, arrived at Fort Laramie on August 10.[22] Convinced that most Indians of his agency wanted peace, he attempted to separate peaceful bands from hostile ones, ordering the former to camp south of the North Platte near the fort. By the early part of September some four thousand Platte Sioux were encamped along the Laramie River above the post. Not included were most Brulés and the Miniconjou bands that frequented the Platte. These remained to the north along the Cheyenne and White rivers around the Black Hills, or farther south along the Niobrara. With them were most of those involved in the Grattan fight.[23]

One band of southern Brulés, led by Little Thunder, was camped near the forks of the Platte hunting buffalo. In mid-August they had been advised to come to Fort Laramie to council and find safety. With much meat to dry and prepare, however, the headmen determined that they could not yet move. On September 2 this band, with about forty lodges and between 250 and 300 men, women, and children, camped along the west side of Blue Water Creek, a tributary of the North Platte, four miles north of its mouth.[24]

The Sioux Expedition under Colonel Harney reached Fort Kearny on August 20 and, after rest and resupply, left on August 24. On September 2 they crossed from the South Platte to the North Platte and camped at Ash Hollow. Learning the location of the Brulé village from a party of traders and from his scouts, Harney prepared his plan of attack. Under cover of darkness on the morning of September 3, the cavalry under Colonel Cooke moved out silently with orders to circle the village from the east and north, and move into position a mile above it, thereby cutting off the Sioux retreat. At 4:30 A.M. Harney marched north with five infantry companies, forded the North Platte, and moved along the east bank of the Blue Water towards the Brulé village. He intended a surprise attack in concert with the cavalry, with the fire of the infantry to signal the cavalry charge. In all Harney had about five hundred effective combat troops.[25]

The plan to surprise the camp failed when the Brulés discovered the approaching infantry. The Sioux struck their lodges and moved rapidly northward, toward the waiting cavalry. Harney then called for a parley with Little Thunder, during which he demanded the surrender of those who participated in the Grattan fight. Because most were with other bands in the north, Little Thunder could not comply. Harney told him to return and prepare his braves for battle. He had scarcely left the field when the infantry opened fire.[26]

The fight was more pursuit and killing than battle. Sounds of the first shots brought the cavalry swiftly into action to intercept the fleeing Sioux. With infantry to their south and east and cavalry advancing from the north, many scaled bluffs to the west and hid in limestone caves and shelters. The infantry turned their new, long-range rifles on them, pouring in a withering fire and causing great slaughter. Cut off from escape to the south and north, those

who could fled across Blue Water Creek and through a draw running east, where survivors dispersed through the sandhills.

The attack killed at least eighty-six Indians and wounded many,
including men, women, and children. About seventy women and
children, five of whom had suffered wounds, fell captive. Male
Indians who did not escape apparently were killed. Army casualties were four killed, four severely wounded, three slightly
wounded, and one missing and presumed dead or captured. The
fight on the Blue Water was variously known as the Battle of Blue
Water, the Battle of Ash Hollow, or the Harney Massacre.[27]

Following the battle, troops burned the Brulé lodges and other
materials, then marched to Fort Laramie. There Harney held a
council with the friendly Indians camping along the Laramie. He
promised similar treatment for any future misbehavior. After rein-
forcing the Fort Laramie garrison, Harney and 450 men marched
northeast by way of an old fur trappers' trail to Fort Pierre.

On March 1, 1856, six months after the Battle of the Blue Water, Harney held a council with Indians at Fort Pierre, which included northern bands of Cheyennes and Arapahoes. After five
days the council ended when the nine tribes present signed a
treaty, dictated by Harney, that promised peace, delivery for trial
by white men of Indians accused of crimes against whites (in direct
contradiction of the Fort Laramie Treaty), restoration of stolen
property, election of chiefs who would be responsible for conduct
of their tribes, and protection of travelers along the overland trails.
During these talks, Harney made a number of demands of Cheyennes and Arapahoes, requiring that they make peace with Pawnees and other enemies, hunt only in their own country as defined
by the Fort Laramie Treaty, and withdraw completely from the road
along the Platte. If they did not, he assured them, he would make
war and "sweep them from the face of the earth." Not satisfied that
the Cheyennes were humbled as the Sioux had been, he recommended an expedition against them in the spring. Harney's words
fell on receptive ears in Leavenworth and Washington, and became
the basis for long-range planning leading to military operations
against the tribe.[28]

The Sioux Expedition, by its blatant use of force, imposed a
temporary peace among the Plains Indians, but it also vastly increased their resentment against whites. Now they could see that
the presence of the whites in their land was not merely a matter of

temporary passage of large numbers of people. It meant permanent military occupation of parts of their country, with swift and brutal retribution upon all Indians for the real or fancied wrongdoings of a few. Buffalo herds were being killed at an alarming rate, the Indians' food supply was being depleted, and they were becoming prisoners in their own land, hostage to an alien people who had said they wanted only the right to cross the plains unmolested.

An Incident at the Upper Platte Bridge

"The Cheyennes" wrote Maj. William Hoffman, commanding officer of Fort Laramie, "are an unruly race and I have little confidence in their promises of good conduct unless they are kept in dread of immediate punishment for their misdemeanors." [29] These words, written on March 31, 1856, echoed earlier statements of Colonel Harney and Agent Whitfield, whose 1855 report had declared that only a "sound chastisement" would bring them to their senses and make them respect the power of the government. [30] Cheyennes held a similar view of whites, based on a history of broken promises, wanton killing of game by immigrants, and increased penetration of their lands on routes other than those agreed to in the Fort Laramie Treaty.

Cheyenne suspicions had been heightened when, in 1855, Lt. Francis T. Bryan of the Topographical Engineers had completed a survey for a wagon road through the heart of the Cheyenne buffalo range. The route ran from Fort Riley along the Solomon, Saline, and Smoky Hill rivers and the Pawnee Fork to Bent's New Fort on the Arkansas. William Bent had tried to arrange for Cheyenne and Arapahoe guides to assist Lieutenant Bryan. However, having already observed the effects of trails on buffalo herds and other game along the Arkansas and the Platte, neither tribe would help, and both indicated their displeasure. [31]

In 1856, construction of bridges began along the route between Fort Riley and Bent's New Fort, further arousing the fury of the Cheyennes. Later in the season, Lieutenant Bryan surveyed another road. This ran from Fort Riley to Bridger's Pass, cutting through the northern part of Cheyenne country by way of the Platte, South Platte, and Lodgepole Creek. On his return, Bryan explored an alternate route, also through Cheyenne country, following the Republican River back to Fort Riley. [32] This confirmed Cheyenne suspicions that whites were about to drive yet another road through some of their best buffalo range.

The first important conflict between Cheyennes and the United States Army occurred in April 1856 at Upper Platte Bridge (Reshaw's Bridge), three miles northeast of present Casper, Wyoming. The bridge was a major crossing for immigrants, and a small detachment of troops from Fort Laramie stood guard. As spring renewed the grass across the plains, the stream of wagons and travelers once again had begun moving slowly along the trails. A few lodges of northern Suhtai* had gone into camp near the bridge to trade. In the camp were four horses said to belong to white men, but which the Cheyennes claimed they had found as strays. The commanding officer of the detachment ordered the horses brought in to be reclaimed by the white man from whose herd they had strayed, assuring the Indians they would be rewarded for finding and caring for the animals.[33]

Although the Indians agreed to the terms, they delivered only three of the horses. The fourth was in the possession of a young brave, then named Two Tails, who was later to gain fame under the name Little Wolf during the Dull Knife outbreak in 1878. Two Tails refused to surrender the horse, declaring that it had been recovered at a different place and an earlier time than the others, and not as described by the white claimant. When the Cheyennes refused to surrender the fourth horse, the commanding officer ordered three young men taken hostage to ensure its return. Neither the Cheyennes, nor indeed most other Plains Indians, understood the meaning of arrest. They seldom took prisoners in war, and they believed that seizure by whites meant certain death. Because of this perception, they usually fiercely resisted any attempt at arrest and imprisonment. When soldiers moved to place the three young braves in irons, they tried to break free on their horses. One, Bull Shield, was shot through the head and killed. Two Tails was wounded yet managed to escape. The third, Wolf Fire, was captured and sent to the guardhouse at Fort Laramie in irons.† There

---

*The Suhtai were one of the ten principal Cheyenne bands. See Appendix A for a brief sketch of the Cheyenne tribe, its history, tribal organization, and way of life.

†Grinnell calls this warrior "Wolf Fire." Fr. Powell translates his name as "Fire Wolf." See Grinnell, *The Fighting Cheyennes*, 112; Powell, *People of the Sacred Mountain*, 1:202.

In April 1856 a detachment of troops from Fort Laramie, guarding the Upper Platte Bridge, shot and killed a young warrior, named Bull Shield; wounded a second, named Two Tails (later Little Wolf); and captured a third, named Wolf Fire, while trying to take the three men prisoner and force delivery of a stray horse claimed by a white man. This was the first serious incident of the Cheyenne wars.

he was kept until he died of the effects of imprisonment on April 16, 1857.[34] The post commandant, Major Hoffman, refused the request of his relatives to recover the body, intensifying hostile feelings already generated by the affair.[35]

When Two Tails reached the small Cheyenne camp with news of what had happened, the people of Wolf Fire's band fled north toward the Black Hills, taking with them only what they could carry on horseback. They feared that soldiers would attack them just as they had the Sioux after the Grattan fight. This belief may have been well founded, for shortly after their departure troops arrived, plundered the abandoned encampment, and burned the tipis and all other articles for which they had no use. All this occurred for the sake of one horse of doubtful ownership.[36]

As they moved northward, people from Wolf Fire's camp came across an old trapper named Ganier who was married to a Cheyenne woman. Blinded by fear and hatred of white men, the Indians killed and scalped him before continuing their flight. He was innocent of wrongdoing, just as Bull Shield and Wolf Fire had been innocent in the matter of the horse. But the trapper became a symbol to the Cheyennes of ills impressed upon them by unwelcome white invaders, and he, too, paid for wanton acts of other men.[37]

Although Wolf Fire's small band moved northward, when other northern bands of Cheyennes, mostly Omissis and northern Suhtai, received news of the incident on the North Platte, they fled southward to join southern bands between the Platte and the Arkansas. The story they carried caused bitter resentment and stirred young warriors to clamor for war. William Guerrier, a trader, was in one of the camps along the Smoky Hill in May 1856 when the wounded Two Tails arrived, bringing word of the attack by soldiers and the death of Bull Shield. This caused such hostility that the chiefs warned Guerrier to take care, and they set their young men to guard him. As the council fires burned, he could hear the chiefs haranguing the young men, urging them to do nothing rash and to avoid further difficulties with the whites.[38]

The admonition not to molest whites was unenforceable. In the tradition of their tribe, hotheaded young warriors believed vengeance a sacred duty. In early June 1856, while searching for their old enemies the Pawnees, a small war party of Cheyennes, Arapahoes, and a few Sioux attacked an immigrant train along the Little Blue River, killing one man.[39] As the party moved west along the

Cheyenne war parties roamed the country in search of intruders on their hunting grounds or seeking vengeance for past losses to tribal enemies.

Platte, they camped near Fort Kearny. A number were summoned to see the commanding officer, Capt. H. W. Wharton, who accused them of attacking the immigrants. When they denied it, suggesting it was the work of Kiowas, he brought out two arrows, placed them on a table, and asked to what tribe they belonged. The arrows were immediately identified as Sioux, and when Captain Wharton asked if there were any Sioux among them, they pointed to a member of their party. This man confirmed that the arrows were Sioux.[40]

A short time later some of the warriors, glancing out a window, noticed six soldiers approaching the building. Fearing trouble, most got up and left. The Sioux and three of the Cheyennes—Big Head, Good Bear, and Black Hairy Dog—remained. Shortly after the others left, the six members of the guard entered the room, arrested the Sioux, and took him out to be put in irons. Meanwhile, the young men who left had run to their camp for horses, and returned mounted and calling for their friends to escape. The three Cheyennes broke free of the guards and ran from the post headquarters with the guards firing after them. Big Head, last of the three to run, was shot several times by the soldiers but managed to reach the waiting horses. Even the Sioux, who was shackled to a ball and chain, managed to break away, carrying the ball in his hands. The waiting Cheyennes helped each in turn onto the back of a horse and galloped away from the post. At a safe distance from the fort they stopped and helped Big Head remove his bloody coat, throwing it on the ground. Then they rode back to camp.[41]

After the escape of Big Head and the other intended hostages, Captain Wharton sent a detachment of mounted troops to the Cheyenne camp located downriver from the fort. Sighting a small herd of Indian horses near the camp, they ran off thirteen and drove them back to the fort corral. The Cheyennes quickly broke camp and fled south to their villages along the upper reaches of the Kansas River.[42] A few days later a second Cheyenne war party moving west along the Platte toward Fort Kearny met the post sutler John Heth, brother of 1st Lt. Henry Heth, former post commander of both Fort Atkinson on the Arkansas and Fort Kearny. Heth told the band of happenings at the fort and advised them not to go there lest they get into trouble. A few young warriors, ignoring his advice, rode close to the fort. On the ground they found Big Head's bloody coat, and nearer the fort they observed the thirteen Cheyenne horses grazing with the army's horse herd. Incensed, they charged the herd and drove off the captured horses, leaving those belonging to the army.[43]

When they returned to the villages in the south, Big Head found that in his absence he had been made a chief. He asked his people to ignore the incident and to bear no ill will toward the whites over the injury to him.[44] The army took a different view. On June 7, 1856, Captain Wharton wrote, "The Cheyennes have been pursuing this same outrageous course for some years past, but this time, in open and daring violation of the treaty just made by them it calls most loudly for punishment."[45]

The Affair near Fort Kearny

Spring is a time of growth on the Great Plains, and, in times gone by, as grasses greened and grew thick, the buffalo fattened. It was time for Cheyennes to end their winter seclusion, moving from isolated camps along small streams all over their country to the site selected by the Council of Forty-four for the great tribal encampment. Family groups met others of their kindred, then kindreds joined with others of their band, and all bands moved slowly to the place ordained by the wise fathers of the tribe. There they would renew acquaintances, socialize, and participate in the great tribal ceremonies pledged since the last gathering. Whether a Renewal of the Sacred Arrows, the Sun Dance, the Massaum, or a combination of these, the event would take place near the summer solstice, when the sun reached its zenith and days were longest. The ceremony would be followed by the tribe's communal buffalo hunt, when the great village moved to a site nearer the buffalo feeding grounds. It was a time of renewal of all life, and, for Cheyennes, an especially important and sacred time.[46]

Following events of the spring of 1856, war parties left the trails along the Platte and Arkansas and concentrated at the tribal encampment somewhere on the upper reaches of the Kansas River, probably on the Smoky Hill, heartland of the Dog Soldier band. There they spent the summer enjoying the camaraderie of the great village, feasting and dancing, and afterward engaging in the tribal buffalo hunt. When it was over, the various bands split up, heading back to their usual haunts along the upper Arkansas, upper Platte, and various branches of the upper Kansas.[47] War parties again roamed the trails, looking for old enemies such as the Pawnees. In the middle of August a band of about seventy or eighty warriors, under Little Gray Hair and Little Spotted Crow, went northeast to the Little Blue River, a favorite hunting ground for Pawnees. Finding none there, the war party followed the Little Blue northwesterly to the Oregon-California Trail and then on to the Platte. There they went into camp on Grand Island, a few miles below Fort Kearny.[48]

About midday on August 24 a group of young warriors from this band observed the westbound mail wagon approaching on the Fort Leavenworth road. Among these young men was a half-blood who could speak English, and his companions persuaded him to go out onto the road to ask for tobacco. In the company of a friend he did so, making signs for the driver to stop. The driver, having heard that the Cheyennes were hostile, became frightened and whipped his horses for a dash to the fort. As he did so he pulled out his pistol and fired at the Indians. The young warriors, angered by the act, jumped out of the way and shot several arrows at the driver, one of which injured him slightly in the arm. Leaders of the party, hearing the report of the driver's pistol, jumped on their horses and rode out to see what had happened. When they discovered that the young men had shot at the driver, they repeatedly struck them with their bows and quirts, driving them back to camp. The day was cool and rainy, so the band remained on Grand Island, intending to continue its journey the following morning.[49]

When the injured driver reached Fort Kearny, he reported the incident to Captain Wharton, the commanding officer, who ordered the post's complement of cavalry to retaliate against the Indians without delay. During the afternoon of August 24, Capt. George H. Stewart led forty-one men, including his Company K, First Cavalry, and a detachment of sixteen men from Companies E and G, First Cavalry, under 1st Lt. Frank Wheaton, in pursuit of the Cheyenne war party. They traveled down the trail to where tracks of the Cheyennes intersected those of the mail wagon and then left the road. As it was nearly dark, the troopers camped at that point, intending to continue the pursuit at daybreak. The next morning they identified the Indian trail and followed it for about five miles before crossing an arm of the Platte to Grand Island. At 11:30 A.M. the detachment reached the camp used by the Cheyennes the night before and found buffalo meat cooking on several fires, with the framework of twelve temporary war-lodges still standing. From that point they followed what was described as a "broad and fresh trail" heading down the island. After traveling about fifteen miles the troopers found themselves within a quarter of a mile of the unsuspecting Cheyennes, who were encamped at the edge of a thick grove of trees. [50]

Dividing his command, Stewart sent Lieutenant Wheaton and his men to charge the camp from the right while he and Lieutenant McIntyre charged from the left. Taken completely by surprise, the Cheyennes abandoned horses and property and ran into the dense undergrowth on the island for safety. About fifteen of them who stayed together were chased for six or seven miles before the pursuit was abandoned. On returning to Fort Kearny, Captain Stewart reported that the cavalry attack had killed ten Indians and badly wounded another eight or ten. In addition, his unit had captured twenty-two horses and two mules and had destroyed fourteen saddles, a number of shields, lances, bridles, and buffalo robes, as well as lodges and their contents. There were no deaths or injuries among the soldiers. [51] A white man named William Rowland had been in the Cheyenne camp at the time, however, and he reported that the number of Indian dead was six. [52]

Whatever the number of casualties, the punishment was entirely out of proportion to the injury inflicted by the Indians. The effect on the Cheyennes was immediate and terrible. This was possibly the major event in a series of unfortunate incidents that spelled the end of peace and the beginning of long years of open warfare between the United States and the Cheyenne nation. Far from serving as a lesson, the actions of Wharton and Stewart would be remembered through the years by Cheyennes, and would lead to death and destruction for whites as well as Indians.

The Platte Raids

Violence begets violence, and the attack upon the resting Cheyenne camp by Captain Stewart and his troops was soon to bear bitter fruit. Crossing the many small branches of the Platte flowing about Grand Island, the surviving Cheyennes reassembled on the north bank and immediately planned revenge. Approximately thirty-three miles northeast of Fort Kearny, where the Council Bluffs Road crossed the Cottonwood Fork of the Platte, they found their first victims. A small four-wagon train carrying immigrants for Utah was encamped next to the crossing. It belonged to Almon

W. Babbitt, Secretary of Utah Territory and its delegate to Congress, and was being used to transport Mormon settlers to their new homes. During the night of August 25, the same day of the cavalry attack upon them, the Cheyennes descended upon the little group of immigrants, killing two men and one child, wounding a man, and carrying off Mrs. Wilson, mother of the dead child. Taking with them all of the train's mules, they returned to their villages in the south. The raiders killed Mrs. Wilson when she proved unable to ride fast enough to keep up with them.[53]

On August 30 a war party of eight Cheyennes attacked a small band of immigrants near Cottonwood Springs, some eighty miles west of Fort Kearny. They killed a woman, Mrs. William Schvekendeck, wounded one man, and carried off Mrs. Schvekendeck's four-year-old boy. They also drove off all of the livestock. On September 6 another party of thirteen warriors attacked a group of Mormons returning to the States, killing two men, one woman, and a child and carrying off a second woman. Once again all of the livestock was driven off and the wagon burned. A small party of immigrants was also reported to have been killed along the Little Blue at about the same time.[54]

On September 2, Almon W. Babbitt and two other men left Fort Kearny in a light carriage bound for Salt Lake City, taking with them a great deal of public money and many valuable papers. Notwithstanding the attack on Babbitt's wagon train eight days earlier, the three refused to heed Captain Wharton's advice to wait for the next patrol to escort them to Fort Laramie. They never arrived there, and on September 26 the bodies of Babbitt and his two companions were discovered in their camp along the Council Bluffs Road on the north side of the Platte near O'Fallon's Bluff, about 120 miles west of Fort Kearny. They had been killed by the Cheyennes, apparently the night before the September 6 attack on the small Mormon party. The carriage had been burned and their horses taken.[55]

Following the attacks of September 6, Cheyenne raiding ended abruptly, and the Indians melted into the plains to the south, moving back to camps along the Smoky Hill, the Saline, the Solomon, and tributaries of the Republican Fork. Newspapers in the States reported that eighteen people had been killed in the raids. The *Council Bluffs Bugle* demanded vengeance, stating that Babbitt's "loss is irreparable, and the government should send at once a

sufficient force to punish, yes to exterminate this tribe who for
the last three months have been murdering and plundering her
emigrants."[56]

What was probably the last confrontation of the season occurred
on the morning of September 20 along the banks of the north fork
of the Republican River, then known as Rock Creek. Lt. Francis T. Bryan and his survey party, charged with locating a good
road from Fort Riley to Bridger's Pass, were returning by way of
a more southerly route than they had followed outbound. After
marching downstream on the right, or south, bank of Rock Creek
for about seven miles, they were suddenly confronted by a large
party of Cheyenne warriors, some of whom had been with the party
attacked by Capt. George Stewart on Grand Island. The Plains
Indians had observed surveyors at work before, and knew their
appearance foreshadowed the opening of new trails and an increased white presence. Bitterly opposed to further roads through
their country, the band prepared to attack, but timely arrival of the
military escort made them think better of the plan. When a cold
rain began falling at 10:30 A.M., the Cheyennes left the survey
party and disappeared into the plains.[57]

While the American press was stirring up public support for a
war of extermination, Cheyenne chiefs were trying to get their
young men back under control, telling them they had enough of
vengeance. Southern bands went into Bent's New Fort to collect
their annuities as usual.[58] Leaders of the northern bands rode north
to Fort Laramie for meetings with their agent, Thomas Twiss, holding three councils with him during the fall of 1856. They wanted
him to understand their side of the story of the summer's troubles—
how the troops had killed Bull Shield without provocation and
taken Wolf Fire prisoner, destroying their camp; how Big Head had
been shot while a guest in the soldiers' lodge at Fort Kearny, the
others chased, and their horses stolen; how Captain Stewart had
destroyed a camp and shot several Cheyennes without reason "after
they had thrown down their bows and arrows and begged for life."
They explained that the young men who wounded the driver of the
mail wagon had not intended harm, that no one wanted trouble,
but that after what happened to Wolf Fire's band and to the camp
on Grand Island, young men could not be controlled and were "hot
for the warpath." It was this, they said, that led to the killing of
Ganier and attacks on immigrant trains.[59]

Convinced the army bore the greater share of blame, Twiss sympathized with the Cheyennes. In September and October 1856 he reported these facts to the Commissioner of Indian Affairs as related to him by the Cheyenne chiefs, along with their expression of deep regret for the attacks. The third council he held, on October 16, when he met with forty-two chiefs and leaders, led to an agreement for the general cessation of hostilities. Twiss laid down four conditions. The Cheyennes were to cease attacks on travelers along the Platte River road, treat all whites traveling through Cheyenne country as friends, make peace with all Indian enemies, and prevent any kind of hostile activity that might threaten peaceful relations with the United States. As a symbol of good faith the Cheyennes and the army agreed to a prisoner exchange.[60]

In the agency report of October 13, 1856, Twiss stated, "The Cheyennes are perfectly quiet and peaceable and entirely within my control, and obedient to my authority." He then told of the escape, to Lieutenant Bryan's surveying party, by the white woman captured on September 6. He also complained of obstacles created by the army that impeded his efforts to perform his duties.[61] It was a valid point, for the army had ignored his efforts to create peace. It had determined to enforce peace by other means.

3

The Cheyennes and the Path to the Solomon

Were all the teeming regions of the dawn
Unpeopled now? What devastating need
Had set so many faces pale with greed
Against the sunset? Not as men who seek
Some meed of kindness, suppliant and meek,
These hungry myriads came. They did but
    look,
And whatsoever pleased them, that they took.
Their faded eyes were icy, lacking ruth,
And all their tongues were forked to split the
    truth
That word and deed might take diverging ways.
Bewildered in the dusk of ancient days
The Red Men groped; and howsoever loud
The hopeful hotheads boasted in the crowd
The wise ones heard prophetic whisperings
Through aching hushes; felt the end of things
Inexorably shaping. What should be
Already was to them. And who can flee
His shadow or his doom? Though cowards
    stride
The wind-wild thunder-horses, Doom shall ride
The arrows of the lightning, and prevail.
Ere long whole tribes must take the spirit trail
As once they travelled to the bison hunt.
Then let it be with many wounds—in front—
And many scalps, to show their ghostly kin

How well they fought the fight they could not
    win,
To perish facing what they could not kill.

So down upon the Platte and Smoky Hill
Swept war; and all their valleys were afraid. (22–23)

The Winter Camps of 1856—57

During September—the Plum Moon, as southern bands of Cheyennes called it—war parties and raiding parties returned to their
bands. Days were shorter, nights cooler, and there was much to do
in preparation for winter. The great herds of buffalo that roamed
the plains in spring and summer were now scattering into smaller
herds seeking the shelter and food supply to be found along the
valleys of rivers and streams. Since first moving out upon the
plains and becoming nomadic buffalo hunters, the Cheyennes had
adapted themselves to the yearly cycle of these movements, gathering for their major tribal ceremonies and hunts in late spring and
summer, and separating into smaller bands or groups for fall, winter, and early spring.

As the native grasses of the plains shriveled and died, first from
the effects of the dry, searing heat of summer, later from the first
killing frosts of midfall, the mobility of the bands grew more re-
stricted. Horses depended on native vegetation, and as their food
supply began to shrink so did their endurance and ability to move
rapidly over long distances. They were the most valuable property
the Plains Indians had, and their condition often meant the difference between life and death. For the band's own survival, horses
could not be worked too hard. This in turn, particularly during the
coldest part of winter, meant that each kindred or group camping
together must find a location suitable for a winter camp. It must be
a place providing the best shelter from winter storms, a stream with
fresh, moving water, a wood supply, grazing for the horse herd,
and cottonwood bark for them to eat in times of deep snow. It must
also be a place where game could be found throughout the entire
period in sufficient abundance to ensure survival of the People.
This was a time of waiting for the sun to move back to the north
and for warmth to return to the land, permitting a renewal of all
life. During this time there could be neither war nor raiding.

The economics of survival usually made living together in a large tribal gathering impossible for Plains Indians during late fall, winter, and early spring. As bands broke into kindreds and the kindreds into family or other small groupings, each selected its own winter campground, far enough from others to ensure that its needs could be met but close enough to afford security against enemy attack. Generally, members of a particular band wintered in their own customary range, with each kindred or other grouping moving to favored campsites within it. For the Hair Rope, Wutapiu, Scabby, Hofnowa, Ohktounna, and Burnt Aorta bands, this was usually at the Big Timbers of the Arkansas or along the Pawnee Fork, Ash Creek,* or Walnut Creek,† important tributaries of the Arkansas, where there were sufficient supplies of wood and water. The Ridge People and the southern Suhtai generally made their campsites along tributaries of the South Platte, those of the Republican Fork of the Kansas River,‡ and along forks of the Solomon, the Saline, the Smoky Hill, and their tributaries. These included such streams as Beaver Creek, Bijou Creek, and Kiowa Creek flowing northward into the South Platte, as well as Rock Creek, the Arikaree, the south or main fork of the Republican, Beaver Creek, Sappa Creek, the Prairie Dog, and other small streams feeding the Republican. The Dog Soldier band favored the Smoky Hill River,§ claiming territory on either side south to Walnut Creek and north to the Republican, along with small streams and tributaries lying between. Their preferred wintering ground was at the Big Timbers of the Smoky Hill (Blue Mound), a short distance east of the present western border of Kansas.[1]

In some years, for security or other reasons, several or all bands might camp close to each other in a string of villages located along a watercourse in a part of their range where hunting could be expected to be reasonably good all winter. Regardless of where they

---

*Ash Creek was called Motoshe' (Where the Ash Trees Grow Thick) by the Cheyennes. Its upper reaches were a favorite camping ground for one of the bands.

†Walnut Creek, known as Otaase-menoshe (Where Walnut Trees Grow Thick) to the Cheyennes, was a favorite camping place for several bands.

‡The south or main fork of the Republican River and the main stream below the forks, was known to the Cheyennes as Mahohevaohe, Red Shield River. The other two forks, Rock Creek (north fork) and the Arickaree, were considered separate streams and had their own names for Cheyennes as well as whites.

§The Smoky Hill River was known to the Cheyennes as Manoiyohe, Bunch of Trees River. It was the heart of the Dog Soldier country.

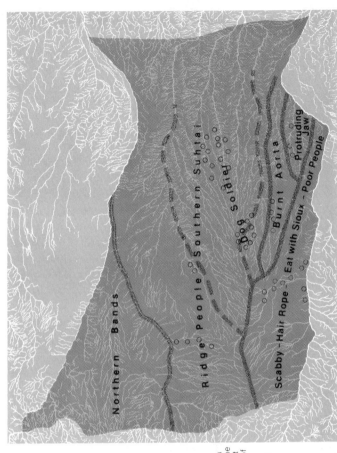

This map presents the areas generally inhabited by the bands of the Cheyenne in the mid-nineteenth century.

Northern Bands
Omissis
Suhtai
Ridge People
Issiometaniu
Dog Soldier
Hotamitaniu
Burnt Aorta
Ivistsitsinihpah
Protruding Jaw
Ohktounna
Scabby
Oivimanah
Hair Rope
Hevatanu
Eat with Sioux
Wutapiu
Poor People
Hotnowa

Each circle, O, indicates a cluster of 10-12 lodges, the campsites of the different bands during the winter of 1856-57. Note that the Northern Bands camped in the area normally used by the Ridge People, Southern Suhtai, and Dog Soldier bands.

| 0 | 25 | 50 | Miles |
| 0 | 25 | 50 | 75 | Kilometers |

Cheyenne Bands Within the Tribe's Territory

camped, they usually continued mobile, wandering and hunting, through October (called the Moon of Dust in the Face in the territory of the southern bands because of the dry dust blowing) and November (the Moon of the Hard Face, referring to the increasing cold). By December (the Moon of the Big Hard Face), with much colder weather dominating the plains, each group was in its camp. There they stayed through January, February, and, depending on the weather, part or all of March (the Buffalo-and-Horse-Begin-to-Fill-Out Moon).[2]

In the fall of 1856, as a result of difficulties with white men, many bands chose to camp together in territory between the Republican and the Smoky Hill. After the fall buffalo hunt, most of these congregated along or near forks of the Solomon. The Hair Rope, Scabby, and Wutapiu bands camped adjacent to each other along a small tributary of the Smoky Hill known to the Cheyennes as Running or Driven (back and forth) Creek.*[3] Some other bands frequenting the Arkansas seem to have camped in the Big Timbers or along the Pawnee Fork, while the Ridge Men band camped for at least a portion of the winter along the South Platte and Beaver Creek, one of its tributaries.[4] The Dog Soldier band appears to have maintained its village at the Big Timbers of the Smoky Hill throughout the winter, while the southern Suhtai camped along small streams feeding the Republican.[5]

In 1856 others who did not usually winter in the south pitched their lodges with those of the southern bands. The northern bands (except Wolf Fire's small family group) had fled south following the incident at the Upper Platte Bridge. They were mostly Omissis, the largest single Cheyenne band, and northern Suhtai, and together they constituted the bulk of the People still living in the north. These bands, who eventually became separately identified as the Northern Cheyenne, appear to have wintered along branches of the Solomon.[6] With them came a few lodges of southern Oglalla Sioux, and in one of these was a young boy named Curley, who had come south to visit relatives and friends among the Cheyennes. He was

---

*Running Creek, known to the Cheyennes as Amaohktsiyohe, was later known as Punished Woman's Creek or Punished Woman's Fork of the Smoky Hill, then as Beaver Creek, and finally as Ladder Creek, its modern name. See George E. Hyde, *Life of George Bent*, 167, Map 2; Mrs. Frank C. Montgomery, "Fort Wallace and its Relation to the Frontier," *KHC* 17:272; John Rydjord, *Kansas Place-Names*, 477; John Rydjord, *Indian Place-Names*, 305–306.

about fifteen or sixteen years of age. Within two years he would earn a new name, Crazy Horse, and become the legendary war leader of the Oglalla Sioux. Scarcely more than twenty years later he would be dead, a great man lost as a result of the tragic failure of two cultures to understand or tolerate each other.[7]

As fall gave way to winter, Cheyenne camps became quiet and immobile, warriors engaging in hunting and caring for horses, women busy with their never-ending cycle of making clothing, preparing food, caring for the young, and generally keeping the camp together. In the evenings around campfires the storytellers spun tales and men talked. This year many stories were of attacks made by the Veho,* white men, upon Cheyennes who had done them no wrong and who had wanted only peace with them. There were stories, also, of raids of vengeance along the Platte River Road. The anger in their hearts grew with the telling of these stories. The keening of mourning women and haranguing by angry relatives of dead warriors reminded them of their losses and of traditions calling for vengeance.

When the southern bands had gone to Bent's New Fort in the fall of 1856 to receive their treaty goods, Col. William Bent had reported that the Great Father was preparing an expedition against them. They told him they had no intention of meeting army troops in a great battle. Now it was not so clear what should be done.[8] As a hard and long winter drew slowly to a close, the Cheyennes were troubled. They wanted no war with the white men, but it seemed whites wanted no peace with them. What they wanted were more roads through Indian territory and more buffalo and other game. What whites wanted *was* the Indian country. Whether the year would bring peace or war would be up to the Great White Father and his soldiers. The Cheyennes would be ready for either.

The Sun Dance and the Summer Camps

The winter of 1856–57 was harsh across the southern plains, with cold lasting much longer than usual. At last, in April (the Fat

*The term Veho means spider. The spider was considered a creature of unique powers, and Cheyennes applied the term to the whites whose inventions so amazed them. It also carried with it the connotation of a trickster, the white man's mind being deceitful and intent upon tricking the Cheyennes and destroying their way of life. See Peter J. Powell, *Sweet Medicine*, 1:299–300.

Moon) grasses began to grow and leaves to bud on cottonwood, hackberry, ash, and willow trees scattered along the few flowing streams. Horses, weak from the long winter, took many days of grazing before they began to regain strength. Rains started in April. Not much fell, but by the standards of the plains it was sufficient to generate growth in what vegetation it sustained. Camps were moved to higher ground to avoid the runoff and the marshlike effect on bottomlands.[9] Finally in May (called the Bright Moon because the sun shines so brightly), Cheyennes began coming together once again. This year, as family joined kindred, and kindred joined together as bands, the movement was toward the upper reaches of the Republican—the Red Shield River of the Cheyennes.

Sometime during the period following the last tribal gathering, a member of the tribe had pledged the Sun Dance, or Medicine Lodge, the Cheyenne ceremony second in importance only to the Renewal of the Sacred Arrows. As days of late winter warmed into spring, this man had sought out camp chiefs of every Cheyenne encampment across the plains and told them his plans and where the ceremony would be held. Then, as if drawn by some irresistible power, small camps broke up and began a steady migration to the rendezvous. There were many camping places along the way as each of the groups and bands moved toward the site selected for the great tribal encampment. As they traveled, they sometimes stopped for a few days to do a little hunting, but most of the camps en route to the tribe's communal village were only to permit a night's rest. Four times they stopped to pray and invoke the blessing of Maheo and the Sacred Persons.[10] Some bands, already camping near the area selected for the Sun Dance village, had to move only a short distance.

As they drew closer to the ceremonial site, the bands prepared for entry into the great circle of the Sun Dance village. At the last campsite before reaching the appointed place, they donned their best clothing. On the following day, with horses groomed and people and horses painted, they completed their journey and entered the waiting camp from the east at the designated opening of the camp circle, riding in a long column and singing songs of joy and happiness.[11] This was the end of a harsh winter.

Cheyennes were a people of action, and they lived with the assurance that through the sacred ceremonies Maheo, the Sacred

Persons, and the Sacred Powers offered them a supernatural power of life. The Sun Dance was intended to revive and renew the people, Grandmother Earth, and all her inhabitants, and to restore the harmony and vitality of life.[12] It was, fundamentally, a celebration of the rebirth of life on earth and the return of the season of growth.

The Sun Dance required eight days. The first four were given to building the Medicine Lodge itself and to secret rites at the Lone Tipi, which symbolizes the Sacred Mountain from which the Sacred Powers instructed Erect Horns (Tomsivsi) in the sacred ceremony that would renew the earth and save his Suhtai people from starvation. The last four days were devoted to the public dance in the Sun Dance Lodge.[13] The village site was moved each of the first four days, although usually the move was very short.[14]

In 1857 the Sun Dance village probably was located first on the upper reaches of the Republican River, possibly along the Arikaree or the south fork, with the various bands coming together about mid-May. Campsites were always close to the final site of the communal village, where the Medicine Lodge would be constructed. The Pledger or Pledgers (no more than three were permitted)[15] had selected a place along the banks of Beaver Creek, a tributary of the Republican flowing from the south.*[16] By the third day of the Sun Dance, the village had been moved to the head of a small stream now known as Big Timber Creek, which flows into the south fork of the Republican from the southeast.[17] On the fourth day, the village moved one last time, to Beaver Creek, site of the Medicine Lodge. On the fourth day of Oxheheom† preparations were complete, and ended with the sacred acts of consecration. Then the dance itself began.[18]

So sacred were the great ceremonies of the Cheyennes that all tribal members were required to attend. Absence from either the Arrow Renewal ceremony or the Sun Dance was believed to bring misfortune not only to the absent members but also, through them, to the entire tribe.[19] All who could attend were expected to be there, and in 1857 the only tribal members known to be absent were those unfortunate people of Wolf Fire's band who fled

---

*The Cheyennes called Beaver Creek Homaiyohe, and they frequently camped and held sacred ceremonies along it.
†The Cheyenne name for the Sun Dance was "Oxheheom," meaning New Life Lodge or Lodge of the Generator.

to the Black Hills after having lost their lodges and personal possessions.[20]

When the Sun Dance of 1857 had been completed, the People once again removed their camp. Following the great tribal ceremonies came the communal summer buffalo hunt, during which the People continued living together as one united tribe. Leaving the sacred village on the Beaver, with the frame of the Medicine Lodge still standing as an offering to Maheo, the Cheyennes moved south and east, making their next camp on the middle fork of Sappa Creek, known to Cheyennes as Stealing Horse Creek.[21] The Sun Dance village along the banks of Beaver Creek was located in one of the very best parts of the Cheyenne and Arapahoe buffalo range. Especially after white men's roads were built along the Arkansas and the Platte, the undisturbed country around the Smoky Hill on the south and the Republican on the north represented to the southern bands of the People the most prized of their remaining hunting grounds. This area lay within the remaining range of the great southern buffalo herd.[22] Thus, when the Cheyennes left their Medicine Lodge behind on the Beaver, they had to travel no great distance to establish a new camp close to vast herds of the shaggy beast that meant survival.

Around the first of June the great tribal village moved from the Beaver to the Sappa. Later in the month they moved to the upper reaches of the North Fork of the Solomon, which they called Turkeys Creek, where once again they set up the camp circle.*[23] Here they spent days hunting buffalo and antelope on the plains, and wild turkey and deer along streams. No one knows how many were there, but only Wolf Fire's band and a few scouting and raiding parties were absent. The Cheyennes were never a large tribe, and their losses to cholera in 1849 and 1850 were so great that in 1857 they probably totaled no more than forty-five hundred people.†[24] Thus, assuming an average of eight persons per lodge, the communal camps of 1857 probably had somewhere between 450 and 550 lodges.

During their visit to Bent's New Fort the previous fall, the south-

---

*The Solomon River was known as Mahkineohe, Turkeys Creek, to the Cheyennes, and was a favored hunting and camping location.

†Whitfield estimated that in the Upper Arkansas Agency there were 3,150 Cheyennes living in 350 lodges; Twiss estimated that 1,400 Cheyennes lived in the Upper Platte Agency in 140 lodges. See letters cited in chap. 3, n. 24.

In May 1857 the Cheyennes held their Sun Dance at a great village on the east bank of Beaver Creek, a tributary of the Republican River. All of the bands and most of the tribal members were present.

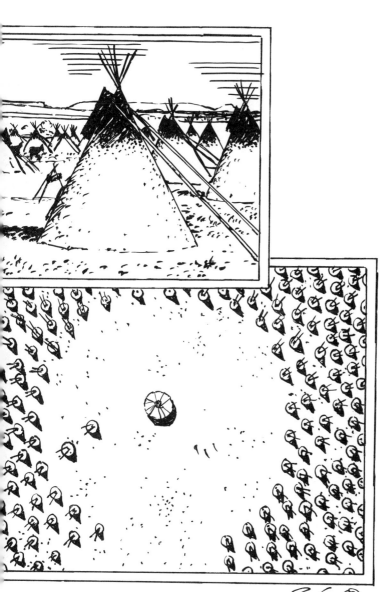

ern bands had learned of the army's intended spring campaign
against them. In anticipation, they sent a small number of scouts
to the trails along the Platte and the Arkansas. Even before cele-
brating had ended in the Sun Dance village on the Beaver, they
had received disquieting news from visitors. From the south came
Arapahoes who brought stories of horse soldiers moving along the
road to Santa Fe near Allison and Booth's trading post on Walnut
Creek. The soldiers said they were looking for the Cheyennes and
wanted to fight. From the north came Oglalla Sioux to visit with
friends and relatives. They too carried news of many horse soldiers
marching along the Little Blue River on the Platte River Road.

After the People had moved their communal village to the Sappa
and then to the north fork of the Solomon, visitors continued to
bring stories of soldiers marching westward along the Arkansas and
the Platte. Scouts were kept in the vicinity of both roads to learn
the whereabouts of white troopers and to report their progress. The
continuing flow of news from scouts and visitors stirred anew a
festering resentment. It seemed that the Great Father in Washington did want war.

Evenings, after the day's hunt, men sat around campfires talking
about attacks upon innocent Cheyennes and about raids of vengeance. They talked of what they would do when the soldiers found
them. Their chiefs and the old men wanted peace and to stay away
from the army. As spring turned to summer, however, voices of
warriors and chiefs of military societies were heard more and more,
and it was war they urged.[25] Cheyennes had done no wrong, they
said, and had wanted nothing of white men except to be left alone
to live in the sacred manner taught them by Maheo in the land He
had given them. The white invaders were the ones who should
leave. The country was not theirs, and they had been first to lift an
unjust hand, when the Cheyennes had tried to be friends. The
Cheyennes were warriors; they would not run.

In late June or early July, the tribal encampment moved again,
this time to the south or main fork of the Solomon, and from there
hunting continued. Now, however, the hunting focused more on
deer, antelope, and other game, because the great herds of bison
were moving steadily eastward, to where grass was thicker and
lasted longer into summer. The debate about the army expedition
against them continued. Even then soldiers were on the Fat River,

the river whites called the South Platte.*[26] Scouts were sent to watch the marching column and to warn the village of its approach. The Cheyennes continued to hunt during the day, but in the evenings, warriors and chiefs sat about council fires making plans for the war they were sure would come.

At the time there were in the camp two prominent young men, Ice (or Hail, later called White Bull), an Omissis, and Gray Beard (or Dark), a Dog Soldier, both eager to prove their power as holy men.[27] From the time the tribe had gathered in the spring for the Sun Dance, these two had thrown their influence behind those calling for war. They had sacred powers that they believed would assure victory by protecting the warriors from white men's bullets. With such assurances they made a powerful argument for fighting against the heavily armed soldiers, whose guns would thus be rendered harmless.[28] The Brulé and Oglalla Sioux bands they had tried to convince to join them in raids along the Platte that summer had refused. While disappointing, this made no real difference, for Cheyennes believed their medicine so powerful that the help of others would not be needed.[29]

Around the middle of July, the Cheyenne villages moved once more to a fresh site farther south, closer both to remaining buffalo, which had moved away from hunting parties along the Solomon, and to the many bands of antelope. This time the People placed their principal village on the north side of Cedar River, called by the whites the Grand Saline Fork of the Smoky Hill.†[30] The vast camp circle, located in the broad bottom of a horseshoe bend in the river extended from its banks one-half mile or more northward to the bluffs.[31] It included between four hundred and five hundred lodges and many small temporary shelters for young bachelors or those not living in a lodge with a family unit.[32] The searing heat of summer lay heavily across the plains, and the great herds of buffalo diminished, most drifting farther east to better grass or north to cooler climes, or congregating along larger streams in areas with stands of timber. Still, food supplies remained adequate and the tribe continued to camp together. The news they received almost

---

*The South Platte River was called Witaniyohe (Fat River) by the Cheyennes.
†The Grand Saline Fork, now known as the Saline River, was called Shistotoiyohe (Cedar River) by the Cheyennes.

daily, regarding the whereabouts of the white troops, compelled the tribe to remain concentrated in one location. By now the determination to fight had spread to all but the few chiefs and older men to whom fighting the Veho seemed futile.

As news of the soldiers' approach continued, councils were held to plan the fight. A great white council lodge was erected within the camp circle; here chiefs and principal warriors met daily to discuss the impending battle and how and where it should be fought.[33] Scouts reported that the troops had left the South Platte and were headed in a southeasterly direction—toward the Cheyenne tribal village on the banks of the Saline. Their medicine men had assured them of the great protective power that Maheo had given them. War leaders were confident in their fighting abilities and those of Cheyenne warriors. When the soldiers came, the Cheyennes would be ready.

4

An Expedition Against the Cheyennes

But half a world away the Mighty Ones
Had spoken words like bullets in the dark
That wreak the rage of blindness on a mark
They cannot know.　　　　　　　　*(226)*

A Punitive Expedition Is Ordered

The concept of a large-scale military operation against the Cheyennes had its origin in the 1855 report by their agent, John W. Whitfield, who found Cheyennes and other Plains Indians of his agency in need of a "sound chastisement" to ensure what he considered proper behavior.[1] Following the Treaty of Fort Pierre in early March 1856, Col. William S. Harney, dissatisfied with a lack of humility on the part of the Cheyennes and believing they deserved some of the same treatment he had given the Sioux, recommended that an expedition be sent against them in the spring. Plans for such an operation had subsequently been deferred because of army problems during 1856 in keeping peace between pro-slavery and free-state settlers of the new Kansas Territory.[2]

The next link in the chain of events culminating in the Cheyenne Expedition was forged later in March 1856, when Maj. William Hoffman, commanding officer of Fort Laramie, delivered Colonel Harney's ultimatum to Cheyenne and Arapahoe camps near the fort. Chiefs of those bands agreed to the demands Harney made and even sent runners to the southern bands advising them of the council at Fort Pierre and requirements the treaty imposed upon them. Major Hoffman remained skeptical and wrote the Sioux Expedition headquarters that Cheyennes were "an unruly race" whose good conduct could be insured only if they were "kept in dread of immediate punishment" for their misdeeds.[3]

In June 1856, Cheyennes attacked an immigrant train along the Little Blue River, and Capt. H. W. Wharton, commanding Fort Kearny, wrote to Capt. Alfred Pleasonton, adjutant of the Sioux Expedition, that such conduct was in open violation of the Fort Pierre Treaty and "calls most loudly for punishment."[4] On September 8, 1856, following the attack upon the Cheyenne camp on Grand Island and subsequent retaliatory raids by Cheyennes, Captain Wharton wrote to Col. Samuel Cooper, adjutant general of the army, reporting recent events and warning of a need for strengthened military presence to protect travelers along the trail. There was, he said, a combination of Cheyennes of the Arkansas with those of the Platte to make war on whites, and this necessitated reestablishing a large garrison on the Arkansas near the site of the now-abandoned Fort Atkinson. He reported the Cheyennes as troublesome since abandonment of that post, which was the location of several of their bands as well as the congregating ground of Arapahoes, Comanches, and several other hostile tribes. He expressed his belief that only with a strong force of cavalry at the new post and a strengthened force at Fort Kearny could the Indians be deterred and punished.[5]

This report of Captain Wharton, transmitted through the usual military chain of command, was endorsed and forwarded by Bvt. Maj. Gen. Persifer F. Smith, commanding general of the Department of the West, from his headquarters at Fort Leavenworth. In his accompanying letter of September 10, 1856, General Smith made clear his belief that a military expedition against the Cheyennes was imperative, and that they must be severely chastised. However, unsettled conditions in Kansas Territory, which required all available troops for keeping peace among the settlers, made immediate action against the tribe impossible. Smith therefore stated his intention to defer any major operations until the following spring.[6]

On September 27, 1856, Major Hoffman, commanding officer at Fort Laramie, wrote: "Anticipating that a campaign will be made against the Cheyenne Indians, I have caused a map of their country to be prepared. . . . They are well armed and well mounted and have the reputation of being enterprising and warlike."[7] The reports forwarded by Captain Wharton and the endorsement of General Smith finally made their way to Washington, and on October 24, 1856, Secretary of War Jefferson Davis gave his approval to the "long-entertained design" and ordered the First Cavalry to mount a campaign against the Cheyennes.[8]

The order from the War Department was issued on October 24, 1856, eight days following the successful conclusion of the peace council with Thomas S. Twiss, Agent for the Upper Platte. The white captives had for the most part been released. The only property of consequence taken by the Cheyennes were a few horses and mules. The punishment to be administered was for activities occurring in the preceding two years (previously settled and forgiven by treaty), and for which the army bore substantial responsibility by its harsh and indiscriminate treatment of Indians. It was the culmination of years of misunderstanding and mistrust, and was grounded on the belief that a whole people should be responsible for the actions of a few; that Indians had no right to move freely through their own lands or hold whites accountable for wanton acts committed by them; and that the appropriate punishment for harm done to the person or property of whites was to kill Indians, any Indians, regardless of their culpability. It was the policy that would persist until well after the Battle of the Little Big Horn, until 1890, in a place called Wounded Knee.

On November 11, 1856, two and one-half weeks following endorsement of the plan for an expedition by Jefferson Davis, General Smith again wrote to Colonel Cooper, the adjutant general of the army. He reported that because civil conflict had been suppressed and order restored to Kansas Territory, it was now possible to proceed with plans for an expedition against the Cheyennes. This must be primarily a mounted force, he said, and ready to move by the middle of April. Details of the force and direction of operations were not then determined.[9]

The expedition was now in the planning stage, and during the winter and early spring its composition and route were determined. Prophetically, General Smith's November 11 report noted that winter had come much earlier than usual, and harsh weather had indeed descended across the plains. Early arriving, it also took a late departure, thwarting plans for the regiment to be in the field by the middle of April.

The First Cavalry troopers commenced what would be a long and arduous march in search of the Cheyennes.

Plans were complete by March 1857 and were forwarded from the Department of the West to army headquarters in New York for approval by the general-in-chief, Winfield Scott. On April 4, 1857, the army issued General Order No. 5 directing the expedition against the Cheyennes, to be under the command of Col. E. V. Sumner, regimental commander of the First Cavalry. It provided that two squadrons of the First Cavalry, equipped and supplied for distant service, should move along the line of the Arkansas River as soon as the season permitted. A third squadron would simultaneously move along the line of the Platte River, to be joined by a squadron of the Second Dragoons at Fort Kearny, and by three of the four companies of the Sixth Infantry stationed at Fort Laramie. The order directed the remaining squadron of the First Cavalry to proceed south under the command of Lt. Col. Joseph E. Johnston to survey the southern boundary of Kansas Territory. It authorized Colonel Sumner to take one or more prairie howitzers with each column and to march with either as he elected. A supply of forage sufficient for ten or more days would be sent out in advance of departure, and each column would commence its march when sufficient grazing could be anticipated.[10]

On April 10, 1857, the new Secretary of War, John B. Floyd, confirmed to Secretary of the Interior Jacob Thompson that the army intended to conduct operations against the Cheyennes during the summer "to keep the peace of the plains and to punish past offenses against the United States."[11] In doing so, Secretary Floyd gave notice that the peace the Interior Department had concluded with the Cheyennes the previous fall through Agent Twiss would be ignored and, in fact, breached.

The judgments of those in high command were now final, the plans made, the orders given. There would be an expedition across the plains to make war on the Cheyennes.

The First Cavalry Prepares

Preparations for the march of the First Cavalry began long before orders for the Cheyenne Expedition were written. Indeed, the army's early belief that there should be such an operation probably resulted in some long-range planning during the spring of 1856. Major Hoffman forwarded his map to the adjutant general of the army nearly a month before Secretary of War Jefferson Davis gave his approval. But serious planning and preparation began only after Davis's order of October 24. The logistics of such operations were staggering, with mules and horses to be acquired and trained and cattle to be purchased, along with all necessary foodstuffs, clothing, shelter tents, ammunition, weapons, wagons, and conveyances. Training of troops had to be accelerated.

The First Cavalry was a new and inexperienced regiment. Though it had participated in a minor way in the Sioux Expedition of 1855, its ranks had never been filled with needed enlisted personnel, and its training was incomplete.*[12] Demands made upon it to keep the peace of Kansas Territory compounded the training

---

*See Appendix B for a brief review of the history and organization of the First Cavalry, along with an explanation and description of its operations in the field.

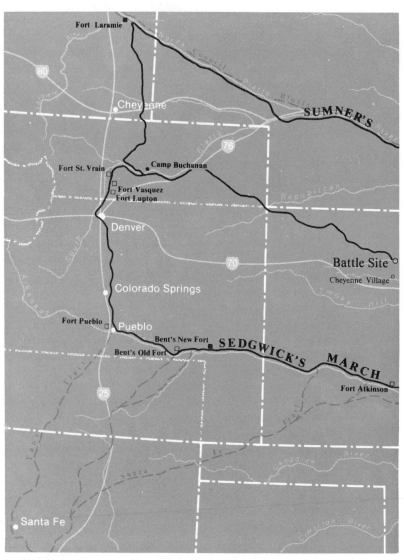

Route of the Cheyenne Expedition

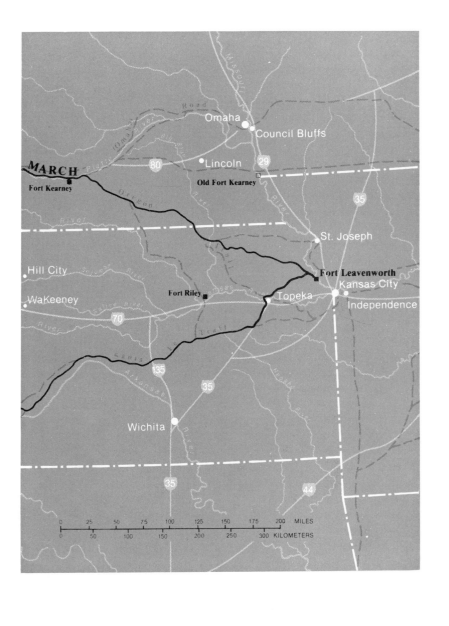

difficulties. New recruits, then being trained at Jefferson Barracks in St. Louis, had to be made into capable, if unseasoned, cavalrymen in short order. This was a complex and time-consuming undertaking.

Notwithstanding a shortage of personnel, 1856 was a busy year for the regiment. Capt. George H. Stewart and his Company K had been sent north to Fort Kearny for a time and while there had made the attack upon the Cheyenne war party on Grand Island. Most of the regiment had been occupied with suppressing violence between pro-slavery and free-state factions among the settlers. It was a rare occasion when a majority of the companies were in garrison at the same time. However, as the year drew to a close, troubles in the territory subsided, and troops returned to Fort Leavenworth to continue training and preparing for the spring campaign. Among officers, talk of an expedition against the Cheyennes had begun almost as soon as the fight on Grand Island had been reported, and it raised eager anticipation among those bored by current policing activities and anxious to make a name for themselves.[13]

Because the onset of winter brought safe navigation to an end on the Missouri, new recruits were kept at Jefferson Barracks until the spring thaw, in the latter part of February 1857. At this time the first group of about three hundred recruits was loaded aboard two chartered steamboats and transported to Fort Leavenworth.[14] Immediately upon arrival they were assigned to the companies for which they had been enlisted, marched to their quarters, and commenced training. On April 20 a group of one hundred fifty men left St. Louis; they arrived at Fort Leavenworth on April 29. Of these, one hundred thirty were assigned to the First Cavalry and twenty to the Second Dragoons. During the evening of April 29, another three hundred recruits arrived for the First Cavalry, which was now filled to its full complement plus four extra men to each company. With departure scheduled in days, training and preparation were at fever pitch.[15]

Since February 1857 it had been proposed that the regiment would march on May 1.[16] When the order for the expedition arrived from army headquarters in early April, officers and enlisted men alike started speculating about the actual departure date. The monotony of the life of constant training while in garrison served to heighten anticipation and eagerness for action. On April 15, eliminating some of the speculation, Colonel Sumner issued orders that

Maj. John Sedgwick would command the southern column consisting of two squadrons (four companies) of the First Cavalry. Originally Sedgwick's column was to consist of Companies A, D, G, and K, but a change in orders altered its composition to Companies D, E, G, and H. Companies A and B were then assigned to the northern column to be commanded by Colonel Sumner, the expedition commander.[17] Companies E and H, Second Dragoons, would join Sumner's command at Fort Kearny, and Companies C, D, and G, Sixth Infantry, would be added at Fort Laramie, bringing the northern column to full strength.[18] Remaining companies of the First Cavalry, C, F, I, and K, were placed under the command of Lt. Col. Joseph E. Johnston with orders to proceed south and survey the south boundary line of Kansas Territory, at the same time keeping a watchful eye out for hostile Kiowas.[19]

Once the composition of the three columns had been determined, remaining plans fell rapidly into place. Each command would be provided with two prairie howitzers, to be hauled by four-mule teams and manned by dismounted cavalrymen detailed from each company.*[20] Each company would be provided two wagons, pulled by six-mule teams, to carry tents, mess kits, extra clothing, and other personal items of officers and men. To minimize the load, clothing for the troops was limited to fatigue uniforms and one change of underclothing. The troopers' best uniforms and extra clothes were packed away in boxes and trunks, to be left with the company laundresses until the regiment returned. Tents and other camp equipment were drawn from the quartermaster, and such horses as were not fit for the expedition were turned in and replacements issued. In short, participating companies underwent a general outfitting to place both troopers and transport in the best possible condition for a long campaign far from Fort Leavenworth.[21]

The overall plan devised for field operations called for Major Sedgwick's command to march west along the Santa Fe Trail and beyond along the line of the Arkansas River to Fountain Creek, and then to move north, parallel with the Front Range of the Rocky Mountains, to the South Platte. Colonel Sumner's column was to

---

*Prairie howitzers were identical to mountain howitzers, except that the carriage was mounted on larger wheels, which permitted rapid movement over the relatively level plains. The smaller wheels used for what were designated as "mountain howitzers" were designed to facilitate movement in mountainous terrain with narrow, rocky, winding trails.

march west along the Oregon-California Trail to Fort Laramie, whence, after resupply, it would move south to the South Platte, there to join with Sedgwick's column on July 4, at the site of old Fort St. Vrain. If neither of the two commands had met and engaged Cheyennes on the way west, the combined column was to scour the country between the Arkansas and Platte until the Indians had been found and severely punished for the previous summer's raids along the Platte River Road.[22]

A late spring slowed the growth of grass on the plains, which in turn delayed the planned departure of the First Cavalry. By May 1, however, the six companies assigned to the Cheyenne Expedition moved into camp on what was known as the "blue grass pasture" south of the post, the two columns camping separately. There they continued to train, and to check, repair, and replace worn or defective arms and equipment.[23] Being close to the garrison, they also continued to perform normal garrison duties, including standing guard. The expectation was a departure on May 16 and a return by November 1.[24]

On May 2, 1857, the paymaster arrived and the troopers were mustered for pay.[25] On the same day an article in the *Kansas Weekly Herald*, published in Leavenworth City, told of a trip from Green River to the Missouri made during the early spring by Tim Goodale, a well-known mountain man and trader. Goodale reported meeting a few Cheyennes on the Platte who were waiting for news of the military expedition and whether it would fight them. They told him that if the government wanted peace, they were willing, but that if the soldiers wanted a fight, they were ready. According to Goodale, the tribe was encamped along the tributaries of the upper Republican and determined to make a fight if the troops disturbed them. Efforts by the Cheyennes to form a working alliance with the Sioux for attacks along the Platte River Road had not been successful.[26]

The days that followed were filled with more intense training and preparation for the march. Finally, May 16 arrived, but once again Sedgwick's column was delayed. However, with word of delay came the welcome news that officers and men should be prepared to march on May 18. Spirits again soared. On May 17, the order was finally passed down. The command would depart the following morning. At last they were going in search of the Cheyennes.[27]

Part Two

The Expedition's March
to the South Platte

5

The March of Sedgwick's Column

By fours and troop by troop,
With packs between, they passed the Colonel's group
....
The regimental banner and the grays;
And after them the sorrels and the bays,
The whites, the browns, the piebalds and the blacks.
One flesh they seemed with those upon their backs,
Whose weathered faces, like and fit for bronze,
Some gleam of unforgotten battle-dawns
Made bright and hard. The music of their going,
How good to hear!—though mournful beyond knowing;
....
The guidons whipping in a stiff south breeze
Prophetical of thunder-brewing weather,
The chiming spurs and bits and crooning leather,
The shoe calks clinking on the scattered stone,
And, fusing all, the rolling undertone
Of hoofs by hundreds rhythmically blent—
The diapason of an instrument
Strung taut for battle music.

So they passed.   (178–79)

The March to the Great Bend of the Arkansas

On May 18, 1857, the Cheyenne Expedition began. Breaking camp at 9:00 A.M., the four companies of Major Sedgwick's command started their march, four men abreast. Company E, mounted on roan horses and with Captain Sturgis, the senior captain, at their head, led the way. They left the bluegrass pasture where they had been encamped and met the mounted band, then marched proudly through the garrison with carbines slung, sabres drawn, and guidons flying. The band, in the lead, played the traditional piece for such occasions, "The Girl I Left Behind Me." As they crossed the old drill ground southwest of the post, the band wheeled off to the north side of the road and struck up "Goodby, John." Colonel Sumner and his staff sat on their horses nearby, taking the salute of the passing companies. As the commanding officer of each drew abreast of the reviewing party, he gave the order "Present-sabres" and, after the last rank had passed, "Carry-sabres." When the rear company had passed, the colonel, his staff, and the band returned to the post. The marching column now returned sabres and continued steadily toward the west. Ahead lay the vast emptiness of the plains—without points of resupply or refuge, without friendly faces.[1]

The last of the troops, by now strung out in a long column, cleared Fort Leavenworth at about 10:00 A.M. Riding far in the front were four Delaware scouts engaged by Major Sedgwick and led by a chief named Fall Leaf. Behind them at some distance rode Major Sedgwick with his adjutant, 2d Lt. Lunsford Lomax of Company D, and his orderly bugler. Following them were the four cavalry companies in their initial order of march: Company E, led by Capt. Samuel D. Sturgis, 1st Lt. Frank Wheaton, and 2d Lt. Eugene W. Crittenden; H, led by Capt. Edward W. B. Newby, 1st Lt. James B. McIntyre, and 2d Lt. Eli Long; G, led by 2d Lt. George D. Bayard;* and D, led by Capt. James McIntosh and 1st Lt. David S. Stanley. Following the rear cavalry company were the two prairie howitzers assigned to Major Sedgwick.[2]

The column marched three miles to the crossing of Salt Creek, where it halted to rest and await the wagon train, the remuda of horses and mules, and the beef herd. When they arrived, the march resumed, following the Fort Leavenworth-Fort Riley Military Road. About twelve miles from the fort, they reached and crossed

---

*Capt. William S. Walker of Company G was at the time on extended leave to be married, and 1st Lt. J. E. B. Stuart of Company G was to accompany Colonel Sumner's northern column as acting quartermaster and commissary of the expedition.

Stranger Creek, going into camp opposite the tiny pro-slavery hamlet of Eastin.* Shortly thereafter a mounted officer rode in, bringing with him several men on foot. These were soldiers whose excessive celebration over their imminent departure had landed them in jail in Leavenworth City. Colonel Sumner had their fines paid so they might rejoin their units.[3]

On the morning of Tuesday, May 19, first call was sounded at dawn's first light, and the troopers turned out, dressed hurriedly, and, after roll call, began their day's routine. At 7:00 A.M., with their horses groomed, watered, and fed, breakfast eaten, and their tents and other gear packed in the company wagons, they broke camp and continued down the trail. During the day's march, they passed three small pro-slavery towns, the first of which as yet had no name, the second was Hickory Point, and the third Ozawkie.† Opposite the last they went into camp on the banks of Grasshopper Creek,‡ a beautiful rock-bottomed stream that ran nearly due south and emptied into the Kansas River opposite Lecompton, the pro-slavery territorial capital.[4]

Hickory Point, the second of the three fledgling towns they had passed during the day, held some interest for the soldiers, because there, on September 13 and 14, 1856, units of the First Cavalry had intervened in a fight between pro-slavery forces, under Capt. H. A. Lowe of the Kansas Militia, and the free-state "army" of James H. Lane, from Indiana. Now eight months later, a cannonball hole in the blacksmith shop was visible evidence of the scrap.[5]

On May 20, Sedgwick's men were back on the trail by 6:30 A.M., which was to be their usual departure time through the re-

*Eastin, a pro-slavery town founded by people from Kentucky, was originally named for Gen. Lucian J. Eastin, editor of the *Kansas Weekly Herald* in Leavenworth. The spelling was later changed to "Easton" at the request of then Territorial Governor Reeder, a native of Easton, Pennsylvania. In 1857 it had no more than twelve houses, a saloon, a sawmill, a blacksmith shop, and a store. See *KHC* 20:645–48; John Rydjord, *Kansas Place-Names*, 269.

†The town with no name was founded by a small group of settlers from Virginia, and later was known as "Winchester," in honor of Winchester, Virginia. Hickory Point disappeared following abandonment of the military road and failure of the railroad to come through it. Winchester and Ozawkie survive to the present day. See *KHC* 7:486; John Rydjord, *Kansas Place-Names*, 300.

‡Grasshopper Creek was later renamed Delaware River because it ran adjacent to and along the west boundary of the Delaware Indian Reservation. John Rydjord, *Kansas Place-Names*, 60.

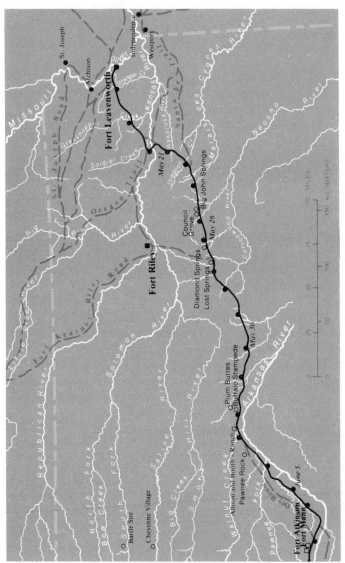

March of Sedgwick's column from Fort Leavenworth to Fort Atkinson

mainder of the expedition. Ozawkie was north of the northwest corner of the Delaware Indian Reservation and several miles east of the Potawatomie Reservation. The Fort Leavenworth-Fort Riley road they were following dropped southwest across the gap between the two reservations, winding through valleys and over rolling, grass-covered hills in a generally southwestly direction until it reached the Kansas River, thereafter running westerly, parallel with the river, until it reached its destination. The troops followed this road through the small pro-slavery town of Indianola, going into camp two miles beyond it.[6]

At Indianola and beyond, the road from Fort Leavenworth to Santa Fe split from the road to Fort Riley at two different points. The first, dropping south from Indianola, crossed the Kansas River via Papan's Ferry; the second, about six miles farther west, crossed at Smith's Ferry. Heavy use of Papan's Ferry by immigrants persuaded Major Sedgwick to use the upstream ferry in the interest of time.[7]

Shortly before their departure on the morning of May 21, the command was passed by four companies of the Second Dragoons en route from Fort Riley to Fort Leavenworth, there to join the Utah Expedition. Once they had moved on, Sedgwick's men left camp and marched to the branch of the trail leading south to the river and Smith's Ferry. This they found to be a flatboat operated by ropes fastened to trees on either bank and with which the boat was pulled back and forth. Wagons, teams, and howitzers were ferried, but cavalry troopers forded the river on horseback, followed by the livestock. The river was difficult to ford because of quicksand.[8] Reaching the south bank, the column followed a road leading southeast to a junction with the trail from Papan's Ferry, going into camp eight miles from the Kansas River, below the fork of the two trails.[9]

Once beyond the river, the trail dropped south-southwest, crossing the Wakarusa River, Dragoon Creek, and Soldier Creek before intersecting the main branch of the Santa Fe Trail. En route troopers passed the small free-state village of Brownsville at the crossing of the Wakarusa,* and, at the junction of the two trails, a new

---

*When an 1857 petition for a post office brought news that there already was a Brownsville in the territory, the name was changed to Auburn. See *KHC* 16:519; John Rydjord, *Kansas Place-Names*, 263.

station operated by Hockaday and Hall, contractors for the Independence–Santa Fe Mail. On May 22 they passed a wagon train of
immigrants moving west, one of many they would encounter during
their march.[10]

The land south of the Kansas River was hilly and rolling, but it
lay below the glaciated region and the rocky deposits of glacial till
marking the hills north of the river. South of the Wakarusa the
landscape changed gradually as the men moved from the border-
lands of the till plains into the Flint Hills.* The grassy hills, tree-
less as a result of periodic drought and regularly recurring fires,
must have looked to the troops like giant waves in an ocean of
grass. All around them was evidence of earlier occupation by buffalo: patches of ground tramped so solid by hundreds of animals
over untold years that no vegetation except prickly pear cactus
would grow on them. These buffalo wallows they would see with
great frequency in the days to come.[11]

Camping successively on Dragoon Creek and 142-Mile Creek,†
the long column of the First Cavalry reached the Neosho River on
the afternoon of May 24. During the march a man named White
deserted, the first of several who would do so as they moved west.
On the east bank of the Neosho they passed a large grove of trees
known as the "Council Grove," site of the famous treaty with the
Osage Indian tribes.‡ On the west bank a small pro-slavery village
known as Council Grove had grown up around the early trading
post of Seth M. Hays, a grandson of Daniel Boone and cousin of
Kit Carson.§ After passing through the little settlement, the troop-

---

*The Flint Hills constitute the western edge of the Osage Plains and consist of
Permian Age limestones that dip gradually to the west. These limestones contain
numerous bands of chert, or flint, and weathering of the softer rock tends to leave
behind a clay type of soil containing much flinty gravel. For eons these deposits
of chert had served the Indians well as a supply of flint for the making of arrow-
heads and spearpoints. Rex Buchanan, *Kansas Geology*, 19–20; Daniel F. Merriam, *The Geologic History of Kansas*, 161, 164–65.
†142-Mile Creek was so named because it was 142 miles from Fort Osage in
Missouri, where the 1825 survey of the Santa Fe Trail began.
‡In 1825 the government commissioners had entered into a treaty at the Council
Grove with the Great and Little Osage tribes of Indians, in whose country it was
located, to secure a legal right of way for that part of the Santa Fe Trail that passed
through it, and also the surrender of a large portion of their lands to the government. Kate L. Gregg, *The Road to Santa Fe*, 33–34, 57–59.
§By 1857 Council Grove, strongly pro-slavery, had buildings on both sides of the

ers went back into camp, picketed their horses, and awaited arrival of the company wagons with their mess kits, tents, and other equipment. Because the wagons usually were about an hour behind the lead companies, going into camp and preparing the afternoon meal took some time.[12]

At Council Grove the men saw their first "wild" Indians, the poor and wretched Kansas, many of whom were lounging around the traders' stores. Destitute, having lost their own country and being confined to a small reservation along the Neosho centered on Council Grove, the Kansas had turned to begging and stealing from white travelers and each other.* Once the troops were in camp, they were nearly inundated by men, women, and children begging and stealing what they could.[13]

On May 25 Major Sedgwick ordered the command to lay by, resting their horses and loading a thousand bushels of corn that had been sent ahead from Fort Leavenworth. For the officers a welcome break occurred when Seth Hays invited several to dinner at Hays House, his new hostelry, where he served an excellent meal. This was a satisfying way to spend their last night in this remote outpost of civilization.[14]

Tuesday, May 26, the troopers left Council Grove bound for the plains. Council Grove was the last town or settlement of any kind along the Santa Fe Trail until Fort Union, New Mexico Territory, and the last white habitation they would see for many days, except for a few scattered trading posts. Beyond the valley of the Neosho the land was an undulating plain, broken here and there by small rock-covered buttes and mesas, and occasionally becoming quite broken and hilly. Most dramatic was the abrupt disappearance of

---

trail. The Hays House was located on the north side, and directly south was the Gilkey House. Beyond was the stage station, the town well, and a great corral. Farther west were a few log cabins, and on the north side of the road, the low, one-story, stone trading post famed in trail history as the "Last Chance Store." See *KHC* 16:556, 558; *KHC* 17:709–10.

*The Kansas had been a semi-nomadic people, living in more or less permanent villages, raising some crops, and going west to the plains two times a year to hunt buffalo and other game. In earlier days they had been noted trappers and had engaged in a large trade in furs and hides. By 1857 they had lost most of their horses, were reduced by warfare, disease, and starvation to no more than 1,000 people, and were almost totally dependent upon an indifferent government for their survival.

trees even along watercourses. Excepting an occasional straggler
or an isolated grove of cottonwood, there were none. Lack of wood
forced them to build fires thereafter by using buffalo chips, the *bois
de vache* (wood of the cow) used by most caravan cooks during trail
days.[15]

The march beyond Council Grove led past Diamond Springs,*
where the men found a mail station and trading post,† and Lost
Springs,‡ both renowned camping places along the Santa Fe Trail.
On May 28, they reached the crossing of the Cottonwood River,
the location of a trading post operated by George Smith and known
as "Smith's Ranch." The "ranch" consisted of a log cabin, where
the proprietor offered supplies, corn, hay, wood, grass and water,
and mail service via the monthly mail run of the Hockaday and
Hall mail wagons. Smith also operated the post as a "woodyard,"
where entertainment and refreshments could be found in the forms

*The government survey party found Diamond Springs and marked it on August
11, 1825, naming it "Jones Spring" because it was discovered by Ben Jones, a
hunter with the party. On June 10, 1827, George C. Sibley again visited it while
correcting errors in the first survey, and this time he renamed it "Diamond of the
Plains," inspired by a spring in the Arabian Desert known as the "Diamond of the
Desert." Numerous well-worn trails of buffalo, elk, antelope, and deer led to it.
It was known to white traders and trappers even before the Becknell Expedition
and the 1825 Survey. The spring, which gushed out of the bluffs at the head of a
draw, flowed in a stream eighteen inches wide and two and one-half inches deep,
running across a rocky bottom into Otter Creek a short distance away. See *KHC*
14:794–97; Kate L. Gregg, *The Road to Santa Fe*, 46, 60, 184, 272.

†In 1850 the firm of Waldo, Hall, and Company entered into a contract with the
government to provide monthly mail service between Independence and Santa Fe.
Sometime between that date and 1854, the company constructed a station at Diamond Springs. This station had at least two large, two-story stone buildings, one
a ranch hotel or stage station, where the horses were changed and where travelers
were served meals and drinks from the bar, and the other a storehouse for supplies, where passing travelers could purchase needed items of food or equipment.
There were other, smaller stone buildings and a large stone corral in which the
livestock for the mail run was kept. The corral was surrounded by a six-foot stone
wall that .encompassed three or four acres of ground. By 1857 the station was
operated by Hockaday and Hall. See *KHC* 14:794–97; Morris F. Taylor, *First
Mail West*, 28–35.

‡Lost Springs also gushed from a small ravine and formed a part of the headwaters
of Lost Creek. In times of drought or extreme heat the waters tended to sink into
the sandy bottom, leaving no surface flow from which to water the livestock and
giving rise to its name. Lost Creek was later renamed Lyon Creek. See *KHC*
14:143–45; John Rydjord, *Kansas Place-Names*, 14.

of gambling and whiskey. The troops paused at the crossing long enough to transfer to the expedition's wagons corn brought by ox train from Fort Leavenworth. Camp for the night was on a water hole three miles southwest of the crossing.[16]

On May 29 the march brought the command to the McPherson Lowlands and the beginning of the Great Plains. The taller blue-stem grasses now gave way to buffalo grass, and the soldiers found themselves in the shortgrass country of the buffalo plains. During the day's march they saw two or three herds of buffalo, the first encountered during the march. Several officers and Delaware scouts, not being mounted on government horses, gave chase. First Lt. James B. McIntyre and a Delaware each killed a buffalo, and a wagon was sent to butcher the fallen animals and bring back the choice parts. That evening the command dined on its first buffalo meat, cooked over buffalo chips. The men were disappointed, finding it lean and tough, not nearly as tasty as their usual ration of fresh beef.[17]

On May 30 the column left camp bound for the Little Arkansas, a nineteen-mile march. They encountered no water and no timber until the Little Arkansas, but there were immense herds of buffalo, and these brought a number of officers into the field for a little sport. After chasing what they took to be buffalo for about six or eight miles they found they were in fact tracking Indian hunters, themselves after buffalo. These proved to be Kansas who had left their village near Council Grove the day before the departure of the troops. Officers and Indians continued together and three miles farther overtook the herd, when each began their own hunt. Some of the enlisted men attempted to hunt on foot, but this proved too difficult and hazardous, a wounded buffalo being a formidable opponent for a man on foot in open country. The hunt was successful, with twenty buffalo killed.[18]

By midafternoon the command made camp on the east bank of the Little Arkansas. This small, shallow stream had box elder, elm, and other scrub timber, and a giant sentinel cottonwood, which stood north of the ford on the east bank.* Directly in front of the cavalry camp was a large mound of stones with a headboard in it. According to the faded headboard, it marked the graves of a

---

*The sentinel or marker cottonwood at the Upper Crossing of the Little Arkansas stands to the present day (1988).

captain and eight privates of a company of Dragoons who had been killed there in an engagement with Indians some years before. The board was too weathered to see a date, the soldiers' names, or the company or regiment of Dragoons to which they had belonged.

A Majors and Russell wagon train, bound for New Mexico, was in camp just above the military encampment. It had stopped in the middle of a large prairie-dog town, where the men were able to observe these interesting little animals barking at and scolding their unwanted intruders. A wagon train full of immigrants with twenty-five hundred head of cattle had arrived the previous evening and gone into camp on the opposite side of the stream. They claimed to be bound for California, but a number of officers believed they were really Mormons on their way to Utah. Because of the Mormon troubles and the pending expedition against them, the travelers were the object of some suspicion.[19]

Sunday, May 31, the column camped on Little Cow Creek. The following morning they departed for the Big Bend of the Arkansas, their next night's camp. En route they hunted, killing six or seven buffalo.[20] During the morning's march the command passed two trains headed east. One of these was Mexican and had lost twenty-five mules stampeded by the movement of a great buffalo herd. As the long, strung-out column of cavalry companies and their supply train, remuda, and beef herd descended into the valley of the Arkansas from the sandhills to the northeast, they were about to experience a similar, far more hazardous meeting with buffalo. The valley spreads out seven or eight miles north of the river, and north of the trail the plain seemed one black mass of animals, so great was the herd. When the lead part of the column was about halfway between the rim of the valley and the river, something startled the bison, causing them to stampede southward, directly at the troopers.

Major Sedgwick was a seasoned soldier, having been with the artillery for nearly twenty years, but he had little experience on the plains. The uneasiness of the older troopers quickly spread, and Sedgwick, apprehensive but not knowing what to do, turned for advice to Sam Sturgis, his veteran senior captain. Sturgis had seen buffalo stampedes before and knew the course of action needed. With the consent of Major Sedgwick, he took command of the column. Being at its head, he directed the orderly bugler to pass the word for all company commanders to take their orders from him,

On Sunday, May 31, 1857, while crossing the valley of the Arkansas River, the four companies of the First Cavalry under Maj. John Sedgwick were threatened by the stampede of an immense herd of buffalo. Capt. Sam Sturgis, the experienced senior captain, took command, corralled the wagons and livestock, and organized a firing party that forced a split in the herd, saving the column from disaster.

and for the wagon master to corral the train as rapidly as possible, with the livestock on the inside. He ordered the cavalry companies back to the train at a gallop and placed them around the corral in a circling line, dismounted to fight on foot. Quickly forming the new line, Sturgis moved the center company out at "double-quick" time to a position about two hundred yards in front of the wagon corral, facing the oncoming herd. He formed the remaining companies into two reserve parties, one on each flank, to prevent the buffalo from closing in on the horses and corral after passing the forward firing party.

When the stampede began the buffalo herd was at least two miles away. By the time the wagon train was corralled and everything made ready, they were nearly upon them, thundering across the plain in a solid, unbroken line, which ran as far to the left and right as the troopers could see. The noise made by the galloping hooves became an enormous rumble, and the earth shook. Stretching back toward the northern horizon without visible break, the oncoming sea of bison seemed as ominous as an approaching tornado, and many feared for their survival.

Captain Sturgis waited until he could delay no longer without courting total disaster, then calmly ordered the lead company to "commence firing." At first it appeared that his plan to force the herd to split and pass around the beleaguered troopers would fail, and they would be engulfed in an avalanche of hooves and horns. But as they furiously fired, reloaded, and fired again, the miracle happened. Almost at the last moment, the sheet of fire from the carbines caused the oncoming herd to split, the maddened beasts savagely crowding their flanks to the right and left, some even climbing over others in an effort to escape the searing pain of the bullets. Though it split, the herd continued to pass without checking its speed or giving other notice. The break was enough, and the gap thus made sufficient to clear the horses, the men, and the corral.

After the herd had split, it became apparent to Sturgis that the firing party had too broad a front. He therefore drew back their flanks to form a wedge in the shape of the letter V with the point toward the oncoming animals. Bringing up other companies, he extended the V to encompass the train and livestock between the flanks. The original firing party continued to do most of the shooting, but others now did so with ever-greater frequency as buffalo began crowding their position. It was like being in a tornado, with an enormous cloud of dust kicked up all about them, choking and blinding the men. Worse, they found themselves forced back step by step until they were closely packed about horses and wagons. So immense was the herd it took more than a half-hour to pass. Finally, when the weary men were beginning to think that doom would envelop them, they perceived a thinning and straggling in the great mass swirling about them. And then the stampede was over. The torrent of brown wool had disappeared to the south, across the river.

It had been a very close call. Troopers had fired as fast as they could, and yet, as rapidly as they were resupplied with ammunition, cartridge boxes seemed almost to empty themselves. The threat ended so suddenly they scarcely realized the herd was gone and they had survived. As the dust cleared, something even more baffling confronted them. For all the fire directed at the oncoming animals, very few had been killed at the point of the V. But a large number had been killed on each flank. This was in part because the great, thick skull of the buffalo was difficult to penetrate with the ammunition of the day, and in part because nearly all frontal shots struck too low to pierce the brain or vital organs. It was the broadside shots that had brought most of the animals down.

When the danger was over, the troops rested a bit, then parties were sent to secure the choicest meat from some of the tender young buffalo. This was packed in the wagons. The rest was left as a feast for the great packs of wolves and coyotes then abounding on the plains. That accomplished, the column regrouped and continued its passage down the trail. They finally struck the Arkansas at its Great Bend of the north at about one o'clock in the afternoon, having traveled twenty-one very exciting and dangerous miles.*[21]

From the Great Bend to Bent's New Fort

Rest revived the exhausted men of Sedgwick's command, and notwithstanding their unnerving experience the previous day, on June 2 they completed their many tasks early in the predawn hours and

*The point along the Santa Fe Trail known as the "Big Bend" or "Great Bend" is near present-day Ellinwood, Kansas. Hobart E. Stocking, *The Road to Santa Fe*, 116.

left camp at 6:30 A.M. The trail now ran parallel with the Arkansas, a stream that impressed the troops with its width, one hundred to three hundred yards, its many channels and small islands, its shallow depth, and the fact that there were a few cottonwoods growing along its banks or out on the islands. The water level was high by the standards of the plains, June being the time of the rise caused by melting snow in the Rocky Mountains. This, in turn, caused it to be muddy and the current swift. The valley through which the Arkansas passed was from six to eight miles wide, with bluffs of the high plains clearly visible in the distance.[22]

At 8:30 A.M., after marching about six miles, the cavalry column reached Walnut Creek. On the east bank, on the north side of the Santa Fe road, was an Indian trading post known variously as "Allison and Booth's Ranch," "The Ranch at Walnut Creek Crossing," and "Allison and Booth's Fort."* The bright sun was causing the rapid rise in the morning temperature typical of the high plains. Lounging about the establishment were several Kiowa Indians, the first the soldiers had seen of any of the fierce warriors of the plains.

*Allison and Boothe's "Ranch" or "Fort" had been built in 1855 by William Allison and Francis Boothe (or Booth), both former employees of Waldo, Hall, and Company as conductors of the monthly mail run to Santa Fe. Allison had lost an arm in a gun fight but was as adept as anyone with a six-shooter and absolutely fearless. The Indians referred to him respectfully as "No-arm."

While a large amount of their trade was with the Comanches, Kiowas, Plains Apaches, Cheyennes, and Arapahoes, Allison and Boothe did not overlook the opportunities afforded by the passing traffic on the Santa Fe Trail. For this purpose they maintained a stock of groceries, provisions, and other supplies suitable to the trade. They offered forage and corrals for horses and other livestock, and they engaged in profitable speculation in trading for the lame animals of passing wagon trains. Following recuperation, these animals were sold to other travelers. The little trading post was the only white installation then engaged in trade with the Indians between Council Grove and Fort Union on the Santa Fe Trail, and between Council Grove and Bent's New Fort on the trail to the mountains. At the time it was also the only mail station between Council Grove and Fort Union.

Evidently the "fort" was enclosed by a palisade of logs set upright in the ground and enclosed by sod slabs. On the inside, built against the walls of the enclosure, were several buildings constructed of adobe in the Mexican fashion. In times of danger livestock could be placed in the open enclosure in the center of the fort. For trading with the Indians a long, narrow opening with a base about waist high was made in the side of the storeroom formed by the enclosing wall. This door was closed, when necessary, by means of a drop-door on the inside. The post probably had a watchtower at one corner of the enclosure. See *KHC* 8:489; *KHQ* 37:121–47; Eli Long, *Journal*, June 2, 1857.

The traders at the post told them the Cheyennes were "ready and waiting" and counted on giving the troopers a "good thrashing." Lieutenant Bayard understood that they had taken their families to the mountains and, with the assistance of young Sioux warriors, were preparing for war. He probably misinterpreted a statement that the Arkansas River bands had gone to the Smoky Hill; certainly the location of the Cheyennes was no secret to the traders or any of the other Plains Indians. The soldiers also were told that large villages of Comanches, Kiowas, and Arapahoes were encamped along the Pawnee Fork above the trail. After learning what they could about the location of the Cheyennes, the troops crossed the Walnut and continued another eight or nine miles, going into camp along the Arkansas about one mile from the road.[23]

As they marched west the men noted many graves along the side of the road. Those for Mexicans were invariably marked by a cross, many with the crossbeam at the horizontal, but most with the crossbeam at a slant. An old trooper who had lived among Mexicans stated that the slanting of the piece meant the deceased had died a violent death, usually at the hands of the Indians, while at right angles it signified a natural death or "died on the square."[24]

From June 3 to June 7, Sedgwick's column stayed with the trail along the Arkansas known as the Wet Route. Though longer than the alternate Dry Route, it had the water of the Arkansas close at hand and avoided the dreary, arid desolation of the high plains. On June 3 they passed the famous trail marker, Pawnee Rock;* the following day they crossed Coon Creek, site of the June 18, 1848, Battle of Coon Creek.†[25]

*Pawnee Rock was so named because a party of Pawnees had once been chased there and wiped out by their mortal enemies, the Cheyennes. Early traditions differ, however, as to whether it was the Cheyennes or the Comanches who were responsible. Henry Inman, *The Old Santa Fe Trail*, 404; John Rydjord, *Indian Place-Names*, 141–42; Robert M. Wright, *Dodge City: The Cowboy Capital*, 25–26.

†The Battle of Coon Creek occurred when a large war party of Comanches attacked a detachment of troops, including seventy-one recruits from Missouri, on their way to Santa Fe under the command of 1st Lt. Wm. B. Royall, Second Missouri Mounted Volunteers, who had been appointed adjutant of the Santa Fe Battalion. These recruits had just been armed with German-made, breech-loading carbines, which could be loaded and fired five times in one minute, and which had an effective range of about four hundred yards. Their use during the engagement was the first time breech-loading rifles were used against the Indians on the

Camp on June 4 was along the Arkansas seven miles beyond Coon Creek. During the night the men were awakened by a shot from a carbine and the call "Sergeant of the Guard, number 7" from the post closest to the Arkansas. The whole force was turned out under arms. The guard had seen an Indian sneaking up and had fired one shot at him with his carbine and two more with his Navy pistol. The next morning they found the man's tracks, a blanket with blood on it, and four arrows he had shot, which, luckily, had missed their intended target. The Indian's tracks led to the river, and no other trace of him was found.[26]

On June 6 the command camped along the Arkansas near where the Dry Route and the Wet Route converged. The next morning, following an eight-mile march, they passed the ruins of old Fort Atkinson. The walls had been knocked down when it was abandoned; only mounds of sod and adobe, no higher than a man's shoulders, marked the outline of the outer walls and some of the adobe walls of the inside buildings. North, in bluffs overlooking the valley, was the first "Point of Rocks," a rocky protrusion that served as a marker on the trail, and nearby the "Caches," a depression created by the caching of trader goods in 1823, but nonetheless a landmark in the empty plains.[27]

No buffalo had been seen for several days, and the troops were now passing beyond the western limits of their range, which that year seemed to be about the Middle Crossing of the Santa Fe Trail. Older soldiers pointed out to the younger men that beyond the ruins of Fort Atkinson the river once formed the international boundary, first with Mexico and then with Texas, prior to its admission to the Union as a state. In camp that afternoon, pistols and cartridges were issued to all the men because they had now reached the point on the trail where travelers were most vulnerable to Indian attack.[28]

Beyond Fort Atkinson the country traversed by the trail took on a more rugged aspect, with rocky bluffs of the high plains moving closer to the river and changing its broad valley into a narrow ribbon. On June 8 the column passed the Middle Crossing of the Santa Fe Trail and climbed the hills onto the high plains along

---

western plains. The result was at least twenty-three dead Comanches and a large number of wounded, for they did not anticipate the soldiers' being able to fire again so quickly after the first volley. See *KHC* 10:409.

Nine-Mile Ridge.* After coming off Nine-Mile Ridge, they passed
an abandoned Indian village near the river with the lodgepoles of
one tipi still standing. From appearances there had been about one
hundred lodges and it had been abandoned no more than a week.
A deep track etched by dragging lodgepoles marked the trail of the
departing band where they crossed the road heading north onto the
high plains. Most likely they were Arapahoes, but they could have
been Kiowas or Comanches. Because the Cheyennes were on the
Sappa for their summer buffalo hunt, this probably was not one of
their bands.[29]

On June 9 the troops made camp below a second "Point of
Rocks." At 10:00 A.M. the next morning a small band of twenty
Arapahoe Indians appeared from the plains and pitched their
lodges just below the cavalry camp. There were seven lodges and
eight families. Watching them prepare a meal, the men were surprised by their method of roasting turtles and prairie-dogs in the
ashes of their campfire without any prior preparation.

The Arapahoes, like most Indians of the southern plains, could
speak some Spanish as a result of long contact with Mexican traders. This group told the cavalry's Mexican herdsmen that five days
earlier they had fought with a Mexican wagon train but that the
Mexicans had beaten them badly and taken all their horses. They
also said the Cheyennes had gone far away, to the Rocky Mountains, but no one believed that story.

About sunset that evening Bill Shaw, whom the officers regarded
as the best of the four Delaware scouts, died of pneumonia, which
he had contracted following a case of measles. Shaw's body was
buried near the upper Point of Rocks, just above the campsite.†[30]

Beyond the upper Point of Rocks the country became hillier and
rockier. The grassland along the trail undulated, looking like huge
swells broken occasionally by protruding waves in the grassy

*The Middle Crossing was about seventeen or eighteen miles above Fort Atkin-
son, and was the latest in a series of "Middle" crossings that had been tried,
having become the primary crossing point by 1853. See *KHQ* 39:345–50; Hobart
E. Stocking, *The Road to Santa Fe*, 140–41, 146.

†The upper Point of Rocks along the Santa Fe Trail on the north side of the
Arkansas River is in Township 24 South, Range 31 West of the 6th P.M. A third
Point of Rocks, located along the part of the original Santa Fe Trail in Kansas
Territory later known as the "Cimarron Cutoff," was just west of the Middle Ci-
marron Spring in present Morton County, Kansas. See *KHQ* 39:353.

ocean. The silver-green of sand sage lent color to the desolation of the plains about them, spiked here and there by the blossoms of yucca plants and cacti.

On June 12 the command passed the Upper Crossing, the one surveyed by Sibley and Brown in 1825. Here the Santa Fe Trail took final leave of them and crossed to the south bank of the Arkansas. The old traders' trail that continued along the north bank was well defined and well traveled, being used both by parties going west to Bent's New Fort and the mountains and by the many immigrants heading for California. This resulted in its being referred to as the "California Trail."[31]

The following day the march took the troopers past Chouteau's Island and Indian Mound,* famous markers opposite which the Santa Fe Trail turned south to cross the Cimarron Desert.† Continuing on the trail along the north bank of the river, the command reached the Big Timbers on June 15 and went into camp at the mouth of Buffalo Creek. Two men from Bent's New Fort who were camping at the site reported to Major Sedgwick that there were

---

*In 1816, Auguste Pierre Chouteau of the famous Chouteau trading family and perhaps twenty other trappers and traders were attacked by some two hundred Republican Pawnees, Otoes, and Rees in the vicinity of Chouteau's Island while returning from the mountains. Retreating to the island and digging three small redoubts, they fought off the Indians, with only one man killed and three wounded. Five Pawnees were killed and many more wounded. In 1825 the surveyor Joseph C. Brown used the island as the marker for the point at which the Santa Fe Trail turned south through Bear Creek Pass, a shallow bed of an intermittent stream, which provided the only firm passage through the extensive range of sand hills south of the river. In 1828, following an Indian attack upon them along the Cimarron to the south in which they lost their livestock, Milton Bryan and his fellow traders cached at least $10,000 of silver on the island. One year later Maj. Bennet Riley and his troops camped by Chouteau's Island and Indian Mound while providing the escort for the 1829 trading caravan to Santa Fe. Louise Barry, *Beginning of the West*, 76, 151–52, 160–63, 202–203; Hobart E. Stocking, *The Road to Santa Fe*, 158–62.

†This was the desolate and dreaded Jornada, or Water Scrape, over which the trail passed for more than fifty miles without water of any kind before reaching the Lower Cimarron Spring at the edge of the bluffs overlooking the valley of the Cimarron River. South of the Arkansas was Comanche, Kiowa, and Plains Apache country. At either the Lower Spring or another a little farther southwest on the north bank of the Cimarron famed mountain man Jedediah Smith was killed by Comanches on May 27, 1831. Hobart E. Stocking, *The Road to Santa Fe*, 148–62.

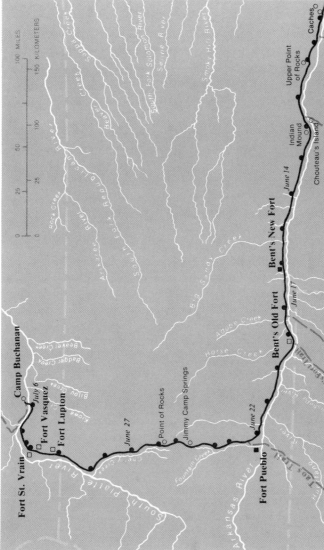

March of Sedgwick's column from Fort Atkinson to Camp Buchanan

fifteen hundred Cheyenne warriors encamped on the Smoky Hill fork of the Kansas River about sixty miles northeast.[32]

The Big Timbers was a continuing grove of cottonwoods, willows, and other trees that grew on the islands and along the north bank of the Arkansas for a distance of at least twenty-five miles, extending from about ten miles above Bent's New Fort to fifteen miles or more below it. Beyond those boundaries the trees thinned gradually until, a few miles to the east, they entirely disappeared. The trees were "big" only in contrast to the scattering of scrub trees found along a few of the smaller watercourses the column passed on its westward journey. This was no forest, but the groves did provide shade and were a favorite winter campsite for some bands of southern Arapahoes and Cheyennes, as well as a handy place to do business with William Bent and his traders during the summer.[33]

On Tuesday, June 16, the command went into camp two miles east of Bent's New Fort. As they approached their campsite, they passed a village of Arapahoes located on the south bank of the river. Soon after the troopers pitched their tents and ate their afternoon meal a large number of Arapahoes mounted their horses and crossed the river to visit the military encampment. There were about two hundred in the party, and they stopped at the upper end of the camp while their chief and eight or ten warriors went to Major Sedgwick's tent to smoke a peace pipe and confer. They had been camping near the post while awaiting their agent with the annual treaty goods. The Indians said they were starving and had been living on roots and rodents for some time, there being no game around Bent's New Fort. They were afraid to go east to the buffalo plains to hunt, the traders having told them the military expedition was going to fight both Arapahoes and Cheyennes. They begged for food and Sedgwick gave them two steers. Following the council, a number of warriors visited the tents to trade, but there was little to exchange except those things neither side would part with. During the afternoon and evening a few soldiers and officers visited the Arapahoe village to trade or just to observe an Indian camp. The Arapahoes could not or would not tell them anything as to the whereabouts of the Cheyennes.[34]

On the afternoon of the sixteenth, some officers rode to Bent's New Fort, two miles distant, and found that Colonel Bent was away from the post, reportedly in Washington. They learned nothing further of value concerning the Cheyennes, but that evening 2d Lt. Eli Long made the following notation in his journal: "The Cheyennes were within 60 miles of us yesterday, north of us, on the Smoky Hill Fork of the Kaw River, 1500 warriors. We have to go 300 miles from here and then go back again before we can touch them 'sic transit gloria belli'."* There was still a long, hard journey ahead.

Bent's New Fort to Fort St. Vrain

Sedgwick's men left their camp below Bent's New Fort at 6:30 A.M. on the morning of Wednesday, June 17, 1857. Immediately after departing, they passed a village of fifty or sixty lodges of Arapahoes, the same band that had visited their camp the previous evening. Apparently they had moved across the river to trade more easily with the soldiers. That the people were starving was evident by the telltale protruding stomachs of the children.

Reaching the fort, the troopers paused to visit. A rectangular limestone structure, it stood on the north bank of the Arkansas at the top of a hill overlooking a bend in the river. There was an abrupt, rocky bluff on its south or river side and a steep rise of limestone on the west, making attack very difficult from those directions. Thus situated, the fort had a commanding view up and down the valley and the inhabitants could see traffic approaching along the trail for several miles in either direction. The location was by far the best natural defensive position the men had seen since the trail reached the Arkansas. They understood that William Bent, the proprietor, was then in Washington trying to negotiate its sale to the government for use by the army.[35]

Bent was absent, but in residence was a motley crew of eight or ten retainers and hangers-on (clothed almost entirely in animal skins), including French-Canadian, Mexican, and white American trappers, as well as a number of Indians. Each of the fort personnel seemed to have at least one Indian wife. Present also was Little Raven, a principal chief of the Arapahoes, whose band was camped above the fort. He was a dignified-looking man, darker

*"Sic transit gloria belli" translates roughly as "so goes the glory of war."

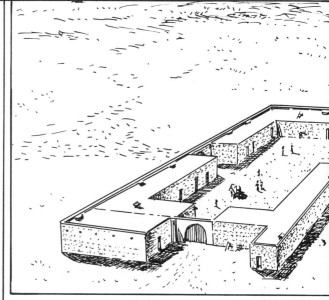

The march of the Cheyenne Expedition's southern column along the Arkansas took the troopers past three early-day trading posts: Allison and Booth's Fort (or Ranch), which they passed on June 2, 1859; Bent's New Fort, which they visited on June 17; and the ruins of Bent's Old Fort, which they reached on June 20.

R.G. ©

than most Arapahoes, with a demeanor at once sad and proud. He wore a medal given him by the President and seemed of friendly disposition. With him were several other chiefs and warriors, one of whom wore an army officer's uniform coat with epaulets. All the Indians seemed very nervous until told that the soldiers were looking for Cheyennes and had no intention of fighting Arapahoes. Little Raven asked where he could take his people to hunt and was very pleased when Major Sedgwick said they were free to go anywhere they could find meat.[36]

The troopers enjoyed their brief visit to the trading post, finding bargains difficult to resist. Buffalo hides were offered at five dollars apiece, and there was a choice of over five thousand hides. Buffalo heads were free for the taking. Following their inspection of the fort and its wares, the column continued the westward march. Three miles beyond the post they came upon the village of Little Raven's band of Arapahoes, consisting of forty or fifty lodges. Little Raven's lodge, located at one side, was larger than the rest and painted red. It was surrounded by five or six smaller lodges, which the men were told contained his wives and children. The Indians were eager to trade, especially for sugar, and would trade nearly anything they had except their horses, to which, in the words of Lieutenant Long, "they cling like grim death to a dead log."[37]

Below Bent's New Fort the Arkansas River had been wide and shallow, but above it the bed was narrower and the waters deeper and swift-flowing, with precipitous banks. In contrast to the flow across the plains farther east, the water itself was now clear and cool. Another change also had occurred. Soon after leaving Bent's New Fort, mountains began appearing on the horizon. The snow-capped peaks at first seemed to be small white clouds, but as the column advanced, the clouds held their positions. Some said it was Greenhorn Peak and the Wet Mountains, others that it was Pike's Peak and the mountains around it in the Front Range. Considering the distance, more than likely what they saw was either Pike's Peak or the Spanish Peaks—Wah-to-yah.[38]

On the morning of June 18 the troopers marched about sixteen miles, halting again at noon. The country continued to be hilly and undulating and the valley of the Arkansas narrower as the altitude increased. Wild roses and several beautiful varieties of cacti began to appear, but many creatures they had been accustomed to on the plains had disappeared almost entirely. They had seen no buffalo since before Fort Atkinson, and antelope had become scarce. Prairie-dog towns, formerly enumerable, were now seen but rarely. On the other hand, deer became more plentiful. [39]

Saturday, June 20, they passed the ruins of Bent's Old Fort, consisting of broken walls of adobe, many of them nearly fourteen feet in height, and with several chimneys and a tower or two still standing. Passing travelers had used the walls as a makeshift post office to leave messages for those who followed, to try out their artistic talents, or just to endow posterity with some graffiti. The size of the ruin impressed the men, for it had been a considerably larger post than its successor some thirty-six or thirty-seven miles downstream.

Beyond Bent's Old Fort they passed one of the fords used for crossing the Arkansas on a trail that followed the Purgatoire River into New Mexico Territory to a crossing of the mountains, and beyond to Taos or Santa Fe. Known as the Bent's Fort Trail, it was little used except by a few trappers and traders. [40]

The trail westward from Bent's Old Fort became progressively more difficult as the ground itself became more rugged. More snow-capped mountains made their appearance on the horizon, and the Arkansas continued its transformation from the broad and shallow river of the plains to a much narrower, deeper, and swifter stream as they drew ever nearer the mountains. Its banks also were becoming much better timbered. However, away from the river the land was arid and the grass generally poor. Eighteen or nineteen miles above the ruins of the old trading post, the column made camp for the evening. While there an enlisted man named Fullmer deserted, probably hoping to join one of the immigrant trains bound for California. [41]

Sunday, June 21, the command passed the remains of an old Arapahoe village a short distance below their evening's campsite. According to the Delaware scouts, it had been abandoned about two months earlier. They said it had been used while the Arapahoes were moving west to find and fight their enemies, the Utes. Still standing was a medicine lodge built in the traditional circular shape. Upright poles four or five inches in diameter, with forked tops, had been set into the ground forming the circle. In the center was a larger pole made from a trimmed tree trunk, which extended perhaps thirty feet above the ground, and from which ran poles four to five inches in diameter, used as rafters or stringers, tied to it by rawhide thongs, and with the far ends resting in the forks of the outer poles. The men thought that the lodge had been covered at one time but that the covering had been removed. Hung at the top of the center pole was the hide of a mongrel silver gray and red fox. Just below it was a large bundle of twigs pointing north and south, and below the bundle a large number of eagle quills were fastened in a buffalo hide. On the ground nearby was a rectangular pit six inches deep, eight and one-half feet long, and one foot wide. Stuck in its sides were strips of wood that arched over the gap. At the head of the pit was a buffalo skull, the eye sockets and horns stuffed with dried grass and the face dotted with spots, one side black and the other red. The Indian scouts told the troopers that this signified a wish for plenty of grass and buffalo.[42]

The country had been changing rapidly, and the valley of the Arkansas was now surrounded by rugged hills barren of grass but covered with sage and sprinkled with cactus. During the afternoon one of the Delaware guides was sent upstream to cross the river to the abandoned settlement on the Huerfano, a few miles above them. There was supposed to be a Frenchman still living there who could be useful as an interpreter with the Cheyennes. Unfortunately, the river being too high to ford, they did not make contact with him—if in fact he was there.[43]

On June 22 the command marched eighteen miles. The country continued to change. Each day the river grew deeper, narrower, and swifter. Trees along its banks became more plentiful, some of the cottonwoods being huge, patriarchal-looking fellows with great, thick trunks. Ahead of them, to the right of their line of march, Pike's Peak was clearly visible, although they were still a considerable distance from it.[44] When they had traveled about six miles, the column was joined by a Taos trader named Thomas Otteby. With him were two Blackfoot Indians he had employed to assist him.[45] Two miles farther the troopers passed the mouth of the Huerfano River, which entered the Arkansas from the south. The Arkansas bottom at that point was rich black soil covered with grass, and it varied in width from a half mile to a mile. Timber was dense along both streams, and the valley was protected on the south by a line of steep bluffs some thirty feet high. A small settlement established in the fall of 1854 along the west bank of the Huerfano near

its mouth had flourished briefly.* In the spring of 1855, following
the December 24, 1854, massacre of the inhabitants of Fort Pueblo
by Chief Blanco's Muache Utes, it was abandoned.[46]

Except for occasional grassy areas, the ground over which they
now traveled was without cover and created a very light dust. The
wind blew for only an hour or two during the day's march. When it
was not blowing, the massive dust cloud kicked up by the passing
column did not settle for two to three hundred yards. The trail
being narrower, the troops were marching by twos; thus, the rear
companies and the rear couples of the leading company were covered and hidden from each other by the dust. In combination with
thinner air at the higher altitude, this made breathing difficult.
Whenever they passed grassy patches and were temporarily freed
from the dust, a new kind of misery took its place: great clouds of
mosquitoes rose to envelop them. During the march a burning sun
was almost directly above.[47]

On June 23, after a march of two miles, Sedgwick's men arrived
at a point across from the mouth of the St. Charles River where a
branch of the California Trail led northwest across the hills to the
Fontaine-qui-bouille, or Fountain Creek.† This cutoff began about
eight miles below the ruins of Fort Pueblo‡ and was a good deal

---

*The little settlement had been formed by Joseph B. Doyle, R. L. ("Dick") Woot-
ton, Charles Autobees, William Kroenig, and Juan ("Guerro") Pais, all men who
were experienced traders and frontiersmen. They built five *placitas*, each consisting of a number of rooms enclosing an open square in the fashion of the Mexican country homes. Doyle, a Virginian by birth, was a noted Indian trader in the
area, and although his *placita* on the Huerfano was known as his trading post, it
was in fact a storehouse for his wares: he did all his trading with the Indians at
their villages. All the *placitas* were more or less fortified for protection against
Indians. They were located at random along the river bottom. To the south,
against the bluffs, were a number of *jacal* cabins for the hired hands, and along
the river were several dugouts where other French and Mexican laborers lived.
Whether any of the hired hands continued to live there following abandonment
of the settlement is unknown, but the expectations of Major Sedgwick and his
men suggests the possibility. Janet Lecompte, *Pueblo, Hardscrabble, Greenhorn*,
234–35, 252.
†Fontaine-qui-bouille means "Fountain That Boils" or "Boiling Fountain."
‡Fort Pueblo was a small trading post built by George Simpson, Robert Fisher,
and two or three associates in 1842. It was abandoned in the fall of 1855 following
the December 24, 1854, massacre of its inhabitants by the Utes. Edward Broadhead, *Fort Pueblo*, 27; Janet Lecompte, *Pueblo, Hardscrabble, Greenhorn*,
35, 45.

shorter than the trail from the mouth of Fountain Creek. The long column of men and animals began ascending the hills almost as soon as they left the river and continued the laborious climb for two or three miles before H Company, the lead company that day, finally reached the top. There, spread out before them, was a sight so magnificent it took their breaths and held them spellbound for a few moments before they were forced to move on by those following. Immediately to their south were the Spanish Peaks, ravines in their sides filled with snow, giving them a striped appearance. West of the Spanish Peaks were snow-capped peaks of the Culebra Range, running south to north, or a little west of north, and disappearing from view behind Greenhorn Peak and the Wet Mountains, the range immediately southwest of the cavalry column. Beyond the Wet Mountains, running in a parallel north-northwest direction, were great peaks of the Sangre de Cristo Range, capped with snow, which glistened in the morning sun like a solid mass of diamonds. Angling off to their right into the distance was the Arkansas, descending from its mountain birthplace as a raging torrent, and farther to the right the southern flank of the great Front Range. Rising majestically above the surrounding mountains, the massive dome of Pike's Peak thrust its snow-capped crest into the clouds at a height of over fourteen thousand feet above sea level, and more than one thousand feet above its neighbors. It seemed to the troopers a Gulliver among the Lilliputians.[48]

To the northeast lay the foothills through which they had come, gradually descending into and merging with the Great Plains. Behind and southeast of the lead company, creeping their way upward along the top of a snake-like ridge, were the other three companies, followed by the artillery battery, the wagon train, the remuda, and the cattle herd, with the guard bringing up the rear. To those looking back they seemed like some great and invincible war dragon. Down the valley of the Arkansas, on the west side of Fountain Creek near its mouth, they could see the walls of the abandoned Fort Pueblo, slowly falling into ruin.[49] Awed by the great wall of rock, the cavalry column continued its march along the ridge until they had traveled twelve miles, then descended into the valley of Fountain Creek. The valley and the stream were beautiful, with more and different kinds of trees along the banks. Eight miles farther they made camp on the banks of the creek, having traveled twenty hard, but spectacular, miles.[50]

Wednesday, June 24, the trail took the troops along the east bank of Fountain Creek, and they made camp at the mouth of Jimmy Camp Creek. The grazing had been poor the entire distance, making travel hard on the livestock. Two or three more men had deserted the previous night, and Eli Long was detailed to look for them in and among several immigrant trains moving along the trail. The presence of such trains created a great temptation for green young recruits wearied by the march and lonely for their families. Their weapons were found, but not the men.

While Lieutenant Long was making his search for deserters, several other officers and Indian scouts rode over to the base of Pike's Peak, some with the thought of climbing it. As they rode up the valley of Fountain Creek, however, they did not take long to realize the folly of the plan. The distance was too great and the mountain too high for them to reach, much less climb, in the one-half day left to them. Fall Leaf, the Delaware chief and guide, had led the party of would-be climbers up the valley, and in passing they visited the "Soda Spring," one of the mineral springs at the site of modern Manitou Springs and a sacred spot to the Utes. While there he shot a mountain lion in a thicket near the spring.[51]

On the morning of June 25, the troopers continued following the trail along the east bank of Jimmy Camp Creek. At Jimmy Camp Spring, source of Jimmy Camp Creek,* they halted for a brief rest, filling their canteens and watering the livestock before continuing. Beyond the spring, the trail entered more rugged country as they approached the divide between the waters flowing south to the Ar-

---

*The springs and the creek took their name from Jimmy Daugherty, a longtime trapper and trader in the Rockies and the South Platte area. During the winter of 1841, while in the employ of Lancaster Lupton, Daugherty and John Brown were trading with Indians from a camp along the Arkansas near the site of present-day Pueblo. The two were sent from this camp in the company of a Mexican to Fort Lupton (Fort Lancaster) to pick up a wagonload of dried buffalo meat and a few trader goods. On Daugherty's return trip (Brown remained behind at Fort Lupton) he was murdered on the banks of the stream by his Mexican companion, apparently for a blanket, a few bolts of *manta*, and the rest of the trader goods. Within a short time of his murder the stream was being called first "Daugherty's Creek," then "Jimmy Camp Creek." See John Brown, *Mediumistic Experiences of John Brown, The Medium of the Rockies*, J. S. Loveland, ed., 23–24, 188–89; Rufus Sage, *Scenes in the Rocky Mountains* (1846), reprinted in LeRoy R. Hafen and Ann W. Hafen, eds., *Rufus B. Sage: His Letters and Papers, 1836–1847*, 4:72; typescript in author's possession.

kansas and those flowing north to the Platte. It was well after 3:00 P.M. when they reached their new camp about one mile beyond the headwaters of Black Squirrel Creek.[52]

Friday, June 26, the march continued through a pine forest. Seven miles brought them to a "Point of Rocks" where they found reasonably good grass and very good water. Here they rested and watered the livestock. Beyond the Point of Rocks, pine trees began to thin, but the ground remained broken and the trail narrow, slowing the march and tiring the animals. During the morning they met a party of twelve gold seekers from Arkansas with two ox-drawn wagons, one driven by a black slave.* They were headed south, en route home. At 10:00 A.M. the troops made camp on the east bank of East Cherry Creek.[53]

On June 27, the slow march continued. The country was very broken and rocky, alternating between patches of pine forest and fine prairie grass nearly the entire distance. About midjourney, West Cherry Creek joined the east branch to form "Cherry Creek." The mountains seemed more remote, their line appearing to angle toward the northwest. On the other hand, hunting greatly improved.[54]

During the morning the party of gold seekers they had met the previous day rejoined the cavalry column. One of their number had accidentally shot himself in the hand while pulling his rifle from a wagon, muzzle first. The hand was so badly injured they hurriedly retraced their steps to permit their companion to be treated by Dr. Edward N. Covey, the army physician assigned to Sedgwick's command. The injury was too severe to save the hand, and Dr. Covey determined to amputate it the following morning.

While the injured man was transferred to an army wagon, some of the soldiers had an opportunity to talk with other members of his party. They said they had been up in the mountains during the winter and spring looking for gold along the headwaters of the Platte, in the Pike's Peak area and along Cherry Creek, and had found some. However, Indians, probably Utes, had harassed them, running off all their livestock except the yoke oxen. Now they were

---

*Eli Long said the party was from Arkansas, while Robert M. Peck said Missouri. As an officer, Long probably spoke to the leaders and should have known. However, it is possible there were men from both states in the group. See Eli Long, "Journal," June 26, 1857; Peck, "Rough Riding on the Plains," March 14, 1901; Peck "Recollections," *KHC* 8:492.

going home to resupply and reequip themselves, intending to return with a stronger party capable of defending itself against the Indians. They exhibited small quantities of gold dust in bottles and buckskin bags, and one of their party gave a small bag of it to Fall Leaf, the Delaware Chief.* A number of troopers had prospected in California some years earlier, and these went down to nearby Cherry Creek and washed out a little sand, finding enough gold to corroborate the report.[55]

When the transfer of the wounded man was complete, the party of prospectors proceeded south en route home while the cavalry column resumed its march north. The next morning, June 28, Dr. Covey and his assistants remained behind to perform the amputation, planning to catch up with the command at the next camp.[56]

Monday, June 29, the column went into camp one-quarter mile above the mouth of Cherry Creek. The location was beautiful, with a clear view of the mountains looming beyond them to the west, and the well-timbered banks of the South Platte curving off to the north. Lieutenants McIntyre and Crittenden had been left behind at the beginning of the morning's march to look for deserters among the immigrant trains. There were a number of immigrant camps near the crossing and several more of their trains were coming up the trail. Among so many immigrants there were a number of pretty young girls, which lifted the spirits of young men who had spoken to no one of the opposite sex except Indian women at the trading posts and in the Arapahoe camps they passed, since leaving Fort Leavenworth.

Game being abundant in the area and the weather pleasant, Major Sedgwick decided to lay by for an extra day to rest the men and animals. Tuesday, June 30, therefore, was a day at ease. The troops were mustered for two month's pay in the morning, army regulations requiring mustering for pay on the last days of February, April, June, August, October, and December, no matter where a unit was. They would not, of course, actually receive their pay until they came within reach of a paymaster.[57]

The California Trail, or Cherokee Trail as it was sometimes

---

*The bag of gold given to Fall Leaf was exhibited by him around the Delaware Reservation and in neighboring Lawrence, Kansas, following his return. As a result, the "Lawrence Party" of gold seekers went to Cherry Creek to prospect in 1858 in the vanguard of the Colorado gold rush. See *KHC* 8:492.

called, made its first and principal crossing of the South Platte just
below the mouth of Cherry Creek. It was here that most travelers
using it separated from the Trappers Trail, the latter thereafter
becoming a dim wagon road following the east bank of the South
Platte. On the morning of July 1, the troopers departed their pleasant camp on Cherry Creek and marched north along the Trappers
Trail. The weather had been and continued to be most pleasant,
with warm days and cool nights, contrasting with the oppressive
heat and monotony of the plains.

During the march on July 2 they came to the ruins of old Fort
Lupton (or Fort Lancaster), built by Lancaster P. Lupton in 1837
and abandoned in 1844. The walls were crumbling but still largely
intact. It was about one hundred feet square in size, built of adobe,
and had a tower at the northeastern corner. Six miles beyond, they
passed the ruins of a second adobe fort, Fort Vasquez. This little
trading post was also approximately one hundred feet square, and
its walls still stood, though in a dilapidated condition. [58]

That afternoon the command camped along the South Platte
across from and a little below the mouth of St. Vrain Creek. This
was a fine campsite, offering good grass and a spectacular view of
Long's Peak and the surrounding snow-capped peaks in that part
of the Front Range, now nearly due west of them. They could see
clouds among and below the peaks, a curiosity to men who had
never seen such great mountains, and during the night flashes of
lightning illuminated them in a most intriguing way. [59]

On the morning of Friday, July 3, the troopers marched only
three miles, passing the ruins of Fort St. Vrain en route and going
back into camp two miles downriver from it at a bend in the stream.
There was a beautiful bottom with fine grass between their campsite and the river, and here the livestock were grazed. Once in
camp some of the officers and men rode back to explore the old
trading post. Though in a state of ruin, it was better preserved than
the other two they had passed. Built of adobe having a reddish
hue, it measured 128 feet north to south and 106 feet east to west.
There were towers or bastions at the southeast and northwest corners, both two stories in height. A small cannon without a carriage,
about a four-pounder, was found abandoned there, half buried in
the crumbling ruins of the walls. [60]

Fort St. Vrain was the intended point of rendezvous with Colonel

Sumner and his column. The plan had called for the two separate arms of the Cheyenne Expedition to meet there on July 4, the national holiday. Sedgwick's men had completed that part of their assigned duty, and now they eagerly awaited the arrival of Sumner and his troops. Somewhere far to the southeast, in the Smoky Hill country, the Cheyennes were waiting.[61]

6

The March of Sumner's Column

And now the restive horses prick their ears
And nicker to the bugle. Fours about,
They rear and wheel to line. The hillsides shout
Back to the party. Forward! Now it swings
High-hearted through the gate of common
                    things
To where bright hazard, like a stormy moon,
Still gleams round Hector, Roland, Sigurd,
                    Fionn;
And all the lost, horizon-hungry prows,
Eternal in contemporary nows,
Heave seaward yet.   *(73–74)*

The March to Fort Kearny

When Major Sedgwick and his two squadrons of the First Cavalry departed Fort Leavenworth on the morning of May 18, 1857, Colonel Sumner and his staff returned to their headquarters at the post. There was still much to be done. Even then his column's wagons were being loaded under the careful supervision of Percival G. Lowe, the First Cavalry's experienced head wagon master. Lowe had served with the First Dragoons for five years and had left the military as a sergeant at the expiration of his enlistment in 1854. His natural ability, good common sense, and vast experience along the western trails had gotten him immediate employment with the army quartermaster's department, with which he had served as a wagon master at both Fort Leavenworth and Fort Riley.

Transportion for Colonel Sumner's column consisted of his four-mule ambulance, fifty wagons drawn by six-mule teams, and twenty extra mules. There were, in addition, two prairie howitzers pulled by four-mule teams, the remuda of extra cavalry horses, and a beef herd to supply fresh meat to the command during the march.[1]

The loading of wagons and other final preparations took the rest of May 18 and 19. Officially the troops were detached from duty at Fort Leavenworth on May 19, but not until 8:00 A.M. on the morning of Wednesday, May 20, did Companies A and B, First Cavalry, leave the post to begin their march as part of the Cheyenne Expedition. This time Colonel Sumner rode at the front of the troops, followed closely by 2d Lt. Albert V. Colburn, of B Company (the regimental adjutant), 1st Lt. James E. B. Stuart, of G Company (acting quartermaster and commissary officer of the expedition), the orderly bugler, and the four-mule ambulance that would serve as mobile headquarters for the next several weeks. Behind them, mounted on sorrel horses and marching by fours, came A Company led by Capt. William N. R. Beall, their first lieutenant, John N. Perkins, and their second lieutenant, Richard H. Riddick. Following at an interval behind A Company came B Company, mounted on grays and led by 1st Lt. Phillip Stockton, the executive officer.*[2]

The regimental band, which was to accompany the expedition, led the way through the garrison playing the traditional "The Girl I Left Behind Me." Once beyond the garrison, the column crossed the old drill field at the southwest corner of the post, following the route taken by Major Sedgwick two days earlier. Just as with Sedgwick's departure, each of the companies marched with sabres drawn and guidons flying, making a grand spectacle for those watching. Waiting to take their salute was Lt. Col. George Andrews, Sixth Infantry, now by virtue of seniority the fort's ranking officer. He and his staff sat mounted at the side of the road until they had passed, then returned to the garrison. The cavalry column continued on with no more than a change in gait to put the horses at a walk, and slowly disappeared into the valley to the west.[3]

---

*The company commander of B Company, Capt. Delos B. Sackett, was in Washington, D.C., on special orders at the time the expedition departed from Fort Leavenworth. See Post Returns, Ft. Leavenworth, K.T., May, 1857 (M617-R611).

With their sabres returned and the band with its instruments at the carry, Sumner's troopers marched three miles beyond the fort to the crossing of Salt Creek. There they too halted, dismounted, and rested their horses until Lowe reached them with the wagon train, the remuda, and the beef herd. When they arrived and the column was closed up and in line, the band stowed their instruments in their wagon, and all the troopers remounted and resumed the march. The Fort Leavenworth–Fort Laramie Military Road on which they were traveling was at one with the Fort Leavenworth–Fort Riley Military Road for the first few miles beyond Leavenworth. Together they angled a little northwest from the fort to a division point eight miles west, where the road to Laramie continued moving northwest, while that to Fort Riley turned sharply southwest to cross Stranger Creek at Eastin. The Laramie road struck Stranger Creek about five miles beyond the division of the roads, thereafter moving parallel with its northern bank. After marching eighteen miles from the fort, Colonel Sumner halted his troops and put them into camp on its banks.[4]

On the morning of May 21, Sumner's command continued to march northwest. After two miles they reached another division in the trail. The older military road followed a small tributary of Stranger Creek in a more northerly direction to a junction with the road from Atchison at a place called Chain Pump. From there it ran northwesterly to the town of Seneca and beyond until it joined the road from St. Joseph at Ash Point. In 1854, by order of Colonel Sumner, a new, more direct route had been surveyed that continued to follow Stranger Creek to its headwaters, whence it proceeded in a generally west-northwesterly direction. It crossed Grasshopper Creek (Delaware River) farther south and east than did the earlier trail, and had no towns along its course until it again rejoined the combined trails from St. Joseph, Atchison, and Leavenworth at Spring Creek, five miles east of Palmetto. Because no known journal or record of the route followed between the camp of May 20 and arrival at Spring Creek has been found, there is no way to be certain which trail they followed. However, because it was the shorter road, was laid out at the direction of Colonel Sumner, and would have avoided the heavy traffic by then moving along the roads from Atchison and St. Joseph, it seems logical that the cavalry column would have followed the newer road.[5]

Whichever route Colonel Sumner chose would have required at least a four- or five-day march to the point where the two trails converged at Spring Creek. Both roads traversed very hilly and rocky country, crowned with a carpet of grass and with trees only along the streams. Deer, antelope, wolves, coyotes, prairie chickens, and other forms of wildlife abounded. Beyond the headwaters of Stranger Creek, the new road to Laramie crossed only one major stream, Grasshopper Creek, and that in its upper reaches. Thereafter it followed the divide between the streams draining the area north and south until it struck the headwaters of the Black Vermillion, along whose north bank it continued until reaching Robideaux Creek. It followed the Robideaux north about four miles, then crossed to the west bank and continued northwest another six miles. At that point it met the road from St. Joseph and Atchison, and the older Fort Leavenworth Military Road, at the south bend of Spring Creek, then followed that stream west to its junction with the Big Blue.

Arriving at the Big Blue, the column first passed through Palmetto on the east bank of the river, then Marysville on the west bank.* Palmetto, the newer of the towns, was pro-slavery in sentiment, and a fierce rival of Marysville, but more because of money and power than politics. Although Marysville was the bigger and more "booming" of the two, as the men of Sumner's column passed through there were only about twenty log houses, a weekly newspaper, and atrocious whiskey.[6]

The Big Blue River, which divided the rival towns, was a beautiful stream with a rocky bottom, clear water, and good timber. It marked the beginning of the buffalo country and the territory of the Pawnee Nation. Immigrant travel from that point to Fort Kearny

*Palmetto was founded on July 8, 1856, by a colony of thirty-five men from South Carolina, mostly from the area of Charleston. Marysville was on the west bank of the Big Blue opposite Palmetto. It was founded in 1854 by Francis (Frank) J. Marshall, for whom the county was named, who had established a ferry along the trail at that point in 1852. The town was next to the ferry, and was named for Marshall's wife, Mary. Marshall was a Virginian, a Democrat, and not antislavery. Sometimes considered a free-state town, in the elections of 1857, Marysville produced only one free-state vote. Aside from its founding Virginian, its early population was primarily from Missouri. See *KHC* 14:135; *KHC* 17:9, 11; *Marysville Advocate*, October 15, 1965.

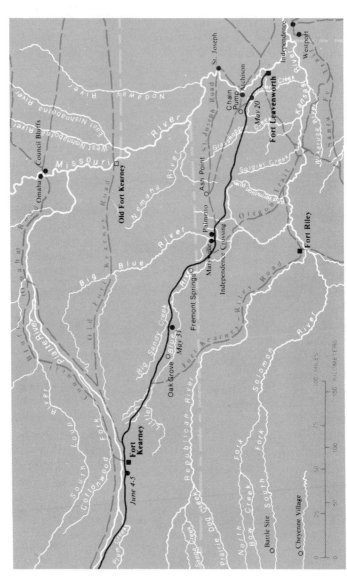

March of Sumner's column from Fort Leavenworth to Beyond Fort Kearny

always carried with it the possibility of stock theft, begging, and extortion, if not outright attack by the Pawnees.[7]

The road followed by Sumner's troops from Fort Leavenworth joined the original Oregon Trail from Independence about nine miles west of the Big Blue Crossing. Marysville and Palmetto, settlements far to the west of other white communities, represented the last outpost of European civilization (if such they could be called) before Fort Kearny. From the junction of the two trails, the road followed a northwest course parallel with and finally adjacent to the Little Blue River and its valley for some 120 miles until reaching Thirty-Two Mile Creek. Thereafter it crossed a twenty-mile-long divide to reach the valley of the Platte seventeen miles east of the fort.

By Sunday, May 31, Sumner had taken his command across the Big Sandy into camp along the banks of the Little Blue about eighty miles southeast of Fort Kearny. From the time the troops had reached the junction with the road from St. Joseph and then the Independence Road, they had met large numbers of immigrants with great herds of cattle. Their presence in Indian country gave Colonel Sumner concern for their safety. To protect them, he decided to slow his march and time it to provide cover along the road up the Platte until the larger part of them had passed.[8]

Beyond the First Cavalry camp of May 31, north of the Little Blue, the country began to flatten out and was less broken. Following a march of fourteen miles, they passed Oak Grove on the north bank of the Little Blue, and in two more miles negotiated "The Narrows." The land beyond became extremely flat, a featureless plateau between the rugged hills of northern Kansas Territory and sand dunes on the south side of the Platte River. Another thirty-five or thirty-six miles across this plain brought them to the first crossing of the west branch of Thirty-Two Mile Creek, a marker on the trail because it was thirty-two miles from Fort Kearny. A few miles before reaching it, the Little Blue had turned almost due west, while the column of cavalry continued marching to the northwest. Ten miles after crossing Thirty-Two Mile Creek, they reached the divide between the waters flowing southeast into the drainage of the Kansas River and those flowing northeast into the Platte. The line of descent beyond was marked by a series of sandy hummocks, one more obstacle against which the wagons and animals had to struggle.[9]

Clearing the chain of sandhills, the column finally descended into the valley of the Platte. The first view of it beyond the dunes revealed a wide plain as level as the surface of a lake, with a long, thin line of timber on Grand Island to the north and east. Away from the island there was no timber, just a flat valley perhaps six or seven miles wide, and the river itself, which was between one and two miles wide from bank to bank. Its waters were shallow and they snaked their way across the bed through innumerable channels.[10]

Shortly after the trail broke free of the sandhills, it turned nearly due west, joining the road from the original old Fort Kearny (Nebraska City) seventeen miles below the new Fort Kearny. The post itself was visible for almost ten miles, with first the flagpole and one or two chimneys making their appearance, and finally buildings attaching themselves to the chimneys as they drew nearer. Sumner's command reached it on the morning of June 4, and went into camp nearby. The fort was a motley collection of frame and sod buildings, the most important of which were scattered around a large parade ground. They were in a dilapidated condition and housed only a small garrison. In the center of the parade stood the flagpole the troopers had been watching grow out of the valley for the last several miles. But the post did offer a substantial point of resupply, one of its more important functions. Best of all for the tired troopers, it meant a brief respite from their march.[11]

Fort Kearny to Fort Laramie

When Colonel Sumner and his troopers rode into Fort Kearny they found, in addition to the garrison of Sixth Infantry soldiers, two companies of the Second Dragoons that were to join the Expedition, and one hundred recruits for Companies B, C, D, and G, Sixth Infantry, stationed at Fort Laramie. The dragoons were in camp near the fort, having been sent there for the travel season to patrol the trail. The infantry recruits, in the charge of 1st Lt. Silas Parsons Higgins of Alabama, were to accompany the cavalry column to Fort Laramie to join their units. Companies E and H, Second Dragoons, on the other hand, were now attached to Sumner's command in accordance with the army's General Order No. 5, establishing the makeup of the Cheyenne Expedition. E Company was commanded by 1st Lt. William Duncan Smith, of Georgia, and H Company by 1st Lt. Bordenave Villepigne, of South Carolina.[12]

The afternoon of June 4 and all of June 5 were devoted to resupplying rations and other consumables, and forage and grain for the livestock. Lieutenant Stuart had resigned as acting quartermaster and commissary on June 1; Lieutenant Riddick, who had succeeded him, was responsible for the resupply and loading. Ten additional wagons were provided to Percival Lowe for the train, and when the loading was completed all was in readiness for an early departure. The men of the First Cavalry, in preparation for continuation of the march, let their mounts and other livestock graze without interruption, except for watering, grain feeding, and currying. That completed, they bathed, washed their clothes, and rested. Troopers of the Second Dragoons also had prepared themselves for departure, packing their wagons and readying their horses. To lead his enlarged command to the Cheyennes, Colonel Sumner engaged the services of five Pawnee scouts under a chief named Speck-in-the-Eye.[13]

On the morning of June 6, Sumner's column, greatly enlarged by the addition of the dragoons and infantry recruits, resumed the westward march. Above Kearny the Platte was braided with islands and filled with sandbars. As with the Arkansas, there was little or no timber along its banks most of the distance from Fort Kearny to its forks. The line of sandhills the troops had crossed to enter the valley of the Platte was clearly visible two or three miles south of the river. The road along the Platte was broad and very hard, the result of years of use by innumerable wagon trains, herds of livestock, military units, and other travelers. As a result of the extreme flatness, its surface was mostly smooth, but frequently it was broken by buffalo trails worn like furrows into the earth as the great herds moved to the river to drink. The view seemed unchanging for as far as the eye could see, a broad plain stretching to the horizon with the sandhills on the left (south) and the wide, shallow, featureless river on the right. The north side of the river was the mirror image of the south.[14]

On the second day out of Fort Kearny the column reached and probably camped beside Plum Creek, about thirty-five miles distant, the first wood and water supply of consequence above the post. Some eighty-six miles beyond Kearny they reached Cottonwood Springs, another likely camping place. It had a fine spring with a small grove of cottonwoods around it.

About nine and one-half miles from Cottonwood Springs, the marching troops passed the confluence of the North and South Platte rivers, known as the "Forks of the Platte." Seventeen miles farther they came to Fremont Springs, beyond which they saw no more buffalo during the march to the west.*[15]

On June 13, after passing two or three early fords along the South Platte above O'Fallon's Bluff, Colonel Sumner brought his troops into camp four miles below the Lower California Crossing. They had traveled a little over 160 miles in eight days of steady marching, and both they and their animals were tired. On June 14, knowing the difficulties attendant to a crossing, Colonel Sumner had the command lay by. This gave the men a chance to clean up and allowed the livestock time to graze and rest. Head Wagon Master Lowe had the covers thrown off every wagon to allow the sun to dry out any dampness that might have accumulated during the march.[16]

Crossing the Platte at any point and at any time was filled with difficulty. It was wide, had a quicksand bottom, and was of unpredictable depth even during dry seasons—anything from a few inches to ten or fifteen feet. The river Sumner's men had to cross in June 1857 was very high, for it was the "June rise," the time when the snow melt in the mountains put great quantities of water into the streams that drained out across the plains. Usually noted for low levels and great numbers of sandbars, the South Platte was now full, one-half mile wide from bank to bank, no sandbars showing, and with a current of three to four miles per hour. There were a great many immigrants, and their trains were backed up near the crossing, waiting for the whims of nature to lower the water level and permit a safe passage. For Sumner, however, time was running short. He was still about one hundred fifty miles from Fort Laramie, and in just twenty days he was due to meet Major Sedgwick and his troops at old Fort St. Vrain. Like it or not, he had to cross promptly.[17]

Rising early on the morning of June 15, Lowe and all his wagon masters and their assistants, except one who remained behind in charge of the train, rode to the crossing at 5:00 A.M. He pointed

*Fremont Springs was named for John C. Frémont, who discovered them in 1842.

out the landing on the north side and ordered a wagon master named Eskridge, a man of quick perception, to remain on the south bank and direct him step by step should he start to drift downstream before the current. Taking the other men with him he waded across to a small island where they cut a number of willow switches ten or twelve feet long from the trees growing along the north side, carefully leaving a few leaves at the top. Moving to the north bank of the South Platte he directed his men in a straight line to Eskridge, having each in turn plant a switch deep in the quicksand to mark a straight trail from the south bank to the north. With a very uneven bottom, the river varied in depth from one to four feet, but was generally two to three feet deep.[18]

Soon after the path had been marked, the cavalry troopers arrived. They were instructed to keep close to the line of willow switches on the downriver side in order to beat down and level the uneven quicksand bottom and thus improve the crossing for the wagons. Before the first riders entered the water, Lowe rode ahead to show the way. As they crossed in a long line, company by company, some of the men had trouble, drifted, and even before the north bank had been reached by the lead troopers, the straight line had become an arc. The center of the line had drifted as much as three hundred yards below the direct line, many horses were foundering in the quicksand, and several men nearly drowned. Though all men and horses eventually crossed safely, their failure to move in a straight line did nothing to help the road bed.[19]

With the cavalry and dragoons safely on the north side, the wagon train was next. So that the Sixth Infantry recruits would not have to attempt a crossing on foot, they were permitted to climb into the wagons, two in each. The river was a boiling, churning cauldron of swift-flowing water and shifting sand, a dangerous place for the strongest and most experienced men and teams. In quicksand, to stop and stand still is to sink. Each man and each wagon and team must keep constantly on the move to avoid a serious problem, if not disaster. When the train was lined up and ready, Lowe started them off one at a time, keeping a distance of about fifty feet between them and taking care that no more than half-a-dozen wagons were in the river at the same time. This he did to avert a blockage by a wagon and team in trouble, which might cause those following to be thrown out of line or forced to stop and sink in the quicksand. In addition to the wagon masters, a dozen teamsters mounted on their saddle mules were strung out along the crossing to assist any who needed help. A strap or rope was tied to the bridle of the lead mule and held by a mounted man who started into the river ahead of each team. One or two other riders stayed downriver of the team to whip up the mules and keep them from drifting, while the teamster on his saddle mule did his best to keep them moving.[20]

Most wagons and teams experienced some kind of difficulty as they entered the water. Outriders had to dismount so frequently to help those in trouble that before long all were completely soaked. The day was dark and cloudy, with a cool north wind blowing, and because the water was still cold from its mountain origins, those who had to stay in it were soon thoroughly chilled and suffering a great deal. As each wagon reached the north bank, the teamster leading it unhitched his saddle mule and returned to the south bank to help the next. Working thus, many among them were in the water almost continuously for three, four, and even five hours. Percival Lowe, a careful and conscientious leader, set an example for his men by remaining in the water for more than six hours, making every effort to ensure a safe crossing. The only men who stayed dry, other than a handful of careful cavalrymen, were the infantry recruits who rode over in the wagons.[21]

Few crossings as dangerous as this failed to take a toll, but so well planned and executed was the crossing of Lowe's train that there was only one serious incident. When about half the wagons were over, the hospital wagon, containing all the medicine and medical equipment for the command, started its crossing. Driven by the oldest of the wagon masters, then making his first trip across, the hospital wagon held the lightest load. When it was in the middle of the river, the team became tangled and the lead mules swung around. This forced the saddle mule to stop, causing him to sink in the sand and then, in his struggle, to go under the tongue of the wagon. As he did so, the front wheels of the wagon sank and, under the force of the current, rolled over. The eighteen-year-old boy leading the team was caught on his saddle mule as it went under and was crying for help as he attempted to free himself. The old wagon master seemed frozen into immobility, and the rider on the downriver side could not reach him. Percival Lowe, about fifty yards distant at that moment, saw what was happening, spurred his horse, and reached the boy in time to keep him from

On June 15, 1857, Sumner's column was forced to cross the South Platte during the spring rise, when it was swollen by the melting snows in the mountains. Bank full, a half mile wide, with no sandbars showing and a swift current, the river caused the troopers great difficulty. In the end, all the men and the wagon train, except the hospital wagon, made it across safely.

going under the wagon tongue with the drowning saddle mule. The other men cut the harness from the rest of the mules and led them to safety. Fortunately the only loss was the hospital wagon, its contents, and one mule.[22]

When the last of the train was over, the remuda and beef herd were driven across with little difficulty. Meantime, the cavalry column, having reorganized itself, had moved out. Colonel Sumner's plan was to march six miles beyond the crossing to a water hole. To do this, however, the troopers and the wagon train had to get themselves up California Hill, which rises 240 feet over a distance of 1.7 miles. Once beyond this hurdle, the land was mostly level for a stretch of about sixteen miles before the travelers descended into Ash Hollow and the valley of the North Platte. Exhausted by the crossing, and in need of a stop to rest and dry out, Sumner's men were going only six miles this day. They did not find the water hole, but even so, because their canteens contained plenty of water for the men, they went into camp for a rest. Some exhausted teamsters changed into dry clothing, and after a hot meal and plenty of coffee, their circulation returned, making them more comfortable and relaxed.[23]

On the morning of June 16, the column of cavalry continued the march. From the campsite of the previous night it was ten miles over a barren plateau to the edge of Windlass Hill, down whose steep grade entrance to Ash Hollow was normally obtained. Ash Hollow itself is about four miles in length, some two thousand feet wide rim to rim, one thousand feet wide at its gateway along the North Platte, and an average of two hundred and fifty feet in depth. The basin within is surrounded by high, white cliffs and in the bottom were patches of trees, shrubbery, and beautiful, clear springs.

Beyond O'Fallon's Bluff the land was more uneven; with California Hill and Ash Hollow the troops were about to enter into a country along the North Platte quite unlike the flat and featureless broad plain they had followed from Fort Kearny. From this point on they would pass many notable and interesting geological phenomena. First, however, they had to take four companies of mounted troops, some sixty wagons, a remuda, and a beef herd down a very steep hill. The slope was twenty-five degrees for about three hundred feet, and negotiating it required the ingenuity and hard work of the

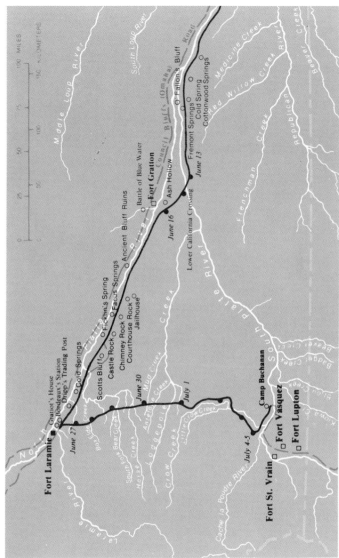

March of Sumner's column along the North Platte to Fort Laramie, and south to Camp Buchanan

whole command and their civilian crew of wagoneers and herdsmen. Doing so took a great part of the day. Afterward the command
probably went into camp near Ash Hollow Spring. It reputedly had
the best water for many miles in either direction, and, with a fine
grove of cottonwood and cedar trees, it was a welcome break from
the exhausting and dangerous march they had just made.[24]

Leaving Ash Hollow on the morning of June 17, Colonel Sumner
and his men found themselves following a trail that was confined
to a narrow strip of land crowded between a line of sandstone bluffs
to the south and the North Platte River on the north. It continued
thus for about twenty-five miles, when the valley began to broaden
and the bluffs retreated from the river. As they cleared the entrance
of Ash Hollow, they could see the sod walls of Fort Grattan standing to the northeast along the river's south bank. This was the small
redoubt constructed by Colonel Harney as a temporary shelter
for wounded soldiers and Indian prisoners after the fight on the
Blue Water.[25]

About forty miles above the mouth of Ash Hollow, the column
passed a landmark formation of eroded sandstone on the north
bank of the North Platte. It was known as "Ancient Bluff Ruins"
because of its appearance. From there the troopers had their first
glimpse of Chimney Rock, a tiny speck in the distance some thirty
miles up the valley, and their first good view of Courthouse Rock
and the neighboring "Jailhouse," about seventeen miles beyond
them on the south side of the river. This was a dramatic introduction to the series of similar, freestanding landmarks forming a part
of a ridge running from that point to Scott's Bluff.[26]

About nine miles beyond Courthouse Rock, Sumner put his men
into camp at a small series of springs, later known as Facus
Springs, four miles below Chimney Rock and eighty miles short of
Fort Laramie. There an express rider brought orders to leave the
two companies of dragoons at Fort Kearny to become part of the
expedition to Utah. Because they were far closer to Fort Laramie
than Fort Kearny, Sumner determined to take them on to Laramie
to await further orders rather than be forced to march over the same
ground three times.

The following day the troops passed Chimney Rock and went
into camp at Ficklin's Springs (as they were later known), the last
good water before Scott's Bluff.[27] The territory beyond and south of

Chimney Rock, a range known as the Wildcat Hills, culminated at
Scott's Bluff, a massive promontory rising about eight hundred feet
above the valley floor. Four or five miles beyond Ficklin's Springs,
the trail divided. Colonel Sumner followed the newer branch,
crossing Scott's Bluff by way of Mitchell Pass. Beyond it, Sumner
quickly regained the valley of the North Platte, and another fifteen
miles brought him and his men to Horse Creek Crossing, site of
the 1851 treaty with most of the Plains tribes.[28]

After Horse Creek the marching column passed Cold Springs,
then three well known trading posts in succession: the first was that
of Maj. Andrew Dripps, where the agent for the Upper Platte Indian Agency generally made his headquarters during the summer;
the second was Bordeaux's station, the trading post near which the
swaggering Lieutenant Grattan and his men met their end; and the
third was Gratiot's House, a trading post four miles west of Bordeaux's station. Three and one-half miles beyond Gratiot's House
was their immediate destination, Fort Laramie.

They reached the fort on June 22, camping a mile and a half
above it on the south side of the Laramie River. Companies E and
H, Second Dragoons, camped separately, having been detached for
service in Utah. They were officially attached to the fort on June
23. The march had been long, tiring, and often tedious for the men
of the First Cavalry. Now, while provisions and stores were being
replenished, they had an opportunity for some well-deserved rest
before moving south to their rendezvous with Sedgwick and his
men and, ultimately, the Cheyennes.[29]

From Fort Laramie to the South Platte

In June 1857, Fort Laramie was still in its infancy as a military
post; nonetheless, it had taken on the general outline that it would
follow thereafter. Though in a state of decay, the outer walls of old
Fort John, built by the American Fur Company, still stood at the
southwest end of the parade ground. Along the northwest side stood
the two-story officers' quarters known as "Old Bedlam," and beyond it the sutler's store. At the northeast end stood a large, two-
story, two-company infantry barracks gazing across the broad parade to the remains of Fort John. On the southeast side were adobe
stables (in poor condition); scattered about the parade ground and

beyond were some twenty other buildings, mostly built of adobe. A large number of the fort's buildings were either incomplete or deteriorating.[30]

For Sumner's column, arrival at Fort Laramie meant a few days' rest, but it also meant work to complete resupply. Fortunately the post maintained a good stock of quartermaster and commissary supplies, and the sutler's store operated by Seth E. Ward had a notably fine selection of campaign goods. The four full days at Laramie were mostly spent replacing teams broken down by the long march, fitting horse and mule shoes, drawing forage for the livestock and provisions for the troops, and generally renewing the supplies they would need when the march continued. The troops had been slaughtering some of the beef herd each day for meat, especially since passing beyond the buffalo range at Fremont Springs, and now they drew 150 more head from the post commissary. Colonel Sumner also employed two additional guides, a Mexican named Armijo and a white mountaineer. Meanwhile the livestock was allowed to graze on the excellent grass found along the Laramie River and to recuperate from the rigors of the march.[31]

General Order No. 5 had provided that three of the four companies of the Sixth Infantry stationed at Fort Laramie were to become a part of the Cheyenne Expedition and that the commanding officer of the post, Maj. (Bvt. Lt. Col.) William Hoffman, would designate the company to remain in garrison. He had selected Company B. Companies C, D, and G were busily packing and preparing to march south with the rest of Sumner's command as soon as the cavalry was ready. The new recruits brought to them by Colonel Sumner posed a problem for the infantry: they had to be assigned to their units, issued equipment, and familiarized with their duties in the very short time prior to departing on their first campaign.

The officer designated by Colonel Sumner to assume overall command of the infantry units was Capt. William Scott Ketchum, of G Company. Company C was commanded by Capt. Rennselaer W. Foote, with John McCleary as its second lieutenant.* Because of the absence of Capt. (Bvt. Maj.) Edward Johnson, of D Company, temporary command had passed to its first lieutenant, Wil-

---

*The first lieutenant of C Company, James L. Corley, having been appointed regimental adjutant of the Sixth Infantry, was stationed at Fort Leavenworth. See Sixth Infantry, Regimental Returns, July, 1857.

liam Passmore Carlin.* Company G was under the command of Captain Ketchum and its second lieutenant was Orlando H. Moore.†

A day or so before departure the infantry moved out of their barracks at the fort and went into camp on the south side of the Laramie River above the cavalry camp. While each infantry company had its own wagons to transport tents and other equipment, the men themselves were afoot and, except when physically disabled, had to march the entire distance during any campaign in which they participated. The journey would be arduous and difficult for the infantry whether or not they engaged an enemy.

With preparations nearly complete, Colonel Sumner sent a report to army headquarters stating his intent to depart Fort Laramie on the following morning, June 27, expecting to meet Sedgwick's column on the South Platte on July 4, then to march to the Cheyenne country. There his plan was to establish a large camp and have two columns, without baggage, constantly in the field in search of the Indians. He noted that, owing to the size of their country and the lack of water and grass, finding and engaging the Cheyennes would be difficult.[32]

On the morning of June 27, Colonel Sumner once more put his troops on the road, this time by marching almost due south to meet Sedgwick's column. Because of their comparatively slow rate of march, the three companies of the Sixth Infantry left at 8:00 A.M. They passed the cavalry camp with the guides and five Pawnee scouts in the lead. Shortly after they were followed by the two cavalry companies, the wagon train, the remuda, and the beef herd. Marching first east and then southeast, they crossed Deer Creek and turned almost directly south, following the trace of the old Trappers Trail to Taos. As Fort Laramie, the only symbol of their civilization that most of the men would see for nearly two months,

---

*Captain Johnson was at the time on detached duty with a survey party under Wm. M. F. Magraw. He was carried on the books at Fort Laramie and of the regiment as "absent without leave," apparently because the survey party had failed to return when scheduled. The company's second lieutenant, Edward Dillon, was at the time on a sixty-day leave of absence. Fort Laramie Post Returns, June, 1857; Sixth Infantry, Regimental Returns, July, 1857; Percival G. Lowe, *Five Years a Dragoon*, 191.

†First Lt. John C. Kelton of G Company was then on detached duty at the United States Military Academy at West Point. See Sixth Infantry, Regimental Returns, July, 1857.

receded in the distance, many doubtless had misgivings about what lay ahead. At the least this would be a time of extreme hardship and ever-present danger.[33]

Following a gradual rise, after about eight miles they reached the top of a steep, rocky hill. Negotiating the abrupt drop on the south side required an hour, during which they traveled only five hundred yards, to the edge of Cherry Creek, a small stream flowing generally east-southeast to the North Platte. Once down, they crossed the creek and camped on its south bank. With their descent they had entered Goshen's Hole.* Except at its northern and southern extremities no natural watercourses ran through it. Of those that did, some flowed through the subsurface sand strata during the heat of a summer's day, leaving only a dry bed to greet a thirsty traveler. According to Percival G. Lowe, it had the reputation of being "the hottest place this side of the home of Dives."[34]

On June 28 the guides, the Pawnee scouts, and the infantry resumed their march at 6:00 A.M., followed by the cavalry and the train at 7:00 A.M. The sun shining on the light, sandy ground created an intense light and stifling heat that grew worse as the sun rose higher. Their course was across the flat of the basin bottom, not difficult terrain but terribly uncomfortable for men and animals, the temperature rising to ovenlike intensity with no breeze to cool them. Worse, no water was found, creating a special hardship for the livestock. After a slow and punishing march, they reached a small stream called Box Elder Creek at a point about a mile from the bluffs through which it emerged from a canyon. There they went into camp. Box elder trees marked the course of the stream, and good grass grew along its banks, but no water washed its sandy bottom. The mountaineer guide told them the water always sank into the sand during the heat of the day, but resurfaced to become a fine running stream by 11:00 P.M.[35]

The waterless march and lack of water at the campsite was beginning to tell on the animals. The men pitched their tents and made use of such shade as there was, and what little bit went

---

*Goshen's Hole is more properly called Goché's Hole, as it reputedly was named for a shadowy French trapper named Goché. It is a large basin measuring more than thirty miles north to south, surrounded by a rim of steep white bluffs. The floor of the basin is a flat plain some 700 to 800 feet below the level of the surrounding country. See *Rufus B. Sage's Correspondence and Papers* 1:217.

unused was given to the cavalry horses. The miserable mules and the beef herd were left standing in suffocating heat, afflicted by a terrible thirst. The weather was so hot and dry that the horses could not swallow the grass they chewed and were forced to spit it out. With the permission of Colonel Sumner, Percival Lowe had the herd of mules turned up the creek to the high point of the bluff a mile beyond them. Scouting up the little creek to deep within its canyon he found flowing water sufficient for the livestock. In a short time all the animals were driven there and their suffering was at an end.[36]

Monday, June 29, after a march of about ten or eleven miles, the troopers reached and watered the animals at a small stream called Willow Creek.* Three miles beyond, they found a pass through the rim of Goshen's Hole between the continuing line of bluffs and Castle Rocks to the east. The pass was only a half mile across, but because its base was quicksand, the train required four hours to climb the hill. Three miles farther they crossed the north fork of Bear Creek (now Fox Creek) and there made camp. A fine location with good water and grass, it permitted them to relax a little following the rigors of Goshen's Hole.[37]

It was a tired group of men who resumed their journey on the morning of June 30. After marching one mile, they reached and crossed the south fork of Bear Creek. Normally only about ten feet across, it was so swollen by recent rains that it had become a bog 100 yards wide. Because the slough grass was as much as five feet tall, the cavalry had to dismount, and all soldiers and teamsters were put to work cutting grass to create a causeway. Although time consuming, the plan worked well and all troops, wagons, and animals crossed without loss or injury. The column then moved south another seventeen or eighteen miles over an undulating plain, crossing five small tributaries of Horse Creek, and made camp on the banks of Mud Creek at 4:00 P.M.[38]

On July 1 the infantry and cavalry continued down the Trappers Trail, but Percival Lowe took his wagon train over a smooth plain on what he called a "hard gravel road." It was much more level and saved considerable trouble for both train and livestock. After

---

*Willow Creek probably was the same stream as the one later named Lone Tree Creek.

eighteen miles they reached and crossed Lodgepole Creek, camping four miles beyond on the banks of "Big Mud Creek."* That night a heavy rainstorm struck.[39]

When the troopers and soldiers roused themselves the following morning, July 2, they found the storm had done more than make the road muddy. The beef herd had stampeded from fright and the butcher in charge of them was forced to acknowledge there "wa'n't a critter in sight." Quartermaster Sergeant Clark formed a search party and by 10:00 A.M. overtook the column with all the cattle. He had found them some ten miles from the camp, nearly in the line of march. The troops meanwhile had continued on and, after ten miles, struck the main branch of Crow Creek. Following its east bank for ten more miles, they reached a slough that ran into the creek from the northeast. The previous night's heavy rain here created more problems; four hours were needed for cutting grass and making a causeway. When they finally reached the opposite bank, they went into camp, very tired and with a number of mules broken down by the hardships of the day's march.[40]

Friday, July 3, brought more of the same. After marching a mile and a half they reached a large slough that took two hours to cross. Ten miles farther they attempted a crossing to the west bank of Crow Creek at the place selected by the mountaineer guide, but it took too much time to cross just nine wagons. In the meantime Captain Beall had found a much better crossing a half mile below, so the rest of the train moved down and crossed there with relative ease.

After the wagons were across, Colonel Sumner summoned Percival Lowe and told him what the guide was now suggesting. Their evening camp was still eight miles distant. According to the guide, the usual crossing of the South Platte, below the mouth of the Cache la Poudre, was twelve miles from the camp, and from there to Fort St. Vrain was an added thirteen miles—leaving a twenty-five-mile march and a river crossing for July 4. The guide believed that a direct route southwest to Fort St. Vrain would be only twenty miles and the crossing better than the one below the mouth of the Cache la Poudre. Lowe was not impressed by the guide, believing he lacked familiarity with the country and the best route through it. Therefore, he suggested to the colonel that he ride the supposed

*Big Mud Creek is now known as Muddy Creek.

twenty miles to Fort St. Vrain, verify the crossings and distance, and be back at camp before starting time in the morning, thus eliminating uncertainty as to the best route. The colonel agreed, telling him to take both guides and any others he might need. Lowe picked Simeon Routh, a teamster in whom he had great confidence, and departed camp. The column continued eight miles farther south, going into camp on the west bank of Crow Creek.[41]

After leaving the cavalry column, Lowe and Routh rode south. They quickly overtook the marching infantry, picked up the two guides, and then struck out southwesterly toward what the mountaineer guide called the "South Fork Peaks." He claimed Fort St. Vrain lay in a direct line between them and the peaks. Since leaving Fort Laramie, they had been moving nearly parallel with the mountain range, which seemed to be about forty miles away, and now they were turning toward it. Moving steadily over a level plain, they alternated going at a walk, trot, and gallop, averaging six or more miles per hour. The grade was slightly upward, and by 5:00 P.M. they had reached the high ground and could see the line of trees marking the channel of the Cache la Poudre. It was a lovely afternoon, and as they looked toward the mountains they saw a spectacular sight, for storm clouds were dodging around the snow-capped peaks in the distance, with rain and vivid lightning clearly visible. Upon it all the sun was shining brightly, creating a kaleidoscopic effect as the clouds churned rapidly.

They reached Cache la Poudre River at 7:00 P.M., having gone at least twenty-five miles and still being a considerable distance from Fort St. Vrain. The distance was of little moment, for the river was so swollen by the mountain rains it had overflowed its banks and was from ten to twenty feet deep. Crossing here was out of the question. Not wanting to retrace his steps twenty-five miles back to Colonel Sumner's camp, Lowe dispatched the Mexican guide, Armijo, with a note to the Colonel advising the Cache la Poudre was too high, likely to remain so, and a crossing there too difficult for the train. With a few instructions as to the route and the star to be followed, Armijo was sent off to Sumner's camp with the message. Lowe, Routh, and the mountaineer guide made camp for the night one-half mile from the river.[42]

By 5:00 A.M. on July 4, Lowe and his two companions had breakfasted on hardtack and were on the trail down the Cache la Poudre River. They arrived at the usual crossing point below its mouth at 8:00 A.M. There they unsaddled and let their horses graze for an hour, then Lowe attempted a crossing of the swollen South Platte with his horse. He made it over and back only with great difficulty, and it was apparent that no crossing could be made there for some time. When he returned to the north bank the dust cloud of the advancing cavalry column was visible four miles north and a little east. Armijo had reached Colonel Sumner in time to ensure that they followed the proper trail along the west bank of Crow Creek, and they expected to meet Lowe at the crossing. Because high water made fording the river impractical, Lowe selected a suitable campground another mile downriver. Then he rode up the trail to meet the Colonel, who was riding in his ambulance at the head of the column. After hearing the information concerning the crossing, Sumner put his men into camp on the site Lowe selected. It was an unexpected problem. They had come this far but could not cross the river and travel the last few miles to meet Sedgwick and his men. [43]

7

On the South Platte

Here they camped,
Rejoicing, man and beast.
....
                    And the trail-worn troopers went
About their duties, whistling, well content
To share this earthly paradise of game.
But scarcely were the tents up, when there
        came—
Was it a sign? One moment it was noon,
A golden peace hypnotic with the tune
Of bugs among the grasses; and the next,
The spacious splendor of the world was vexed
With twilight that estranged familiar things.
A moaning sound, as of enormous wings
Flung wide to bear some swooping bat of death,
Awakened.   *(63–64)*

The Two Columns Meet

Dawn of July 4, 1857, found the troopers of Sedgwick's column in camp two miles below the ruins of old Fort St. Vrain, on high ground overlooking the east bank of the South Platte. According to plan, Colonel Sumner's column was to join them there, and the combined command would then strike southeast across the plains in search of the Cheyennes. Major Sedgwick therefore kept his men in camp throughout the day in anticipation of the imminent arrival of Sumner and his troops. At twelve o'clock noon the battery of two prairie howitzers was ordered to commence firing a thirty-one-gun salute in honor of the national holiday. No sooner had the sound of the last gun begun to die than it was answered by the measured firing of an identical salute downriver. Sumner had arrived, or at least was close.[1]

Even before the booming report of Sumner's howitzers was heard in Sedgwick's camp, the major had sent Fall Leaf, the Delaware guide, to scout down the South Platte and find him. With him he sent a letter to the colonel, requesting orders for the joining of the two commands. Fall Leaf probably left camp about 9:30 or 10:00 A.M., as it was a good fifteen miles to the point where the Trappers Trail crossed the South Platte below the mouth of Cache la Poudre River. Shortly after the howitzer battery in Sumner's camp fell silent following the firing of the "National Salute," someone cried, "A horseman on the south side of the river!" Everyone rushed to the river's edge to catch sight of him. By then Fall Leaf, the rider, was at midstream. The depth and the swift current made the crossing difficult and dangerous, and several times the waiting troopers thought him lost. But at last he reached the north bank and delivered Sedgwick's message to Colonel Sumner. Sumner immediately wrote a response instructing Sedgwick to move downstream and make camp opposite him. The faithful Fall Leaf took the message and once again plunged into the river, fighting its swift current until he reached the south bank and disappeared to the west. He arrived in Sedgwick's camp with the letter at 4:00 P.M.[2]

Back at Sedgwick's camp a number of his officers took lunch on the banks of the South Platte and had some claret to celebrate the nation's birthday. The remainder of the day they spent preparing for the next morning's move or else resting. However, their rest was disrupted by wind, rain, and hail, followed by rainbows and a tornado funnel. A stampede of horses and mules, caused by the storm, also ruined the afternoon's rest for the tired men of Sumner's column. Fortunately all mounts were recovered and only two or three horses were hurt, the result of flying picket pins.[3]

On the morning of July 5, Sedgwick's men marched about sixteen miles downriver, reaching a point opposite Colonel Sumner at twelve noon and going into camp. Once in the new camp, the colonel sent word that, in view of the information received as to the whereabouts of the Cheyennes, he was going to leave behind the wagon train, tents, and other encumbrances, and form a mobile

On July 4, Sumner's column reached the South Platte. There Sedgwick's faithful guide, the Delaware chief Fall Leaf, crossed the swollen river to obtain Sumner's orders for the joining of the command.

column supplied by a train of pack mules. This would permit them
to strike fast and hard, with any luck surprising the Cheyennes.[4]

During the morning, while Sedgwick's men were moving downriver, troops under Colonel Sumner attempted a crossing of the
South Platte. A work detail was formed from each company of cavalry and infantry. Using three of the light, watertight, metallic
wagon beds and six coils of rope, they tried to build a rope ferry
with which to transport the wagons. First they stretched a rope from
the north bank to an island in mid-river, but this took until noon
and was much hard work under a hot sun. Their intention was to
lash the three wagon beds together, forming a raft, then attach it
by two pulleys to a rope at each end, which would be pulled back
and forth by men on the raft. Unfortunately, one of the wagon beds
got away from them and floated downriver. Worse, three men working with the rope in mid-river became exhausted, lost their hold on
it, and were swept away by the swirling waters. One managed to
catch a low hanging willow branch with his left hand and the hand
of one of his comrades with his right, hanging on tightly until they
were finally pulled in by men on shore. The third, a cavalry trooper
named Daugherty, was pulled under by the current and drowned.
A search party was unable to recover his body. Further efforts to
effect the crossing proved futile, and were abandoned altogether at
5:00 P.M. The men returned to their camp disheartened by their
failure and saddened by the loss of Trooper Daugherty.[5]

The water was too high and the current too strong to justify the
added danger for the troops and loss of time that would result from
further attempts to cross at their present campsite. Sumner therefore ordered both columns to proceed downstream until they found
a more suitable ford. On the morning of July 6 they moved an
additional eighteen miles downstream, although Sedgwick's officers thought it more like twenty. They passed the mouth of Crow
Creek during the march, and were surprised to find it dry, although
there was running water above.

The new camp was at a point where the South Platte was wider
and shallower and the current less swift. To celebrate, Lieutenants
Bayard and Lomax of Sedgwick's command swam across to the
north bank, carrying their clothes clenched in their teeth. Because
Major Sedgwick's wagons were nearly empty, his forage and provisions exhausted by the long march, a decision was made that his

troops and wagon train would cross to the north bank the following morning. The wagons were to be sent back to Fort Laramie anyway, while the combined column continued its search for the Cheyennes with pack mules.[6]

On the morning of Tuesday, July 7, Sedgwick's wagon train began crossing after breakfast, with Sumner's wagon masters and teamsters mounted on saddle mules along the banks and in the river to assist. The water proved no more than four feet deep, although nearly one-half mile wide. By 10:00 A.M. all wagons were over, and the four companies of cavalry, the remuda, and the beef herd quickly followed. The metallic wagon bed lost the previous day was found on a sandbar by "Big Nick" Beery, chief wagon master of Sedgwick's column, who brought it with him.

Once across, all wagons were turned over to the quartermaster to be taken back to Fort Laramie. There they were to be refitted and loaded with provisions and forage and then to proceed to the Lower California Crossing, where they were to meet the expedition in twenty days. Except for the cattle herd, the cavalry and infantry were to take rations for only that period of time. This should provide for their needs until they again met the wagon train and would lighten the load for the pack mules. Most officers considered the march a wild goose chase and ridiculed or grumbled at the idea of using a pack train.[7]

When Major Sedgwick's men reached the north bank of the South Platte, they went into camp adjacent to and upstream from Sumner's troops. Now they were one for the first time since leaving Fort Leavenworth. Their next task, using mules largely trained as saddle mules or as teams and with few real packsaddles, was to make up a mule train and renew their search for the enemy. The Cheyennes, they knew, were far to the southeast, somewhere in the country between the Republican and the Smoky Hill, and were expecting them.

That evening Colonel Sumner, having named the new, combined encampment "Camp Buchanan" in honor of the President, issued his first written order from it. Dated July 7, 1857, it informed the men that pack and riding mules must be made ready to accompany the six companies of cavalry and three of infantry, to create a mobile and fast-moving column to find and engage the Cheyennes. Calling his officers together to publish the order, he followed it with an invitation to take wine with him from his Fourth of July box, which he had intended to open at Fort St. Vrain. This was a fitting climax to the day's events.[8]

The Days at Camp Buchanan

Wednesday, July 8, started a period of preparation and rest for the men of the Cheyenne Expedition. Colonel Sumner divided his troops into two commands, infantry and cavalry, with Captain Ketchum in charge of the Sixth Infantry troops and Major Sedgwick in command of the six companies of the First Cavalry. For the military this was primarily a day for rest and tending horses. However, for the farrier-blacksmiths, saddlers, teamsters, and other civilian support personnel, it was a day of hard work. A blacksmith shop was set up in a central location and immediately put to work. It was a makeshift affair, with awnings made of wagon covers supported by poles, a portable anvil, bellows, and other equipment, and a small coal pit that burned through the night. Once established, this enabled blacksmiths to reshoe any horses and mules needing it, and to fit and repair wagon tires for the return trip to Laramie. A saddler shop was set up nearby, also using awnings made of wagon covers. There the saddlers made crosstree or sawbuck packsaddles out of a large number of saddletrees they found at Fort Laramie. Unfortunately, only a few real packsaddles were available at that post and because a march with a pack train had not been contemplated, none had been brought from Fort Leavenworth. The carpenter and his helpers spent the day fitting panniers (packbags), everyone involved doing his best with the materials at hand.[9]

July 9 was largely devoted to selecting mules to be used for the march across the plains. Percival Lowe and those among his crew knowledgeable about mules made a careful search for the best of them, insofar as possible using those broken for riding, including saddle mules belonging to teams. To fill in the gaps, he put teamsters to work breaking other mules. Packing presented an even greater problem: except for a few Mexicans, not a man among them, military or civilian, was a practical packer. To overcome this deficiency, Lowe established a sort of school on packing, using the Mexicans as instructors and, because they spoke little English, officers who spoke Spanish as interpreters or as student-instructors who then passed on to a few of their men the knowledge thus gained. What was needed were 100 packsaddles, ten apiece for each of the six cavalry and three infantry companies, and ten to be used to carry food and supplies for the officers, each company's officers being assigned one mule and a packsaddle. In addition, there were several pack mules for the blacksmith, complete with farrier equipment, and others for use by company cooks and the mule train cook.[10]

While work progressed in training pack mules and preparing packsaddles and packs, Colonel Sumner reorganized the command in anticipation of the forthcoming march. Second Lt. Albert V. Colburn was appointed acting adjutant general of the expedition, with 2d Lt. Lunsford Lomax acting adjutant of cavalry and infantry. First Lt. Frank Wheaton became acting quartermaster and commissary officer. Second Lt. George D. Bayard was placed in charge of the artillery, now consisting of the combined complement of four prairie howitzers. First Lt. J. E. B. Stuart was returned to his own G Company as the acting commanding officer, replacing Lieutenant Bayard.[11]

Friday, July 10, the command remained in camp, most of the troops spending their time washing clothes, cleaning weapons, repacking the limited gear they were taking with them, and attending to the horses' daily needs. That completed, the remainder of the day was spent at leisure. At the blacksmith shop and the saddler shop, work proceeded unabated, the men trying to minimize delay in resuming the march. Teamsters continued to work with the mules in an effort to accustom them to carrying the weight of packs. Each mule was expected to carry 150 pounds, not an undue burden but a problem nonetheless for mules unused to packsaddles and packs, and because of the tendency of some packs to produce strange noises as they jogged. Minimal equipment was to be taken: no more than one change of clothing per man and no tents. Even so, the necessary provisions, grain, and ammunition made a tight fit.[12]

Preparations continued at a feverish pace until the 12th, when all saddles and packs were finished and mule training was as far advanced as might be expected. In the afternoon, 180 pack and riding mules, 170 blind bridles, and all saddles and saddle blankets belonging to the mule train were turned over to Lieutenant Wheaton, the quartermaster, along with personnel to look after the

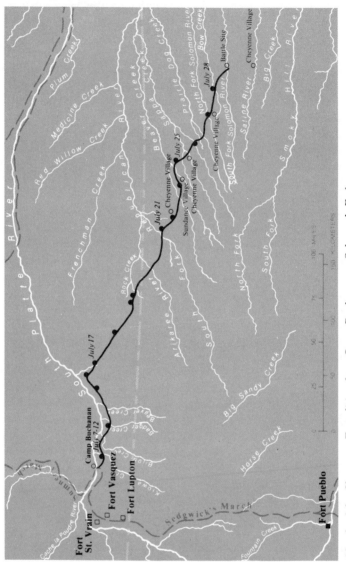

March of the Cheyenne Expedition from Camp Buchanan to Solomon's Fork

train. "Big Nick" Beery was to be the pack master (chief "mule-teer"), and he took with him Simeon Routh, as assistant pack master, and his pick of other teamsters and herders to fill the requirement of one packer for every five mules. Except for a small number of steers left with the wagon train, the beef herd was to accompany the cavalry column along with the remuda of replacement cavalry horses and mules. Training was continued to the last moment, and men assigned to the job packed and repacked the mules for practice. The mess mule was packed as an experiment and the job was very well done, to the gratification of those dependent upon its future services.[13]

With preparations complete and the mule train organized, Colonel Sumner issued his last orders from Camp Buchanan. The Cheyenne Expedition would depart camp the following morning. Infantry and packs would be crossed first, by wagons, and they would be followed by the mule train, cavalry companies, artillery, remuda, and beef herd. As soon as the mules were across, the packsaddles were to be placed on their backs and the packs strapped to the saddles. After they had taken their proper place, the column would move out, the course to be a little north of east, following the line of the South Platte River to the point where Lieutenant Bryan and his survey party had left it the previous year. Thereafter, they would strike southeast across the plains to the upper reaches of the south fork of the Republican, again following the trail of Lieutenant Bryan. The Pawnee scouts said the Cheyennes were camped along Beaver Creek, east of the south Republican, or at least they had seen their large communal village there in May. Wherever they were, the command would stay on their trail until they were found, then strike hard. The day of reckoning was at hand.[14]

Part Three

A Rendezvous with Destiny

8

Across the Plains in Search of the Cheyennes

And thither pressed the horse and foot . . .
Their pack mules, lighter for a greater speed,
With scant provisions for a fortnight's need
Upon their saddles.　　　　　　　*(209)*

The March Along the South Platte

Monday, July 13, men of the Cheyenne Expedition rose early, struck their tents, and carefully returned them to the company wagons along with anything not essential to a march supplied only by pack mules. That done and each company's packs complete, they tended to their horses, breakfasted, then answered the clear, resonant sounds of "Boots and Saddles." At 7:00 A.M., Percival Lowe and his men, using the best six-mule teams they could rig up, began crossing the infantry troops and the packs for the pack train to the south bank of the South Platte. These were followed by the pack mules and then by the cavalry companies in their day's order of march. Once over, farewells were said to Lieutenant Riddick, Percival Lowe and his crew, the band, and the approximately fifty men of the First Cavalry who were sick or injured or whose horses were disabled. The wagons and teamsters then returned to the north bank to prepare for their return to Fort Laramie.

The crossing, including remuda and cattle herd, was completed by 9:00 A.M., and once on the south bank, the troopers and soldiers loaded their packs on the blindfolded pack mules. Loading or unloading pack mules was nearly always done while they were blindfolded, to avoid alarming or agitating them. That completed, the bugler sounded "Advance," and the long column of the Cheyenne Expedition began its march eastward, Indian scouts in the lead, infantry, artillery battery, cavalry, mule train, remuda, and beef herd following.[1]

Mules usually were not placed in a pack string until they had completed a thorough course of training. Well-trained mules were a marvel; once they understood what was expected of them, they often could perform their work without further guidance. A green, or unbroken, mule, however, was dangerous, particularly to those following too closely. The mules in Colonel Sumner's packtrain were not really green, but few had been pack mules, and the change in their duties had been abrupt. Most adapted with little difficulty, but some became quite obstreperous: once they heard the jingling of pots or other metal articles, they began kicking and soon relieved themselves of their loads. These few caused the packers considerable grief.[2]

The trail Sumner's men were following, the same used by Lieutenant Bryan in the fall of 1856 during the return of his survey expedition, was originally an Indian trail. Tracks left by the travois of migrating villages were cut deeply into the ground. There were also ruts left by the wagons of Indian traders. The Cheyenne Expedition, minus its wagon train, now had only one vehicle, an ambulance, pulled by a four-mule team and heavily loaded with ammunition, medical supplies, and two tent-flies, one for use as the headquarters and adjutant's office, and the other as the hospital. There were also the four prairie howitzers. The absence of large numbers of wagons, while a logistical disadvantage, did create greater mobility for the column and made crossing streams and rough terrain faster and easier.

The Indian trail the troops followed generally took the best route along the river. It alternately traversed sandy or hard and gravelly soil, except in bottoms close to the river, and there were frequent patches of prickly pear cactus on the uplands. The only grass for grazing the animals was close to the river, and there the camps were made. The nearby South Platte was higher than usual, spreading out over its broad bed, but even at high water remained shallow from this point to its junction with the North Platte.[3]

On July 14 the column crossed Kiowa Creek and Bijou Creek, hardly more than dry arroyos with steep banks and no trees. The day was excessively hot and dusty, and as a result three or four men collapsed from heat exhaustion and had to be carried in the ambulance. Captain Sturgis also was affected by the sun but required no assistance. The men saw a few antelope as they marched, but there was little else in the way of wildlife, possibly because the timber was thinning out dramatically. Five miles beyond Bijou Creek they made camp on the banks of the South Platte.* [4]

On July 15 the trail took the command across Badger Creek and Beaver Creek, each having water but no trees. At the mouth of the latter, scattered along the banks of the South Platte, were a few trees that had been used as a burial site by a band of Cheyennes the previous year. Probably they were Ridge People, a band that regularly camped and hunted in the country between the Republican and South Platte. At least one tree burial was visible, and near the river they found a tripod consisting of three old lodgepoles (the remains of a burial lodge), from which were suspended some bloody blankets and skins. On the ground beneath were the bones of a human body with some of the cartilaginous matter still attached. At one side, staring toward the remains of the body, were a number of buffalo skulls set in a line. One of the civilian packers with the column said the bones were those of a young Cheyenne chief named Young Antelope, who had died or been killed in the vicinity the previous summer.† [5]

That afternoon Sumner's command made camp seven miles beyond Beaver Creek. Timber along the river had given out almost entirely, and the mountains to the west had faded from view. They were back on the plains. On July 16 they marched along the river for another seven miles, then went into camp at the site where Lieutenant Bryan and his party had camped the previous year. The following day they would take leave of the South Platte to march

*The camp of July 14 would have been on or very close to the townsite of present Fort Morgan, Colorado.

†These burials undoubtedly were among those seen by Lieutenant Bryan and his party when they camped at that location on September 12, 1856. See Report, Secretary of War, 1857, House Ex. Doc. 2, 35 Cong., Sess. I, 2:469 (Serial 943).

Near the banks of the South Platte, a short distance from the mouth of Beaver Creek, the troopers came upon a tripod of three old lodgepoles (the remains of a burial lodge) from which were suspended some bloody blankets and skins. On the ground below were the bones of a young Cheyenne chief, named Young Antelope, and nearby were a number of buffalo skulls set in a line facing the remains.

southeast across the plains. Once in camp, the horses, mules, and steers were turned out to graze on what would be their last good grass for a long time.[6]

From the South Platte to the South Fork of the Republican

The road that Colonel Sumner intended to follow away from the South Platte was one established by Lieutenant Bryan the previous fall while making his survey of a road from Fort Riley to Bridger's Pass. It, too, followed an old Indian trail that appeared not to have been used for some time. As might be expected of a practical people, forced at every turn to consider their welfare and survival and that of their animals, this trail crossed the ranges of sandhills lying between the South Platte and the Republican at their narrowest points. Its route followed the most level of the lands between and had at least a small supply of water at critical intervals before striking the upper reaches of the closest stream draining into the Republican.

Sumner's men began their passage to the waters of the Republican on the morning of Friday, July 17, at 7:00 A.M. The road appeared to be nearly perpendicular to the flow of the South Platte, running southeastward onto the plains and into country that was dreary, desolate, and barren, without trees, without game, without much water, and with little grass. After two or three miles they reached and passed through a range of sandhills, thereafter emerging onto a flat and sandy plain dotted with the mounds of gopher holes and prairie-dog towns. They went into camp on the headwaters of a small, running stream Lieutenant Bryan had named "Parker's Creek." The ravine from which it emerged was not more than one hundred yards wide: after flowing past their campsite, it sank into the sand, apparently making the rest of its trip to the South Platte underground.[7]

Beyond the sandhills the marching troops saw their first buffalo signs in many days, Sumner's column having seen no more beyond Fremont Springs and Sedgwick's none after Fort Atkinson, roughly the line of the 100th meridian. But the chips they now saw were a few months old, indicating that it would be some time before fresh buffalo meat would again be available. There were no other signs of game, but the Indian scouts (who had gone ahead the previous day) reported they had seen a herd of wild horses while looking for water. Captain Beall took a few men and rode ahead to try to catch some, but had no luck. Before getting into camp, three of the men became ill and had to be carried in the ambulance, the result of drinking water from a contaminated water hole the previous night. Once in camp, to escape the punishing sun, officers and men alike hurriedly fixed shades for themselves, using pack covers and blankets laid over sabres driven into the ground. Under these they crawled like so many ants.[8]

When the march continued the morning of July 18, the troops found themselves on a high, rolling plain with a smooth and hard surface, less sand, and more and better buffalo grass. During the day they passed several small ponds of standing water, probably old buffalo wallows, and a number of prairie-dog towns. At 11:00 A.M. they made camp in the narrow ravine of a creek Lieutenant Bryan had called "Dog Creek," which had only a few water holes in its bed. A densely populated prairie-dog town nearby provided them with a little entertainment and relief from the boredom of the march. The location of Lieutenant Bryan's camp of the previous September was clearly visible, as was the site of his Sibley tent.[9]

On Sunday, July 19, the command broke camp and resumed their march at 6:00 A.M. to take advantage of the cool of the morning. Ascending from the valley of Dog Creek, they found themselves once again on the level and grass-covered plain. About a mile and a half beyond the camp and perhaps four hundred yards to the north of the road was a large pond of water that appeared to be quite deep. Here they paused to water the pack mules. The hard, sandy soil beyond, almost dead level, was thickly covered with weeds.

At 1:30 P.M., after a march of twenty miles, the column halted at a series of small ponds with poor water. The heat across the plains in midsummer begins to rise from its overnight low almost as soon as the sun's rays first break across the eastern horizon. From about noon to 5:00 P.M. it is at its maximum, often well above the 100 degree mark. In combination with the nearly constant south wind, it creates a blast furnace effect that makes activity during the afternoons both difficult and dangerous. Because of this, Colonel Sumner kept the troops at rest around their water holes until 5:00 P.M., allowing the animals time to find a little nourishment from the sparse grass. Then they re-formed their column and continued the march along Lieutenant Bryan's road.[10]

Seven or eight miles from the water holes, they struck another range of sandhills that were several miles across. About an hour after dark they became lost, the trail having been covered by the shifting sands. Their guides were scouting the country in advance of the column and no one else was familiar with either the trail or the territory. When they realized their predicament, they stopped and conducted a search for the lost trace, but because of darkness and the elusive and impermanent quality of any road through sandhills, more than an hour passed before it was again found. Once back on the trail they marched for another hour or more in the hope of finding the water the Indian guides had told them would be there. They finally gave up at midnight and went into camp on top of a hill.[11]

The long march, the lack of water and the travel through the sandhills had been exhausting for both men and animals. But the greatest of their difficulties was the lack of fresh, potable water, of which there had been little since the previous morning. So thirsty were they that some of the men tried to dig for water, but found none. They had some Gutta Percha tanks with them with six gallons of water, but these had not been previously used and the very disagreeable taste they imparted served to increase, not satisfy, their extreme thirst.* One or two of the infantrymen were driven nearly to the edge of sanity for want of water, and one of these asked Captain Newby of H Company if he had any. When told no, he promptly went to the Captain's striker and examined the canteen for himself.† At about 2:00 A.M. a light rain began and the men spread their talmas to catch as much as they could.‡ This gave some relief, enabling them to sleep.[12]

*Gutta Percha was a trade name for cloth waterproofing of material made from the milky juice of certain Malaysian trees. See Randy Steffen, *The Horse Soldier*, 2:38.

†A striker was an enlisted man who volunteered for or was detailed to perform various chores for the company commander or other important regimental or company officers. This duty included looking after the officer's gear and equipment while on the march. See Ben Innis, *How T' Talk Trooper*, 39.

‡A talma was a waterproofed raincoat, which had been authorized for the First and Second Cavalry only, the Dragoons and Mounted Rifles of that day still being

At daybreak on July 20 the command was preparing for departure when some of the Indian guides returned and told them they were very near water. A mile and a half from camp they reached Chief Creek,* where they immediately went back into camp. By now the men and animals were near exhaustion and Colonel Sumner kept them there the rest of the day. Food and water revived the soldiers, but the animals were beginning to wear under the strain of the march and the lack of grain, forage, and good grass.[13]

On Tuesday, July 21, the troops entered what proved to be very rugged country, uphill and downhill nearly all the way. After six miles they struck the main branch of Rock Creek, which came in from behind a ridge to the right of their line of march. It was a fine stream flowing over a sandy bed, about eight or ten inches deep and six or eight feet wide, but there was no timber along its banks. They crossed this stream without difficulty, then turned almost directly south. Here they left the road made by Lieutenant Bryan, which continued along the south bank of Rock Creek, first to its junction with the Arikaree Fork, then with the main or South Fork of the Republican,† and finally to Fort Riley. Sumner and his men now followed their Pawnee scouts in search of the place where they had last seen the Cheyennes in the spring.[14]

After about five miles the march turned from a southerly to a southeasterly direction, following the valley of Willow Creek,* a small stream that emptied into the Arikaree,* the Ree River of the Cheyennes. They camped at the mouth of this stream on very good grass. At the time the Arikaree had no running water and no timber, but both were found along the little creek, as were gooseberries and wild grapes. These provided a needed supplement to the

---

equipped only with ponchos. The talmas were waterproofed with Gutta-Percha. See Randy Steffen, *The Horse Soldier*, 2:37.

*Chief Creek was a small stream running almost due east to a junction with Rock Creek, the latter flowing from the southwest. The combined streams continued on as Rock Creek, for white mapmakers of that day, and is the same known in later times as the north fork of the Republican. For the Cheyennes it was Wihiuniyohe, the Chief River.

†The main or South Fork of the Republican was then simply referred to as the "Republican," because the north and middle forks bore the names Rock Creek and Arikaree Fork respectively.

‡Willow Creek was known to the Cheyennes as Minoshe.

§The Arickaree River was known as Ononiohe (Ree River) to the Cheyennes.

soldiers' meager diet. Some officers and men found the tree burial of a Cheyenne baby nearby, the dead child having been wrapped in five blankets and buffalo robes to protect its flesh from predators. The wind had blown it out of the tree, probably the previous fall. Shortly after midnight a sudden storm struck, and two or three hours of rain left the men and their bedding completely soaked.[15]

On July 22 the course the column followed was generally east-southeast and, for most of the march, over very high hills. About nine miles from the Arikaree, they struck flowing water and crossed two small creeks (probably intermittent streams brought to life by the previous night's rain), finally reaching and following the creek into which they emptied. This stream, the Hackberry,* flowed almost due east until it reached the South Fork of the Republican. The Cheyennes camped along it from time to time. Four or five miles down this stream the hunters killed two or three antelope, the first large game they had seen in several days. They followed the creek to its junction with the South Fork of the Republican. There they went into camp in a fine grove of small cottonwood trees with plenty of grass for the livestock.

The Hackberry had running water, but at its mouth the men once again observed one of those curiosities of the plains: the water sank into the sand shortly before reaching the Republican. The Republican itself had a broad, sandy bed but no visible flowing water. It was, in the words of Eli Long, "a foot deep, i.e., you have to dig a foot deep in the sand before you come to it, it being perfectly dry on top." Although not impressive for the surface flow of its waters, the Republican was an important marker for another reason. On it the troops were deep in Cheyenne country.[16]

*The Cheyennes called Hackberry Creek Kokoeminoshe (Where Hackberries Stand Thick).

9

The Wagon Train Moves
to the South Platte

Once more the solitude . . .
Was startled with a brawl of mules and men.
The Long Knives' wagons clattered there again. . . .

(93)

The Return to Fort Laramie

The troopers and soldiers of the Cheyenne Expedition marched away from Camp Buchanan and down the South Platte on July 13, 1857, beginning the last leg of their long journey in search of the foe. Behind them they left the wagons of the two trains that had supplied Sumner's and Sedgwick's columns on the way west, the company wagons with tents, extra clothing, and other gear not essential for the movement to combat, the remaining mules, and a number of broken-down horses. With these remained 2d Lt. Richard H. Riddick as acting commissary and quartermaster of the train, Percival G. Lowe and his teamsters, the regimental band, and about fifty other men, who, having bunged up either themselves or their horses, were no longer useful to the expedition and hence were left dismounted with the train.[1]

As soon as the last of the pack mules, packs, and infantry had been crossed to the south side of the river, Colonel Sumner issued orders for Lowe and Lieutenant Riddick to return with the train to Fort Laramie, there to turn in all surplus wagons and harness, refit the train, make as many six-mule teams as possible, and load the wagons with corn and commissaries. That completed, the train was to proceed down the Oregon-California Trail to the Lower California Crossing and meet the mobile column of the expedition in twenty days. Before he took his final leave, Sumner complimented Lowe on the fine work he had done and told him he had increased his pay to $25 per month, effective June 1. With that he shook his hand and rode off to take his place at the head of the troopers of the First Cavalry.[2]

The long column—cavalry, infantry, howitzer battery, and pack mules—quickly faded in the distance, a great cloud of dust marking their progress. With their departure, Lowe turned his attention to preparations for the return to Fort Laramie. An inventory showed that the train now consisted of 109 wagons, 25 six-mule teams, 18 five-mule teams, and 66 four-mule teams, with a total of 504 mules. The only horses were those of Lowe and Lieutenant Riddick, plus a few broken-down cavalry mounts. There were neither saddles nor saddle blankets for the teams, and the train was 170 bridles short. To remedy this some of the men were put to work rigging bridles by using ropes and straps. Others were busy breaking leaders and saddle mules, a task they had been working at since arriving at Camp Buchanan. By noon the train was reorganized and began moving upriver. They traveled twelve miles and camped above Cottonwood Grove on the South Platte. While scouting the area about the campsite, Lieutenant Riddick found the remains of drowned Private Daugherty on an island in the river a little below camp. Riddick had him buried there and called it "Daugherty's Island."[3]

Leaving camp on the morning of July 14, the train retraced the route followed by Sumner's command on the march from Fort Laramie to the South Platte. They arrived at Laramie on the nineteenth, going into camp along the Laramie River one mile above the post. On July 20, Lieutenant Riddick and Lowe started the process of refitting the train. They turned in twenty-nine wagons, the traveling forge, and all surplus harness. After drawing necessary equipment, Riddick, Lowe, and their men found themselves with eighty wagons complete with six-mule teams, including saddles, blankets, bridles, and a few inferior surplus mules drawn from the quartermaster at Fort Laramie. They also drew all necessary commissary, medical, and other stores and loaded everything but the corn. On July 21, they loaded 1,030 pounds of corn, drew fifty rifles, two boxes of rifle ammunition, and eight boxes of cartridges for the Navy pistols. Rifles were issued to the teamsters, and they made ready to start down the Platte road the following morning.[4]

From Fort Laramie to the South Platte

The train of the Cheyenne Expedition left Fort Laramie on the morning of July 22, with orders to move to the Lower California Crossing of the South Platte to meet with Sumner's command on or about August 2. They proceeded down the trail nineteen miles beyond the fort, passing Bordeaux's trading post and camping below the trading house of Maj. Andrew Dripps. The following day, they traveled another fifteen miles and camped at the mouth of Horse Creek. Anticipating that hostile Indians might attempt to capture the train's many desirable supplies, Lowe made a practice of establishing each night's camp in a square, with the wagons forming the east, west, and south sides and with the river to the north. There were twenty-six wagons on each side at intervals of about twenty feet, and the mess wagons were placed on the inside along the river. The mules and horses were herded into the enclosure an hour before sundown, then picketed on half-lariat.

Lieutenant Riddick established a guard at each camp, with sentinels well out from the wagons from sundown until sunup. Lowe supplemented these with two teamster sentinels on the east, two on the south, and two on the west, with a change of the guard once each night. In addition, two or three men mounted on mules were sent to the highest points in the area of the campsite from the time they made camp until sunset. These men were instructed to dismount and let their mules graze while they kept a lookout.[5]

The train continued its movement down the North Platte without incident from July 24 to 27, camping each night along the river. On the morning of July 28, soon after leaving camp, the soldiers observed a party of Sioux Indians on the north bank of the river, with a number of their women moving around the bluffs. Lieutenant Riddick and Lowe crossed over and learned that the Indians were after rattlesnakes sunning themselves on the rocks. The women were very adept, using a forked stick to pin down the snake's head just before it would strike, then cutting off the head with a knife.

Killing them in this manner prevented the snakes from biting themselves, which they might do if hurt or angry, thus poisoning the meat. The meat of the rattlesnake was sweet and considered a delicacy, providing a welcome variation in their diet.

The train reached Ash Hollow at 10:00 A.M. on July 28 and went into camp. Moving the heavy wagons, an average of 3,500 pounds of supplies in each, up "Windlass Hill," the usual route, promised to be very difficult and time-consuming. Therefore, after lunch, and after a sudden thunderstorm had passed, Lowe and "Billy" Daniels went in search of a better way out of the hollow. Five hours of hard riding was required before Lowe found and staked out a route that could be traveled without much difficulty. The following morning they broke camp at 5:00 A.M., and by 8:00 A.M. all the wagons were safely at the top of the hill.

The train had just been straightened out for the continuation of their journey when a band of Indians came into sight from the east, riding at a fast gallop. Uncertain of their intentions, Lowe ordered the wagons into corral, signaling his instructions by riding his horse in a circle. The teamsters promptly obeyed and Lieutenant Riddick immediately formed his detachment of the "sick, lame and lazy" into a line to defend the train if necessary. Lowe rode to a high point with his interpreter, Manuel Vijil, and motioned the Indians to stop and for the chief to come in. He proved to be Man-Afraid-of-His-Horses, a principal chief of the Oglalla Sioux, with his band. They had no hostile intentions and were simply hoping for something to eat. When told it was Colonel Sumner's supply train and that all of the food must be kept to feed his hungry troops, the chief promised to come no closer, shook hands with Lowe, and departed. Lowe galloped back to the train and straightened it out, and they continued down the road another fourteen miles, going into camp one mile above the crossing of the South Platte.[6]

10

On the Trail of the Cheyennes

And oft by day upon a distant rise
Some naked rider loomed against the glare
With hand at brow to shade a searching
    stare,
Then like a dream dissolved in empty sky.   (65)

Sumner Finds the Cheyenne Sun Dance Village

On Thursday, July 23, Sumner's troops crossed the sandy bed of the Republican River, then turned abruptly south and marched upstream for two or three miles. There they turned southeast, moving at an angle almost perpendicular to the riverbed and, taking leave of its valley, ascended into hills flanking it to the east and southeast. These hills were more gentle and rolling than those west of the river, rising only one to two hundred feet above the surrounding plain. The weather, though hot, was pleasant, with low humidity and a moderate breeze. Seven miles beyond the river the command went back into camp on top of a high hill.[1]

Crossing the Republican marked Sumner's entry into the area where the Cheyennes were known to be present in force. The colonel issued orders cautioning all men and officers to keep their arms and ammunition in good order and ready. Equally worrisome was the fact that many horses and mules were beginning to fail, the result of poor grazing and lack of forage and grain.* To avoid weak-

---

*Cavalry horses used on long marches, particularly when they were away from a wagon train carrying grain and forage, were generally weighted down with a heavy

ening them unduly, Sumner ordered the troopers to dismount and walk, leading the horses, every alternate hour during each day's march. He set the example himself at the head of the column. At first a few officers assumed the order did not apply to them because they supplied their own horses. Colonel Sumner soon gave them to understand that the order applied to every mounted officer and trooper in the command, and that all officers were required to so march at the head of their companies.[2]

The command reached the new camp at 11:00 A.M. At the foot of the hill were the upper reaches of a small stream known to Cheyennes as Thickwood Creek and to white men as Big Timber Creek, which wound off through the hills north and northeast until turning back northwesterly to join the Republican. The stream was well timbered with cottonwood, but it had little grass. Adjacent to the stream were remains of an old Cheyenne village, with a broad circle of tipi rings and fire pits marking its location. Though obviously abandoned for many weeks, it convinced Colonel Sumner to take added precautions both in camp and on the march.[3]

Concern for security resulted in a number of new orders. Because of the heightened alert, cavalrymen slept each night thereafter with their heads on their saddles, their saddle blankets serving as both mattress and cover. Firearms were kept at their sides where they could be reached at a moment's warning. No longer could they remove any clothing, not even their boots, and preparing to sleep meant nothing more than removing belts and spurs. The guard was ordered to be extra vigilant, and the cavalry was henceforth to march en echelon, with three parallel columns of two companies each moving abreast so as to be able to move quickly into line to meet an attack from front or rear, left or right.[4]

---

pack, plus the weight of the trooper and his equipment. To maintain weight, size, and health, these horses had to be fed about twelve pounds of grain (usually oats, corn, bran, or sometimes barley) and fourteen pounds of hay per day. In the field and away from a wagon train there was no way to provide forage or hay other than what the country offered by way of grazing, and the grain ration usually was reduced if not eliminated. As a consequence of the inadequate diet and the exhaustion, overexertion, and extreme heat associated with the march, the horses lost weight, their health deteriorated, and they broke down. Loss of weight caused the saddles to fit poorly, and this in turn caused sores and other problems. See 1st Lt. John J. Boniface, *The Cavalry Horse and His Pack*, 377, 400, 423; W. H. Carter, *Horses, Saddles and Bridles*, 82, 84, 188, 192.

The following morning, July 24, the command broke camp and marched across a high and level plain in an east-southeasterly direction. The day was typically hot, but a fine breeze made it more tolerable. The Pawnee scouts had told the colonel the village where they had last seen the Cheyennes lay within the day's march, so they were expecting to find and attack them when they reached the stream upon which it was located. After traveling about eighteen miles, the column reached Little Beaver Creek,* a small stream flowing east-northeasterly to a junction with the Beaver. Here they stopped for an hour to water and rest their livestock. The ambulance, heavily laden with ammunition, had broken down during the march, and its remains were brought along on just two wheels. The ammunition and other contents were repacked on the mules.[5]

Moving five or six miles farther southeast, the column reached the edge of the valley of the Beaver, the stream where the Cheyenne village had been seen by the Pawnees the previous May. The returning scouts reported it abandoned, so the troops went into camp on high ground overlooking the creek at that point. All their camps from this time on were to be made on high ground, to reduce the possibility of a surprise attack. There was timber and grass along the Beaver, and a good flow of water.

Saturday, July 25, the march continued along the lodgepole trail they had been tracking from the Arikaree. It now turned northeast along the high ground overlooking the valley of the Beaver. Two miles beyond, the valley broadened and the trail descended into it, crossing the stream to the site of what had been a great Cheyenne village. Hundreds of tipi rings and fire pits forming a great circle marked the site, and in the middle and toward the east side of the camp circle stood a Medicine Lodge of about the same size and form as that of the Arapahoes Sedgwick and his men had seen during their march along the Arkansas. The centerpole was the trunk of a young cottonwood tree, forked at the top, and set about it were four major poles. Between these were forked uprights into which were placed support beams that ran to the next upright and supported the stringers or rafters, which were secured to the centerpole. There was an opening on the east, just as there was a gap in the line of tipi rings on the east side of the former camp circle.

*The Cheyennes called this creek Homaiyohekis, which meant "Little Beaver Creek."

On Saturday, July 25, 1857, the expedition came upon the remains of the great Cheyenne Sun Dance village. The medicine lodge was still standing, with three Pawnee scalps attached to the center pole.

At the fork of the centerpole were bundles of cottonwood and willow brush. Inside the lodge on the ground was a buffalo skull and around it a pile of sod. Affixed to the centerpole were three Pawnee scalps, an offering by Cheyenne warriors to Maheo.[6]

After they had inspected the remains of the Cheyenne village, the troops moved on. The trail led up out of the valley, moving toward the southeast; on high ground it turned to the northeast, running parallel with the Beaver. They followed the Beaver downstream for about ten or twelve miles, until they reached the forks of the Beaver and the Little Beaver, and there made camp. Believing they were in the vicinity of the Cheyennes, Colonel Sumner prohibited the discharge of firearms for fear of revealing their presence. This made it impossible to hunt for fresh game, at least by all but the Pawnees, so the beef herd was the only supply of meat. That night a heavy rain struck, soaking everyone's bedding (the saddle blankets).[7]

The Trail to the South Fork of the Solomon

On Sunday, July 26, the search for the Cheyennes resumed. The Indian trail the troops were following led downstream a short distance, then turned sharply southeast, or a little south of southeast. After passing through hills flanking the valley of the Beaver, they came to a high level plain that, except for the streams they crossed and the hills and ravines about them, they stayed on most of the day. Still, the land was rougher than that over which they marched en route to the Beaver. As they moved along the trail, they could see valleys of what appeared to be several streams at a distance of a mile or two. After ten or eleven miles of marching, they reached the north fork of Sappa Creek,* and in another mile or so the middle fork,† for they were close to the confluence of the two streams. On the middle fork of the Sappa they passed the remains of another abandoned Cheyenne village that they estimated to be about three hundred yards in diameter and to have had four hundred or more lodges. From there the trail continued almost due southeast, taking them through beautiful, rolling hills covered with

*The north fork of Sappa Creek was known as "Short Nose Creek" to the Cheyennes.
†To the Cheyennes the middle fork of the Sappa was known as "Horse Stealing Creek."

a much-improved growth of buffalo grass. Buffalo signs were getting fresher, indicating they were approaching their range and fresh buffalo meat might soon be available. At the crossing of a small tributary of the Sappa, Fall Leaf, the chief Delaware scout, said there had been some old buffalo bulls along the stream when the Cheyennes had crossed.[8]

About five miles beyond the middle fork of the Sappa, the column reached the south fork, a fine stream with good grass and timber, and here they went into camp. At officers' call, Colonel Sumner announced he was considering sending an express to Lieutenant Riddick and the wagon train (which should arrive at the Lower California Crossing of the South Platte within the next four or five days), directing them to move due south to the Expedition's trail and then follow it southeasterly until they caught up. The train would take at least twelve days to reach the mobile column but would bring badly needed food supplies. The twenty-day rations they had brought with them were being depleted rapidly. After some discussion Colonel Sumner decided to wait a day or two to see if they could locate the Cheyennes before ordering the train down.

At midnight that night a young German recruit on guard duty fired his carbine. First Lt. David S. Stanley, officer of the guard, jumped on his mare and rode to the guard's post to learn the cause. The guard reported that a man on horseback had ridden up in the dark, halted and dismounted, then spoken to him in a strange tongue. When challenged, the man leaped back on his horse and fled into the night, the guard firing after him. Colonel Sumner and most other officers thought the young man was merely frightened and had fired at a buffalo moving down to the stream for water. But at dawn the next morning the Pawnee scouts soon found the tracks of an unshod horse. They were being observed. Shortly after dawn, Indian scouts were seen on the horizon.[9]

On July 27, the march to the southeast continued. The morning's weather was pleasant with warm temperatures and a light breeze from the south. The country through which they passed was much the same as it had been, a rolling plain broken by rough hills and ravines about the streams, but with few trees. The trail led them on a winding route that nevertheless kept to a generally southeasterly direction. After four miles they came alongside a small stream running parallel with their line of march. In two more miles it

Although the Cheyennes had, in fact, been scouting and observing both columns of the Expedition from the time they reached their country, it was not until they reached the Republican River that the men of Sumner's command realized that they were being watched.

joined the north fork of Prairie Dog Creek. There they stopped to water the animals.

Four miles beyond the north fork they crossed the main or south fork of the Prairie Dog. Seven miles farther, after following the line of another small creek, they reached the north fork of the Solomon River and went into camp in a small stand of ash trees. Across the creek, on the south bank, was yet another large Cheyenne village site with several hundred tipi rings and fire pits, and some discarded Indian equipment. A few of the men examining the great campground found items of interest—one an axe and another a letter, unfortunately too rotten to be read. The closeness of this latest Cheyenne village and its obvious recent occupancy persuaded Colonel Sumner that they were nearing their quarry, and he decided against sending for Lieutenant Riddick and the wagon train. The expedition's Indian scouts and hunters found and killed two buffalo during the day, adding a little variety to their supper.

Anticipation that the Cheyennes would soon be found caused mounting excitement among the troops as they left camp the following morning, July 28. The trail now ran east-southeast. Shortly after they departed, they saw fresh tracks of unshod horses, doubtless the Cheyenne scouts who had been observing them, and this intensified the excitement. Fifteen miles beyond camp, they struck Bow Creek, the middle fork of the Solomon, and marched down it for five miles, following the Indian trail. At 2:00 P.M., they went into camp on high ground overlooking the stream. It had good water but no trees or grass along or near its banks. This posed a serious problem for the already weakened livestock, but nothing could be done: they had found no good grazing en route, and both men and animals were spent.[10]

During the evening, two Indian dogs came to the camp, another sign the Cheyennes were near. Colonel Sumner issued orders that all cooking was to be completed during the daylight hours and fires extinguished before dark. The guard was strengthened, and the men slept with their belts on and carbines at their sides. The cavalry horses and mules were brought in close and picketed at half-lariat. No one knew with certainty where the Cheyennes were, but none doubted they would soon be found.[11]

Wednesday morning, July 29, the men rose early. They were called by a verbal command passed down each company's line, no bugle calls being permitted. Silently they hurried through their morning duties, the cavalry having the added chore of stable call. Each man was ordered to take a little food in his haversack in case there was a battle and they became separated. At 6:30 A.M., they left camp and struck off to the east-southeast, following a fresh trail made by five or six unshod Indian horses. This day they were formed into three columns, with three cavalry companies forming each of the outside or flanking columns, and the cavalry guard, the artillery battery, and the three infantry companies forming the center column. The mule train was kept close to their rear.[12]

Because the country was much more broken than it had been, the infantry and the artillery had difficulty keeping up. Although marching only at a fast walk, the cavalry periodically was forced to take short halts to enable the others to stay abreast of the outside columns. With the trail growing fresher every mile, the soldiers were eager to press forward. Unfortunately, this compounded the suffering of the horses, for they had not grazed the previous night, and the speed of the morning's march permitted no water stops.

At about 10:30 A.M., a Delaware scout came back to report to Colonel Sumner that five or six Cheyennes had been sighted and had seemed to retreat as the scouts advanced. Eleven or twelve miles from the camp on Bow Creek, they struck the upper reaches of a small stream flowing almost due south.* The Indian trail now followed its west bank, and there they found fresh horse manure and other Indian signs, and also a puppy the Indians had somehow left behind. As they were preparing to resume the march, one of the Pawnee scouts rode up and reported to the colonel that the five or six Cheyennes were now clearly visible, moving east along the north bank of the south fork of the Solomon, into which the stream emptied. Clearly the Cheyennes were very close, and now it was time to prepare for battle.[13]

*This small stream is known now as Rock Creek.

Main parade at Fort Leavenworth, looking from the southeast across to the southwest corner, circa 1858. In coming from their encampment on the bluegrass pasture on the south, the departing troopers of the First Cavalry would have marched north along the road in the foreground, passing through the garrison, and then moved south again on the road on the opposite side of the parade and exited the post on the right of the small building seen at the left of the photograph. *Fort Leavenworth Frontier Army Museum*

1858 view of Fort Kearny, looking northwest. The back of the officers' quarters is shown in left center, facing north, and at the extreme left the commanding officer's quarters face east across the parade ground. The post appears here much the same as when visited by the troopers of the Cheyenne Expedition in 1857. *Collections of the Library of Congress*

This view of Fort Laramie, the earliest known, was made in 1858. The slowly disintegrating walls of Fort John are shown at left, Old Bedlam is in the center, and the soldiers' barracks are on the right, each fronting on the parade. A few tipis and a log trading post may be seen in the foreground. The fort is as it appeared in 1857. *Collections of the Library of Congress*

Edwin Vose Sumner, the "Bull of the Woods," commanded the First Cavalry and the Cheyenne Expedition of 1857. He is shown as a colonel in a photograph taken about 1855 when he had just assumed command of the new First Cavalry. A stern, dedicated soldier, many officers considered him a martinet, but enlisted men thought him fair and high-minded as he shared the hardships and rigors of compaigning with his men. *Massachusetts Commandery Military Order of the Loyal Legion and the U.S. Army Military History Institute.*

164

John Sedgwick, of Connecticut, the junior major of the First Cavalry, was second in command of the Cheyenne Expedition under Colonel Sumner. A bachelor, he was gentle, courageous, and well liked by officers and men, but on the plains he seemed indecisive and ineffective when faced with a crisis. *Massachusetts Commandery Military Order of the Loyal Legion of the U.S. Army Military History Institute*

Capt. Samuel D. Sturgis, of Pennsylvania, the senior captain with the Cheyenne Expedition, was a brave and resourceful officer who repeatedly proved his common sense and ability during the time the First Cavalry was in the field in pursuit of that tribe. He became a major general of Volunteers in the Union Army and after the war served as the colonel and second commanding officer of the new Seventh Cavalry, with George Armstrong Custer as his lieutenant colonel. *National Archives*

William N. R. Beall, from Arkansas, a captain in the First Cavalry in 1857, was a courageous and effective soldier and field commander. On the Cheyenne Expedition he proved both resourceful and adventurous. Following the secession of the southeastern states, Beall left the army and offered his services to the Confederacy. He rose to the rank of brigadier general, Confederate States of America. *Collections of the Library of Congress*

J. E. B. Stuart, a first lieutenant in the First Cavalry during the Cheyenne Expedition, suffered a near-fatal wound during the fight on the Solomon. He was a gallant and dashing cavalry officer. When his native Virginia seceded from the Union, he offered his services to the Confederacy and became the premier cavalry leader of the Army of Northern Virginia. *National Archives*

9

David S. Stanley, from Ohio, was a first lieutenant in the First Cavalry during the 1857 Expedition. A highly competent cavalry officer, he spent many years serving in the West during the Indian Wars. *National Archives*

Frank Wheaton, a first lieutenant at the time of the Cheyenne Expedition, was one of the company-grade officers who had been commissioned from civilian life. Well liked and capable, he remained with the Union and rose to the rank of brevet major general with the United States Volunteers. *National Archives*

George D. Bayard, an 1856 graduate of West Point, was twenty-one when he served with the Cheyenne Expedition as a second lieutenant in the First Cavalry. To his chagrin, Colonel Sumner placed him in charge of the howitzer batteries immediately before the fight on the Solomon, which he consequently missed. He was killed in action at the Battle of Fredericksburg on December 13, 1862, while serving as a brigadier general of United States Volunteers. *National Archives*

Eli Long was a twenty-one-year-old second lieutenant in the First Cavalry during the Cheyenne Expedition. Appointed from civilian life, he made the army a lifetime career and was a major general of the United States Volunteers during the Civil War. He kept a daily diary during the expedition, which is an important source of information about what transpired and gives interesting insights into his character and gentle good humor. *Massachusetts Commandery Military Order of the Loyal Legion and the U.S. Army Military History Institute*

Percival G. Lowe, the intrepid head wagon master of the Cheyenne Expedition, served for five years as a dragoon before leaving the army, attaining the rank of sergeant. His common sense and vast experience on the plains proved invaluable to Colonel Sumner. *The Kansas State Historical Society, Topeka*

11

The Cheyennes Move to Solomon's Fork

When the pale-faced sun arose—
A spectre fleeing from a bath of blood—
It saw them like a thunder-fathered flood
Surge upward through the sounding sloughs
  and draws—
Afoot and mounted, veterans and squaws,
Youth new to war, the lowly and the
  great—
A thousand-footed, single-hearted hate
Flung fortward. Now their chanted battle-
  songs
Dismayed the hills. Now silent with their
  wrongs
They strode, the sullen hum of hoofs and feet,
Through valleys where aforetime life was sweet,
More terrible than songs or battle cries.   *(79–80)*

Preparation for Battle

During mid-July scouts had brought back word that the soldiers had left Fat River, the South Platte of the whites, and were marching southeast, toward the headwaters of Red Shield River, the south fork of the Republican. Some old men wanted to move the village and stay away from the white soldiers, but hot-blooded young warriors would have none of it. It was their country and the Veho were intruders. If they wanted a fight, they would have it. The medicine of Ice and Dark was strong; with it would come a great victory, and perhaps white men would stay away from the

People forever. Then the old times could come again, buffalo and other game would multiply, and the life of the People would be good once more.

In following days, news received almost daily was that horse soldiers and walking soldiers were drawing ever closer—now on the Republican, now on the Beaver at the sacred Sun Dance village. Still they came. Warriors spent many hours each day in preparation, checking bows and bowstrings, setting arrow makers to work making more arrows, and selecting their finest war-horses to take into battle. Each day chiefs met in council, discussing the progress of the soldiers and reports from the scouts. There was the matter, too, of where the battle should be fought; it should be far enough from the village to avoid danger to their families, near enough that their return would not take too long. Finally a decision was made to fight in the broad valley of the south branch of Mah-kineohe, Turkeys Creek, fifteen miles north. Here they often camped, and they knew it well. Some thought the village should be removed to a more remote and safer haven, but this was not seriously considered, because the medicine of Ice and Dark assured the People of a great victory. The Veho offered no real danger.[1]

During late July (Moon-When-the-Buffalo-Bulls-Are-Rutting), news came that the soldiers had crossed Short Nose Creek (the Sappa) and were moving to the north fork of Turkeys Creek. The battle would be very soon. Ice and Dark again spoke of their medicine and instructed warriors how to invoke its powers. Few of the People had rifles or pistols in that day, and those they did have were mostly old short-range, flintlock, smoothbore, muzzle-loading rifles and a handful of old-fashioned, hand-cocked Allen's six-shooters obtained from traders. These were not very accurate, even when fired from a standing and braced position, and the Cheyennes were well aware of these deficiencies. To overcome this, Ice and Dark told those warriors having such weapons that they would load them with a magical white powder that, with the aid of the Sacred Powers, would make it impossible for the owner to miss a shot. Afterward ceremonies were performed to guarantee the result.[2]

The magic powder was only part of the medicine by which Ice and Dark intended to bring victory to the People. Of even greater importance was the medicine they would make to render white men's weapons impotent and cause their bullets to roll harmlessly

On the morning of July 29 the Cheyenne warriors prepared themselves with prayer, song, and paint for the battle they were certain would come.

on the ground. Following sacred ceremonies in the camp, each warriors' hands must be washed or dipped in sacred waters known to the holy men. This would be done the day of the battle, to ensure the power of the medicine.[3]

Finally, on the evening of July 28, scouts reported that the soldiers were encamped on the banks of Bow Creek, the middle fork of Turkeys Creek. They thought the troopers would reach the valley of the south fork, the selected battleground, by late morning or early afternoon the next day. At the words of the scouts, the fighting spirit surged in men eager for the honor and glory earned in battle, men determined to teach the Veho to stay away from the People and their country. After their council the warriors prepared paints for their war-horses and themselves, prayed to Maheo and the Sacred Persons for strength and victory, and readied their weapons and battle dress. With the help of Maheo and the Maheyuno, tomorrow would be a great day for the Cheyennes.

The Wait

Before dawn on July 29, 1857, the Cheyennes were awake and readying themselves for battle. Women had the day's first meal cooking in the pots, while warriors and their military society chiefs ritually prepared themselves with prayer, song, and paint. Excitement filled the air throughout the great Cheyenne village on the Saline, for the time had come to force the Veho from their land forever. Their deep belief that Maheo would look after the People and that the wonderful medicine of Ice and Dark would protect them, filled their hearts with a profound confidence.

At first light, following the lead of Ice and Dark, the warriors formed into a large band and filed out of the valley on their war-horses. With them rode a small number of Sioux friends and a few teenage boys eager to witness the great fight. One of these was the young Crazy Horse. Those warriors who could, took at least two horses, to provide a fresh one for pursuing the fleeing soldiers once they discovered the power of the Cheyennes and the impotence of their own weapons. Their strength probably was between three hundred and three hundred fifty, at least half the fighting men the tribe could muster. Riding away from the village, they left the valley of the Saline, moving a little east of north. Three or four miles of travel brought them to a small lake with clear water, situated on the upland, where they had a sweeping view of the plains. The rays of the rising sun struck the water, making it sparkle and dance; truly, this was a place of magic. The warriors dismounted and, as Ice and Dark sang a song to the Sacred Powers, dipped their hands in the waters. This medicine, they were told, was so strong that when they raised their hands toward the weapons of the white men, their bullets would drop and roll harmlessly at the feet of the Cheyennes. An easy victory would follow once they got close enough to use arrows and fight the soldiers hand to hand.[4]

When Ice and Dark had made their medicine at the little lake,

At first light the Chey-
enne warriors left their
village on the Saline en
route to the valley of the
south fork of the Solo-
mon. Three or four miles
northeast, they came to a
sacred lake, where they
were instructed to wash
their hands by Ice and
Dark, the holy men whose
medicine was supposed
to bring them victory.
Reaching the Solomon,
they waited and rested
until their scouts brought
word that the cavalry was
nearly there. Then they
mounted their horses and
formed a grand line of
battle.

the men once again mounted their horses and started for Turkeys
Creek. This time they followed their war leaders, chiefs of the military societies, not Ice and Dark. After a ride of ten or eleven miles,
they descended into the east end of the valley on the south fork of
the Solomon selected as the battle site. There was no timber along
this part of the river, except a scattering of cottonwood trees and
willows at the east end, where they camped from time to time.
When they reached the trees, the warriors dismounted, removed
the saddles from their horses, and turned them out to graze. The
"wolves," or scouts, had told them that the soldiers were on their
way but would be some time reaching the Solomon.

As they waited, warriors and those accompanying them rested
in the shade of trees. The time for battle was near, and they would
need their strength, just as their horses needed rest and the grass
and water along the river. Some men entertained themselves with
talk, others by playing games. The soldiers, they knew, were slow.
They rode large, grain-fed cavalry mounts that lacked the stamina
of the tough Cheyenne war-horses.

At noon some men ate a little jerked buffalo meat they had
brought, then continued to rest and talk. Finally, a little before
1:00 P.M., the wolves came galloping over the bluffs at the west
end of the valley, periodically riding their horses in a circle, the
Plains Indian sign for "many buffalo sighted," to indicate the
enemy was approaching. The men sprang to their feet, caught their
favorite war-horses, armed themselves, and mounted. Then they
trotted their horses into a long line, with their left flank against the
river and their right against the bluffs to the north. As the rest of
the men rode up, they were formed into a great body of four or five
loosely constructed ranks. There they stopped and waited, lances
and other weapons at the ready, watching for the white troopers.
The south wind now blew gently across them, making feathers on
their lances flutter. With painted faces and bodies, colorful shields
and lances, war bonnets, and other finery of battle, and mounted
on their painted horses, they presented a splendid, warlike appearance. The thrill of impending battle spread among them. This
was a good day for war, a good day to die.[5]

12

The Battle

They formed behind him in a solid wall
And halted at a lifting of his hand.
The troopers heard him bellow some command.
They saw him wheel and wave his rifle high;
And distant hills were peopled with the cry
He flung at Death, that mighty men of old,
Long dead, might hear the coming of the bold
And know the land still nursed the ancient breed.

(127–128)

The Charge of the First Cavalry

When the Pawnee scouts reported the party of Cheyennes in view ahead, the troopers of the First Cavalry were just reaching the head of Rock Creek. There they would have to halt and wait for the infantry and artillery battery to close up. Concealment or effort to achieve surprise no longer served any purpose. Colonel Sumner therefore directed his orderly bugler to sound "Halt," and when the command had halted, he called out in his loud, parade-ground voice, "Company commanders will see that their men are prepared for action." Each commanding officer quickly issued orders: "Prepare to dismount!" "Dismount!" "Prepare for action!" That done, the company officers passed along the ranks of their troopers giving instructions: "Tighten up your saddle girths," "See that your accoutrements are in good shape and your arms in good working order!" "Noncommissioned officers will see that the men have a good supply of cartridges." When preparations were complete, each company commander rode to the head of his company and gave the command "Prepare to mount!" then "Mount!" With the troopers back in their saddles, each commander in turn saluted and reported to the colonel, "My company is ready for action, Sir!"[1]

When the last commander had reported, Colonel Sumner turned to his orderly bugler and said, "Bugler, sound the 'Advance'!" With that the column moved out at a brisk walk, proceeding south parallel with Rock Creek. As they began their march, 2d Lt. George D. Bayard, commanding the artillery battery just then catching up with the rear of the column, came galloping up to the colonel. Upon seeing him, Sumner asked, "Mr. Bayard, is your battery prepared for action?" Bayard answered, "Not only prepared, Colonel, but my men are just fairly spoiling for a fight!" "That's right," responded the colonel, "We will try to give you a chance before long." A number of the other officers of the command had come to the front of the column and were gathered about the colonel, who was riding at its head. To these he said in his booming voice: "Gentlemen, you will probably soon have something to do. My instructions from the War Department are to use all means to conciliate the Indians. But if conciliation fails, then to use my discretion and do the best I can for the safety of my command and the honor of the government." At that moment another of the Indian scouts came back to report that the party of Cheyennes continued to retreat slowly. Obviously they were scouts. Sumner again spoke to his officers: "I have implicit confidence in my officers and men. I don't know how many warriors the Cheyennes will bring against us, but I do know if you will all pull together, and obey orders promptly, we can whip the whole tribe." With that he ordered his bugler to sound "Trot-March." The command was repeated by each company commander, and they moved out at a trot.[2]

With the increased rate of march, the cavalry companies quickly outdistanced the infantry and the artillery battery. Colonel Sumner did not want to delay lest the Cheyennes evade them, and not wanting his command strung out, he sent word back to Captain Ketchum that the infantry should make no attempt to keep up but march steadily at a normal pace. Lieutenant Bayard and his battery were struggling valiantly to match the speed of the cavalry but could not. After about two miles the troopers reached the mouth of Rock Creek and the valley of the south Solomon, at that point quite narrow. Here some of Bayard's mule teams bogged down trying to cross to the east bank of Rock Creek and the colonel, much to Bayard's chagrin, ordered him to halt the artillery and wait for the infantry. The cavalry then formed itself into three columns of two companies each and continued eastward on the north bank of the Solomon, followed closely by the pack mules, also at a trot. Bayard was left behind "swearing like a pirate" at his misfortune.[3]

As the troopers trotted eastward along the Solomon, they could see a small party of Indians going over a large hill on the north side of the river perhaps two miles beyond them. The army's Indian scouts were in between, and as they approached the point where the river made a bend to the south to clear the same large hill, they suddenly slowed their advance, indicating that the foe was near. At about the same time, Fall Leaf began riding his horse rapidly in circles, signaling Cheyennes ahead and that the soldiers should hurry. But the cavalry horses, already worn from their day's march and lack of water, could not be pushed any harder if there was going to be a battle. The troopers continued to move ahead at a steady trot.[4]

Without Bayard's artillery and the three companies of infantry, the six cavalry companies were more mobile but less effective in terms of men and firepower. Troopers from each company had been detailed to man the artillery battery, some were assigned as packers to the mule train, and fifty or so sick or disabled had remained behind with the wagon train. Without these men, Sumner's command had an effective fighting force of approximately three hundred cavalry troopers, scarcely fifty per company, as they trotted bravely down the valley of the south fork of the Solomon toward their unseen enemy.[5]

Their rapid pace soon brought the column of cavalry close to the large hill that sliced across the valley floor, forcing the river to make its turn to the south. Now they could see that it had a rocky projection extending into the valley and obscuring their view of what lay beyond. The river itself, shallow at that time of year, wound its way through a broad, sandy bed, arcing sharply southward for more than one-half mile before turning back to the east. Forced into a narrow gap between the face of the rocky hill (Stony Point) and the sandy riverbed, the advancing companies formed a single column in order to pass into the valley beyond, the center column entering first, followed by the left and then the right.[6]

At about 1:00 P.M. on July 29, 1857, the troopers of the Cheyenne Expedition came around a projection of rock, Stony Point, which had obscured their view down the valley of the south fork of the Solomon. Beyond it the valley widened out for two or more miles to the east. At the far end, in front of a scattering of cottonwood trees, more than 300 Cheyenne warriors were formed in a line for battle. The troopers, on Colonel Sumner's command, fronted into line preparatory for a charge.

At about 1:00 P.M., the six companies of the First Cavalry came around the rocky projection. Before them the valley widened out to between one-half and three-quarters of a mile in width on the north bank of the river for a distance of two or more miles to the east, after which the river turned sharply north. At the far end of this expanse Colonel Sumner could see a scattering of cottonwood trees and in front of them a dense mass of moving animals that appeared like a herd of buffalo. The column halted long enough to reorganize itself. As it did, Sumner and several officers, using field glasses, determined that what they saw was a large body of mounted Indians. Formed loosely in a long line, they started moving toward the troopers.[7]

As soon as he had confirmed that the Cheyennes were found and had apparently picked their own ground for a fight, Colonel Sumner ordered the column to "Front into line." Each company wheeled to the right by fours and, with its guidon on the right, was conducted by its captain or commanding officer to its battle position. When this movement was complete, they formed a long line of six companies, their flanks four men deep, facing the Cheyennes. The packtrain was halted at this point to await results of the impending combat. That done, Sumner again bellowed in his great voice, "Trot-march," and the line of cavalry began a steady and rapid movement directly toward the Cheyennes. Ideally, at a trot they would have covered one mile in about eight minutes.[8]

At the east end of the broad valley, the Cheyennes sat easily on their horses watching the great column of troopers turn the point at the west end and form themselves into a long line. None had ever seen so many Veho soldiers in one place and at one time, nor had they ever been in a real battle with them, their only fights with the military having been those in which soldiers attacked them by surprise while they were in camp. To see such a great number was troubling, for they had many powerful guns—far better than the few the Cheyennes had. Still, this advantage was offset by the wonderful medicine made by Ice and Dark, medicine that would render the soldiers' guns harmless. Moreover, they were Maheo's people and He was with them. In that belief they moved forward in their long line, the left flank brushing the stream, the right against the bluffs to the north. In front rode the chiefs of their military societies—the Kit Fox, the Crooked Lance, the Red Shield, the Bow Strings, the Dog Soldiers, and the Crazy Dogs. These chiefs

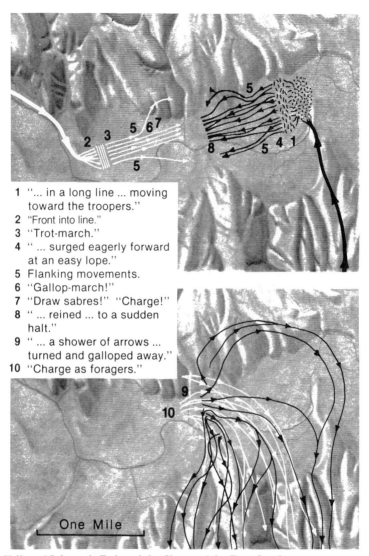

1 "... in a long line ... moving toward the troopers."
2 "Front into line."
3 "Trot-march."
4 " ... surged eagerly forward at an easy lope."
5 Flanking movements.
6 "Gallop-march!"
7 "Draw sabres!" "Charge!"
8 " ... reined ... to a sudden halt."
9 " ... a shower of arrows ... turned and galloped away."
10 "Charge as foragers."

One Mile

Valley of Solomon's Fork and the Charge of the First Cavalry

were their war leaders. The line of warriors was not so tightly
formed as that of the soldiers. Although it was four or five warriors
deep, they were not ranks, because Plains Indians did not fight in
a uniform and disciplined order. Behind them, looking on, were
the teenage boys who had come to observe the great battle and
witness the defeat of the Veho.[9]

It was, for a brief moment, a magnificent warlike spectacle. The
soldiers, clad in their blue fatigue uniforms, with glinting buckles
and accoutrements, the plumes in their hats tossing in the wind,
moved steadily forward following their officers and guidons in a
great disciplined line.* Opposite, the colorful line of Cheyenne
warriors, their greatest leaders wearing brilliant warbonnets, their
bodies and horses painted for war, their medicine shields and
lances with colored feathers fluttering, likewise surged forward at
an easy lope. Never before had horse Indians formed in such a
grand line of battle against white soldiers. As the two lines moved

---

*The hats of the First Cavalry were referred to as the Kossuth, Jeff Davis, Hardee,
or War Hats, and were prescribed by General Order No. 13 of the adjutant general's office, dated August 15, 1855. At the time, they were the only regulation
headgear authorized for use by cavalry, although a soft cloth fatigue hat was issued
to the men. The visored fatigue hats, or "Bummer" hats, familiar in the Civil War
were not introduced until after November 30, 1858. While some other units of
the mounted service in that day permitted a mixture of issue and non-issue articles
of clothing during field operations, including broad-brimmed hats, the First Cavalry seems not to have done so. Colonel Sumner was well known as a martinet, a
"spit-and-polish" officer devoted, says Brackett, to "the minutiae of his profession," who tolerated no variance from regulations. Peck stated that enlisted men
were not permitted to have any clothing that was not government issue and were
required to dispose of any that was not. Captain James McIntosh, who commanded
D Company in the charge on the Solomon, wrote the quartermaster general in
June 1859 that, because most of the hats had no chin straps, if there were any
wind at all they blew off in a charge. Captain Thomas J. Wood, commander of C
Company, though not a participant in the Cheyenne Expedition, likewise wrote
the quartermaster department in 1859 complaining that the original-issue chin
straps were too short and, being made of patent leather, soon broke. In August
1859 the Secretary of War directed that strong leather chin straps thereafter be
used with the cavalry hats. It is thus apparent the hats themselves were in field
use with the First Cavalry. The plumes, however, may have been removed prior
to departure, for Brackett noted that the feathers developed a bedraggled and
wilted appearance after one or two wettings. See Albert G. Brackett, *History of
the U. S. Cavalry*, 141 and 161; Robert M. Peck, "Rough Riding on the Plains,"
The National Tribune, February 14, 1901, 6; Randy Steffen, *The Horse Soldier*,
2:34–45; Robert M. Utley, *Frontiersmen in Blue*, 121.

toward each other across the long valley, the warriors began to sing their war songs and death songs, wild and eerie to the ears of the white troopers. [10]

At the ferocious appearance of the Indians, anxiety and uneasiness gripped many of the troopers. Most had never been in battle, and the sight and sounds of the advancing line of Cheyennes directly in front of them had an unsettling effect. If Colonel Sumner felt any anxiety, he never showed it. He seemed eager to close with the enemy. As the distance between the two lines lessened, a body of Indians detached themselves from their left flank and crossed the river to the south bank, then moved steadily to the west preparatory to a flanking movement. From their right another body of warriors ascended the hills, obviously intending to turn the other flank. Sumner detached the two flank companies, A and B, to deal with those Indians while the main body continued forward, still at the trot. Captain Beall and his A Company formed the left, and their advance soon turned back the party riding along the edge of the hills. [11]

The gap between the lines quickly narrowed, and as they drew closer, the Indians began to shout their battle cries, setting up a great din. When the distance separating them had closed nearly to rifle range, a figure dashed out from the right of the cavalry line, galloping toward the Cheyennes. It was Fall Leaf. At a point almost midway between the two opposing forces he halted, raised his rifle, and fired at the advancing Indians. Colonel Sumner observed this with relish and, turning slightly in his saddle toward 1st Lt. David S. Stanley, on his right, he said in a loud voice, "Mr. Stanley, bear witness that an Indian fired the first shot." Pretending not to notice that the Indian was one of his own scouts, the colonel thus relieved himself of the obligation to wait for peace overtures from the Cheyennes were they so disposed. [12]

After firing the shot, Fall Leaf turned his horse and rode back to the cavalry line, followed by a few desultory shots from the advancing Indians. At this time the cavalry weapons were still at the carry, and officers and men alike confidently expected they would draw their carbines, halt to fire a volley, then return the carbines and charge with pistols. However, sometimes it is the unexpected, the surprise, that wins the battle. For the moment Sumner did nothing, and the cavalry line moved on as if at a garrison drill. The war cries of the Indians were building to a crescendo, and the

Colonel Sumner, to the surprise of his own men as well as the Cheyennes, brought his troopers to a gallop, then ordered them to draw sabres and charge. Three hundred sabres came to the tierce point, and with a mighty yell the cavalry charged across the valley of the Solomon, directly at the astonished Cheyennes.

barbaric splendor of their line was becoming clearly visible to the troopers. The war chiefs were in front yelling defiance, shaking their spears, and shouting encouragement to their men. Behind them the mass of painted warriors, bows strung and lances at the ready, continued their forward surge. Now only moments separated the foes. [13]

In the ranks of the cavalry there was no talking; the men sat in their saddles tense and alert. Then Sumner turned his head and said something to his orderly bugler. Across the line came the call "Gallop—march!" The men rose in their saddles, and the horses, feeling the excitement, let themselves out as they began the gallop. The distance separating the lines closed rapidly. Now the troopers could see the painted faces and bodies of the Indians. Then came the booming voice of the "Bull-of-the-Woods," somehow strong enough to be heard above all the din: "Draw sabres!" quickly followed by "Charge!" The bugler echoed the commands. As one the troopers reached down, and then 300 sabres arced above them, the bright afternoon sunshine flashing across the burnished steel as if the air were torn by a shower of flame. For an instant the blades were held aloft, then came down to the tierce point. At the same time the troopers in unison gave out a mighty yell. And so they thundered across the valley of the Solomon, directly at the oncoming Cheyennes. [14]

Opposite the charging cavalry, the Cheyenne warriors reined their horses to a sudden halt. The sight of the sabres, the "long knives," surprised and troubled them. It was for rifles and pistols that Ice and Dark had made their mighty medicine to ensure that the soldiers' bullets would roll harmlessly at their feet. There was no medicine for the long knives and no way to fight them. This must mean that Maheo did not want His Cheyenne children to fight the Veho this day. Otherwise he would have given them a sign or a vision—and strong medicine for their protection. An uneasy murmur arose in the ranks of the warriors as they stared at the oncoming line of cavalry troopers. Then one of their war leaders, chief of a military society, rode up and down their line on his spirited horse, shouting at them, gesturing wildly, obviously urging them to stand their ground and fight. He was a splendid-looking man, with a warbonnet that had a long tail or trailer that flowed behind him. Even as they were charging, the troopers could not help admiring his superb horsemanship as he wheeled his mount, charging back and forth, twirling his long war lance over his head. His efforts were of no avail. [15]

The Cheyenne warriors stood with remarkable boldness for a few moments, facing the charging troopers. When the lines were no more than a hundred yards apart, they fired a shower of arrows at the advancing cavalry, then turned their horses and galloped away. Few of their arrows had any damaging effect. The departing Indians now broke into small groups that scattered in different directions. Some went north, through the many ravines and arroyos leading into the hills; some went east, down the valley of the Solomon. But by far the greatest number splashed across the river and beyond into the line of hills on the south. The Cheyenne will to fight had been broken. [16]

A Running Fight

When the Cheyennes scattered before them, the charging cavalry troopers returned their sabres to their scabbards, for they were useless in pursuit of a fleeing enemy. The clear call of the bugle penetrated the noise and confusion about them, this time sounding "Charge as foragers." This command directed all the troopers to disperse and direct themselves in couples upon the point each wished to attack. It enabled them to split and follow whatever foe they believed themselves capable of catching. However, they were required not to lose sight of their officers and the other members of their units. The Cheyennes who moved north into the hills or who had gone east were too few and had disappeared too quickly to make pursuit profitable. Doing so, moreover, would fragment the command. Therefore, they kept themselves together as a more-or-less organized force, crossing the river and following the main body of warriors southward. [17]

The south fork of the Solomon was a small stream, particularly during the hottest part of the summer. As with most watercourses across the plains, however, a large part of its flow was subsurface. At water level its broad, sandy bed was filled with quicksand. The Cheyennes knew it well, and few of them had any difficulty getting their horses across. In this they were aided by the fact their horses were fresh, having spent the morning resting and grazing. Even so, a number did become mired and, eager to evade the cavalry, their riders abandoned them. Most of these warriors escaped by riding

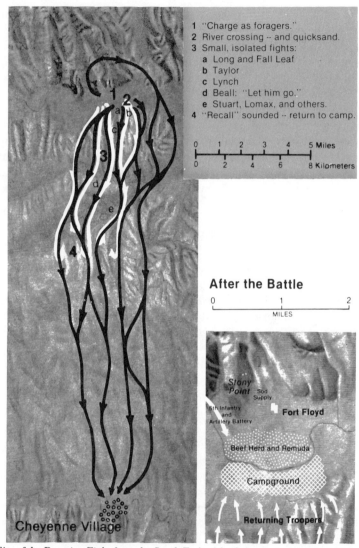

1 "Charge as foragers."
2 River crossing -- and quicksand.
3 Small, isolated fights:
   a Long and Fall Leaf
   b Taylor
   c Lynch
   d Beall: "Let him go."
   e Stuart, Lomax, and others.
4 "Recall" sounded -- return to camp.

0   1   2   3   4   5 Miles
0   2   4   6   8 Kilometers

After the Battle

0   1   2
MILES

Stony Point   Sod Supply

6th Infantry and Artillery Battery

Fort Floyd

Beef Herd and Remuda

Campground

Returning Troopers

Cheyenne Village

Site of the Running Fight from the South Fork of the Solomon to the Saline River

double with comrades who had already crossed. But the extra load slowed the horses, making capture more likely. [18]

The fight that followed was on the run, primarily a chase. Unfamiliar with the Solomon or the better crossings at that point, the troopers had a great deal of difficulty with quicksand. Most became bogged down for at least a brief period, during which the fleeing warriors gained an insurmountable lead. However, not all the Indians ran without a fight. Scattering into many small groups, the Cheyennes forced the troopers to do the same. From time to time small parties would stop and there would be a sharp fight. Some were probably warriors who would not leave a battlefield without having made the enemy pay a price; some doubtless were performing rear-guard or delaying actions, to permit the main body time to return to their village and take those steps necessary to protect women, children, and the elderly. [19]

The first among the cavalry to reach and cross the Solomon was 2d Lt. Eli Long, who, along with Fall Leaf, had outdistanced their comrades. Lieutenant Long was the officer of the cavalry guard for the day. In the charge he had served as bodyguard for Colonel Sumner, but at the command "Charge," his horse had let itself out and soon outdistanced the colonel and others at the center of the line. Long and Fall Leaf reached the south bank of the river together and commenced firing at three or four Indians. There were about eight or ten in the vicinity, most trying to help others whose horses were mired. All but three soon left, disappearing into the hills. Long fired eight shots at the remaining three, one of which struck and wounded an Indian. Finally only an older warrior remained, and before he left he delivered a parting salute with his muzzle-loader, which to Long had the appearance of an old-fashioned carbine. Fall Leaf and Lieutenant Long were together at the moment, but the shot missed them both. The warrior then rode off into the hills, no doubt bitterly disappointed by the results of the magic white powder given him by Ice and Dark. [20]

After thwarting the flanking movement attempted by the Cheyennes across the hills, the men of A Company had turned and moved eastward at a gallop behind the charging center of the cavalry line. The result was that when the Indian line broke and the warriors scattered, pursuing troopers of A Company found themselves next to those of E Company. The men of the two companies

After the charge of the First Cavalry, the Cheyennes broke and dispersed, most going south. The fight which followed was primarily chase and individual combat.

were able to get close to a number of warriors bringing up the rear and, although they apparently did not kill any, observed many remarkable feats of horsemanship. Some warriors slipped down on the side of their horse and shot arrows back at them from the underside of the animal's neck while at a gallop. The troopers saw others pick up dropped weapons from the ground while their horses were running, and, even more impressive, reach down from the back of a running horse, pick up wounded comrades, and carry them off. One warrior was seen running his horse at a gallop while his broken leg flopped at the animal's side. Perhaps most astounding was the feat of one young Cheyenne being chased by Captain Beall, of A Company, and Privates Muniky and Peck, of E Company. Seeing that the three were gaining on him, he began to lighten the load on his horse. First he threw away his bow and arrows, still keeping his long war lance in his bridle hand. Then he slid out of his saddle onto the horse's back just behind the saddle, without checking its speed, and reached down and cut the girth. That done, he threw away the saddle and blanket and sprang back to where the saddle had been. Next he passed his lance to his right hand, whirled it about his head, let out a few yells, and left his pursuers behind in a cloud of dust. Captain Beall reined in his horse and said: "Men, that fellow deserves his life and liberty! Let him go." The other Indians in their area having disappeared, the three retraced their steps, picking up the warrior's bow and arrows and other equipment for souvenirs as they went.[21]

Another member of E Company was less fortunate during the pursuit. Private Rollin M. Taylor had a desperate hand-to-hand fight with a warrior shortly after crossing the Solomon. His horse, like most cavalry mounts, had becomed mired in quicksand. Many men left their horses to get out as best they could, but Taylor stayed with his, and after a struggle managed to extricate him and reach the south bank. By that time, his comrades having gone on in pursuit of the Indians, he found himself alone. Looking about he spotted a lone warrior on foot trotting up a slope not far away, having apparently lost or abandoned his horse in the quicksand. Taylor let his sabre drop, hanging by the sabre knot tied to his wrist, and galloped after the Indian with drawn revolver. Before he had gone far, his horse stumbled in a prairie-dog hole, pitching Taylor over his head and throwing his pistol some distance from him. The warrior observed the fall and turned back toward Taylor, shooting arrows at him as he came.[22]

Private Taylor jumped up but, failing to find his revolver, was left with only his sabre to defend himself. His horse had broken a leg and was useless for an escape. Arrows were whizzing about him, one passing through his sleeve, another through the shoulder of his jacket, where it broke the skin, and the last striking him on the forehead, splitting the skin, parting his hair, and coming out through the top of his hat. At that moment Taylor found an empty carbine dropped by a passing trooper. Having no ammunition, he threw it at the advancing Indian, who nimbly dodged the weapon, picked it up, and threw it back. He also missed. Then realizing the warrior was out of arrows, Taylor rushed him with his sabre. The Indian proved nearly a match for him even without a weapon other than a knife, for he parried each blow with his wooden bow, then slashed at the trooper with the knife. This continued for some minutes, until the bow had been hacked nearly to pieces. Finally the sabre glanced off the bow and took a large slice from the Indian's right arm, which began bleeding profusely. Standing his ground with great courage he deftly switched the blade to his left hand and continued the fight. Once he grabbed for the sabre, badly cutting his right hand as he attempted to twist the blade from Taylor's grasp.

By this time both men were nearly exhausted, and they drew back to catch their breaths. As they did, Taylor observed that the severe loss of blood was having an effect on the Indian, who had begun to stagger. Seizing the opportunity, he rushed forward and aimed a blow at his opponent's head. The Indian saw him coming and sprang back to avoid the blade, but tripped and fell on his back. In an instant Taylor was on him and drove his blade through him deep into the ground. He then sat down on his foe, completely spent. With his last remaining strength the dying warrior made a sign asking if Taylor intended to take his scalp. Taylor assured him by signs that he would not. With that the Indian smiled, laid back his head, and died. Shortly, one of the Pawnee scouts appeared, and wanted to scalp the dead warrior. Taylor refused to allow it, threatening to use his sabre if the man attempted to take it. He had given his word.[23]

When the cavalry charge had begun, G, H, and D Companies were to the right of A and E Companies, and as the fastest horses

began to pull away from the main body during the pursuit, their
men gradually became mixed. Jeb Stuart had led G Company after
the larger body of warriors who had crossed the river and headed
south from the battlefield. The chase took them toward the right
and front. Officers, riding their own, well-bred horses, outdistanced the enlisted men, and in a short time Lieutenants Stuart,
Stanley, McIntyre, and Lomax, along with Captain McIntosh, were
near each other and frequently side by side. After crossing the
river and chasing the Indians for about five miles, Stuart's horse,
Dan, having set the pace the entire distance, failed. To avoid missing the action, he stopped a private and commandeered his horse,
then galloped after the others.

At the time they were pursuing about fifty Indians who seemed
to be staying together. As Stuart caught up, he saw an older warrior
jump from his horse and advance on foot toward Lieutenant Lomax,
attempting to shoot him with an old Allen's revolver. Stuart charged
the Indian and shot him with his pistol, striking his thigh. By now
surrounded by Lieutenants Lomax, Stuart, Stanley, and McIntyre,
as well as Corporal Boggs of G Company, the warrior fired his revolver at Stuart but missed. Stanley fired a shot in reply, but also
missed, then called out: "Wait! I'll fetch him." He dismounted to
take deliberate aim, but as he tried to fire, the pistol remained
firmly cocked and would not discharge. Seeing this, the Indian ran
toward Stanley with his own pistol raised. On his horse, Lieutenant
Stuart again rushed the man, this time striking him with his sabre
and inflicting a severe head wound. At the same moment the Indian
turned and fired his revolver at Stuart from a distance of no more
than a foot. The ball struck Stuart in the center of the breastbone,
then glanced to the left and embedded itself beneath his rib. Lieutenant McIntyre charged the Indian from horseback and ran him
through with his sabre, then with a man from D Company finished
him off with a pistol. After being hit, Stuart dismounted and lay
down on the ground. Lomax had several sabres stuck into the
ground and rigged up a shade to protect the wounded officer until
the abbreviated ambulance could reach him.[24]

The charge of the First Cavalry had brought casualties to the
troopers as well as to the Cheyennes. Private George Cade, of G
Company, was killed by an arrow that pierced his heart and passed
completely through his body. Private Martin Lynch, of A Company,
was also killed. Detailed for that day to lead pack mules, he was

Lieutenant Stuart charged the Cheyenne warrior with his sabre, seriously wounding him in the head. At the same moment the Cheyenne turned and fired his old Allen's revolver at Stuart, striking him in the chest.

in the rear of the mounted companies as they were ordered to front into line before the charge. When he saw his orderly sergeant pass nearby, he called out: "Sergeant, can't you send some other man here to hold these mules? I want to get into the fight." The sergeant responded that there was no time to make a change, that Lynch would just have to stay where he was and hold the mules. As the sergeant left to join his company, Lynch was heard to say: "Hold hell in a fight! Do they suppose I've come all this way across the plains to hold pack mules in a fight?" With that he dropped the leading strap, drew his sabre, and dashed off with the rest when the charge was ordered.

Once beyond the Solomon, Lynch's horse, fiery and hard-mouthed, took the bit in its teeth and ran away. He soon outdistanced his comrades and overtook a small party of Cheyennes. These warriors, sensing his problem, split to left and right, allowing his horse to dash in between them. Then they shot a few arrows at him and hit him in the head. When he fell from his horse, one of the warriors dismounted, withdrew Lynch's pistol from the holster, and shot him through the chest, killing him instantly. The Indian started to scalp the dead trooper, but the approach of several cavalrymen forced him to stop before he had completed the job. He jumped back on his horse and escaped with Lynch's horse and pistol.[25]

The running fight with the Cheyennes continued over a distance of some five to seven miles, becoming progressively more disorganized as the quarry scattered or outran their pursuers. Encounters were mostly a matter of small, isolated fights involving only a few of the officers and men, those who had horses fleet enough and with the endurance to overtake any of the fleeing warriors. Well aware of the danger of allowing the command to become too widely separated, at three o'clock Colonel Sumner had "Recall" sounded. Most of the Indians had disappeared, and both troopers and mounts were exhausted. The fight was over, and the time had come to return to camp for a well-earned rest.[26]

The Dead, the Wounded, and the Building of Fort Floyd

For the tired men and horses of the First Cavalry, the walk back to the banks of the Solomon must have been tedious and wearisome.

Their energy had been spent in the charge and pursuit, and all this after a considerable march in which neither they nor their mounts had food or water. Colonel Sumner established a camp on the south bank of the Solomon directly across from the ground where the charge had been made, and here the hospital tent-fly was erected to receive the wounded. The camp itself was spread along the river bank to take advantage of water for men and animals, but there were no trees to shade them and only buffalo grass in the river bottom.

The companies established their own separate campsites within the assigned area, and as the men straggled into their company locations they unsaddled and watered their horses, then picketed them to graze. The infantry and artillery had just arrived in the valley and were crossing the river to the camp, cursing their luck at having missed the fight. Once all companies were in place and the mules of the packtrain, the remuda, and the steers were "in herd," the camp of the Cheyenne Expedition had a circumference of two to three miles. Lieutenant Eli Long, as officer of the guard, was required to check sentries at the various posts, by walking around the entire camp, an onerous task after the exhausting activity of the day.[27]

As soon as the worn troopers had reached camp and picketed their horses, most headed for the hospital tent to determine how many casualties they had suffered and if any close friends were among them. The still forms of Privates Cade and Lynch, lying on the ground side by side at the corner of the tent, were covered by a saddle blanket. The small hole in Cade's chest, over the heart, showed where the Cheyenne arrow had gone through him. Lynch had several arrow wounds on his head and had been shot twice with his own pistol. A cut around the edge of his hair, with the front of the scalp turned back, gave mute evidence as to how close the warrior who killed him had come to taking his scalp.[28]

During the afternoon eight enlisted men and 1st Lt. J. E. B. Stuart rode or were carried to the hospital tent for treatment. The wounds that they had received ranged from minor to serious, but, aside from the ever-present possibility of infection, most were not considered to be dangerous. Three of the men, however, had critical wounds, and for the moment their lives seemed to hang in the balance. First Sgt. George C. McEawen, of D Company, had a very serious rifle wound through his arm and chest, and Pvt. Franz Piot, of B Company, had been wounded by an arrow that passed completely through his chest. Private James M. Cooke, of G Company, suffered an arrow wound in his abdomen. The arrow passed all the way through his body, and that it had not killed him seemed a wonder. However, there he sat on the ground under the tent-fly, apparently comfortable and talking cheerfully, though occasionally spitting up blood.[29]

The other First Cavalry wounded included 1st Sgt. Henry B. Robinson, of H Company, with a sabre wound to his hand, Pvt. Francis T. Freer, of B Company, with an arrow wound deep in his hip, Pvt. Alexander Wilkey, of B Company, with a slight arrow wound to his face, Pvt. Rollin Taylor, of E Company, who had received arrow wounds to the shoulder and head before killing his opponent with his sabre, and Pvt. Thomas Wilson, of D Company, with a wound to his arm where an arrow had passed through it. All these men were receiving medical treatment from Doctors Brewer and Covey, the Expedition's physicians, and had been ordered to rest as best they could. It was an insufferably hot day, the sort expected on the high plains in midsummer, and the likelihood of infection in wounds was even greater than usual.

Soon after the injuries had been treated, Colonel Sumner made his appearance, circulating among the wounded, speaking words of comfort and cheer as he passed each man in turn. When he reached Private Cooke, the colonel paused, noting the location and seriousness of the wound, and spoke to him. "How are you feeling, my man?" "All right, Colonel, but a little weak," Cooke answered. "Not going to give up and die, I hope?" asked Sumner. "Not much, Sir," Cooke responded with a smile. "I'll live to eat lots of hardtack and sowbelly for Uncle Sam yet." "That's right, never give up" the colonel said. "I hope you'll be able for duty soon." Then turning to the doctor he commented: "He'll do. Such men are not easy to kill." And so he passed through the little hospital, having a kind word and friendly encouragement for all his wounded troopers.[30]

Also wounded, of course, was a man who in time would become one of the most famous among them. J. E. B. Stuart had been shot in the chest at point-blank range, and that he survived at all was doubtless because the weapon was an old-fashioned Allen's self-cocking revolver of the "Pepperbox" pattern, probably with a very weak charge of powder in the cartridge. After he had dismounted and lain down, Dr. Charles Brewer was sent for, but because the hospital was to be established several miles away, he had taken some time to arrive. After the sounding of "Recall," a large number of the returning troopers gathered about Stuart, all trying to help and to make him as comfortable as possible. Soon Colonel Sumner appeared among the troopers of the returning cavalry companies. He moved up from their rear and greeted Lieutenant Stuart with great affection and concern. He ordered him taken back on a blanket to the banks of the Solomon, where he intended to establish the Expedition's camp, the horses being too used up to continue the pursuit. After about three miles, they met Dr. Brewer, who examined and bandaged the wound. Soon after, they met the ambulance, which now consisted of the two rear wheels of the original wagon with a tongue attached and with the cushions fastened to the spring. On this Stuart was borne to the camp with its small hospital tent. He suffered far more from the new form of transportation than from the hand-carried blanket.[31]

Once the troopers had reached the camp and tended their horses, they were to report to their company officers what they had observed during the engagement. Individual company reports were to be given to Colonel Sumner in order for him to prepare his report to army headquarters. This process reduced itself principally to a summation of Cheyennes killed, wounded, or captured, along with the number of horses captured. No attempt had been made to bring back bodies for verification, and individual fights had occurred over a great distance and wide area; thus the number each trooper believed that he had killed or seen killed was the best available estimate. Inevitably men who had witnessed the same fight or seen the same body duplicated reports. Some, too, doubtless saw wounded Indians whom they thought dead who later were carried off by comrades, or, having successfully played dead, made good their escape.

The officers did their best to screen for duplication, but figures turned in by each were estimates at best, and doubtless the report by one company included one or more dead Indians reported by another. An accurate report of wounded was hopeless, for the same reasons as with the dead and with the added difficulty that the wounded were gone and not available to verify troopers' accounts.

In the end, the number Colonel Sumner thought to be reasonably accurate was nine killed and "a great number" wounded.*[32]

The number of captured horses did not involve the guesswork required of Indian casualties. The troopers and Indian scouts jointly accounted for about thirty head. Most were extras left grazing prior to the charge and those abandoned when they became mired in the Solomon. The cavalry itself lost three horses, those of dead or wounded troopers that had been captured by the Indians. One Cheyenne also had been captured. He was among those whose horses had become mired. Finding escape impossible, he had thrown away all weapons except his knife, then lain on the ground and feigned death. Probably he was waiting for an opportunity to escape into the hills when the troopers had passed beyond him, but as it happened 1st Sgt. George C. McEawen, of D Company, had been shot and seriously wounded nearby just after crossing the river. Trying to make the best of a bad situation by dispatching McEawen and lifting his scalp, the warrior had worked closer by crawling at intervals. Some returning troopers noticed this and raced over to him. Once he realized he was discovered, he jumped up and surrendered. This was most unusual; Cheyennes greatly feared imprisonment and believed a warrior should fight as long as there was breath in his body.[33]

The Delaware scouts had performed admirably during the charge and the fights that followed, as they had throughout the expedition. The Pawnee scouts, on the other hand, were not held in such high esteem. They had followed in the rear, scalping dead Cheyennes and rounding up lost and abandoned horses. When they heard that a Cheyenne had been captured, they went to Colonel Sumner's headquarters seeking possession of the prisoner so that they could put him to death by torture at their war dance. Sumner, of course, refused, whereupon the Pawnees offered to ransom him by turning over the horses they had collected and foregoing pay they were to

*In later years attempts to verify the number of Indian dead through the Cheyennes produced the information that four of their warriors had been killed—Coyote Ear, Yellow Shirt, Carries-the-Otter, and Black Bear. The daughter of She-Bear, brother to Coyote Ear, later married George Bent, son of William Bent. The son of Carries-the-Otter, Two Moons, became the well-known Chief Two Moons of the Northern Cheyenne. See George Bird Grinnell, *The Fighting Cheyennes*, 120.

receive when they returned to Fort Kearny. This greatly angered
Sumner, who sent them back to their camp empty-handed and
embittered.[34]

As with all soldiers, return to camp brought an exchange of experiences and, for some, a swapping of yarns. Friends wanted to
know how their comrades had fared and what they had seen or
done. Some had incredible experiences that grew with the telling,
but most merely wanted to share events they had observed that now
formed a common bond between them. Because few had been close
enough to any warrior to engage in individual combat, the stories
were of the chase and not of heroics. E Company counted in its
ranks one of the greatest braggarts in the regiment, a wild Irish
private by the name of James Murphy, but even Murphy was at a
loss for bravado, though not for words. When asked how many
Indians he had killed in the fight, Murphy responded: "Well, really
I didn't count them. But I'm dead sure of one thing, and that is
that I killed as many of them as they did of me."[35]

During the early evening, after the troops had an opportunity to
rest and freshen up, they were ordered out for an "undress parade," in the fatigue or combat uniforms they wore, which were
their only clothing. With the command drawn up in parade order,
the adjutant, 2d Lt. Albert V. Colburn, read an order from Colonel
Sumner commending the officers and men for gallantry in action,
and expressing deep regret over the deaths of two brave men and
the wounding of nine others. Following that he read a separate
order, which detailed Capt. Rensselaer W. Foote and his C Company, Sixth Infantry, to remain at the present location to protect
the wounded until they were able to travel. Then, if the command
had not returned by August 20, they were to make their way north
to the Lower California Crossing of the South Platte, there to meet
Lieutenant Riddick and the supply train. Doctor Covey and the
wounded were to be left with the train before the company returned
to Fort Laramie, their duty station. The adjutant read a further
order directing the command to remain in camp the following day
for rest and to bury the dead, after which they would pursue the
Cheyennes to the south.[36]

Following the evening parade, the men were given their last substantial meal, for by this time they were near the end of the twenty
days' rations brought with them from the South Platte. Although it
refreshed and revitalized them, it caused some concern and gloom.

The dwindling beef herd was now almost the sole remaining source of food, and they were far from white civilization and any possible point of resupply. For them, near-starvation and great hardships seemed a certainty, because they would be going away from their supply train, not toward it. Despite this unhappy prospect, only a rare trooper did not sleep the sleep of the dead when "Taps" sounded. Around their campfires before "Taps," they could plainly hear snarling wolves tear at the bodies of dead Cheyenne warriors who had been left where they fell. Terrifying as the sound was, it could not keep them awake.[37]

On Thursday, June 30, the command remained in camp throughout the day. After breakfast the infantry companies and those among the cavalry enlisted men not otherwise occupied with care of horses and mules or the burial of the dead, began construction of a small sod fort for the protection of the wounded. This was done under the supervision of 2d Lt. John McCleary of Captain Foote's company. It was built on the north side of the river just to the east of "Stony Point," the rocky hill they had passed on entering the valley, and near the area where they had formed their line prior to the charge. The sod for construction was dug from the side of the hill to the north. The little fort had walls two feet thick and five to six feet high, with bastions at the southeast and northwest corners. By the end of the day it was more than half completed, and sod for finishing it had been cut from the hill and brought to the construction site.[38]

While other men were busy building the field fortification, which was designated "Fort Floyd," officers and troopers of A and G Companies were occupied with the burial of their dead comrades. Two graves were prepared, side by side, on the western slopes of "Stony Point." That completed, each company in turn buried its own man, A Company burying Private Lynch, and G Company Private Cade. Each was buried with honors, albeit an abbreviated form of what this would have been in garrison. A howitzer was dismounted and the gun carriage used as the hearse. Because there were no coffins, each body was wrapped in a blanket, laid on the gun carriage, and the flag laid over it. An escort had been selected for each from among men of the company, and these marched on either side of the dead trooper with their carbines carried at "reverse arms," with muzzles pointing down. Company buglers preceded them sounding the "dead march," and the rest of their comrades followed.

In this manner the procession for each of the dead men sadly and slowly wound its way up the hill to the grave site overlooking the route of their march to battle on the previous day. There each body was lowered into a grave after the flag was removed, and the burial service was read by a commissioned officer of the company, there being no chaplain with them. For Private Lynch, 1st Lt. John N. Perkins read the service; for Private Cade, it was done by 2d Lt. George D. Bayard. Bayard had been returned to the command of Company G following the wounding of Lieutenant Stuart. When the burials were completed, the escort fired a salute with blank cartridges, and the graves were filled nearly to the top with dirt, the remaining space being filled with prickly-pear cactus to keep out the wolves. Finally, the buglers sounded "Taps" as a last farewell, following which the escort and procession faced about and marched back to camp at quick time accompanied by lively music.[39]

The Pawnee scouts spent the day stretching and drying the Cheyenne scalps they had taken. For the rest of the command, once their duties had been performed in construction of Fort Floyd and burial of the dead, this was a day of rest. They had come far and performed well a difficult and dangerous duty. Tomorrow would bring more hardship for them, because tomorrow they would start in pursuit of the fleeing Cheyennes.[40]

Part Four

The Pursuit

13

The Flight of the Cheyennes

What hope was left in anything but flight?
And whither? O the world was narrow now!
South, east, the rat-like nibbling of the plow
Had left them but a little way to go.
The mountains of the never melting snow
Walled up the west. Beyond the northern haze,
There lay a land of unfamiliar ways,
Dark tongues and alien eyes.

As waters keep
Their wonted channels, yearning for the deep,
The homeless rabble took the ancient road.   (208)

The Southern Bands

The shock of the charge of the "long knives" had filled the hearts of the Cheyenne warriors and accompanying Sioux with fear and bewilderment. The fear was not of battle or death, for these were men who had gladly faced many fierce and unyielding foes in mortal combat with the sure knowledge that Maheo would give them victory or a warrior's death. Rather, it was a fear that somehow they had displeased Maheo and the Maheyuno—that they had made the wrong medicine to invoke the help of the Sacred Powers, or that their medicine had failed because of something they had done or failed to do. Some believed there was a traitor in their midst who had somehow slipped away to the soldier chief and told him of their medicine that rendered bullets harmless. They thought this must be why he ordered his men to use the long knives for which there was no medicine to help the People.

Now, as they came racing back to the great village in the bend of the Cedar River, the Saline, they were also swept with a feeling of shame and humiliation. But of greater importance were their families, within striking distance of the soldiers against whose weapons they no longer had a defense. Uncertain how long they had before the soldiers came, fear for the safety of their wives and children led many into precipitous flight. Some took with them only what they could carry in packs on their horses. Others, less sure the soldiers would be there soon, packed their belongings, rested the night in camp, and the following morning took down their lodges and began a rapid but deliberate movement away from the Saline.[1]

Most of the southern bands fled directly south, back to the Flint Arrowpoint River (the Arkansas),* and beyond. They knew their friends the Kotsoteka and Yamparika Comanches and the Kiowas were camped along the upper reaches of Crooked Creek, country into which the Veho seldom went. With so large an encampment they believed the soldiers would not follow and they would be safe. There, with the help and protection of their friends, they would be able to hunt and begin to restore the grievous loss of their lodges and possessions and the great supply of cured buffalo meat they had accumulated from the summer's hunt to take them through the time of the Cold Maker.[2]

Leaving the Saline, at first in small groups and then in a great, long column, the Indians left a wide, deep trail of lodgepole tracks scarring the earth as they fled southward to the Bunch of Trees River (Smoky Hill) and beyond. Eleven or twelve miles south of the village they crossed the upper reaches of Big Creek, dry this time of year except for a few scattered water holes in the bed. Here they drank, watered their horses, rested a little, then plunged on south. Those with travois were slowest, but laden though they were, the hardy Indian horses made excellent time. Various bands camped on the upper reaches of Walnut Creek on August 1 and 2, probably on Wild Horse Creek, one of its tributaries. Here

---

*The Cheyennes, and other tribes of the southern plains, called the Arkansas River the Flint Arrowpoint River. For the Cheyennes it was Mutsitooniyohe.

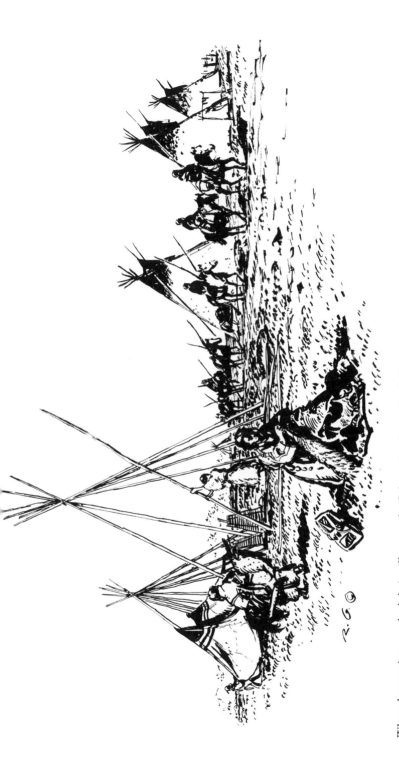

When the warriors reached their village on the Saline, the demoralized Cheyennes, anxious to move their families from harm's way, began a precipitous flight. Some left their lodges and belongings, taking with them only the bare necessities. Others dismantled their lodges, packed their belongings, and began a rapid and deliberate movement away from the Saline. The southern bands fled south toward the Arkansas, and the northern bands northwest to Lodgepole Creek and beyond.

the bodies of three dead warriors were placed on scaffolds along the creek.[3]

As they continued south from the Walnut, one of several groups of stragglers met a Mexican and an Arapahoe sent by their agent, Robert C. Miller, to invite them to Bent's New Fort for talks and distribution of their annuities. Miller, of course, had no knowledge of the fight on the Solomon or the destruction of the village on the Saline. The stragglers told these men the story of their misfortune, adding that they were going to Crooked Creek to camp with the Kiowas. The Kiowas, they said, had promised to join with them against the whites, and as soon as they could do so they were all going to the fort to take their goods, along with the scalps of the agent and everyone with him. Obviously this was the ill-considered talk of angry young warriors.[4]

By prearrangement the bands split into smaller units or family groups as they approached the watershed of the Pawnee Fork (Red Arm's Creek), a few leaving the main body about every one-fourth mile. Most went west, just far enough to be clear of the trail left by the greater number that continued southward. With small groups continuing to move away from the trail to the south, visible evidence of their movement became less and less apparent, and finally vanished. Like quail scattering before a predator, the Cheyennes melted into the emptiness of the plains.[5]

After leaving the main body, the small groups of fleeing Cheyennes followed an erratic course west-southwest along the various branches of the upper Pawnee Fork. Finally they again joined a common trail that moved southward and struck the Santa Fe Trail about ten miles west of the Middle (Cimarron) Crossing of the Arkansas. Carefully scouting the trail to ensure that no soldiers or large trains were moving along it, they quickly crossed the road, splashed across the broad but shallow river, and disappeared into the sandhills to the south. Another twenty miles brought them to the upper reaches of Crooked Creek, and a few miles more to the safety of great camps of Kiowas and Comanches.[6]

When they reached the Kiowa and Comanche villages, the frightened Cheyennes were at last relatively secure and able to rest, eat, and reorganize. Many were without those things they needed most—shelter and food. Therefore most bands elected to stay with their allies in the country south of the Arkansas until they could rebuild their supplies and replace lost lodges. It would take

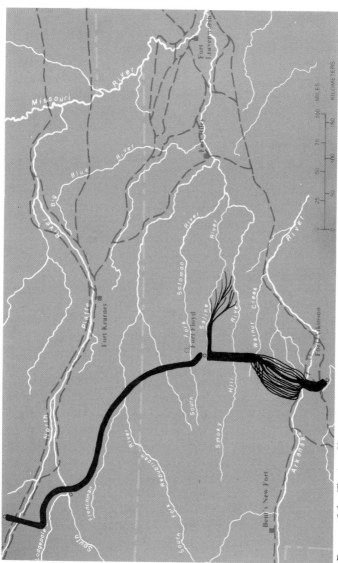

Routes of the Fleeing Cheyennes

many months to restore these losses, because between all of the bands more than 350 lodges had been abandoned and later destroyed by the soldiers. An average of 14 or 15 hides were needed to replace each lodge, requiring that at least 5,250 buffalo be killed, their hides laboriously scraped, cured, and tanned, and the long process of making the lodge covers begun. Then, too, there were lodgepoles, lodge furnishings, skins and hides (for clothing and robes), cooking utensils, and many other items to be replaced. To regain the comfort and security they had known before that day on the south fork of the Solomon would take many months of hard work and patience.[7]

Those of the People who went to Crooked Creek stayed south of the Arkansas for the rest of the summer and well into fall, hunting and restoring their losses. For all the fiery talk of young braves, no white men or white installations were attacked. When leaves began to fall and the Cold Maker touched the grasses of the plains, the bands who had gone to the Comanche and Kiowa country gradually moved back north to their own lands and their usual camping grounds.[8]

Not all the southern people moved south of the Flint Arrowpoint River. Some, probably Dog Soldiers and southern Suhtai, seemed to have stayed in their own land along the Smoky Hill and between Walnut Creek and the Republican. When the battle was over and the flight of the People began, these bands doubtless moved quickly to a location not far away, possibly along one of the branches of the Solomon farther east, or to the Saline or Smoky Hill. These people may already have been camping in one or more satellite villages farther down the Saline. Wherever they were, after watching Colonel Sumner's troops march away to the south, they evidently felt secure enough to send out war parties.

On August 2 a large band of warriors attacked a party of nineteen drovers herding 824 head of cattle along the Oregon-California Trail as beef for the Utah Expedition. With them were twenty horses and mules. The attack took place at about 11:00 A.M. only twenty-eight miles west of Fort Kearny and nearly one hundred miles northeast of the site of the battle on the south fork of the Solomon. One drover was killed and another wounded, and all the cattle and all but two of the horses and mules were taken. The drovers reported the strength of the attacking party as 150, highly unlikely in view of recent events. Probably there were about 25 or 30. The captured animals were trailed in a south-southeasterly direction, leading the commander of the garrison at Fort Kearny to conclude there was a sizeable Cheyenne village somewhere south of the Republican. Between 43 and 65 cattle were later found roaming aimlessly through the sandhills south of the site of the attack. The numbers and the character of the raid suggest that a large village did exist south of the Republican and east of that destroyed by Colonel Sumner.[9]

One day following the raid on the army beef herd, two Cheyenne warriors attempted to stampede the livestock left at Fort Floyd as food and transport for Captain Foote's company and the First Cavalry wounded. They met with indifferent success. On August 4, several small parties of Cheyennes were seen in the hills at some distance from the little post, apparently scouting or hunting, perhaps searching for their dead or wounded. That night twenty or thirty Cheyennes attempted an attack on the fort. Clearly a sizeable group had remained in the vicinity. The following day, five Pawnee scouts dispatched by Colonel Sumner two days earlier with letters for Captain Foote and the commanding officer of Fort Kearny, were attacked by Cheyennes a few miles south of Fort Floyd and their horses stolen. This seems to have happened close to the site of the destroyed village on the Saline. Possibly some Cheyennes had remained in the area to see if anything could be salvaged. Whatever luck they had there, they must have replaced a sizeable portion of their losses in buffalo meat with the capture of the government beef.[10]

The bands remaining in the country south of the Republican did not become quiet until well into fall. A war party attacked a government train near Ash Hollow in early September, killing three white teamsters and seizing a large quantity of arms and ammunition, along with fifty head of cattle. About September 10 a small wagon train that included the son of William H. Russell of Russell, Majors, and Waddell, government freight contractors, was fired on by seventeen warriors thirty miles west of Fort Kearny. On September 15, small parties of warriors roaming the Platte River Road came within a mile of Kearny while firing at two different express riders.[11]

Whether the Dog Soldiers and southern Suhtai eventually moved south of the Arkansas with other southern bands is unknown, but in view of their activities after the battle and into the fall, this seems improbable. No more soldiers entered their country in 1857, and it is likely they stayed where they were, trying to replace their substantial losses. With the arrival of fall they probably would have been found within their usual range, living much as they always had.

The Northern Bands

The precipitous flight from the village on the Saline was not entirely to the south. Northern bands, mostly Omissis and northern Suhtai, also abandoned many of their lodges and possessions. Some were so fearful that they packed only a little food and other necessities, then took their families with them in a dash northward to safety. Others, perhaps finding that the soldiers had ceased pursuit and returned to the Solomon, took down their lodges and started a rapid but orderly flight toward the Platte. Their course was north-northwest, passing west of the battlegound on the Solomon and the great encampment of the First Cavalry. Crossing the forks of the Solomon, probably following an established trail, they moved beyond the Prairie Dog, the Sappa, the Beaver, and the Republican, then followed the trail along the line of Frenchmen's Creek* until they turned north to the South Platte. This they struck opposite the mouth of Lodgepole Creek.† [12]

When the first parties reached the Platte, on July 30, they established a small village, erected the few lodges they had saved, and rested a day before continuing the journey. The chiefs had decided, even as they left the Saline, to follow the Lodgepole until arriving opposite Smith's Fork, then to move north across the North Platte into Oglalla and Brulé country. As a guide for those following, the people of the first village painted a map of the route on a bison skull and set it in the center of the camp. Another party, probably Suhtai, arrived soon after, and they too made camp on the south bank of Fat River (South Platte) across from the mouth of the Lodgepole. The same evening yet another group arrived, including one of the important chiefs. This group had seven lodges, which they pitched a little downstream from the other two sites. Their intention was to provide those following with something to eat, needed rest, and the location of the new village. The day after

*The Cheyennes called Frenchmen's Creek Wihioiyohe—White Man's River.
†The Cheyenne name for Lodgepole Creek was Oohkoiyohe.

their arrival the other two bands left, anxious to be away from the trails and the threat of pursuing soldiers.[13]

Once the seven lodges were in place at the third camp, the son of the chief, his cousin, and two other warriors, followed the South Platte downstream, toward the crossing of the Oregon-California Trail. There they hoped to find a wagon-train encampment where they might obtain food for their people or at least a good meal for themselves. They had eaten nothing but a little jerky since leaving the Saline. The chief learned later the same night that the train in camp on the north side of the crossing was that of the soldier chief, and that his son and a nephew were now prisoners of the soldiers. The train being too strong to attack, there was nothing to be done for the young men.[14]

The small encampment of seven lodges remained at the site opposite the Lodgepole for several days, helping many Omissis and Suhtai in their journey north. Then, on the morning of August 5, scouts watching Colonel Sumner's train returned to report a body of armed Veho approaching the camp from the east along the south bank of the river. So close were they that, fearing another attack while their medicine was weak, all the people in camp mounted their horses and fled across the river, abandoning the seven lodges and their possessions. They were only a few miles west along the Lodgepole when they saw smoke rising from the burning village. They felt fortunate to have escaped before the Veho arrived, but now they were even poorer.[15]

The northern bands remained above the North Platte for a while, in familiar country they once had called their own. But by fall they were back in the lands between the forks of the Platte, preparing for the long winter, as they had done for years beyond telling.

14

The Trail to the Arkansas

Still wearily the main trail lengthened east
By hungry days and fireless bivouacs;
And more and more diverging pony tracks,
To north and south, and tangent lodge pole trails
Revealed the hunted scattering as quails
Before a dreaded hunter.   *(209–10)*

Destruction of the Cheyenne Village

At about 6:30 A.M. on Friday, July 31, 1857, the six companies of
the First Cavalry, a cavalry detail with two prairie howitzers, and
Companies D and G of the Sixth Infantry broke camp and began
their march to the south, the direction in which most fleeing Cheyennes had disappeared. The country ahead consisted of rolling
hills, broken here and there by small streams that fed the Solomon
and the Grand Saline farther south. As far as the eye could see it
was covered with buffalo grass, brown from the scorching sun of
midsummer, and sprinkled with prickly pear cactus, yucca, and
sagebrush. In a short time the long column of marching men and
animals had passed beyond the valley of the Solomon's south fork,
leaving behind the still incomplete Fort Floyd with its company of
infantry and the cavalry wounded.[1]

After a march of about fourteen miles, the valley of the Saline
came into view and a mile ahead, nestled in a horseshoe bend in
the river, the great Cheyenne village with many lodges still stand-

ing. There were no horse herds, however, and no other signs of life. Fall Leaf and his Delaware scouts rode ahead to reconnoiter and soon came back to report the village abandoned. Descending into the valley, the troopers passed the village and went into camp in an adjacent bend of the river. Three mounted Cheyennes were seen watching from the village as they approached, but the Indians crossed the river and moved south before the first troops arrived, and no one could catch them. Except for those three, the only living things in and about the camp were a few female dogs with fresh litters of pups, and a number of old, broken-down horses.[2]

Once the cavalry horses had been picketed and camp established, the troops examined the village and its surroundings. What they saw indicated a precipitate and panicked flight by the inhabitants. On actual count they found more than 170 lodges still standing, with about an equal number taken down but then abandoned in place. One lodge, still standing inside the circle, was more than eighteen feet in diameter and at least as tall, made of new and beautifully dressed buffalo skins. There were, in addition, a large number of small, temporary shelters for tribal members without family lodges, as well as many sweat lodges. Clearly a great many more lodges had been dismantled and removed. On the opposite bank of the Saline was a very large and concentrated trail made by horses trailing lodgepoles as they fled southward.[3]

After completing an examination and inventory of the village, the troops searched the standing lodges for items of value or use to them or the expedition. In these were found every manner of Indian property. The supply of cured buffalo meat they had laid in for winter during the summer hunt had nearly all been left behind, packed neatly in beautifully dressed and painted leather parfleches. There were buffalo robes, buckskins, antelope skins, wolf, coyote, and fox skins, blankets, moccasins, leggings, and other articles of clothing, all in great quantity. Many lodges still contained family cooking utensils, children's playthings, lodge furnishings, and other belongings. In front of a few were small, slim poles from which were strung the scalps of fallen enemies.[4]

So great was the amount of property left behind that searching the lodges and removing souvenirs and what was of use took a long time. Estimates of the quantity of buffalo meat varied wildly, ranging from 3,000 to 20,000 pounds.[5] The troops took as much of this

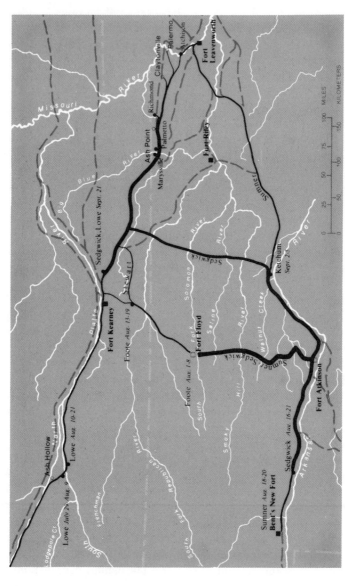

Lines of march of the First Cavalry after the battle on Solomon's Fork

as could be packed on the mules. All remaining Cheyenne property was thrown into piles, along with the lodges and lodgepoles, and set ablaze. The loss to the tribe in lodgepoles alone was enormous, for they were long, prime poles, about twenty-five feet in length and as thick as a strong man's arm. With that the men returned to their camp for a meager supper of biscuits, meat, and a little coffee, and prepared to continue pursuit of the Cheyennes.[6]

Across the Smoky Hill to the Arkansas

Saturday, August 1, Colonel Sumner's command broke camp at 6:30 A.M., crossed the Saline, and began the march to the Arkansas, or wherever the very deep and visible trail of the Cheyennes might lead them. The country continued hilly and broken, with a barren and desolate appearance. As the day progressed, it became increasingly hot, probably well over 100 degrees. One or two infantrymen gave out from heat exhaustion and had to be carried on the mules. A cavalry sergeant, hit suddenly with cramps, nearly died during the course of the march; 2d Lt. Orlando H. Moore, of G Company, Sixth Infantry, had his legs badly poisoned, probably from insect bites or contact with poisonous plants, and gave out two or three miles before they reached their next camp. Both required transport the rest of the way.

The day's march was about twenty miles and lasted until three o'clock in the afternoon. Twelve miles from the destroyed Cheyenne village, they struck the dry bed of Big Creek. In the sand they could clearly see where fleeing Cheyennes had stopped to water their horses from a few pools of standing water. The column continued south following the Indian trail, stopping eight miles farther along the banks of a small stream, probably Downer's Creek. There they picketed the horses, established the guard, and started their evening meal. Bunking arrangements were simple, with just the saddles as headrests. All men slept with boots on and carbines and pistols at their sides.[7]

On Sunday, August 2, the march resumed at 7:00 A.M. The first six or eight miles were over moderately rough ground. One small stream they crossed, which flowed into Downer's Creek, had a barely drinkable, soapstone-tasting water. After ten miles they reached and crossed the Smoky Hill. Its bed was between thirty

R. G. ©

On July 31 the troopers of the Cheyenne Expedition resumed their march in pursuit of the fleeing Cheyennes. Fifteen miles from the Solomon they found the abandoned Cheyenne village with more than 170 lodges still standing and about an equal number taken down but abandoned in place. The former were

filled with all sorts of Indian property. A great many lodges had been removed. Colonel Sumner had everything that remained that was not useful to
the troops put to the torch.

and forty yards wide, but nowhere was the yellow and muddy water more than eighteen inches deep. It, too, tasted of soapstone, but was very sweet.

The land beyond the Smoky Hill leveled out, giving a great, unbroken vista to the south. The trail of the Cheyennes continued ahead, visible to the horizon, and this the soldiers followed. Several men whose horses were fatigued fell behind, but a pleasant south breeze made the incessant heat more bearable, and no one experienced serious heat exhaustion. After traveling another eleven or twelve miles, they camped on a small stream forming part of the headwaters of Walnut Creek, probably Wild Horse Creek.[8]

The new campsite had no trees but did have reasonably good grass, affording the livestock some much-needed grazing. One horse had given out during the day, and the rest were in a weakened condition. In camp the day's second meal was prepared, three biscuits apiece, meat without salt, and coffee. The lack of decent, balanced rations, combined with effects of the long, arduous march in baking heat, was beginning to tell on men as well as animals.

As darkness fell across the plains the wind began to blow and soon became a violent gale. Within a short time rain started, then it began to pour, adding to the soldiers' misery. They could do little but roll up in their blankets, put their oilcloths over them, their talmas over those, and hope for the best. As sometimes happens when men are at the brink of exhaustion, many slept well despite the pelting rain.[9]

After a time the storm passed. But the night's problems were not at an end: a sentry coming off post carelessly lifted his carbine by the muzzle and it went off, wounding his arm so severely it required amputation the following morning. As a result, on Monday, August 3, they remained in camp on Wild Horse Creek to permit Dr. Brewer to perform the operation. The misfortune did aid the livestock, allowing a full day of undisturbed grazing. Soldiers scouting along the stream during the day found three Cheyenne scaffold burials near a site where some of them apparently had camped during their flight south.*[10]

---

*The Cheyennes buried their dead in various ways, depending upon the nature of the environment, materials available, and the like. Security of the body was an important consideration, to ensure that wolves and other predators could not reach

On the afternoon of August 3, 2d Lt. Albert V. Colburn, Colonel Sumner's adjutant, prepared a dispatch to send to the commanding officer of Fort Kearny.[11] It gave an account of the battle, provisions made for wounded soldiers, subsequent pursuit of the Indians, and the destruction of the Cheyenne village. He also wrote a letter to Captain Foote at Fort Floyd conveying Colonel Sumner's order that C Company and the wounded march northeast to Fort Kearny rather than north to the wagon train on the South Platte. The dispatch and letter, along with personal correspondence written by members of the command, were sent in care of the five Pawnee scouts. They were directed to return to Fort Floyd, deliver the letter to Foote, then lead the occupants of the little post northeast to Fort Kearny. They left that night.[12]

Colonel Sumner was eager to get back on the trail and take advantage of the relative cool of morning, so on Tuesday, August 4, the command broke camp at 6:00 A.M. They marched in a southwesterly direction for about twenty miles, crossing the north and south forks of Walnut Creek and two or three other small streams and arroyos, and made camp at 1:00 P.M. Thanks to the recent rain, these streams now had a good flow of water. There was a little scrub timber along some of them, and on one they found wild chokecherries. Except for the streams, travel was mostly over high and level tableland, still following the clear Cheyenne trail. That night camp was on the banks of a small stream, probably Guzzler's Gulch, a tributary of the north (Heth's) branch of the Pawnee Fork.[13]

Wednesday, August 5, the command first moved due south, then southeasterly, and finally nearly due east. En route they crossed two or three small running streams and a few dry arroyos. They made camp at 10:00 A.M. on Heth's branch of the Pawnee, the

---

it and destroy the remains. Burial was practiced where the ground was sufficiently soft to permit it and materials were available to protect the body from being uncovered. Burial in holes or clefts in rocky projections of hills was common. Tree burials and scaffold burials were used where the ground was hard and the protection of the body in a shallow grave questionable. Burial within the lodge, usually by suspension from the lodgepoles, was practiced for very important warriors or tribal leaders. Burial on scaffolds in the area of the high plains was common, not for religious reasons, but because there were no trees and because prior to introduction of agriculture, the ground was extremely hard.

On August 3 soldiers scouting along Wild Horse Creek, a tributary of Walnut Creek, found three Cheyenne scaffold burials.

north fork, having traveled about ten miles. The trail of the Cheyennes had been dwindling steadily and, by the time they reached the north branch of the Pawnee, had disappeared altogether. Delaware guides told them small parties of Cheyennes had dropped away from the main body all along the course of the day's march. These were too small to pursue individually and left such a light trail as to be almost imperceptible. Finally, so many had left that the trail of those remaining completely disappeared. The only sign of them near the night's camp was a pillow lost or abandoned as they passed.[14]

The lack of a meaningful trail convinced Colonel Sumner that direct pursuit should be abandoned and the column should proceed to the Arkansas and go into camp for rest. There he would send a dispatch seeking resupply so the column could stay in the field and again find the Cheyennes. He was convinced the Indians would reassemble on the river, because there were no buffalo that far west so late in the summer, and they would need to hunt to sustain themselves. Thinking them insufficiently punished, he wanted to strike them hard one more time.[15]

Thursday, August 6, the command marched almost due south for fifteen miles, camping on Buckner's Branch (the middle branch) of the Pawnee Fork. Although recent rains had put plenty of water in the streams, the grass was very poor and shriveled by the intense heat, compounding the problems of the livestock. No game was to be found, and the command's larder was nearly bare, with only a few steers remaining. So desperate was their situation that the troops were killing for food almost any form of wildlife they could find, including coyotes, skunks, and buzzards. Lack of salt also created a craving that some tried to satisfy by sprinkling gunpowder on their meat. That night another hard rain added to their discomfort.[16]

On August 7 the column marched about fifteen miles, first moving due south, then southeast. Camp was made on the south branch of the Pawnee Fork, known as Shaff's Branch or Saw Log Creek, the latter name because the troops from old Fort Atkinson got their wood supplies from along its banks. During the day one of the men of B Company, Private Garber, fell behind his fellows because his old horse was too run-down to keep up. Company H was rear guard for the day, and when they came upon the horse they found it without rider, saddle, bridle, or halter. This led the troopers to conclude that the Indians had taken Garber. First Lieutenant Stockton, temporarily commanding B Company, detailed twelve men to look for him, but they found no sign of either the man or his equipment. [17]

On Saturday morning, August 8, Colonel Sumner detached Companies B and H to search for Private Garber. The rest of the troops left camp about 7:00 A.M. and marched in a southwesterly direction along the north bank of the Saw Log for eight or nine miles, then crossed to the south bank and moved south-southwest to the Arkansas along the old wagon trail from Fort Atkinson. When they reached the site of the abandoned post, they moved upstream along the Santa Fe Trail three miles, to camp on better grass. The exhausted infantry stopped seven miles from the Arkansas and camped, planning to rejoin the cavalry the following morning. An Indian, tribe unknown, attempted to sneak up on a sentinel at the cavalry camp during the night, but was spotted and frightened off by shots from the man's pistol.

When the rest of the command left for the Arkansas, Companies B and H began their search for Private Garber. First they backtracked six or eight miles to the point where they had found his horse, then struck off to the right (west) and made a circuit of the country, again reaching the Saw Log at 1:00 P.M. at a point about five miles above the previous camp. They roamed all around this area for approximately four hours, then went into camp three miles downstream without having found any trace of Garber. [18]

Sunday, August 9, the search resumed. The troops moved twelve miles downstream along the Saw Log, then sent Lieutenant Long, with twelve men and two Delaware guides, to its junction with Buckner's (the middle) Branch of the Pawnee. Long and his party followed Buckner's Branch upstream for about two miles before cutting back over to the area they had searched earlier. There they rejoined the remainder of the squadron and marched sixteen miles back up the Saw Log, where they made camp. No trace of the man had been found, and the two company commanders concluded they should abandon the search and rejoin Colonel Sumner and the others on the Arkansas. During the day the search party met three Kiowa warriors and asked them to watch for Garber, but were suspicious that they might in fact have killed him. [19]

At 4:45 A.M. on Monday, August 10, B and H Companies broke camp and moved upstream, crossing the Saw Log to the old wagon road and following it down to the Arkansas. They reached the First Cavalry camp a little before 11:00 A.M., very tired and glad to have an opportunity to rest. The day was extremely hot, too hot to chase Cheyennes, and they were glad the pursuit was over.[20]

15

The Wagon Train's Encounter on the South Platte

Then at last
They came to where another band had passed
With shoeless ponies, following the sun.
Some miles the new trail ran as lean creeks run
In droughty weather; then began to grow.
Here other hoofs had swelled it, there, travaux;
And more and more the circumjacent plains
Had fed the trail. . . .   *(118)*

Lowe Captures Two Young Cheyennes

About 1:00 P.M. on July 30, Percival Lowe retired to his tent for some needed rest. The climb out of Ash Hollow the preceding day had exhausted him, and he gave orders to his cook that he be awakened only for a good reason. At 5:00 P.M. the cook did wake him, stating that Lieutenant Riddick wanted him to come to the riverbank, as there were Indians on the other side. Lowe went to the river, and seeing four mounted Indians on the south bank observing them, sent a man out to a small island to wave a white flag and invite them to cross over. From the Indians they hoped to learn something of the whereabouts of Colonel Sumner and his troops. When they were beckoned, one of the Indians wheeled his horse and galloped off upriver. The other three dismounted, removed their saddles, and crossed the river bareback, it being much easier and safer to do so without saddles.

When they reached the north bank of the river, the three Indians accompanied Lowe, Lieutenant Riddick, and the others back to camp. They claimed to be Sioux, but proved in fact to be Cheyennes. The Mexican interpreter, Manuel Vijil, had lived with the Sioux at one time and understood a little of the Cheyenne language. It was enough to enable him to identify them and translate some of what they said. Learning that the three were Cheyennes, Lowe advised Lieutenant Riddick to take them prisoner since this might help Colonel Sumner gain the tribe's submission and force them to make peace. At the same time, he knew this must be done with care to avoid injuring them, bearing in mind their instinctive fear of imprisonment.

In camp, the teamsters were bringing mules into the enclosures and picketing them on half-lariat between the men and the river; the soldiers, who had been cleaning their weapons for inspection, stood around watching the proceedings. Lieutenant Riddick, Lowe, and Vijil sat on the ground facing the three Indians, preparing to council with them. Two were about twenty-two years of age, tall, well-built, and very handsome. The third was older, a large, powerful man, six-foot-four-inches in height, and deeply pockmarked. Lowe began questioning them, asking why they had come to the camp and where their people were. Speaking through the interpreter, they said they had thought the camp to be that of a freight or immigrant train and hoped for something to eat. Other members of their band, they said, were camped on the south bank of the South Platte across from the mouth of Lodgepole Creek, about twenty miles upriver. This confirmed Lowe's belief that the fourth Indian had ridden off to a camp farther up the South Platte. The three Indians were informed the train was that of Colonel Sumner with supplies for his command, that they were his prisoners, and that they would be well treated and fed, and their horses and weapons cared for until Colonel Sumner returned in a day or two.

While the Indians appeared to agree to this, the older one spoke softly to the other two, stating something to the effect, "You young men can do as you please, but I am no longer a boy to give up my bow." With that he leaped to his feet, jumped on his horse, and made a dash for the river, more than twenty shots being fired after him. His horse became entangled in the lariats with which the mules were picketed, and fell, throwing the Indian into a channel of the river separating some small islands from the mainland. Although most of the men rushed after him, he was neither found nor seen. The discovery two days later that his saddle was gone from the south bank showed that he had made good his daring escape.

When the older man jumped on his horse, Lowe and Vijil seized the other two and, after a sharp fight in which Lowe had to be assisted by Billy Daniels, they were subdued and tied hand and foot. Using small chains and padlocks from the front boxes of the wagons, they were finally "placed in irons" and a tent pitched over them. A soldier sentry was placed at the front and rear to guard against any escape attempt. This completed, Lieutenant Riddick, Lowe, and the interpreter interrogated the two prisoners. They learned that Colonel Sumner's troops had battled the Cheyennes the previous day and that several Indians and some soldiers were killed and wounded. The Cheyennes were said to have scattered, with many going north, crossing the South Platte near the mouth of Lodgepole Creek. The young man captured by Lowe was the son of the principal chief of the band, and the other was his cousin. Incredibly, these men obviously had participated in the battle, no more than thirty-two hours before, and had ridden the distance between the Solomon and the South Platte in something less than that time.

Fearful that capture of a chief's son might bring warriors from a large camp to their rescue, and an attempt to stampede the animals or capture the train, Lowe set about making a secure corral with the wagons. Each wagon was placed with its left front wheel against the right rear wheel of the wagon in front and with its tongue on the outside. Within two hours the circle was complete with all livestock and men inside for security. All arms were checked and each man, soldier and teamster alike, was issued fifty rounds of ammunition. A strong guard was posted, and with that the rest of the men tried to get a little sleep.

During the night the two young Cheyennes whispered together a good deal, and seemed to listen expectantly to the howling of the wolves all about the camp. One in particular had a peculiar howl, and howled at intervals from the south side of the river directly opposite the camp. Many of the teamsters, including Lowe, were convinced that they were very near a large band of Cheyennes, and they got scant sleep in their effort to remain vigilant. An hour before dawn on July 31, the camp was roused in anticipation of an Indian attack, dawn being a favorite time to surprise the unwary. No attack came, however, and after breakfast, with lookouts posted, Lowe rode upriver a couple of miles to reconnoiter, finding nothing but the tracks of two horses that had crossed the river during the night. At 4:00 P.M. an Indian approached on the opposite or south bank of the river, watched for a while, then rode away. At 5:00 P.M. a mountaineer named Charles Gardner, called "Big Phil" because of his Philadelphia origins, arrived from Fort Laramie in the company of a Sioux Indian, with mail for Colonel Sumner's command. They had no news of Colonel Sumner or his troops. The mules were grazed nearby under a strong guard, who were prepared to corral them in a hurry if necessary.

On the morning of August 1 a Majors and Russell train with military supplies passed en route to Salt Lake City. Lowe crossed to the south bank of the river and scouted about five miles upriver, finding many tracks of unshod Indian horses. During the day, "Big Phil" and the Sioux were allowed to talk with the two prisoners in the belief that on their return trip they would tell all Indians they met that the two young Cheyennes were safe and well cared for, and this might induce their band to come in and make terms for peace. In the evening, Lieutenant Riddick sent the two Mexican scouts, Vijil and Malquis Mestos, to find the Cheyenne camp if possible, count the lodges, note every ravine or pass leading to their camp, and return by the evening of the third. The two left camp at midnight.[1]

At the Crossing Point of the Northern Bands

At sunrise on August 2, "Big Phil" and the Sioux left on their return trip to Fort Laramie. During the day the camp was moved a mile and a half upstream for fresh grass, and the teamsters practiced driving the wagons into their tight circle for security. Lowe and two of his wagon masters did a little scouting, but there was no sign of the Cheyennes. On the night of August 3 the two Mexican scouts returned, reporting they had located the camp of seven lodges opposite the mouth of Lodgepole Creek, and had found remains of two other recent camps nearby. In one of the abandoned camps they found a chart marked on a buffalo skull, showing the route taken by the Cheyennes up Lodgepole Creek to a point opposite Smith's Fork, then north across the North Platte. They had seen only one Indian that day and could not get close to him.

At one of the campsites used by the fleeing northern bands, across from the
mouth of Lodgepole Creek, Lowe and his men found a buffalo skull with a
map of the route taken by the Indians painted on the forehead. It was intended
to guide those who followed.

The following day, August 4, Lowe organized a party of twenty
volunteer teamsters and the two Mexican scouts to go to the Cheyenne camp. Armed with rifles and revolvers, they left at sunrise on
August 5, crossed the South Platte opposite the camp, and followed
the south bank of the river toward the seven lodges. When they
had traveled this distance, they found the lodges still standing but
hurriedly abandoned, with fires burning and cooking equipment
and other useful articles in place. Someone noticed a party of Indians some two miles away retreating rapidly up Lodgepole Creek.

Undoubtedly they had discovered the approach of Lowe and his men and had made a precipitate departure. They seemed a large band and apparently were very demoralized. A trail coming from the south was broad and quite well-worn, showing that many had traveled that way since the rain two nights earlier. So many seemed to have passed recently with horses and lodgepoles that Lowe anticipated seeing Sumner and his men coming after them in hot pursuit.

Saving one fine lodge, a packsaddle, and a bushel or more of Kinnikinnick, the Plains Indians' version of tobacco, Lowe and his men piled all the rest together and burned it. Lowe, Billy Daniels, and the two Mexican scouts then rode upriver two miles to the next abandoned campsite, picked up the buffalo skull "chart," and returned with it to their own camp. On the trip back they noted tracks of many Indian horses up and down the south bank of the river opposite their camp, including tracks of what appeared to be two American cavalry horses with shoes, indicating that Colonel Sumner must have lost some horses.

From August 7 to 9, little happened except a few false alarms. The two young Cheyenne prisoners, by then overcoming their fear of their captors, became much more communicative and started talking about the fight with Colonel Sumner's troops. They said the northern bands had scattered, agreeing to go north and come together again at some point beyond the North Platte. The buffalo skull with the chart they identified as the map of the route, and the camp of seven lodges as a sort of supply point, where necessaries and information could be had. They believed their people too scattered to be a threat to the train, and indicated the peculiar wolf howl heard the night of their capture was the chief of the band, father of the prisoner taken by Lowe, giving assurance they would not attempt to attack it. Satisfied, Lowe and his men settled down to await the expected arrival of Sumner and his troops.[2]

Part Five

The Finale

16

Sumner's March to Bent's New Fort

The draggled column slowly making head
Against the muck; the drooping horses, led,
Well loaded with their saddles; empty packs,
Became a cruel burden on the backs
Of plodding mules with noses to the ground.
....

Here the long pursuit,
It seemed, had come to nothing after all.   *(210)*

Agent Robert C. Miller and the Cheyenne Annuities

On June 20, while Sedgwick's division of the Expedition was passing the ruins of Bent's Old Fort on the way west, and Sumner's column was along the North Platte two day's march short of Fort Laramie, Robert C. Miller, Indian agent for the Upper Arkansas, left Westport, Missouri. With him went a large wagon train carrying annual annuity goods for the Comanches, Kiowas, Plains Apaches, Cheyennes, and Arapahoes. The train proceeded down the Santa Fe Trail without incident until it reached Walnut Creek on July 3, camping near Allison and Booth's Ranch. From there Miller sent a runner ahead to notify the Comanche, Kiowa, and Plains Apache camps along the Arkansas of his approach so they might gather near the ruins of old Fort Atkinson to receive their treaty goods. On the morning of July 4 a war party of Kiowas stopped by the trading post while returning from a long search for Pawnees, their traditional enemies. After being fed and given a few presents by Miller, they departed for their village near Fort Atkinson, from all appearances well pleased.[1]

Proceeding from Walnut Creek, the train arrived at the villages of the Comanches and Kiowas on the morning of July 8, the Plains Apaches at the time being encamped a few miles above the ruins of Fort Atkinson. Because several important bands of both tribes were not yet present, Miller declined to distribute the annuity goods until they had arrived. The Kiowas were greatly irritated and threatened Miller and his men with strung bows, demanding their goods immediately and proposing to seize them if they were not delivered. Unable to resist their superior numbers and far distant from any possible help by the military, Miller was about to give in to their demands when the Comanches offered to protect the train. A grateful Miller accepted, and the crisis quickly passed.[2]

By the morning of July 12, all bands of Comanches and Kiowas had arrived, and a council was held with them before annuities were distributed. The Comanches were friendly, but the Kiowas were sullen and resentful, keeping their bows strung and their hands full of arrows. To Miller's admonishment that the Great Father was angry over their attacks on travelers along the Santa Fe road and would send soldiers against them if they continued, the Kiowas contemptuously replied that the Great Father feared them and sent presents to placate them. They said they had heard before that soldiers would come but had never yet seen them. Miller later found that on the very day he distributed treaty goods to the Kiowa tribal encampment on the Arkansas, a Kiowa raiding party attacked and destroyed a ranch near Mora, New Mexico Territory. When he prepared his annual report on October 14, Miller therefore recommended that the Kiowas be soundly punished and that no more treaty goods be sent to them until they had been brought to submission.[3] This report doubtless was responsible in part for the Comanche-Kiowa Expedition of 1860.

After completing distribution of annuities to the Kiowas, Comanches, and Plains Apaches, Miller and his train resumed their journey on the morning of July 13. Their next stop was Bent's New Fort, where distribution of annuity goods to Cheyennes and Arapahoes was to take place. Ten miles west of Fort Atkinson, however, they came upon a large village of Arapahoes, numbering approximately three hundred lodges. Because they were starving, they were moving eastward to the buffalo plains, to hunt. They said they had been waiting in the vicinity of Bent's New Fort for many days to receive their gifts, and that they could wait no longer as "their women and children had become very faint and hungry." They pleaded that they not be required to return to Bent's Fort to receive the presents. The Arapahoes were agreeable and pleasant, and Miller consented to make the distribution immediately in order that they might proceed with their buffalo hunt.*[4]

With the Arapahoe annuities distributed, Miller and his train continued on their way, now bearing only Cheyenne goods. They arrived at Bent's New Fort on July 19, at which time Miller applied to William Bent for permission to store the Cheyenne goods within the fort until he could communicate with Colonel Sumner concerning their disposition. To Miller's surprise, Bent refused without hesitation, stating that if the Cheyennes learned the goods were there and would not be distributed until the soldiers came, they would attack the post, seize both government property and that belonging to Bent, and massacre all within. Miller next attempted to persuade Elijah G. Chiles, the wagon train contractor, to remain in the area with the wagons until he could contact Colonel Sumner. Chiles also refused. To the frustration of Chiles, Miller then refused to accept and receipt for the goods carried by the train and claimed the right to detain the wagons until distribution had been made.[5]

His dilemma compelled Miller to make contact with Colonel Sumner as soon as possible. He tried to find an express rider to carry his message to the First Cavalry camp, wherever that might be. This too was difficult, because the plains were aswarm with small bands of hostile Indians roving to and fro, making a trip by a single person or a small party extremely dangerous. Finally Miller persuaded a French trapper by the name of Antoine (Chet) Dubray to make the trip, provided he could induce two Mexicans to accompany him. He succeeded and left at daybreak on the morning of July 20, expecting to find Colonel Sumner's command at or near old Fort St. Vrain.[6]

On the evening of July 19, at about 9:00 P.M., fearful for the safety of his family and property if the annuity goods remained at his fort undistributed for any length of time, William Bent ap-

---

*The Arapahoe village doubtless included all the bands encountered by Sedgwick's column on June 10, 16, and 17.

proached Miller and proposed to rent the fort to the government.
Miller accepted the proposition and, on the morning of July 20,
entered into a written lease agreement with Bent. The Cheyenne
presents were unloaded from the wagons and stored in the fort.
That accomplished, Bent packed all his goods into his wagons and
left for Westport, Missouri, on the morning of the twenty-first,
taking with him his family, cattle, and horses. Doubtless the government contractor's train left with him. As per the agreement,
Bent left behind sufficient wagons and teams to transport the annuity goods and other government property to the States in the
event Colonel Sumner determined they should not be given to the
Cheyennes.[7]

On July 27, after riding night and day, the express rider, Dubray, returned to Bent's New Fort. He had not found Colonel Sumner nor had he learned anything as to his whereabouts. This left
Miller alone at the little stone trading post with only four white
men and a Negro slave. Two of the white men were independent of
Miller's control, and his situation was indeed serious. Nonetheless,
he believed the goods to be safer behind the stone walls of the fort
than in wagons moving along a road infested with hostile Indians.
This proved correct, for on the day after the empty wagon train left
its camp near Fort Atkinson, most of the Cheyennes fleeing south
after the battle on the Solomon crossed the trail approximately
twenty-five miles west of that abandoned post.*[8] Had the wagons
been loaded with the treaty goods and traveling more slowly because of the weight, they might have had a disastrous encounter
with the Cheyennes.[9]

A few days following departure of the Bent wagons, Miller talked
with two Plains Apaches who had come from the Cheyenne village.
They claimed that several important chiefs and a number of influ-
ential younger men among the Cheyennes were eager for peace and
actively trying to bring it about. Thinking this a real opportunity to
invite the headmen to meet him in a peace council at Bent's New
Fort, Miller obtained the services of a Mexican and an Arapahoe
to deliver his invitation to the Cheyennes. After they had journeyed

---

*Agent Miller stated forty miles in his annual report, but the journal of Eli Long
demonstrates that the great trail left by the Cheyennes could not have been more
than twenty-five miles beyond old Fort Atkinson. This would be the correct path
for a movement to the headwaters of Crooked Creek. See Eli Long, "Journal,"
entry for August 13, 1857.

for several days toward the village, these two met a party of straggling Cheyennes who told them a great battle had been fought, six
of their leaders killed, and their village burned. They said that
though they had lost many horses and lodges, they were not subdued and had gone over to Crooked Creek to join with the Kiowas,
who had promised to unite with them for war against the whites.
As soon as they regrouped, they said, they would come to the fort
to "help themselves to the goods, and take the scalp of the agent
and everyone with him." This report was verified and repeated by
various Indians who came to the fort within the next few days.[10]
Miller's situation seemed critical.

Colonel Sumner Seizes the Cheyenne Annuities

The campsite established by the Expedition in the valley of the
Arkansas on August 8 was three miles west of the ruins of Fort
Atkinson.[11] Colonel Sumner's intention was to give his troops a
brief respite here after their arduous journey across the plains,
then find the Cheyennes and fight them again. He believed traffic
along the Santa Fe Trail to be in danger from them, and thought
the presence of troops would protect travelers and trains. Except
for beef sufficient for twenty-four days, his supplies were now exhausted. To relieve the hardships of troopers and animals, he dispatched an express rider to Fort Leavenworth with orders to have
additional supplies sent out as soon as possible. With them he
hoped to keep his force in the field.[12]

The troops remained in camp August 9 and 10, resting and tending to maintenance chores. Very high temperatures made this an
uncomfortable task. At 11:00 A.M. on August 10, Companies B
and H returned from their unsuccessful search for the lost Private
Garber. On Tuesday, August 11, the reunited command broke
camp at 7:00 A.M. and marched slowly down the river for nine
miles, going back into camp six miles below Fort Atkinson.* Just
before reaching their campsite, they met the United States mail
coach for Santa Fe, from which they obtained some news and tobacco. The mail party told them that Robert Miller, agent for the

---

*The camp located six miles below Fort Atkinson was approximately two miles
east of present-day Dodge City, Kansas, in the vicinity of what later would be Fort
Dodge.

Cheyennes, had gone to Bent's New Fort with the tribe's annuity presents, and that the Cheyennes had told him they would not go to the fort to get them but that he was not to take them away. Hearing this and thinking the agent and the property in his charge were in jeopardy, Sumner decided to proceed at once to Bent's Fort with the best of his cavalry. He believed he could at least protect the agent and property and defend the road from attacks by hostile Indians. With luck he might find the Cheyennes in the vicinity and deliver them another blow. Accordingly he dispatched another express rider to Agent Miller, advising that he was marching to his relief and would arrive on August 18. The message reached Miller on August 15.[13]

At the time, the Expedition was in no condition to undertake rapid marches and still be prepared to engage a highly motivated and mobile enemy. Many men were sick from the effects of a limited diet, no shelter, and constant marching. A number of horses and mules were suffering from want of sufficient forage and were too weak for service; others had become lame. The infantry and the artillery detail were worn down and unable to keep up with the cavalry. Sumner therefore directed Captain Ketchum to take his two companies of the Sixth Infantry, the artillery, and those cavalrymen who were not fit (the latter under the command of 1st Lt. David S. Stanley), along with the disabled horses and mules, and proceed by easy marches to Walnut Creek, there to camp and await the return of the rest of the command. This they did, going into camp a mile below the mouth of Walnut Creek.[14]

While the expedition, minus the unfit and those afoot, was preparing to march west, the express rider selected by Colonel Sumner, "Big Nick" Beery, had left camp heading east to Fort Leavenworth. Beery took with him Sumner's August 9, 1857, report of the fight on the Solomon.* He first went to Fort Riley to see if there were supplies available that could be sent to the camp on Walnut Creek, thus saving valuable time. Finding none, he procured a fresh horse and set out for Fort Leavenworth. Beery rode his horse

---

*Sumner's report of August 9, 1857, pointed out that no Cheyenne women or children had been killed in the course of the expedition, an obvious reference to the record of the Sioux Expedition of 1855 and to General Harney, with whom he had a long-standing feud. Sumner, in turn, was criticized by Harney and other military leaders for having ordered the famous sabre charge when the use of firearms would have killed far more Indians.

the 130 miles in twenty-four hours, causing the exhausted animal to drop dead at Salt Creek, three miles short of the fort. He hiked the last three miles carrying saddle and bridle. Once there he hastily secured available supplies, loaded them into a new train of wagons, and headed back for Walnut Creek. They arrived on September 1, bringing needed rations and forage, but only a scant amount of clothing and blankets.[15]

The six companies of the First Cavalry, now at reduced strength, left camp six miles below Fort Atkinson on August 12 and marched to a point two miles below the lower Middle Crossing of the Arkansas.* En route they met the eastbound mail from Santa Fe five or six miles west of Fort Atkinson. The mail party told them Kiowa warriors had killed the driver of Lt. Col. Joseph E. Johnston's private ambulance on July 30, while the survey expedition was working along the Cimarron valley. They also reported four or five American merchant trains eastbound near the Middle Crossing of the Arkansas. Two or three of these trains came into sight just before the marching column made camp, and Lieutenants Wheaton and McIntyre rode ahead to purchase provisions from them. They were successful in buying 1,100 pounds of flour and a little salt and coffee from a Mexican train. Thinking the supplies too scant to divide meaningfully among the entire command, McIntyre first proposed to assign them entirely to the officers' mess. Colonel Sumner, discovering McIntyre's intentions, grew angry and ordered the supplies divided equally between officers and enlisted men. "I don't propose to feast while my men are starving," he stated, "and I don't intend that any officer in my command shall do so." McIntyre quickly rectified his mistake.[16]

On August 13 the column marched about twenty-four miles and made camp five or six miles west of the upper Point of Rocks.* Nine or ten miles above the lower Middle Crossing of the Arkansas, they found the trail of a large body of Indians who had crossed the Santa Fe Trail with many lodgepoles and horses. These were the Cheyennes who had moved to Crooked Creek to camp with the Kiowas and Comanches following the battle on the Solomon.[17]

---

*The camp two miles below the lower Middle Crossing was approximately two miles east of present Cimarron, Kansas.
†The camp west of the Upper Point of Rocks was about three miles west-northwest of present Pierceville, Kansas.

The command marched nineteen miles on August 14. En route they met two Mexican traders who told them that a small Comanche village was on the south side of the Arkansas a few miles beyond, and that about ten Cheyennes were with them. The traders said there were no Indians at Bent's New Fort, but that Agent Miller had all the Cheyenne presents there, with plenty of sugar, coffee, and flour. Captain Beall, commander of A Company, rode out to reconnoiter the Comanche camp during the afternoon, thinking of attacking it during the evening or at first light to flush out the Cheyennes.[18]

On August 15 the command left camp at 7:00 A.M. Companies A and G crossed the river and marched along the south bank parallel with the other four companies. Those on the north bank, not having the delay of crossing the river, were abreast of the Comanche village first after going only four or five miles. The Cheyennes had left; those remaining were all Comanches, perhaps twenty-five or thirty men and thirty or forty women. Five or six of the warriors—tall, stalwart, handsome fellows mounted on magnificent horses—crossed the river to talk. When they observed the other two companies moving along the opposite side of the river, they dashed back to their camp, very frightened, ready for either fight or flight. After a brief search the column moved on, leaving the Comanches to themselves. A and G Companies recrossed to the north bank, and the command then continued down the trail, going into camp across from Chouteau's Island just beyond Indian Mound. They had traveled twenty miles, and it was midafternoon when they arrived. The rigors of the trip were beginning to tell on the horses. Even though they had enjoyed excellent grazing since reaching the Arkansas, many were beginning to break down, as were a number of the remaining steers.[19]

Just after reveille on August 16, several Arapahoes came into camp to talk. The parley completed, the column continued its march along the trail to Bent's Fort. When they had gone eight or ten miles, another group of Arapahoes crossed to the north side of the river to talk, apparently to satisfy themselves that the military had no intention of attacking them. After traveling twenty-two miles, they went back into camp.* By then there was more sick-

---

*The camp for the night of the sixteenth would have been immediately south of the townsite of present Syracuse, Kansas, along the river.

ness among the men and more horses were disabled. Because dysentery and cramps were common, as was scurvy, Colonel Sumner decided that he should leave A, E, and H Companies encamped at that site to look after the ill and the lame.[20]

On August 17, Colonel Sumner, with Companies B, D, and G, left camp at 7:00 A.M. intending to complete the journey to Bent's New Fort by the eighteenth, although they still were nearly fifty-five miles away. The pack mules went with him to transport food and other materials he intended to confiscate. That evening he was in camp twenty-five miles below the fort, and by late afternoon of the eighteenth he had made camp along the river just east of it.[21] Upon arrival he conferred with Agent Miller to determine what government property was in his custody. After receiving Miller's report on the annuity goods and what he knew of the whereabouts of the Cheyennes, Sumner drew a written order, dated August 19, directing him to turn all subsistence stores over to Lieutenant Wheaton, the commissary officer, and to destroy all ammunition. He further directed Miller to load all guns and as much of the annuity goods as the quartermaster could transport on wagons and to take them out of the country to Fort Leavenworth. The balance Miller was free to distribute, as an advance on the succeeding year's annuities, among those Indians he deemed worthy. Finally, because Sumner had no authority to leave troops behind for his protection, Miller was ordered to accompany the command back to Leavenworth.[22]

Agent Miller had been in a precarious position until the arrival of the First Cavalry troops, and he knew it well. Upon receipt of the written order from Colonel Sumner, which was a formality for the protection of each, Miller promptly complied. All sugar, rice, coffee, hard bread, and flour were turned over to the quartermaster, and the powder, lead, and flints were thrown into the Arkansas. A few Arapahoes had arrived in the vicinity, and to these Miller gave all remaining goods, except what could be transported in two wagons. These he intended giving to any Arapahoes they might meet on the road.[23]

Sedgwick's Brush with the Plains Apaches

Following departure of Sumner and the other three companies, Major Sedgwick and Companies A, E, and H continued camping at the same location, tending the sick and letting the animals graze and rest. In midmorning of the seventeenth, rain began falling lightly, making conditions disagreeable and turning the trail into a muddy trace. Many officers and men were suffering from dysentery; without tents, their only shelter was that provided by their oil-cloths. It was a miserable scene.

On the morning of the eighteenth, the camp was moved upriver a few hundred yards to provide sufficient grass for the animals. The rain had passed, making everyone feel somewhat better. At noon an express rider from Bent's New Fort stopped briefly, reporting he had passed Colonel Sumner and his troops that morning just leaving camp twenty-five miles east of the fort. August 19 brought more pleasant weather, less intense heat, and no rain. With the opportunity for leisurely and extended grazing, the condition of the horses, mules, and steers was improving. The companies therefore remained there that day and on the twentieth. [24]

Because the area around their current camp was by then over-grazed, Major Sedgwick ordered another move on the morning of August 21. This time they moved only one and a half miles downstream. As the line of companies turned the bend of the river, the men suddenly saw a large body of Indians on the south bank moving westward. There seemed to be 300 or 400—warriors, women, and children—driving or leading pack animals with their camp equipment. They were strung out downriver as far as the troopers could see, moving their camp westward, away from the buffalo range. Some thought they were Apaches, others Comanches. It is unlikely that these Indians had any intent to cause trouble, their families and worldly possessions being so close at hand. The troopers, however—150 strong and with only half their weapons in good working order—were highly nervous and suspicious. The Indians, no doubt equally alarmed at finding a large force of troops so close to their wives and children, sent runners back to hurry up stragglers and put the women and children to work moving the pack animals on up the river as rapidly as possible. At the same time, warriors were gathering opposite the troops, and several could be seen riding back and forth on top of the sandhills on the south bank, watching the cavalry and giving the appearance of holding a council of war. [25]

Major Sedgwick halted the column as soon as the Indians on the opposite bank were noticed. For a time everyone sat motionless on his mount, watching their movements. Then the major called an officers' conference, and they gathered around him, sometimes observing the Indians through their field glasses. Although Sedgwick had been on the plains for some three months, his understanding of Indians and of warfare against them was limited, and he seemed indecisive about what to do next. After more warriors had come up to lend support, some of them started crossing the river and rode boldly up to the major, saying their usual "How, How" and making a pretense of friendship.

Finally, so many had crossed that the officers and men were alarmed. Captain Sturgis, exasperated by the delay, told Sedgwick he should do something or there could be "an unfortunate fight." Not knowing what should be done, Sedgwick turned command over to Sturgis at the latter's urging. Quickly issuing orders, the captain called for the interpreter and had the officers return to their posts and quietly prepare their men for action. That done, he gave the command "Prepare to dismount and fight on foot!" In that movement every fourth man remained mounted and took the reins of the other three of his set of four, to retain control of their horses. At the command "Dismount! Form ranks!" the other three troopers dismounted and formed ranks, drawn up in a line of companies and ready for action.

Sturgis next directed the interpreter to tell the Indians to get back across the river, that if any remained on the north side after five minutes, they would be killed. When the words were translated, the ultimatum caused a visible ripple of excitement. Casting anxious glances across the river, they appeared hesitant as to what to do until their chief gave a clear command. Backing away, the warriors looked sullen and grim. When they reached the bank of the river, they wheeled and rushed splashing across to the other bank, anxious to be out of rifle range. After the Indians had cleared the north bank, the men again mounted and formed into line, then moved on to their evening's camp. An extra-strong guard was mounted to protect against a night attack or a livestock raid, but fortunately nothing happened. Before sundown, one mounted warrior was observed on top of a sandhill on the opposite side of the river a mile off. He stayed there watching the cavalry camp for about fifteen minutes, then disappeared. The rest of the night passed without incident.[26]

On August 28, 1857, the worn troopers of Sumner's command passed the ruins of old Fort Atkinson while en route to Walnut Creek. The expedition was about to enter its final phase.

Return to Walnut Creek

On August 20, Sumner and his three companies, accompanied by Agent Miller, started back down the trail. The column moved slowly because some of the wagons were pulled by oxen. Early on August 22 the oxen pulling the two wagons filled with annuity goods gave out. There had been rain during the night and the wagons soon became mired to the axletrees. Attempting to move them, the poor beasts were quickly overcome with exhaustion. There seemed no alternative to abandoning the wagons, but at just that time a band of Plains Apaches appeared moving westward along the south side of the river. Miller sent for their chiefs and delivered to them all the goods except the guns. These he kept, and eventually they were taken to Fort Leavenworth and stored. As he distributed the goods to the Apaches, Miller gave them to understand that

the presents had been intended for the Cheyennes but were being withheld from them as punishment for violations of their treaty. They were being given to the Apaches, he stated, as a reward for their good behavior. Ironically, this must have been the same band of Plains Apaches that Sedgwick and his men had found threatening the previous day.[27]

A little before 10:00 A.M. on August 22, Captain Beall, Lieutenant Wheaton, and Agent Miller arrived in Sedgwick's camp in advance of Colonel Sumner's column, delivering orders from him to move the camp downriver a few hundred yards to better grass. The colonel and the other three companies, along with twenty-three wagons and two ambulances, reached the camp at noon. With them they brought an ample supply of flour, sugar, coffee, blankets, shirts, and hardware for the messes.[28]

Once more reunited, the six companies of cavalry and their new

wagon train of supplies broke camp at 7:00 A.M. on the morning of
August 23, bound for Walnut Creek. The day continued rainy and
cool, and problems with the slow ox-drawn wagons so disgusted
Colonel Sumner that he placed them at the front of the column,
vowing to keep them there until they were completely out of Cheyenne country. By the twenty-sixth they had gone into camp just
below the upper Point of Rocks. During the day, smoke thought to
be from signal fires was seen in different directions, and near sunset some of the men saw Indians in the hills. They feared there
might be an attempt to stampede their livestock, but nothing
happened.[29]

On August 27 the command camped three miles below the lower
Middle Crossing; the following day, eight miles below the ruins of
Fort Atkinson. They made another sixteen miles on August 29, and
seventeen miles on the thirtieth, camping next to the river about a
mile and a half from the Santa Fe road. On the thirtieth they passed
a Majors and Russell train of thirty wagons on its way with supplies
for Colonel Johnston's survey party, and a smaller, fourteen-wagon
train bound for New Mexico. From the two trains they heard news
of the army bound for Utah to fight the Mormons, along with disquieting news that some troops from the Cheyenne Expedition
would go to Utah as well. An express rider with orders for them
was said to be awaiting their arrival at Walnut Creek.[30]

With no rain and good weather the column moved faster now,
reaching Coon Creek on August 31, and Pawnee Rock on September 1. Finally, on Wednesday, September 2, they went into camp
a mile below the mouth of Walnut Creek, next to the camp of the
two infantry companies. First Lt. David S. Stanley rode out to meet
them when they were still ten miles from Walnut Creek, bringing
them mail and news. What he said was not what they wanted to
hear. Four companies of cavalry and the two infantry companies at
Walnut Creek, plus the third company of infantry now at Fort
Kearny, were ordered to Utah. The Cheyenne Expedition was to be
broken up.[31]

17

The Wagon Train's Return

*What screaming thunder when the pack-mules
      brayed
And all the six-mule wagon teams replied!
The popping of the whips on sweaty hide,
How like a battle when the foe is bold!*   (165)

A Long Wait

The morning of August 9 saw one of Chiles's ox trains passing the wagon train's camp on its way back to the States. The following day, Lowe moved the train across the South Platte, its flow greatly reduced by the heat of summer. They went into a new camp five miles below Lower California Crossing, a mile east of their June 13 and 14 camp. Lieutenant Riddick requisitioned 211 sacks of corn from a passing Majors and Russell train in the belief that Sumner and his troopers would soon arrive with many horses and mules in need of nourishment. The following morning, August 11, a band of Sioux under "Man-Afraid-of-His-Horses" crossed from the north to the south side of the river. The teamsters hastily corralled their mules, by this time trained to make for the enclosure at the ringing of a bell, heading for it at a gallop from their grazing grounds. Only the chief was allowed to come to the camp, and he was told to prevent his men from approaching the mule herd. The Sioux soon left, and the mules were again turned out to graze.

At noon on the eleventh, Col. Wm. M. F. Magraw and his survey party, en route to California, arrived and went into camp nearby.

With him were Tim Goodale, the mountaineer, and Capt. Edward Johnson, commanding officer of Company D, Sixth Infantry, on detached duty with the survey party. Colonel Magraw and his men crossed to the north side of the river on the twelfth, with assistance and guidance from Lowe. During the two nights they were in the vicinity, Colonel Magraw, Goodale, and Captain Johnson dined with Lieutenant Riddick and Lowe, passing on news and speculating on the whereabouts of Colonel Sumner and the Cheyennes. They departed for Ash Hollow on August 13, using Lowe's new route avoiding Windlass Hill.

On the evening of August 14, while pursuing an errant mule, Lowe and two of his men found Capt. Stewart Van Vliet, assistant quartermaster of the Utah Expedition, camped at Nine Mile Tree. Although he knew nothing of Sumner's whereabouts, Van Vliet did impart the news that four of the six companies of cavalry with the Cheyenne Expedition, along with the three companies of infantry, were to go to Utah, and that Colonel Sumner and the other two cavalry companies were to return to Fort Leavenworth. Van Vliet and his men departed on the morning of the fifteenth, crossing the South Platte with the assistance of Lowe. On the sixteenth the train remained in camp with little to break the boredom, but on the seventeenth, "Big Phil" once again arrived from Fort Laramie with mail. There was still no news of Sumner and his men. From then until the twenty-first the wait once again lapsed into monotony.

During the day on August 21 a welcome break in the quiet occurred. Lieutenant Col. Edmund B. Alexander arrived with troops of the Tenth Infantry en route to Utah, and Lowe used his expertise to help them cross the river. Then came a Mr. Andrew Gartin and son, beef contractors from Clay County, Missouri, driving a large herd to Fort Laramie under the escort of the Tenth Infantry. Finally came Lt. Francis T. Bryan and his survey party on their return trip to Fort Leavenworth from Bridger's Pass, and they made camp nearby.

The morning of the twenty-second, Colonel Alexander and his troops marched for Utah, and Lieutenant Bryan's party departed for Leavenworth. Later in the day, Capt. John H. Dickerson, quartermaster of the Utah Expedition, and Capt. Henry F. Clarke, commissary, arrived and crossed to the north side of the river on their way to Utah. They brought news that Colonel Sumner had fought the Cheyennes July 29 on Solomon's Fork, charging a large body of warriors in battle array with drawn sabres. They reported twelve Indians killed and many wounded, while two cavalrymen were killed and Lieutenant Stuart and eight enlisted men wounded. Captain Foote and his infantry company were taking the wounded to Fort Kearny. Colonel Sumner and his troops were known to have found and burned the main Cheyenne village and were following the Indians to the Arkansas. This news made Lieutenant Riddick and Lowe doubt that Sumner would be coming for them; consequently, for sanitary reasons, they moved their camp five miles upriver.

On August 24 and 25 the Fifth Infantry arrived on its way to Utah, crossing the South Platte and marching toward Fort Laramie. After that, there was nothing but the interminable wait until August 28. On that day an express arrived from Fort Kearny bringing letters from Captain Foote and Lieutenant Stuart to Lieutenant Riddick, and orders from Colonel Sumner to Lieutenant Riddick for the train to move out immediately for Fort Kearny. There they were ordered to turn in all unnecessary stores and to proceed to Fort Leavenworth. At last the monotonous wait was at an end. [1]

Homeward Bound

On the morning of August 29 the supply train began moving eastward toward Fort Kearny. They had gone only nine miles when they were met by an express rider bearing orders from General Harney at Fort Leavenworth, directing the train to proceed to Ash Hollow and remain in camp there pending arrival of the four companies of the First Cavalry and the three companies of the Sixth Infantry ordered to Utah. Because the order presupposed that the train was at Kearny, however, and because Lieutenant Riddick was directed to draw supplies from that post sufficient to meet the needs of the command until they reached Fort Laramie, Riddick determined to continue on, procure the supplies, and then, unless the orders were changed, return to Ash Hollow.

The afternoon of August 29 found the train camped at Nine Mile Tree. By the thirty-first it had gone into camp below O'Fallon's Bluff at Fremont Springs. As they were coming into camp that day, the soldiers encountered a Cheyenne warrior, with two women and a packhorse dragging a lodge and lodgepoles, preparing to cross the Platte to the north side. Frightened by the troops, the three abandoned their possessions in midstream and ran.

During their march on September 1, Riddick, Lowe, and their men met Captain Foote, Lieutenant McCleary, and the men of C Company, Sixth Infantry, probably at Cold Springs. With them came Dr. Edward N. Covey, who was now ordered to stay with the train until it was joined by Sedgwick's command bound for Utah.* By September 7 the train had reached Fort Kearny. The two Indian prisoners were turned over to the commanding officer, and necessary supplies were drawn for a journey to Utah. The loading was completed on the eighth, and on September 9 the train once again started for the crossing of the South Platte. That night they camped seventeen miles above the fort. During the afternoon, Lowe and Dr. Covey went on a buffalo hunt and were joined by Dr. Summers, post surgeon at Kearny, and John Heth, post sutler.

The movement back to the South Platte continued from September 10 through 13. On the thirteenth, while they were camped near Fremont Springs, one mile below O'Fallon's Bluff, an express rider from Fort Kearny arrived with orders from Colonel Sumner directing the train to remain at that post pending the arrival of Major Sedgwick and his four cavalry and two infantry companies. The return to Fort Kearny began the following morning, and they moved steadily until the seventeenth. On the sixteenth they met an express rider, George Cater, en route from Fort Kearny to Fort Laramie with dispatches and mail. He dropped off letters advising Lieutenant Riddick that all cavalry and infantry units detached from the Cheyenne Expedition for service in Utah were now ordered back to Fort Leavenworth.

On the seventeenth the train again went into camp on the Platte, one day's march short of Fort Kearny. During the afternoon, Lt. John S. Marmaduke and a detachment of recruits from the Seventh

---

*Lowe states that Dr. Covey arrived with Lieutenant Bryan's party on August 21, but this is impossible. Dr. Covey was not with Lieutenant Bryan, but was with the Cheyenne Expedition, originally attached to Sedgwick's column and then, following the battle, staying at Fort Floyd to attend the wounded. He accompanied Foote's Company C to Fort Kearny, arriving at that point on the morning of August 21. In accordance with orders, after he had seen to the needs of the First Cavalry wounded, he would have accompanied Foote and his men westward along the trail to Fort Laramie until they met the Expedition's wagon train.

Infantry bound for Fort Laramie arrived and camped with them. The morning of September 18 brought rain, forcing the train to lay by. In the afternoon, Marmaduke joined Lowe on a buffalo hunt. The two parties bade farewell on the morning of the nineteenth, Marmaduke and his men heading west and the train continuing east to Fort Kearny. Before leaving camp, however, Lowe gave Lieutenant Marmaduke two good wagons with fine teams in exchange for two dilapidated wagons, each drawn by six broken-down pack mules. It was a grateful Marmaduke who proceeded west.

On the road back to Kearny the train was met by "Sim" Routh and Sarcoxie, one of Major Sedgwick's Delaware guides, with letters from Major Sedgwick advising that he and his command were waiting for them thirty-two miles below Fort Kearny. They arrived at Kearny midday and camped at the edge of the post. Lieutenants Wheaton and Bayard met them there with orders for Lieutenant Riddick to turn the train and all of its property over to Wheaton. Except for the return trip to Leavenworth, the adventures of the Cheyenne Expedition were at an end for Lieutenant Riddick, Lowe, and his hardy crew of teamsters.[2]

18

The Expedition Ends

The fight was done;
No victory to boast about, indeed—
Just labor. Sweat today, tomorrow, bleed—
An incidental difference. And when
The jaded troopers trotted home again
There wasn't any cheering.   *(70)*

The Breakup of Sumner's Command

When the cavalry column arrived in camp on Walnut Creek on September 2, the express rider sent from Fort Leavenworth was waiting to deliver orders from the adjutant general to Colonel Sumner. These directed him to break up the Cheyenne Expedition, and from the six cavalry companies to make up four full companies. These, along with the three companies of the Sixth Infantry, were to be sent to Fort Laramie under the command of Major Sedgwick as part of the Utah Expedition, there to await orders from General Harney. Colonel Sumner and the remaining two cavalry companies were ordered to return to Fort Leavenworth.[1]

Sumner lost no time implementing the order, notwithstanding his personal disappointment. The same day he designated Companies A, B, E, and G as those to become a part of the Utah or Mormon expedition. Lieutenant Wheaton was appointed adjutant and quartermaster for Major Sedgwick, and Lieutenants McIntyre and Lomax were made quartermaster and adjutant respectively for Colonel Sumner's remaining command. Because they were returning to Fort Leavenworth, Companies D and H were directed to turn over their best horses, arms, and equipment to the four cavalry companies going to Utah. To make them as complete as possible, the Utah companies also were given what they needed of the supplies and clothing brought back from Leavenworth.[2]

The news was disheartening for the men in the four cavalry and two infantry companies affected. They had now been in the field away from family and friends three and one-half months, and the new orders seemed to make prospects poor for seeing them before another two or three years had elapsed. Even the best horses were near a broken-down condition, and the men were suffering from scurvy and various other ailments resulting from malnutrition, bad water, and hard marching. But soldiers are expected to obey orders without questioning their wisdom, and the men of the First Cavalry did so, albeit with the usual grumbling.[3]

Arrival at Walnut Creek brought other news. Private Garber, the soldier lost around the upper reaches of Saw Log Creek on August 7, had been found. When lost he had been fully equipped with horse, saddle and bridle, carbine, Colt's navy revolver, and sabre. When found he had only his hat, shirt, drawers, and shoes, with his pistol slung at his side by a saddle strap. He had thrown away all his other equipment and ammunition. Evidently he had followed the line of the stream eastward hoping to find the Santa Fe Trail, but without food and in the intense heat of midsummer on the plains, he had "gone loco." He was found by the eastbound mail coach from Santa Fe seven days after he became lost. The men on the coach spotted him running about aimlessly several miles west of the road, and they drove over to find out what kind of creature he was. When they got close they found he was catching grasshoppers, which were in great numbers, then stuffing them into his mouth and eating them voraciously. He paid little attention to them as they drew near, continuing to catch and eat the hoppers. The men put him in the coach and took him to Allison and Booth's Ranch at Walnut Creek. After a few days of good food he recovered, and following arrival of the infantry and cavalry sick, he went into camp with them. When his own outfit, B Company, returned on September 2, he rejoined it and prepared for the march for Utah.[4]

On September 3 the command remained in camp, preparing for the new assignments. Word had been awaiting Captain Sturgis that two of his three children were very sick, and he was granted a short leave to return to Fort Leavenworth to see his family. He left in an ambulance that day with Agent Miller. While preparations were progressing for breakup of the command, Colonel Sumner sent a letter to army headquarters, in New York, acknowledging receipt of the order and expressing his regret that the matter could not have been finished. He reported the Cheyennes more hostile than ever and stated his belief that another severe blow would be required to make them sue for peace.[5]

On the morning of September 4 the command moved downriver about a mile to secure a good stand of grass for the horses and mules. Except for the move, all personnel remained in camp that day. On September 5 they were busy with final preparations, exchanging arms and accouterments and generally doing everything necessary to equip the four cavalry companies for the trip north to Fort Kearny and then on to Utah. When the exchange of horses had been completed, Companies D and H had only eight or ten viable horses left in each. The balance of the troopers, now mounted on mules, good-naturedly received the title of the "Light Mules."[6]

The March of Sedgwick's Command

September 6, 1857, was departure day from the camp at Walnut Creek. The two infantry companies left at 7:00 A.M. and started their slow march north and east, camping that afternoon on Cow Creek about fourteen miles distant. At the same time the six cavalry companies were drawn up in a line and old "Bull of the Woods" rode out in front to deliver a parting word to the men who had served him so well and so faithfully during the expedition. "My men," he said in his deep stentorian voice, which could be heard all along the line, "you have now made a march of near 1,800 miles. You have not only undergone privations and dangers, including even the want of rations, but you have done it willingly and cheerfully and in a manner that does honor to yourselves and to your Colonel and he is grateful for it. One word more. I part from you with great unwillingness and will do my utmost to bring you back to the Regimental Headquarters as soon as it is possible to do so. Farewell." With that he turned and moved eastward along the Santa Fe Trail at the head of his two remaining cavalry companies, their small train, the remuda of broken-down horses and mules, and about fifteen steers. For Companies D and H the march home had begun.[7]

As Colonel Sumner and his companies moved eastward, the four companies under Major Sedgwick headed north-northeast. Following the trail of the infantry, they camped on Cow Creek the night of September 6. Arcing slightly to the northeast, Sedgwick's command marched to the Oregon-California Trail, reaching it shortly after crossing the Little Blue, on September 14.[8] After striking the trail, probably at Oak Grove, the column turned to the northwest and Fort Kearny. While on the road, on September 15, they received word that orders awaited them at Fort Kearny cancelling the previous orders for Utah and directing them to return to Fort Leavenworth. Nonetheless, Sedgwick continued toward Kearny until the seventeenth, when he put his troops into camp thirty-two miles below the fort. There was no good reason for the cavalry and infantry companies to go on in, only to turn about and march back over the same country. But it was necessary to secure the orders and, more important, to bring down the expedition's wagon train, in which were the tents, clothing, and other gear the troops had left behind when they departed the South Platte. Accordingly, Sedgwick ordered Lieutenant Wheaton, acting quartermaster of his command, to proceed to the fort and bring back the train.[9]

Wheaton left the camp, probably the morning of September 18, and arrived at Kearny that afternoon. The indefatigable Lieutenant Bayard, expressing a desire to see the fort, accompanied him. They took with them "Sim" Routh, the teamster who had been with Lowe's wagon train and later with the packtrain, and Sarcoxie, one of the Delaware scouts. When they reached Fort Kearny, they found the wagon train had not yet returned. On the morning of the nineteenth they dispatched Routh and Sarcoxie west along the trail to find Lieutenant Riddick, Lowe, and the train and to deliver letters telling them Sedgwick was waiting thirty-two miles below Kearny. They met the train midmorning and it pulled into Fort Kearny in early afternoon. When they reached the post, Lieutenant Wheaton presented orders from Major Sedgwick to Lieutenant Riddick, directing him to turn the train and all other property over to Wheaton. The remainder of the afternoon was spent unloading and delivering to the commissary officer of Fort Kearny all stores not necessary for troops returning to Fort Leavenworth.[10]

The unloading of extra commissary supplies was completed on

the morning of September 20, and the train, accompanied by Lieutenants Wheaton and Bayard, left Kearny at noon. On the twenty-first they reached Thirty-Two-Mile Creek and joined Sedgwick and his men, delivering the new orders to him. These were brief and to the point. Sedgwick's command was to return to Fort Leavenworth. With the orders received, the unified column of infantry, cavalry, and supply train continued on a few miles, camping on the Little Blue. On the morning of the twenty-second, four wagons and teams were turned over to Captain Ketchum for use by the two infantry companies, and the command proceeded down the trail, again camping on the Little Blue.[11]

While leaving camp on the morning of the twenty-third, the column met Col. Albert Sidney Johnston of the Second Cavalry, commander of the Utah Expedition, his adjutant, Maj. Fitz John Porter, their train of twenty four-mule ambulances, several officers, and an escort of the Second Dragoons. Johnston and his party were headed for Utah, where he was to assume control of the army's efforts to put down the Mormon rebellion. Watching the teams and wagons pass by, Johnston called for Percival Lowe, the wagon master, and told him that he had heard that the train of the Cheyenne Expedition was the finest on the plains. Lowe advised him that, except for a few good teams exchanged to Lieutenant Marmaduke for broken-down ones, the teams and equipment were complete. Johnston issued orders to Lowe to select twenty-five of his best mule teams for service in Utah. These were to be left with a small cavalry escort to await the arrival of Lt. Col. Philip St. George Cooke and his six troops of the Second Dragoons, some days behind on the trail. Sedgwick's command proceeded on another eighteen miles and again went into camp on the Little Blue. That afternoon, Lowe caused twenty-five wagons to be unloaded and the property repacked in the remaining wagons of the Cheyenne Expedition. He selected the best teams and equipment, obtained volunteers to drive them back to Utah, and drew rations for those men. All were now ready to be turned over the following day.[12]

On the morning of September 24 the twenty-five wagons selected for delivery to Colonel Cooke's command were turned over to 1st Lt. John N. Perkins, in charge of the cavalry detail, along with two wagons for their own use. Mr. Patrick remained as wagon master for the train, with Billy Daniels as assistant wagon master. Perkins was ordered to remain with the wagons awaiting arrival of Colonel

Cooke and his troops, which occurred on October 1. Major Sedgwick's column then continued down the trail for Fort Leavenworth,
camping that afternoon along the Little Blue. By the twenty-sixth
they had gone into camp on Snake Root Creek (Horseshoe Creek).
   During the evening of September 26 an express rider arrived
from Fort Leavenworth bringing new orders. Sedgwick's command
was to be broken up and temporarily stationed at various border
settlements in extreme northeast Kansas Territory to ensure that no
violence attended forthcoming elections. The two infantry companies were to camp on the Big Blue at Marysville-Palmetto until
after the elections, which were scheduled for the first Monday in
October. Company A, First Cavalry, was to go to Claytonville in
Brown County, Company B to Palermo in Donovan County, Company E to Atchison, county seat of Atchison County, and Company
G to Richmond, then the county seat of Nemaha County. Palermo,
a small village and landing point on the Missouri River, was free-
state in sympathy. The other towns were then strongly pro-slavery
in sentiment, inviting trouble with the more fanatic abolitionist
"border ruffians." News of this assignment was discouraging to the
troopers, worn from the rigors of a long and hard campaign. But at
least it did not mean as long an absence from Fort Leavenworth as
would an expedition to Utah. [13]
   Nine and one-half miles west of Marysville the Fort Leavenworth–Fort Kearny Road separated from the main branch of the
Oregon-California Trail, which continued to the southeast. Proceeding along the road to Leavenworth, Sedgwick's troops met Colonel Cooke and his Dragoons three miles west of the Big Blue.
First Lt. John Buford, regimental quartermaster of the Second Dragoons, had orders to change all the mules he needed, taking the
best remaining of the Cheyenne Expedition's teams and leaving his
worst. This he did, and the last of the "best train on the plains"
was gone. That afternoon, September 27, the column crossed the
Big Blue, going into camp on Spring Creek five miles east of
Palmetto. [14]
   Beyond Spring Creek the road divided, the older branch turning
north and then east, leading to St. Joseph, Missouri, Atchison, and
Fort Leavenworth. The south branch represented the new military
road surveyed in 1854 upon orders of Colonel Sumner. Because of
the new assignment, the four cavalry companies and supply train
took the old road on the morning of September 28, camping that

afternoon at Ash Point, where the road to St. Joseph split from that
to Atchison and Fort Leavenworth. Following the lower road, the
command moved to Seneca and camped on the south fork of the
Nemaha River on the twenty-ninth. The morning of the thirtieth
the companies split up, G Company moving north along the Nemaha to Richmond, the other three continuing down the road until
leaving it for their respective destinations. Major Sedgwick went
on to Atchison with E Company, whose mess facilities he had
shared during the campaign.[15]

On October 4, Lieutenants Wheaton and Riddick, with Percival
Lowe and the wagon train, arrived at Leavenworth and turned in
the remaining wagons, mules, and other property charged to the
Expedition. The two officers and Lowe made their reports to Colonel Sumner, who was most complimentary on the manner in which
they had discharged their duties. A few days later, with the elections over, the two infantry companies and four companies of
cavalry under Major Sedgwick's command arrived at Fort Leavenworth, completing their official duties with the Cheyenne Expedition. The only difficulty they had experienced during the election
was an incident on election day, when some drunken abolitionists
had induced several soldiers from G Company to break into the
home of Mr. Cy Dolman, the pro-slavery Democratic representative
from Nemaha County, and rough up both Dolman and his clerk,
Joseph A. Brown, originally from South Carolina. A message from
Dolman to Lieutenant Bayard brought the young officer to his rescue, and the matter was resolved without bloodshed.[16]

Colonel Sumner's Return to Fort Leavenworth

When Colonel Sumner and his two companies of cavalry left the
camp near Walnut Creek on September 6, they marched steadily
eastward, reaching the Little Arkansas and going into camp on the
afternoon of September 7. They were in buffalo country now, and
each afternoon after making camp the officers went on a hunt to
secure fresh buffalo meat and provide a little variety in the troopers' diet. Because Colonel Sumner was considering going in ahead
of the troops, he placed Captain Newby in command of the two
companies. Lieutenant Long succeeded to command of Company
H, Lieutenant McIntyre being too busy with his duties as quartermaster to undertake the added burden. On September 8 they broke

camp and marched to a branch of Turkey Creek about three miles east of Big Turkey. It was a small stream with good grass but very bad water, the result of heavy fouling by the great herds of buffalo. During the afternoon the men tried hunting the shaggy beasts with their howitzers, firing ten or twelve shots with grape, cannister shells, and spherical case, but they were too inaccurate and put no meat on the table. First Lt. David S. Stanley, needing to get back to regimental headquarters sooner than travel with the command would permit, left that evening with a Sergeant Madden. They made the trip of more than two hundred miles in three days, alternately riding three hours and resting one, and using two horses per man. [17]

Sumner's command made another twenty-five miles on September 9 and camped on the Cottonwood. An expressman passed the camp in the afternoon on his way east to meet William Allison, who was then returning to the trading post on Walnut Creek after purchasing supplies in St. Louis. The news carried by the expressman was that Francis Booth, Allison's partner, had been murdered on the night of September 6 by a Mexican employee with whom he had an argument. The man secured an ax, came back at night, and split Booth's head open while he was sleeping. [18]

On September 10, Sumner's men marched to Six-Mile Creek west of Diamond Springs. After watering at Lost Springs, two wagons in the small train parted from the rest, turning off at the Fort Riley military road a few miles east of Lost Springs. With them went about twenty infantrymen who had served as escort for the supply train that met the command on Walnut Creek. The train was now reduced to five wagons, two for each company and one for Colonel Sumner. In successive days they retraced the route of Sedgwick's column in May, camping at Big John Springs on September 11, Prairie Chicken Creek on September 12, and the Wakarusa, next to Brownsville, on the thirteenth. While at Big John Springs they bought corn, chickens, and buttermilk from the store at Council Grove, enjoying their first food of that kind in four months.

On the road fifteen miles west of Elm Creek, an express rider arrived bearing orders for the two companies to return to Fort Leavenworth as rapidly as possible, along with news that Sedgwick's command had been detached from the Utah Expedition and ordered back to the post. Because of the slow rate of march imposed by the wagons and steers, Lieutenant McIntyre, the acting quartermaster, was left with them at Elm Creek under orders to bring them in at fifteen miles per day. As the rest of the column moved ahead at a faster pace, they noted that, in the interval since May, a new town with three or four houses, Wilmington, had grown up at the junction of the Fort Leavenworth Road and the Santa Fe Trail. The bottomland along the rivers and streams in the area was rapidly being claimed by white settlers, and farming had begun.[19]

Monday, September 14, the column crossed the Kansas River and camped three miles east of Indianola on Indian Creek. Marching through Indianola, which had doubled in population since May, they met a column of infantry recruits with twenty or thirty officers and a good many ladies riding in ambulances. The new recruits drew up in a line and gave the rifle salute, which the cavalry returned by drawing sabres and giving the sabre salute as they passed.[20]

Sumner's command spent one more night on the road, probably making camp on Stranger Creek, and marched into Fort Leavenworth on the morning of September 16, 1857. Sumner wrote his final report of the expedition on September 20, and it was forwarded to the General-in-Chief of the Army, Winfield Scott. With the piecemeal return of Sedgwick's command some three weeks later, the Cheyenne Expedition passed into history.[21]

19

The First Cavalry's Wounded

Now when the work about the camp was done
And all the wounds had got rude handed care,
The Colonel called the men about him there. . . . (131)

Fort Floyd: Sod Refuge on the Solomon

Watching the six companies of the First Cavalry and Companies
D and G of the Sixth Infantry march southward on the morning of
July 31, 1857, must have given those remaining at Fort Floyd* a
tremendous sense of loneliness and insecurity. They were surrounded by the vastness of the plains, with a seemingly endless
sea of grass stretching beyond them in every direction. Rolling
hills, like waves in an ocean, were the only relief in this picture of
solitude, concealing even the periodic breaks and small streams
where only a thin trickle of water still showed on the sandy beds.
No trees, no green—just blue sky and brown buffalo grass met to
form the horizon. At the east end of the valley of the Solomon was
the scattering of cottonwoods beneath which the Cheyennes had
rested and waited for the soldiers, but from beyond the valley even
these could not be seen. Adding to the discomfort of those left
behind was the summer sun, by then having seared the native
vegetation to a bleached golden hue, as if to take back the promise
of life it brought in the spring. The heat bore down relentlessly,

---

*Fort Floyd doubtless was named for the then Secretary of War, John B. Floyd.

and the only shade was that made by stringing up blankets or oilcloths.

No game was in the vicinity of Fort Floyd, heat and poor grazing having driven the great herds of buffalo and antelope farther east or north. Each night brought forth great numbers of wolves and coyotes that howled in unseen chorus all around them. No doubt these predators, too, were suffering from the lack of game. Though it is unlikely the soldiers discussed it, their vulnerability must have been painfully apparent to them. With only two officers and sixty-eight enlisted men, three of whom were sick, Captain Foote's Company C could hope for little more than survival in the middle of hostile country. The eight wounded enlisted men of the First Cavalry were in no position to help; in fact, their condition made the plight of all more critical, for some could not be moved even if the need arose. Somewhere in the surrounding vastness, the Cheyennes may well have been waiting for an opportune moment to attack.[1]

Before Colonel Sumner left, he had given Captain Foote orders to proceed to the Lower California Crossing of the South Platte if the command had not returned by August 20. There he and his company were to meet the supply train, leave with it the wounded First Cavalry personnel and Dr. Covey, and proceed to Fort Laramie, their duty station. Sumner also left with Foote's small detachment two of the prairie howitzers and the now-abbreviated ambulance for use in moving the wounded, along with a number of pack mules and, as their share of the remaining rations, about a dozen beef cattle.[2]

Sumner's column broke camp and moved out at 6:30 A.M. on Friday, July 31. As soon as they had disappeared over the hills to the south, 2d Lt. John McCleary put his men back to work finishing the field fortification. It was completed at midday, with sod walls two feet thick standing five or six feet in height, and with bastions at the southeast and northwest corners. The northwest bastion was made into a combination hospital-blockhouse to provide security and shelter for the wounded and sick. This structure, about twenty-five feet square, projected on the north side, and its walls were somewhat higher than the rest of the fortification. The roof had a ridgepole in the center and one of the same size on either side. Smaller poles, probably lodgepoles found at an old Cheyenne village site near the east end of the valley, served as rafters. Willow

branches were used as sheathing, and these were covered, first by
a layer of grass from the banks of the stream and then by strips of
sod. Over the last was placed a coating of clay. Entrance to the
blockhouse was only from inside the walls of the fort proper. The
outer walls of the fortification measured approximately 80 feet by
120, sufficient to accommodate all men and animals.[3]

When the fort was complete, the wounded were moved to it from
the original hospital site south of the river. First Lt. J. E. B. Stuart,
in high spirits, was moved by litter to the former hospital tent-fly,
which was stretched a few paces outside the east wall near the
entrance. There he and Dr. Covey established their "ranch."
Stuart's bed was inclined so that he had a good view down the creek
for nearly two miles. Saturday, August 1, moved slowly, with nothing for the wounded to do, and for the fit little but keeping watch.
Stuart amused himself by reading his only written material—his
Anglican prayer book, his army regulations, and a few sheets of
Harper's Weekly. All wounded appeared to be doing well, although
those with dangerous injuries had to remain immobile and were
experiencing considerable pain and discomfort. When night fell, a
full moon bathed the land around them with "a veil of enchanting
beauty," obscuring the harshness and desolation so apparent by
day. As they enjoyed this peaceful scene, the calm and serenity
was suddenly shattered by the howls of a hundred wolves.[4]

On Sunday, August 2, Captain Foote held a short religious service in the morning, following which the routine and boredom of
the previous day repeated itself. A brief thunderstorm struck in
late afternoon, breaking the monotony, and the wolves resumed
their serenade after sundown. August 3 brought an unwelcome di-
version. As the little encampment basked in the relative cool of
the morning, two Cheyenne warriors rode out of the hills firing
weapons and attempting to stampede the livestock. A few mules
were lost, and for a while it looked as though Lieutenant Stuart's
two horses were gone also. However, Stuart sent out the two Mexican guides assigned to them, and they recovered the animals. The
wounded continued to make a remarkable recovery, and Dr. Covey
ventured the hope that even those with the most severe injuries
would survive.[5]

During the day on Tuesday, August 4, a number of passing Indians were spotted by the lookouts, but no attempt was made to
stampede the grazing livestock. Some speculated that they were

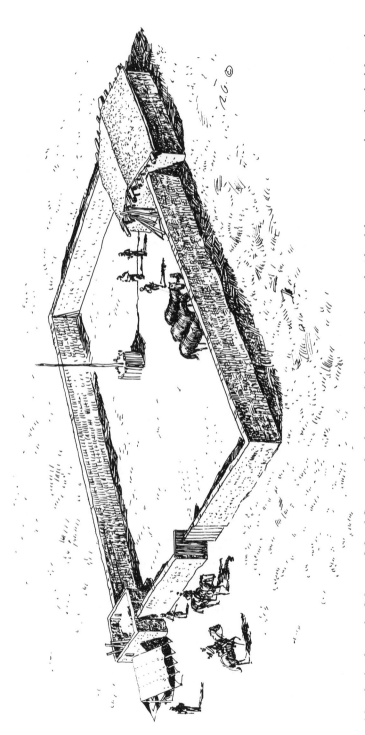

After the battle on the Solomon, Colonel Sumner ordered a sod redoubt built on the north side of the stream near where they had formed to make their famous sabre charge. Dubbed "Fort Floyd" in honor of the Secretary of War, it was garrisoned by Company C of the Sixth Infantry and served both as a hospital and as protection for the wounded of the First Cavalry until they recovered sufficiently to be moved. The former hospital tent-fly was erected at its southeast corner and was established by J. E. B. Stuart as his "ranch."

hunting parties unaware of the fight, but that seemed unlikely. Most probably they were stragglers moving north, scouts from a war party, or perhaps a burial party looking for their dead. Whatever they were, at about midnight the little fort was attacked without warning by a party of twenty or thirty Cheyennes. The guards quickly carried J. E. B. Stuart into the fort, and Lieutenant Mc-Cleary had the howitzers fire a "blizzard or two" into the night in the general direction of the war cries. The attack ended as suddenly as it had begun, with no damage or casualties on either side. Stuart was returned to his "ranch," where he spent the rest of the night undisturbed except by the usual serenade of the wolves.[6]

A little before daybreak on August 5, the alarm was again sounded and the troops turned out with their weapons ready for another Cheyenne attack. This time, however, the party of five Indians approaching the fort on foot and at a run could be heard yelling "Pawnee! Pawnee!" They proved to be the Pawnee scouts that Colonel Sumner had sent on August 3 with letters and dispatches for Captain Foote and Fort Kearny. They had been attacked an hour or two earlier by a band of Cheyennes, who had taken their horses, probably in the vicinity of the burned Cheyenne village. Some letters had been captured with the horses, including the one for Captain Foote, but the Pawnees said that Foote and his command were to go directly to Fort Kearny rather than to the crossing of the South Platte. They said they had managed to kill one Cheyenne but had barely escaped.[7]

With the excitement over, the encampment settled down to its daily routine of resting, trying to stay cool, and keeping a lookout for hostiles. J. E. B. Stuart was by now so much improved that he ate his first meal since the battle and did a little walking. The following day, August 6, Captain Foote held a "council of war" with Dr. Covey and the other officers. His original orders had been to stay at Fort Floyd until August 20 and then, if Colonel Sumner and his troops had not returned, proceed to the Lower California Crossing of the South Platte. There he was to meet the supply train, get the Company C wagons, and proceed to Fort Laramie, at the same time sending Lieutenant Riddick and the train to Fort Kearny. The news brought by the Pawnee scouts altered those orders, if what they said was true. Except for a little beef, the remaining food supplies were nearly gone. It seemed imperative to head northeast to Fort Kearny as soon as possible, thus bringing them back into the buffalo range and a fresh food supply. Doctor Covey stated his belief that after another day's rest, the most seriously wounded would be sufficiently healed to be moved. With this information they determined to leave Fort Floyd on the morning of Saturday, August 8.[8]

Friday the seventh was spent preparing for the next day's departure. Doctor Covey did what he could to improve the lot of the wounded and sick, and the men of Company C got their gear ready for the march. A search along the valley during the building of the little fort had turned up an old Cheyenne village site at the far end, and there the men found a supply of abandoned lodgepoles. Because the "abbreviated" ambulance had a capacity of only one person, the soldiers rigged up a modified travois for each of the other two seriously wounded men, to transport them as comfortably as possible. Two poles were to be lashed to a mule, like the shafts of a wagon, with one end dragging. Between the poles a basketwork of rawhide strips was to be woven, upon which the wounded man would be placed. Infantrymen were detailed to walk behind each travois and lift up the end when they came to rough ground. With the plans completed, all was in readiness for an early-morning departure on the eighth.[9]

The March to Fort Kearny

Company C, Sixth Infantry, with the First Cavalry wounded and sick, the garrison and occupants of Fort Floyd, abandoned the sod redoubt on the Solomon early on the morning of Saturday, August 8, 1857, and began their slow march to the northeast. Ahead of them lay the great, empty plains, without landmarks to guide them or friends to help. And somewhere, perhaps over the next hill or beyond, might be a vengeful band of Cheyenne warriors waiting to strike during an unguarded moment.[10]

Except Lieutenant Stuart, who had his own horses, and the three most seriously injured, who had to be transported, all the wounded were mounted on mules. The need to prevent further damage to wounds still painful and dangerous required a very slow pace. Consequently, at the end of the first day's march, the company went into camp on a small mudhole approximately ten miles northeast of Fort Floyd.* Without a compass, they were dependent on accurate readings of the stars and on recognizing streams and trails. The plan was to find the Oregon-California Trail and to follow it in to Fort Kearny.[11]

On August 9 the party made another fourteen miles and camped on a creek, probably the north fork of the Solomon. Monday, the tenth, they continued moving northeast, striking what was described as a "finely timbered creek" tributary of the Republican, undoubtedly Prairie Dog Creek. This they followed downstream and to the northeast, and soon they found themselves in the vicinity of a great herd of buffalo. Lieutenant Stuart, vastly improved, gave chase and killed a fat cow, which he later described as the finest meat he ever ate. Their food supply had been nearly exhausted, with only a small quantity of fresh beef remaining, and the buffalo meat was a much-needed supplement. The presence of the buffalo proved a mixed blessing, however: their constant bellowing kept the soldiers awake much of the night.[12]

The following day, August 11, they continued to follow the Prairie Dog toward the Republican. In the afternoon, Lieutenant Stuart and Dr. Covey each killed a buffalo, ensuring a continued supply of fresh meat. On the twelfth they found they had passed the buffalo region; no animals were to be seen anywhere. Late in the morning, they reached the Republican, which they crossed with some difficulty. The Pawnee guides told them they were only four or five miles from Fort Kearny. Probably, though, this was a misinterpretation.† The following morning the detachment started early and moved almost due north. After a march of fifteen to eighteen miles, they made camp in the middle of the plains where there were no streams or springs. Fortunately they had a supply of water sufficient to meet their needs. Shortly after dark, as if to replenish that supply, a tremendous storm arose, drenching everyone with a downpour of cold rain lasting nearly the whole night.[13]

---

*The encampment probably was near the springs at the head of present-day Spring Creek.

†The Prairie Dog, or Wolf Creek as it was often called in that time, does flow into the Republican River almost due south and a little west of Fort Kearny, but the distance was more nearly forty or fifty miles from the point of junction, rather than four or five. The disparity in measurement may well be explained by the inability of the Pawnees to communicate in multiples of ten in English.

At dawn on August 14 the land was enveloped in a heavy fog that obscured the sun and any landmarks that would indicate their location. To make matters worse, the Pawnee guides had left in the night. The little command was lost, and as a result, the wounded, particularly First Sergeant McEawen, who was in the most serious condition, were in great danger. Captain Foote, who Stuart disliked and mistrusted, had been badgering the Pawnees since their arrival at Fort Floyd, and Stuart was convinced that they simply became disgusted by it and left when they had the opportunity. Without the Pawnees or anyone else who knew the country well, the troops were forced to seek the help of the Cheyenne prisoner. Because none of them spoke Cheyenne and he spoke no English or Spanish, they were obliged to use sign language. He seemed to understand what they wanted, and they followed him in what they hoped was the direction of Fort Kearny. After traveling fifteen or twenty miles, they camped by a dry streambed with only a little water in a pool, having seen nothing to indicate they were nearer Fort Kearny. Finally, after dark, the fog cleared and the stars came out, giving them the opportunity to mark north.[14]

The party was nearly out of meat again, and, after the long march of the last three months, many of the infantrymen were actually barefooted. To save them from unnecessary travel and hardship, Lieutenant Stuart volunteered to ride ahead in search of the road to Kearny. McCleary, too, wished to go, and Captain Foote gave his consent, authorizing him to take a cavalry sergeant and a cavalry corporal along with a Mexican guide from Fort Laramie. Stuart had little confidence in the guide, who had contended continuously that they should be marching south to find Fort Kearny. As the morning of the fifteenth dawned, the fog returned, keeping the volunteer party in camp. But when it had not lifted by noon, the suffering of the wounded convinced Stuart and McCleary that they should proceed anyway and take their chances on finding the road. Lieutenant Stuart wanted to travel to the northeast, thinking Kearny lay in that direction, but Captain Foote insisted they move eastward, which he believed to be the proper course. They did as he ordered.[15]

Although the fog finally lifted, the sky was overcast, and Stuart and his men were still unable to tell directions. The only way they could remain on their chosen course was to keep two men successively stationed on line, with the others moving as rapidly as they could in the direction marked. This continued until about 5:00 P.M., when a new storm struck. Lieutenant Stuart had their direction marked on the ground, then they waited under some trees until the storm passed. After that they continued their march for another half hour, until it became too dark to go farther. They planted stakes to mark their direction of travel and picketed the horses and mules along the edge of a ravine. They had hardly finished when the storm rose again with great fury. Each man squatted on his saddle, head bowed, trying to wait it out. So exhausted were they that most were dozing despite thunder, lightning, and rain. Suddenly a flash of lightning revealed the ravine filling with water, which already was halfway up the horses' bodies and rising rapidly. The men ran to them, pulled the picket pins, and got them to higher ground just in time to avoid disaster. [16]

By the morning of the sixteenth the storm had passed, but the skies remained cloudy. Stuart, McCleary, and their men saddled up at dawn and started off on the same course they had followed the previous day. At about 7:00 A.M. the sun made a brief appearance, showing them that they were moving south-southeast instead of east. While the sun remained visible, Lieutenant Stuart hastily established an east-west line, and the party started a movement northeast. Stuart suspected that the Mexican guide had intentionally deflected the line of march to the right when taking the point of direction, in accordance with his false belief that Fort Kearny lay to the south. As the party moved, they could see both buffalo and elk in the distance. At 4:00 P.M. they came to an impassable stream in flood stage, very deep and with precipitous banks. They moved upstream to a point where it was narrow and shallow enough to cross, their direction being southeast according to their calculations. Soon they struck a plain wagon trail, which Stuart believed to be the road from Fort Riley to Fort Kearny. They followed this for some three hours before they were overtaken by dark and the need to make camp. [17]

During the night the skies cleared, and the watch, the cavalry corporal, awakened Stuart to show him the stars. They were overjoyed to find, by dead reckoning, that their course was now due north, which Stuart knew to be safe. At dawn on August 17 the party saddled up and followed the trail two or three miles, when they struck a good-sized stream overflowing its banks with a very swift current. Lieutenant Stuart believed it had to be crossed, and, for the sake of the suffering wounded in Foote's camp, the crossing could not be delayed. All but the Mexican guide, who claimed he could not swim, plunged into the waters with their horses and mules and struck out for the other bank. The current bore them downstream a good distance, and in the process Stuart was un-horsed and had to swim the rest of the way. Finally all made it over safely, including the animals, leaving only the Mexican guide on the opposite side. Just as Stuart was about to heed his pleas by using a human chain and ropes to help him over, the guide jumped into the water and swam over more skillfully than any of the others.[18]

While the rest of the party was recovering from the wet and dangerous crossing, the cavalry sergeant went up the bank to re-connoiter. There he discovered that they were next to a well-established wagon road and a fresh trail. Stuart identified it as the road from Fort Leavenworth to Fort Kearny and beyond—the Oregon-California Trail—and the stream as the Little Blue River at a point at least fifty miles south and east of the fort. Then, at 7:00 A.M., wet and cold as they were, the party set out for Kearny, traveling about five miles an hour. At noon they met the mail party bound for the States, and the driver gave them both news and some hard bread. They arrived at Kearny late in the afternoon, having traveled fifty-five miles since morning. There they found the offi-cers much concerned with the whereabouts of the entire party, as the Pawnees had arrived three days earlier and reported them close behind. They had sent out search parties and scoured the country to the south for twenty-five miles, but with no success.[19]

A relief party was soon sent to bring Foote and the rest of his company and the First Cavalry wounded into Kearny. It consisted of an ambulance and two wagons loaded with hard bread and other luxuries, and was accompanied by Jeffries, the interpreter, the best of the Pawnees, and a military escort. Their instructions were to proceed to the point at which the Pawnees had left Captain Foote's party, then follow their trail until they were found. With their departure, Lieutenant Stuart and his little band pitched tents at the edge of the post and dubbed their encampment "Camp Shep-perd." They settled in for a well-deserved rest, enjoying the mail, news, food, and relaxation they found at Fort Kearny. They ex-pected the arrival of Captain Foote and the others on the nineteenth or twentieth.[20]

After Lieutenant Stuart and his party had departed on the fifteenth, Captain Foote and his company remained in camp tending the wounded and waiting for either the return of Stuart with accurate directions, or a relief party from the fort. When no one came for them, they broke camp on the morning of August 19, marched about ten miles northeast, and halted. The next morning they started early, following a course due north, as they reckoned it, and struck the Platte Road about seven miles below the fort. There they camped for the night. They arrived at Kearny on the morning of August 21, much "wearied and broken-down" from the rigors of the march and the protracted lack of a healthful diet. After turning the Cheyenne prisoner over to the post authorities and making appropriate arrangements for care of the First Cavalry wounded, Foote and his company went into camp, trying to rebuild themselves with nourishing food and rest. * [21]

The orders given Captain Foote by Colonel Sumner were to deliver the First Cavalry sick and wounded to the supply train, pick up the C Company wagons, and then return to Fort Laramie. At Kearny the wounded were in better hands than they would be with the wagon train and much nearer their duty station at Fort Leavenworth, to which they must in all events return. Accordingly, following a week's rest and refitting and resupply of the company, Foote, McCleary, and their troops departed for Fort Laramie on August 27, leaving the wounded behind. By August 31 they were encamped three miles above Cottonwood Springs, eighty-six miles west of Fort Kearny, and by September 17 they had reached Laramie. For C Company, Sixth Infantry, the Expedition was over. [22]

The First Cavalry wounded made a rapid and, for some, a near-miraculous recovery, considering the state of medicine in that day and the conditions under which they suffered their wounds. There were no serious infections and, notwithstanding the appalling conditions to which they had been subjected and the lack of food, even those dangerously wounded were able to undertake the trip back to Fort Leavenworth by the end of August. On August 29, Lieutenant Stuart led his tiny command away from Fort Kearny and back over the trail he had followed west the previous May and June. In less

*The Indian prisoner captured on the Solomon, along with the two later brought to the fort by Lieutenant Riddick, Lowe, and the wagon train, subsequently escaped by digging under the sod walls of the post guardhouse. See Peck, "Recollections," 506.

than two weeks they reached Leavenworth and the relative comfort of barracks, quarters, and regular army meals. For Stuart it meant reunion with his beloved Flora and their new child, born at Leavenworth during the first week in September. But life in the military never leaves much time away from duty. When Sedgwick's command was diverted to northeastern Kansas to supervise elections, Stuart rejoined his G Company at Richmond on the Nemaha. With their return to Fort Leavenworth following the elections, the last chapter was complete.[23]

Epilogue—The Last Song

The First Cavalry

> *. . . riding up a shining steep of sky*
> *As though to join the dead that do not die*
> *But haunt some storied heaven of the bold.*
> *And then it seemed a smoke of battle rolled*
> *Across the picture, leaving empty air*
> *Above the line that slowly shortened there*
> *And dropped below the prairie and was gone.* *(174)*

The end of the Cheyenne Expedition brought no placid garrison duty for the men of the First Cavalry. Along the eastern border of Kansas Territory, where white settlement was occurring, the struggle between pro-slavery and free-state immigrants became more intense, compelling a policing role for the army in general and the cavalry in particular. The First Cavalry played its part in this. The arrival of large numbers of white settlers also made the plight of the immigrant Indians, those confined to the reservations adjacent to the eastern border of Kansas Territory, more desperate. Whites stole their livestock, cheated them in their business transactions, and tried to homestead on their reservations. Repeatedly the cavalry was called upon to maintain peace between these unfortunates and their new neighbors. However, it was out on the plains where the most dangerous duty was to be found, for if the Cheyenne Expedition imposed a period of relative quiet on that tribe, it brought neither peace nor meek submission by any of the Plains Indians.

Following the return of the First Cavalry to Fort Leavenworth, a series of events began to shape the course that the regiment would pursue for the coming years. Fall Leaf, the Delaware chief who had served so well as a guide to the Solomon, displayed some of the gold given him by the small party of Arkansas prospectors along Cherry Creek. Bands of men from Missouri and from Lawrence, Kansas Territory, responding to the news, organized themselves into the Green Russell Party, the Missouri Party, and the Lawrence Party and headed for Cherry Creek. The Colorado gold rush had begun. It lured thousands of men across the trails along the Arkansas and Platte, and it opened a new trail along the Smoky Hill, directly through the last great, untouched hunting grounds of the southern bands of Cheyenne and Arapahoe.[1]

The gold rush brought further conflict between travelers and Indians as the wanton slaughter of buffalo and other wildlife greatly increased and as alien eyes looked covetously on Indian lands. The Comanches and Kiowas reacted with rage and hostility, and the Arkansas again saw fresh attacks on travelers. The Cheyennes for the most part remained passive through 1858 and 1859. Colonel Sumner found them to be "perfectly humble" when he met a party in the vicinity of old Fort Atkinson in mid-August of 1858. After passing out the 1858 annuity goods, Robert C. Miller, their agent, noted that Colonel Sumner had worked "a wondrous change" in their dispositions. Their heavy losses in lodges, lodgepoles, camp equipment, and food supplies in 1857 kept them poor for nearly two years as they struggled to replace their needs.[2]

The continuing problems along the trails gave the First Cavalry much to do in trying to protect lives and property of gold seekers and other travelers. In 1858 the Kiowas and Comanches were so hostile they attacked two Mexican wagon trains within sight of the camp of Agent Miller, once more leading him to recommend a "thorough chastisement" as the only proper solution. In June 1859, three companies of the First Cavalry from Fort Riley, upon orders of Colonel Sumner, established a summer camp near the ruins of Fort Atkinson to protect the middle section of the Santa Fe Trail, and later they were joined by a fourth company. During the summer, one of these companies was sent to the Pawnee Fork to provide protection for Hall and Company's new mail station, which the Comanches and Kiowas had threatened to destroy. In October this encampment was moved to a different site and established as a military post, first called "Camp on Pawnee Creek," then "Camp Alert," and finally, on May 29, 1860, "Fort Larned."[3]

On March 10, 1860, army headquarters ordered a summer expedition against the hostile Comanches and Kiowas, to consist of three mounted columns operating independently of each other. Companies F, G, H, and K, First Cavalry, marched from Fort Riley on May 15 and scoured the country south to the Antelope Hills, west to the Purgatoire, and north to the Smoky Hill River. Except for a minor skirmish, the pursuit was mostly unsuccessful, and the column returned to the Pawnee Fork near Fort Larned on August 11. In the meantime, on June 6, Capt. Samuel D. Sturgis, the experienced Indian fighter who had served under Sedgwick during the Cheyenne Expedition, led the remaining six companies of the First Cavalry north from Fort Cobb, and in July his troops had a sharp but indecisive fight with the Kiowas between the Solomon and the Republican. A third column consisting of six companies of the Mounted Riflemen operating out of Fort Union had even less success. The expedition thus concluded with little in the way of tangible results.

Major Sedgwick and his four companies of the First Cavalry were later ordered to the Big Timbers of the Arkansas, arriving there on August 29. At a point just west of Bent's New Fort, the troops established "Fort Wise," later renamed "Fort Lyon." On September 9 they entered into a lease with William Bent for his "Bent's New Fort" and made it part of their facility. Soon Companies C and H of the Tenth Infantry joined them to assist in completing the post and to serve as its garrison. Their duty completed, the First Cavalry troops returned to Fort Riley.[4]

In 1861, with the eruption of the War Between the White Men, the War of Secession, the First Cavalry and the entire American mounted force was torn asunder. One hundred four of the 176 officers in the five mounted regiments were from the South, and most, including four of the five colonels, offered their services to their native states. Of the five only Colonel Sumner remained loyal to the Union. His own family was split, for he had two daughters married to young officers from the South who joined the Confederate Army, a fact that caused him great personal sadness. So few were the officers who stayed with their units that, for the next two years, most mounted regiments were led by green and untried officers.

On May 4, 1861, Army General Order No. 16 created the Third Regiment of Cavalry, making a total of six mounted regiments in the regular army. On August 3 of the same year, Congress directed reorganization of the mounted service, with all regiments to be known thereafter as "cavalry." Following a numbering system based on seniority, Army General Order No. 55, issued on August 10, redesignated the regiments, the First and Second Dragoons becoming the First and Second Cavalry, the Mounted Riflemen the Third Cavalry, and the former First, Second, and Third Cavalry becoming the Fourth, Fifth, and Sixth Cavalry. Colonel Sumner's old regiment, the veterans of the Cheyenne Expedition, were thus turned into the Fourth Cavalry, and so they continued to be known for as long as the United States used mounted troops.

The long trial of the War Between the States diverted the attention of the regular army from wars with the Indian inhabitants of the Great Plains, but during most of that time conflict with immigrants was eased as the white population in the East was absorbed in the great struggle. When the war ended at Appomattox Court House, however, westward expansion resumed with increased vigor, as did demands for the removal or extermination of the Indian population and the appropriation of their lands for white settlers, who would, most said, use it properly and as God intended. Back to the West came the army, and with it the Fourth Cavalry. Now the real era of the Indian Wars had begun, and it would not end until the tragedy at Wounded Knee, on December 29, 1890.

The service of the First, now Fourth, Cavalry during the Indian Wars, measured in military terms and by the standards of the day, was distinguished. Like most regiments of that time, it was rarely together as a unit, its companies being scattered across the plains and the Desert Southwest, wherever the need was greatest. From 1870 to 1882 they fought in New Mexico, Texas, Kansas, and across the plains to the Dakotas, under the overall command of Col. Ranald S. Mackenzie, and were reputed to be the "best cavalry regiment in the Army."

In part because of their great skill, experience, training, and ability and in part because of the fortunes of war, most officers who participated in the Cheyenne Expedition went on to gain fame and glory in the Civil War. Colonel Sumner himself became a major general and commanded a corps in the Army of the Potomac, participating in the battle of Antietam. He died suddenly but peacefully at home on March 21, 1863. By a strange twist of fate he fell victim to the flu, not the battlefield bullet he had hoped for. Major John Sedgwick also became a major general commanding a corps. He was killed in action at Spotsylvania on May 9, 1864. Of the captains of the cavalry companies assigned to the expedition, Delos B. Sackett, Samuel D. Sturgis, and Edward W. B. Newby remained with the Union during the war; the others offered their services to the Confederacy. Sackett became Inspector General of the United States Army, Sturgis a brigadier general, and Newby a major. After the war, Sturgis became the colonel and second commanding officer of the Seventh Cavalry, with one George Armstrong Custer as his lieutenant colonel. William N. R. Beall and James McIntosh served the Confederacy as brigadier generals, and William S. Walker became a colonel.

The first and second lieutenants serving with the Expedition also produced distinguished officers. John N. Perkins became a captain in the Alabama Cavalry, C.S.A., and Philip Stockton, colonel of ordnance, C.S.A. David S. Stanley and Frank Wheaton each rose to the rank of major general in the Union army. James B. McIntyre served as a major and brevet colonel, United States Army. The best-known and most dashing of these men was J. E. B. Stuart, who became a major general in the Army of Northern Virginia and the premier leader of the Confederate cavalry forces. He was wounded at Yellow Tavern, north of Richmond, on May 12, 1864, and died the following day. Richard H. Riddick, who had charge of Colonel Sumner's supply train, became a colonel of the North Carolina Volunteers and was killed at Gaines Mill on June 27, 1862. Albert V. Colburn became a staff lieutenant colonel, United States Army, and Eugene W. Crittenden, a major, United States Army.

Perhaps the most surprising in terms of rapid advancement were Eli Long, George D. Bayard, and Lunsford L. Lomax, each aged twenty-one and a second lieutenant in 1857. Bayard and Lomax had graduated from West Point in 1856, and all three were commissioned and joined the First Cavalry that year. Long rose to major general of the United States Volunteers. He died in 1903. Bayard was a brigadier general of volunteers when he died of wounds received at the Battle of Fredericksburg on December 14, 1862. Lomax became a major general, C.S.A.

The officers and men of the First Cavalry probably constituted

as capable a mounted force as those of any regiment that ever took
the field against the Indians. Brave, willing to endure hardships
far beyond those envisioned by most soldiers today, they were committed to the performance of the duties to which their country
called them, whatever sacrifice it might entail. If, measured by the
standards of a later day, their operations against the Indians seem
inhumane, shortsighted, and lacking in compassion and understanding, it was not because they were unprincipled men. Rather,
it was the natural result of the times in which they were born. And
if their attitudes towards the tribes of the plains mirrored those of
their white countrymen, it was not for want of conscience or vision,
but because they were themselves only a reflection of their society's
beliefs. For who among us, recalling that dramatic moment when
they charged with sabres across the valley of the Solomon and
into the pages of history, can say they were less than the best
among us?

The Cheyennes

"Hey—hey'-hey! *So laments an aging man*
Who totters and can never more be free
As once he was. Hey—hey'-hey! *So may we*
Exclaim today for what the morrow brings.
There is a time, my brothers, for all things,
And we are getting old. Consider, friends,
How everything begins and grows and ends
That other things may have their time and grow.
What tribes of deer and elk and buffalo
Have we ourselves destroyed lest we should die!
About us now you hear the dead leaves sigh;
Since these were green, how few the moons have been!
We share in all this trying to begin,
This trying not to die. Consider well
The White Man—what you know and what men tell
About his might. His never weary mind
And busy hands do magic for his kind.
Those things he loves we think of little worth;
And yet, behold! he sweeps across the earth,
And what shall stop him?   *(52–53)*

For the Cheyennes the battle on the Solomon was the beginning of
the enforced destruction of their traditional way of life, and only

the first act of a long tragedy that, in a real sense, continues to this day. When they lived life in their own land in the age-old manner, they were called barbarians, heathens, animals; when they made war on ancestral enemies, they were considered savage, impediments to progress; when they stole livestock, an ancient and honorable pastime among all Plains Indians, they were judged thieves and worse; and when they resisted white encroachment, fighting and killing in an effort to stem the invasion, they were called murderers. The same willingness to risk life and limb for one's country earned white men accolades and the title "hero."

During the fall and winter of 1857, the various bands of Cheyennes did the same things they had always done, except that year the heavy loss of lodges, lodgepoles, camp equipment, and food forced them to work hard to replace what the soldiers had destroyed. Even so, the Ridge People, camping along Lodgepole Creek, managed to send out at least one war party against the Utes in October. During the winter the members of Wolf Fire's kindred group came south from the Black Hills to rejoin the Omissis, and when they reached Fort Laramie they were stopped and four men were arrested, apparently still because of the missing horse. The following summer they were released after the Omissis had made peace with the soldiers there.[5]

In the summer of 1858, with white men stampeding through their lands on the way to the gold fields of western Kansas Territory (present-day Colorado), Cheyennes and Arapahoes nonetheless kept the peace. Except for the Dog Soldiers and southern Suhtai, who stayed in their usual territory, along and between Walnut Creek, the Smoky Hill, and the Republican, southern bands camped and hunted along Red Arms Creek, the Pawnee Fork of the Arkansas. In July they were joined there by others to form one great camp of all the southern tribes—Comanches, Kiowas, Plains Apaches, Arapahoes, and Cheyennes—and were met by their agent, Robert C. Miller, who distributed their treaty goods. Some of the old chiefs talked of peace, of the tribe's settling down to adopt the white man's ways and learning to farm. But there were few for whom they spoke, because the Cheyennes still were a warrior people and hunters; to them farming was not for men but was woman's work.[6]

In 1859 the great flood of gold seekers crossing their lands reached new heights as more than 150,000 people headed for the diggings along Cherry Creek. This mass migration astonished the Cheyennes, who found more than a few men wandering delirious from want of food and water in the lands between the headwaters of the Smoky Hill and the Republican. These they helped, and they made no war. By 1860, with game depleted as a result of wanton killing, the old restlessness and desperation began to set in. William Bent, who had become the agent for the Upper Arkansas tribes in the summer of 1859, declared them troublesome and troubled, but entirely at peace.[7]

In 1861, Bent engineered the so-called Treaty of Fort Wise, by which both the Cheyennes and Arapahoes were to cede all lands guaranteed to them by the Treaty of Fort Laramie in exchange for a small reservation along the Arkansas centered, not surprisingly, on Bent's New Fort. Only government employees and licensed traders would be allowed there, providing a secure trading monopoly for Bent. However, the treaty was doomed from the beginning, for no more than six chiefs signed it and they represented only Black Kettle's band of Wutapiu and a part of the Ridge People under White Antelope. The Council of Forty-four absolutely refused authority for a treaty or to give away any of their lands or compromise on the way they lived their lives. Black Kettle and the other five signers, who had no authority to commit the tribe, were viewed with contempt by the rest of the southern bands, and both the treaty and the reservation were ignored. The government, however, deemed it binding and designated five of the signers the five principal and ruling chiefs of the Cheyennes, even though they represented only a small part of the tribe.[8]

With the increased inflow of whites, and with new trails and greatly diminished supplies of buffalo and other game, the lot of the Cheyennes rapidly deteriorated. Often they were reduced to near starvation despite their efforts to provide for themselves. Increasing friction between the tribe and white intruders, especially after the start of the War Between the States, led to hysterical demands for their extermination or removal. This prompted the atrocious Sand Creek massacre of Black Kettle's peaceful Cheyennes by the Methodist minister turned volunteer soldier, Col. John M. Chivington. William Bent recognized the uselessness of trying to maintain a reserve for Cheyennes in an area close to a major trail and growing white settlements. In his testimony before the commission investigating the Sand Creek Massacre, Bent stated:

In my opinion the reservation now set apart for the Cheyennes and Araphoes is not suitable. The best place for a reservation for them, in my opinion, would be on Beaver Creek, between the Smoky Hill and the Republican. This would be in their own country, where the buffalo abound, and where they will probably last be seen. This reservation would be off from all the roads and all the great thoroughfares, and distant from all settlements. The land would be suitable for them, but not for the whites, and contains no minerals. On this reservation the agency should be established, and the agent should always be with them; grass and timber abound.

Unfortunately, Bent's opinion was ignored.[9]

After Sand Creek the story of the Cheyennes could lead only downhill. There were many more fights and battles, but for the People the end was already a certainty. The southern bands signed the Treaty of the Little Arkansas in 1865, giving them a new reservation in south-central Kansas and north-central Oklahoma. Few made any effort to settle on the reservation, continuing to live life in the manner they believed Maheo had designed for them, and in the lands He had given them. In 1867, following Hancock's War against them, they were forced once again to sign a treaty, this time at Medicine Lodge, whereby they surrendered all their land in Kansas. Even the Dog Soldiers signed the latter treaty, giving up their beloved valley of the Smoky Hill.

The Treaty of Medicine Lodge did not long satisfy the whites, and in 1869 President Ulysses S. Grant signed a presidential executive order assigning them to a new reservation in western Oklahoma. No formal treaty was deemed necessary. They resisted a few more years, stubbornly clinging to their old haunts and ancient ways, but the rush of settlers claiming their land soon put an end for all time to the buffalo range and to the free life of the southern bands of the Cheyennes. By the summer of 1875 they were permanently settled on their reservation. The northern bands, being further removed from the great trails, lasted a few years more, but by 1879 they too were confined to a narrow strip of land in Montana, eventually (in 1884) consolidated into a small reserve centered on Lame Deer, near the Crow Reservation and the Little Big Horn.

Ironically, the southern bands of the tribe were not allowed to settle on land that had been a part of their own tribal territory, and the northern bands were placed on a reservation in an area also claimed by the Crows and the Sioux. On these two reserves the

Cheyennes lived, year after year, surrounded by white settlements, unable to support themselves, without hope of renewing their way of life, without the pride that brave men need. For many years this desperate condition continued, the People living in despair as wards of a paternalistic government that wanted to turn them into white men, suppressing their religious beliefs and practices and keeping them dependent upon it for the necessities of life. The Great Father and his minions could not, or would not, understand that for people of a warrior culture to give up the old ways and abandon life by the hunt in their own country was against the natural order of things, was demeaning and dispiriting. For the Cheyennes the new path would prove a difficult and impoverished way of life that even today brings them sorrow and hardship.

The great Cheyenne warriors and leaders who faced the charge of the First Cavalry rode off to other battles and frequently to death. Only a few among them—men such as Roman Nose, Tall Bull, Dull Knife, and Little Wolf—had names familiar to the encroaching white settlers. However, many others were equally brave, as much respected, as ready to fight and die for family, people, and homeland. Of the best-known of the Indians present at Solomon's Fork, the Dog Soldier chief Tall Bull would lead his people in battle after battle—until Summit Springs, July 11, 1869; Roman Nose, the renowned Cheyenne warrior, would fight well for his tribe until his medicine failed him at Beecher's Island on September 17, 1868; and the young Crazy Horse would go on to victories at the Rosebud and the Little Big Horn, victories that soon turned to dust and brought him to his death at Fort Robinson on September 5, 1877. Considering their small numbers, the Cheyennes produced a disproportionate number of singularly brave and dedicated warriors, willing to die protecting that which they loved, and earning their reputation as the "fighting Cheyennes."

In 1878 a former participant in the Cheyenne Expedition was stationed with a company of the Fourth Cavalry (the old First) at Fort Reno, Indian Territory. Captain Sebastian Gunther, who had been a sergeant in 1857, was escorting a small band of northern Cheyenne warriors west on a vain expedition to find buffalo along Wolf Creek in the present-day Oklahoma Panhandle. In camp one evening, as he and his company were watching over their charges, an old Cheyenne warrior began to tell a story to his fellows. In the course of the story, he drew a map in the sandy soil with a stick.

Clearly outlined were the Platte, the South Platte, the Republican, the branches of the Solomon, the Smoky Hill, the Arkansas and its tributaries, the "soldier towns" or forts, the line of march of the soldiers, and the charge with the "long knives." Gunther immediately recognized the story and told one of the chiefs, Standing Elk, that he had been among the soldiers making the charge. The Indians were both astonished and delighted, and they told him how they had watched Sedgwick's command all the way out to his meeting with Sumner on the South Platte, and then across to their country. It was, in a sense, the last phase of the Cheyenne Expedition, when old-timers from both sides joined in recalling the happenings of a day long ago.[10]

The Battleground

But there were those—and they were human
*   too—*
For whom the memory of other springs
Sought vainly in the growing dusk of things
The ancient joy. Along the Smoky Hill
The might they could no longer hope to kill
Brawled west again, where maniacs of toil
Were chaining down the violated soil,
And plows went wiving in the bison range,
An alien-childed mother growing strange
With younger loves.   *(140–41)*

For many years the valley of the south fork of the Solomon lay in peace, as if brooding over the events of July 29, 1857. Doubtless great herds of bison and antelope disturbed the solitude from time to time to feed on valley grasses and drink from the river, as did wolves and coyotes. Doubtless various bands of Cheyennes came back and camped by the little grove of cottonwood at the east end of the valley as they had done for many years before that fateful July day. No one knows what their thoughts were as they recalled the march of the "long knives" and the day the medicine of Ice and Dark failed them. Looking up the valley they could see the little sod fort, empty and silent, mocking them from the very battleground where they first had learned of the deadly and irresistible power of the Veho.

As the seasons succeeded each other, and one year gave way to

Some years after the flight on the Solomon, Capt. Sebastian Gunthner, who had served with the First Cavalry as a sergeant during the Cheyenne Expedition, led a party of Fourth Cavalry troopers escorting a party of Northern Cheyennes on a proposed buffalo hunt in the present-day panhandle of Oklahoma. One evening he observed an old Cheyenne warrior telling a story and illustrating it with a map he drew with a stick in the sandy soil. Gunthner instantly recognized the story as that of the sabre charge of the First Cavalry at Solomon's Fork.

the next, change came gradually to the Solomon. Cheyennes no longer came to camp, to hunt, or to hold their great ceremonies. In their place, by the middle of the 1870s, came white buffalo hunters seeking tongues and hides, leaving carcasses to rot or be eaten by coyotes and wolves. The last of the buffalo roaming in the wild were soon gone. Then came the settlers. At first they made claims along the rivers and streams, finally on the high plains themselves. By the 1880s all the land had been reduced to private ownership, and the wide, open expanse of the plains gave way to farms and fenced-in ranches. The time of the Cheyennes had gone.

The field fortification known as Fort Floyd continued to stand into the 1890's. When the first white settlers came, part of the blockhouse roof was gone, but for the most part the structure was intact. The walls were still sound enough and high enough that for a time it was used as a corral by cattle drovers and mustangers. By the early 1890s the walls were badly deteriorated and could no longer serve any useful purpose. Because the landowner wanted the site for farming, located as it was in the bottomland, he had it leveled. A young neighbor, Carl Kobler, did the work. In later years, for the benefit of the Kansas Historical Society, Mr. Kobler recalled the story of the fort and its ultimate destruction. He and others old enough to remember gave affidavits to the effect that its location was in the center of the Southeast Quarter of Section 13, Township 8 South, Range 24 West of the Sixth Principal Meridian, Graham County, Kansas, and he made a small model of the fort from memory.[11] That model remained in the possession of the Hill City, Kansas, library for many years, but unfortunately was later destroyed. Even after its leveling, the outline of Fort Floyd remained visible for some time, and could be seen clearly in early aerial photographs. Finally, after continual cultivation and the effects of wind and rain had taken their toll, even this last vestige disappeared.

Not all physical reminders of the battle were entirely removed when the last trace of Fort Floyd was plowed under. In 1934 the graves of the two soldiers killed in the fight were discovered on the west side of the hill whose southern projection was locally known as Stony Point. Works Progress Administration workers, engaged in construction of U.S. Highway 24, came across the graves and turned over their contents to the sheriff's office of Graham County, Kansas. The same year, while obtaining materials to be used in the highway, these workers also uncovered the skeletal remains of two Cheyenne warriors, each with bone breastplates intact. One was found approximately a mile and a half southeast of the point at which the battle began; the other, two miles due south. The first, found by a dynamiter named Louis Legere, was in a crevice in the rocks along the bluffs paralleling the river on the south. The second was in the area where the WPA dug a sandpit. Whether these burials represented warriors killed in the battle is, of course, speculation. They might have been burials of men who had died or been killed at an earlier or later date, and whose village was at the time on the same stretch of the Solomon's south fork. Nevertheless, they were of the right era, and it is possible that the terrible tearing and snarling of the wolves heard in the First Cavalry camp the night of June 29, 1857, involved dead horses and only some of the Cheyenne dead. Or perhaps the skeletons of the two remained largely intact and were buried by returning tribal members. Their true story will probably never be known.[12]

Other evidences of the battle have also been found. In recent years local residents have found fragments of weapons of the era, including part of a sabre and lead bullets. In the late 1960s county construction workers preparing the approach for a bridge across a small tributary of the Saline River in present Trego County, Kansas, directly south of the battle site, uncovered and destroyed one hundred or more lodge sites, having blackened fire pits and traces of considerable burning in the area. The Saline contains the remains of numerous Cheyenne village sites of great size, and no one can say with certainty that this was the one destroyed by Colonel Sumner and his troops. It was in the right vicinity, however, and on a horseshoe bend in the river. It is just possible that what was found and destroyed were in fact remains of a part of the great camp put to the torch on the afternoon of Friday, July 31, 1857.[13]

Mysteries always will surround events that preceded photography, modern means of determining direction and distance, and modern communication. One of those relating to the battle on Solomon's Fork is the location of the "small and beautiful lake" in which the Cheyennes dipped their hands to immunize themselves against the effect of white men's bullets. The high plains are not known as "lake country," and those unaccustomed to the rolling vastness and the lack of trees and green vegetation would likely be unable to appreciate the beauty. But for the Indians and later settlers, who heard the song of the plains, it was assuredly there. Approximately twelve miles southeast of the battle site, on the high plains north of the Shistoloiyohe (Cedar River), the Saline to white men, there once were two small and clear lakes that probably were formed by great buffalo wallows. The larger covered nearly five acres; the smaller, possibly an acre. Both had what, to an Indian, must have seemed a glorious view of the plains, the waters, the buffalo herds, and the great blue sky of the country that Maheo had given him. After the site had been homesteaded, the lakes were drained and filled in for cultivation. Over the years many projectile points, both stone and steel, were found there, along with other evidences of long years of Indian visitation. Probably no one will ever know with certainty, but this seems a likely spot for the making of great medicine.[14]

A Moment In History

Who knows the crumbling summit where he lies
Alone among the badlands? Kiotes prowl
About it, and the voices of the owl
Assume the day-long sorrow of the crows,
These many grasses and these many snows.   (231)

In terms of history the First Cavalry's campaign against the Cheyennes was but a moment. That moment, however, was a microcosm of relations between white civilization and the Plains Indians—of the best and worst of both worlds. It saw the end of one era in relations with the Indians of the Plains and the beginning of another. It saw change in the methods of warfare. Never again would a large cavalry unit charge an Indian foe with sabres; never again would the Indians believe they could hold white soldiers at bay without paying a price in blood and sacrifice.

Most of those involved in the expedition, warrior and trooper alike, participated in other notable moments in history, some more significant, some more dramatic, but none more illustrative of the struggle for survival in which the Cheyennes were now involved. This was a struggle to maintain their traditional way of life in the lands Maheo had given them, a struggle they would lose before a generation had come to maturity. The Treaty of Fort Laramie, and those they would sign later, promised them their lands as long as the winds blew, the grass grew, and the rivers flowed, or so the interpreters told them. But grass does not always grow nor winds always blow, and rivers run dry. So it would be for the Cheyennes. The story of Solomon's Fork thus was but a moment frozen in time—a slice from the lives of those on both sides who did their duty for their people as God gave them the light to see it. It told and foretold their story well.

For the Cheyennes, Solomon's Fork was the beginning of the end of their traditional way of life. Proud, honest, incredibly brave, devoted to family and tribe, true children of Maheo, the People deserved better from the white nation that grew around them and overwhelmed them. Their old ways are gone now, just as the buffalo and the great unbroken expanse of grass they roamed are gone. The old ways died a little at a time in the struggle between a people who would not willingly yield the gifts they believed God had given them and a people for whom there could be no way except their own.

Perhaps the most fitting way to leave the story of Solomon's Fork is with the words of Percival G. Lowe, the wagon master for Colonel Sumner, who many years later wrote:

> The Cheyenne and Arapahoe were the habitual occupants of these plains from the Platte to the Arkansas, and from the forks of the Solomon to the mountains. I then thought, and still believe, that the Cheyenne were the handsomest, noblest and bravest Indians I ever saw in a wild state. I met them often, knew them well and their way of living. They fought their enemies with an unrelenting vigor—that was their religious duty from their standpoint. They were as virtuous as any people on earth; whatever civilized man may say of their table manners,

their family government was perfect—perfect obedience to parents, and child whipping unknown; veneration and respect for old age was universal. In their relations to each other crime was practically unknown. They worshipped God, in whom they had implicit confidence. They hated a liar as the devil hates holy water, and that is why, when they came to know him, they hated the white man so intensely. For fortitude, patience and endurance, the sun never shown on better examples. They did not crave stealthy murder for the sake of murder; in which they were unlike . . . the doughty hero of Sand Creek. . . .

These Indians knew no suffering except what the white man brought them. . . . [A]nd the Cheyenne never sinned until the white man, with his tyranny and fraud, forced it upon them.*

Hena haanehe!
(That's the end!)

*Address delivered at annual meeting of the Kansas Historical Society, January 14, 1890. See *Sixth Biennial Report*, 361–62.

Appendix A

The Cheyennes

"Grandfather, I have filled a pipe to smoke,
And you shall smoke it first. In you we trust
To show good trails." He held it to the dust.
"Grandmother, I have filled a pipe for you,"
He said, "and you must keep us strong and
    true,
For you are so." Then offering the stem
To all four winds, he supplicated them
That they should blow good fortune. Then he
    smoked;
And all the Fathers after him invoked
The Mysteries that baffle Man's desire.
Some women fetched and set beside the fire
The steaming kettles, then with groundward
    gaze
Withdrew in haste. A man of ancient days,
Who searched a timeless dusk with rheumy
    stare
And saw the ghosts of things that struggle
    there
Before men struggle, now remembered Those
With might to help. Six bits of meat he chose,
The best the pots afforded him, and these
He gave in order to the Mysteries,
The Sky, the Earth, the Winds, as was their
    due.
"Before I eat, I offer this to you,"
He chanted as he gave; "so all men should.
I hope that what I eat may do me good,
And what you eat may help you even so.

I ask you now to make my children grow
To men and women. Keep us healthy still,
And give us many buffalo to kill
And plenty grass for animals to eat.   *(48–49)*

The Path to the Plains

They lived their lives in an ancient way, a sacred way. It was a way only dreamed of now—free, filled with the majesty and harshness of nature, with a spirituality created by closeness to the land and the creatures who lived upon it. They lived as they had been taught by Maheo—God, the All Father—and by Sweet Medicine and Erect Horns, their culture heroes. They were the Cheyennes. They belonged to the western branch of the great Algonquian-speaking people, sharing common blood and a common root language with such famous peoples as the Algonquians, Arapahoes, Chippewas (or Ojibwas), Crees, Blackfeet, Atsinas, Sacs and Foxes, Potawatomis, Delawares, Shawnees, and many others.[1]

The name "Cheyenne" is not their own; it is the English corruption of the Sioux term Shahi'ela or Shahi'ena, meaning "red speech"—speaking a foreign tongue. They called themselves Tsistsistas, "people alike," or "the People."[2] No one knows with certainty where they came from, but in the remote past they must have separated themselves from a larger Algonquian body living to the north and east, possibly north of the Great Lakes or the drainage of the upper Mississippi River and its eastern tributaries. From there they evidently moved gradually westward, first to the northwest, then arcing south. In 1673 they appear to have lived along the Wisconsin bank of the Mississippi River, above the mouth of the Wisconsin River and north of the Sioux, where they were still located in 1680. By 1684 they had moved to the Minnesota River valley, and thereafter to the western reaches of the Minnesota River, between the Iowas to the east and the Otoes to the south and west.

Before the end of the seventeenth century the People had moved northward to the Sheyenne River in eastern North Dakota. They probably moved further up the Minnesota River and eventually to the Sheyenne River because of pressure from the Sioux to their east or the Crees and Assiniboines to the north and east. At least some Cheyennes lived on the Sheyenne River for fifty to seventy

years. Their villages were fortified, evidencing their constant concern over attacks by larger and more powerful neighbors. They
lived in large, earthen lodges and practiced agriculture, raising
corn, beans, and squash. As they moved onto the plains, they became increasingly dependent upon the great herds of buffalo in
whose midst they now found themselves, hunting them first on foot
and later from horseback.

The Cheyennes acquired their first horses during the middle of
the eighteenth century. This was one of the most significant oc-
currences in their history, for it marked the beginning of their
transformation from a semi-nomadic people practicing agriculture,
making pottery, and living in fixed villages, to the archetypical
nomadic buffalo hunters of the plains.[3]

Attacks by the Ho hé (Assiniboines) or the Chippewas seem to
have forced the People to move once again—this time to the Missouri River near the present boundary of North and South Dakota.
The villages along the Missouri were occupied during the period
from about 1750 to 1780, and by at least a portion of the People
much later. First they constructed villages on the east side of the
river and practiced agriculture, then gradually they crossed to the
west bank and established new villages. During this period they
became friends and allies of the Mandans, Hidatsas, and Arikaras.
In time the new mobility they acquired with the horse led them
farther onto the plains, and bison became an increasingly important source of their food supply. Indeed, it is more than likely that
some Cheyennes hardly paused at the Missouri, continuing to roam
and hunt ever farther south and west.[4]

While living near the banks of the Missouri, Cheyennes first met
and became close friends of two separate tribal groups. The first of
these was the Moiseyu, probably a Siouan band from the lake
district in present northwestern Minnesota. These people hunted
and camped with the Cheyennes from time to time, but eventually
they moved back to the north. They left behind a Cheyenne clan
or band called Moiseyu, said to be of mixed Cheyenne-Moiseyu
blood. The second group were the Suhtai, or Sutaio, another Algonquian tribe, whose language, though harsher and more guttural,
was understandable to the Cheyennes. The Suhtai, called the "Buffalo People" by the Cheyennes, had moved onto the plains west of
the Missouri earlier and were nomadic hunters when the tribes first
met. Thereafter the Cheyennes and the Suhtai often roamed and

hunted together but considered themselves separate, allied tribes. Then, in "the year in which the stars fell," 1833, they were incorporated into the Cheyenne tribe as a separate band. In time the language and cultural differences faded, and they became one. The Suhtai gave to the Cheyennes the great legacy of Is'siwun, the Sacred Buffalo Hat, brought to them by Erect Horns, their culture hero, as well as the Sun Dance, Sweat Lodge, and Buffalo ceremonies.[5]

What causes a people to move their homeland or to adopt a different culture or manner of living is never easy to determine. In all probability the change results from the gradual interaction of many varied factors. Removal of the Cheyennes from the Missouri River was doubtless an extended process, occurring over generations, with first a few and then many of the People moving onto the plains and into that course destiny had devised for them.

Possession of the horse gave the Cheyennes a previously unimagined mobility, providing the opportunity to supplement their diet with buffalo meat. The buffalo gave them more than food. It provided warm robes for clothing, bedding, and saddles; leather for lodges, clothing, and shields; bones for soups, tools, and decorations; hoofs for glue; muscle and sinew for wrapping and binding and for bowstrings; and many other useful articles. The Indians' use of almost every part of this remarkable animal made it seem the most valuable gift from God, and each band of Cheyennes devoted ever greater amounts of time to the hunt for bison. As they began to roam the plains, they had less time for agriculture, coming to depend more on wilding fruits and vegetables and those obtained by trading. Occasional extended periods of drought probably accelerated the transition to an entirely nomadic life.

The distance and time involved in finding and killing buffalo, butchering them, and preserving the meat and by-products created an ever greater need for more and better horses, animals suited to specific purposes such as hunting, transport, and warfare. The greatest supply of horses lay to the south, with the Comanches and Kiowas, or in Mexico. When trading could not satisfy the demand, horse-stealing raids drew the People into journeys farther to the west and south. Such travels exposed them to milder winter climates and even larger herds of buffalo and other game, tempting them to return south and remain. The absence of warriors on such ventures meant prolonged exposure of fixed villages to attacks by unfriendly neighbors, with consequent death or capture of wives and families. Attacks by larger tribes living farther to the north and east were a constant threat, for such powerful peoples as the Assiniboines and Chippewas had come into early possession of firearms from white traders. Eventually the larger part of the Cheyenne tribe abandoned fixed village life along the Missouri and moved southwest across the plains. At the beginning of the eighteenth century most Cheyennes were living a nomadic life, hunting buffalo in and about the Black Hills.[6]

While living in the vicinity of the Black Hills, the Cheyennes developed a lasting relationship and alliance with the Arapahoes. The Arapahoes were a kindred Algonquian-speaking people, but unlike the Suhtai, their dialect and words were sufficiently different that the two tribes never could understand each other except by use of the universal Indian sign language. Although they were basically a warrior culture, the Arapahoes were also deeply religious, much given to ceremony, and in general peaceable, usually managing to coexist with even the most warlike neighbors. They had moved south and west much earlier than the Cheyennes, but once neighbors on the plains, the two tribes became staunch allies. From the Arapahoes, as from the Suhtai, the Cheyennes learned much of the culture so typical of the nomadic Plains Indians. During this same period the Cheyennes also developed a lasting and friendly relationship with the western Siouan bodies (Teton Lakota), particularly the southern Oglallas and Brulés. These alliances continued through the remainder of their free period to its climax at the Little Big Horn.[7]

Once the greater part of the tribe had abandoned agriculture and fixed villages, the Cheyennes took on all the trappings of nomadic Plains Indians—the dress, the buffalo-skin lodge or tipi, the buffalo culture, the horsemanship, the skill with weapons—and they became a true warrior society. Hunting west of the Black Hills brought them into conflict with the Crows, who, claiming the same lands as their own, became one of their great traditional enemies. Battles with the Crows to their west, and conflict with various other Siouan bodies to the north and east over common hunting grounds, eventually caused both the Arapahoes and the Cheyennes to start a general southward movement. This migration began slowly but gained momentum rapidly, with the Arapahoes in the lead. By 1804 large numbers of Arapahoes and Cheyennes were inhabiting the country on either side of the North Platte River, although most Cheyennes still remained farther north, around the Cheyenne River in what is now eastern Wyoming and western South Dakota. Nevertheless, by the turn of the century bands of Cheyenne had moved as far south as the Arkansas River to trade with Kiowas and Comanches, generally returning to their homes in the north when the trading was completed.[8]

The year 1812 found Arapahoes roaming the country about the upper Arkansas in considerable numbers, and not long afterward small bands of Cheyennes began to appear on a more permanent basis. Captain John R. Bell, journalist of the 1820 Stephen H. Long Expedition to the Rocky Mountains, reported meeting a mixed encampment of Kiowas, Kiowa-Apaches, Arapahoes, Shoshonis, Crows, and Cheyennes on July 26 at what was probably the Big Timbers of the Arkansas River. On August 1, 1820, while moving eastward along the north bank of the Arkansas, a short distance west of present-day Garden City, Kansas, Captain Bell's party encountered a small war party of approximately forty Cheyenne warriors who were returning to their village after having fought the Pawnees to the north. Such encounters illustrate the gradual movement of small bands and the southward shift of their homeland and hunting grounds.[9]

By 1821 large numbers of Cheyennes had moved down to the Arkansas, and by 1826 the river had become a permanent part of the Cheyenne range. Theirs was a vast domain, for some of their tribe remained in the old villages along the Missouri until well into the 1830s. By then they roamed and hunted over an area extending from about the northern border of South Dakota southward to the Arkansas River, and from the foothills of the Rockies on the west to about ninety-eight degrees longitude on the east (roughly a north-south line intersecting the Little Arkansas River approximately at the crossing of the Santa Fe Trail). Eventually the preferences of the various bands as to hunting ranges began to create a division within the tribe. Those preferring to live and hunt south of the Platte and South Platte rivers became the Southern Cheyennes, and those who continued to inhabit the territory north of those rivers, in eastern Wyoming, northern Colorado, and western Nebraska, became the Northern Cheyennes. A similar division occurred among the Arapahoes for the same reasons, but neither body ever thought of themselves as other than one tribe, despite their geographical preferences.[10]

Life and Conflict on the Southern Plains

The People came to the valleys of the Platte and Arkansas rivers late in their free existence, but once there they quickly adapted and asserted their right to the new territory. Doing so brought them into conflict with earlier claimants—nomadic Kiowas, Comanches, and Plains Apaches who had roamed and hunted much of the same territory for generations before the arrival of the Cheyennes; and seminomadic Pawnees, who had come to the plains each summer to hunt buffalo from their villages to the north and east for as long as their old people could remember. There were also occasional brushes with the Kansas, Osages, and Otoes, seminomadic Siouan peoples who lived in fixed villages east of the buffalo range but generally moved west for two buffalo hunts each year. More ominous was the incipient conflict with whites, who were even then beginning the great westward expansion that someday would engulf all the great Indian nations and deprive them of their homelands.

The earliest contacts between Cheyennes and the allied Kiowas and Comanches occurred when the latter tribes still roamed as far north as the Black Hills. Initially these encounters were mostly friendly, and it is said the Kiowas and the Comanches taught the Cheyennes the best means of dressing and softening buffalo hides. In time they developed a comfortable trading relationship whereby the Cheyennes would obtain horses from the Kiowas and Comanches in exchange for foodstuffs, clothing, weapons, and other trade goods that they had received from northern tribes and white traders through barter for buffalo hides. This mutually beneficial trade continued after many of the Cheyennes had moved down to the Arkansas, but terminated abruptly around 1827 or 1829, when the Cheyennes began raiding Kiowa and Comanche camps for horses and war broke out between them. Horses were the principal form of wealth for all Plains Indians, and raiding increased that wealth far more rapidly than trading the surplus from a year's hunt. When successful, raiding brought glory and acclaim to the returning warriors and increased the material welfare of the band.[11]

Following nearly thirteen years of intermittent warfare, a permanent peace was made between the Cheyennes and the Kiowas and Comanches in 1840. Through the mediation of the Plains Apaches and the Arapahoes, a council was arranged with the leaders of all five tribes—Cheyenne, Arapahoe, Comanche, Kiowa, and Apache. They met for several days at the treaty grounds suggested by William Bent, a few miles downstream from Bent's Old Fort. After the peace pipe had been smoked, the tribes took turns presenting gifts to each other, and holding feasts and dances. From that time on the five tribes were not only friends but allies, helping each other in times of need and in their wars.[12]

The Pawnees were enemies of the Cheyennes at least from the time when the latter began roaming the valleys of the Platte and other rivers and streams of the region, and conflicts between them increased when the Cheyennes continued south and claimed as their own the vast buffalo plains lying between the Platte and the Arkansas. The two tribes remained enemies, fighting whenever they met, for as long as they roamed and hunted on the plains. Nevertheless, the Cheyennes always respected the Pawnees as brave and worthy opponents. Treaties were made between them on several occasions, but real peace never came before the reservation era.[13]

While their traditional foes, the Crows and Pawnees, fought them and raided in the manner that the Cheyennes understood and expected, a new kind of opponent was appearing to the east. Immigrant Indians, driven from the east by the whites, had been placed in reservations adjoining the eastern boundary of Indian Territory, present-day Kansas, Nebraska, and Oklahoma. Greatly diminished in numbers, these tribes were remnants of great and proud peoples, many of whom in earlier times had been fierce fighters and implacable foes of white expansion. Their power broken, they now were confined to small reserves, where they were expected to sustain themselves with little government help. Not surprisingly, they frequently had to organize hunting parties and venture onto the plains in search of game. For this purpose the government permitted them to acquire modern rifles and other firearms, with which they became very proficient.[14]

The advent of hunters from immigrant tribes soon brought conflict. The efficient weapons of the eastern Indians had a further impact on already depleted numbers of buffalo and other game animals, angering the plains tribes. Occasional encounters brought sharp fights in which the firepower of the intruders frequently wrought havoc on the Cheyennes and their allies, who were armed with little more than lances and bows and arrows. These fights gave the Plains Indians a healthy respect for their eastern brethren and their skill with firearms. [15]

Most mysterious and dangerous of the people intruding upon the Cheyenne lands from the east were white men. The Cheyennes' first contacts with them had been with French and English traders and trappers while they were still living in the north. After large numbers of Cheyennes had moved down to the Arkansas they almost immediately encountered Mexican soldiers patrolling the border along the river, as well as traders and trappers moving along the Santa Fe Trail and the trail to the mountains.

During the early 1830s, Charles and William Bent and their partner, Ceran St. Vrain, had begun trading on the upper Arkansas, with their first post located on Fountain Creek near present-day Pueblo, Colorado. Subsequently they built a stockade about nine miles below the mouth of the Fountain. Sometime in 1833, at a site approximately seven miles east of modern La Junta, on the north side of the Arkansas, they began to build the great adobe post that they dubbed Fort William in honor of William Bent, its resident manager. The traders called it "Bent's Fort." Later, following its abandonment and the building of a successor post downstream, it was known as "Bent's Old Fort."

The sites for the original posts near Pueblo had been chosen to facilitate trade with both mountain and Plains Indians. Unfortunately, they were too close to the mountains and too far from the buffalo range to attract the Plains Indians. After conferring with a noted Cheyenne chief, Yellow Wolf, the Bents and St. Vrain selected the location below the mouth of Timpas Creek. Yellow Wolf had actually recommended a location somewhere in the Big Timbers, a favorite winter camping ground for certain bands of Cheyennes and Arapahoes, but the Bents compromised by staying some thirty-five miles west of the Big Timbers, a site closer to Taos and Santa Fe and one that they probably hoped would allow them to continue trading with the Utes and Shoshonis. However, the Utes and other mountain Indians were much too wise to venture that far out onto the plains, where their traditional enemies, the Plains Indians, might attack them. The result was that the new fort was neither fish nor fowl—too far east to have much trade with mountain Indians and too far west of the buffalo range to be in the mainstream of Plains Indian life. Nonetheless, it was far enough east to do a substantial business with the Plains Indians in its early years and at least some profitable business before its abandonment in 1849.

When William Bent built his "Bent's New Fort" in 1853, he followed the advice of Yellow Wolf and moved east to a well-situated location on the bluffs overlooking the Arkansas near the west end of the Big Timbers. Cheyenne contacts with white traders and others at both of the Bents' trading posts were agreeable, despite the disparity in real value between the buffalo robes, skins, and furs traded for relatively inexpensive utensils and trinkets, or, worse, cheap whiskey.[16]

Other white traders, trappers, explorers, and adventurers, of course, intruded upon or passed through the lands between the Platte and the Arkansas. Some came to trade with the Plains Indians, some were on their way elsewhere, some were there to observe. More clearly a harbinger of trouble was the occasional march of troops along the Santa Fe Trail and through the Indian country: United States troops along the north side of the Arkansas, Mexican troops on the south. During the early years there were no serious clashes between Cheyennes and the military, but all that was to change.

The People, Their Tribal Organization, Religion, and Art of War

Conflict between the Euro-Americans and the Cheyennes and other Plains Indians was inevitable. The explanation is simple: the Indians occupied and claimed as their own the vast stretch of open land that we call the Great Plains. It was territory the whites first wanted only to cross, but later to occupy; ownership rights of prior inhabitants made not a whit of difference. With their firm belief that God had chosen them to possess and cultivate the earth and had given to them alone the key to truth, many whites regarded the indigenous Indian peoples as little more than another species of wild animal. Whites, therefore, could in good conscience confine or exterminate Indians, as most expedient, to prevent them from retaining possession of their lands and impeding development of the country. Few seem to have realized that the hostility and warfare they encountered was the natural result of their intrusion, or that they were in conflict with brave peoples who had different yet noble cultures of their own, and who now were fighting to protect their lands and ways of life.

The Cheyennes, like most Plains Indians, were democratic and deeply religious. They were not ruled by hereditary chiefs vested with the powers of an absolute monarch, nor were the daughters of chiefs princesses of royal blood. In fact, their social structure was firmly grounded in a strong sense of freedom and family. Marriage was a formal and very serious matter, the bedrock of the family unit. Cheyennes had a strict code of morality and were renowned among Plains Indians for the virtue of their women. Their families were close, and each member played a part in the continuing struggle for survival. Men did the hunting, raiding, and fighting, took care of the horses and mules, and made the major decisions affecting the tribe. Women were responsible for clothing, feeding, and housing the family as well as rearing the young. The elderly played their part, including the care and training of children. Divorce was permitted under proper circumstances when a marriage did not work, but extramarital relationships were dealt with harshly.[17]

Beyond the primary family unit was the kindred, the larger family group that camped together within the band. Normally it consisted of the lodge of the family head, the lodges of his other wives and their children, and the lodges of daughters with their husbands and children. The preparation of food and the making of lodges, clothing, and necessary implements usually were cooperative activities within the group. Sometimes, as the size and number of its lodges grew, the kindred might become the nucleus of a new band. When they camped away from their band, kindred groups often had their own names.[18]

Above the kindred in the tribal social organization was the band. Generally this consisted of several closely related kindreds, although families did have the right to attach themselves to any band. Because of the blood relationship, young men usually married outside the band into which they were born, living instead with their wife's band. Each band had its traditional place in the camp circle when the tribe gathered together each year for the important religious festivals and the annual communal buffalo hunt. The camp circle always opened to the east or southeast, and the lodges were pitched around the periphery of the circle, two or three deep within a band's assigned area.

Inside the camp circle and toward its southern border, about 150 feet from the lodges, were the two sacred lodges containing the most powerful and sacred medicine of the Cheyennes, the two great tribal fetishes that, when properly used, brought divine aid or protection. The lodge containing the Sacred Medicine Arrows was always the easternmost, and that housing Is'siwun, the Sacred Buffalo Hat, the westernmost. No other lodges were within the circle, except when a large lodge might be erected at the center of the circle for a council, a dance, or other important event. Sacred lodges also were erected there for ceremonies such as the Arrow Renewal and the Sun Dance.[19]

Traditionally there were ten main Cheyenne bands: (1) Omissis (Eaters), (2) Oivimanah (Scabby), (3) Hevataniu (Hair Rope Men), (4) Issiometaniu (Ridge or Hill People), (5) Wutapiu (Those Who Eat with the Sioux), (6) Hofnowa (Poor People), (7) Ohktounna (Protruding Jaw People), (8) Ivistststinihpah or Heviqsnipahis (Burnt Aorta), (9) Suhtai (the Suhtai tribe), and (10) Hotamitaniu (Dog Men). The Dog Men were actually the famous Dog Soldier Military Society, which became a band when the men of the older Mahsihkota (Gray Hair) band joined up en masse. There were lesser bands, sometimes kindred, sometimes groups of friends, sometimes having a common bond with a different tribe. These included the Anskovinis (Narrow Nose Bridge), Mohkstahetaniu (Ute People), Moisiyu (the band of mixed Cheyenne-Sioux incorporated into the tribe), Nakoimanah (Bear People), Wohkpotsit (White Crafty People), Notamin (Facing the North—possibly of Arapahoe descent), and Honisku (meaning unknown).[20]

The economics of life on the plains did not permit the tribe to camp together during most of the year. When they did, it could not be for long periods. The various bands and kindreds joined together in the late spring or early summer after the grass had been growing long enough to permit their horses to regain strength and stamina and the buffalo to become fat, usually in May or June. After the important tribal rituals, they stayed together for a great buffalo hunt. But such a large encampment could not last long, even during the height of the growing season. The vast herds of horses and mules quickly ate the grass around the village site. Sanitation and disposal of human waste was a problem. Game was rapidly killed off or fled the area, requiring that the hunters move farther afield. This meant the encampment had to move with some frequency or split up. After the communal hunt, some bands moved away to their own favored hunting grounds, and by October all bands had scattered to other parts of the Cheyenne country where the game and forage would be sufficient to take them and their horses through the rigors of winter. There they would camp, as bands, kindreds, or lesser groupings of as few as eight or ten lodges. Thus they would remain until spring when the cycle would repeat itself.[21]

Running through all parts of the tribal organization were the military societies, organizations of warriors charged with performance of ceremonial functions, protection of the tribe, and maintenance of tribal discipline. According to Cheyenne mythology, their legendary culture hero, Sweet Medicine, originally established four military societies, the Swift Fox or Kit Fox Society, the Elk Horn Scraper or Crooked Lance Society, the Red Shield or Bull Soldiers, and the Dog Men or Dog Soldier Society. Later a fifth society, the Bow Strings, was formed, and still later the northern bands formed the Crazy Dogs. The Dog Soldiers were the most important and most aggressive, and theirs was the only society that also constituted a distinct band within the tribe with its own chiefs. Each of the societies had four chiefs selected by the members, and these acted as the principal war leaders of the tribe.[22]

At the pinnacle of tribal organization was the Council of Forty-four—the forty-four chiefs charged with civil leadership of the tribe. Sometimes they were referred to as peace chiefs, to distinguish their responsibilities for religious and secular affairs from the responsibility for leadership in war exercised by the chiefs of the military societies. There were four such chiefs from each of the ten principal bands and four head chiefs, considered the wisest in the tribe, who presided over the council. Unlike the military societies, which elected their chiefs, the Council of Forty-four was a self-perpetuating body in which existing members chose their successors (who might be themselves) for a ten-year term of office. Rigorous requirements of even temper, good nature, wisdom, courage, humor, concern for others, kindliness, generosity, and a high sense of honor were established for the chiefs. In their conduct they were expected to provide a sound example for all the people.

In addition to exercising authority over the movement and location of camp sites, the time and place for hunts, tribal religious ceremonies, and other matters of concern to the tribe as a whole, the council acted as a court, judging conduct that violated tribal law and custom. The four chiefs from each band exercised similar authority within the band during the greater part of the year when the tribe was scattered. Although the Council of Forty-four established the policies to be followed, the military societies exercised the power of enforcement and discipline, and in times of war their chiefs were responsible for protecting the tribe and leading its warriors in battle.[23]

Religion was of supreme importance to the Cheyennes. It pervaded all aspects of their lives, from the hunt and warfare to the simplest actions and relationships. The ancient Cheyenne name for God was Maheo—the All Father, the Supreme Being who created earth and all things upon, above, and below it. Maheo created the Maheyuno, the four Sacred Persons, whom he set to guard the four quarters of the universe, and the Maiyun, the Sacred Powers, who live above and below the earth. The earth itself was referred to as Esceheman, "Our Grandmother," the source of food and drink for all creatures. Prayers invoking the blessings of Maheo, the Sacred Persons, and the Earth were offered through smoking the sacred pipe and offering it to each in turn, asking for health, plenty, and safety. The Sacred Person dwelling in the southeast was Esseneta'he, who lived where the Sun rises and spreads his renewing rays across the Earth. Esseneta'he originated life and light, and his color was white. Sovota was the Sacred Person who lived in the southwest, home of warmth and thunder and the source of the rain and warm weather that nourished the earth's vegetation. The symbolic color for Sovota was red. The Sacred Person guarding the northwest, the place where the sun sets, was Onxsovon. His color was a golden yellow, the color of sunset, representing ripeness, perfection, and beauty. Last of the four Sacred Persons was Notamota, who dwelled in the northeast. His color, black, symbolized cold and death. From his home came storms, cold weather, snow, disease, and death.[24]

The Sacred Persons were protective and helpful to men but had to be respected and propitiated through prayer, fasting, and sacrifice. When properly invoked they shared their wisdom and power through visions and dreams. The Maiyun, the lesser Sacred Powers, included those that lived above and below the earth and served the Sacred Persons. Greatest of the Above Powers was the Sun, giver of life-renewing power, which the Cheyennes invoked through the Sun Dance. Thunder and Whirlwind, other strong Above Powers, were the protectors of the Sacred Arrow bundle. In general the Maiyun were beneficent and not intentionally harmful to Man. They were in a sense the extension of Maheo's power working through natural forces. Often they appeared as one of the creatures that lives on or above the earth.[25]

To the Cheyennes the real soul or spirit of a person was called the Ma'tasooma. At death the soul separated itself from the body and traveled across Seozemeo, the Milky Way, to Se'han, the place of the dead, where the deceased was reunited with those who had gone before. Here all dwelled happily, close to the presence of Maheo, very much as they had on earth. They had fine white lodges, plenty of buffalo to hunt, fast horses, and an abundance of the good things of life. Only suicides and the very bad were barred from this peaceful existence. There was no hell or punishment after death; wrongdoing was atoned for during this life by enduring both the punishment meted out by the tribe and the ostracism of tribal members. Goodness and rightness were sought for their own sake and for the approval of one's fellow beings; recognition, honor, and positions of respect and leadership provided strong motivation for people to whom material wealth meant little.[26]

Death was not a fearful event to the individual Cheyenne, but it was a difficult time for the survivors. The tribe was small, and every death was felt keenly by those who remained, particularly by the women of a deceased male's family who were dependent upon him for food and other necessities. As an expression of grief, female relatives usually cut their long hair and gashed their foreheads, breasts, arms, or legs, sometimes even cutting off part of a finger. The dead person, body extended full length with arms at the side, was wrapped in skins and placed upon a scaffold or in a crotch of a tree, or was covered with rocks on the ground, depending upon what was available. The deceased's favorite horse was shot and left at the grave site, along with his weapons, if a man, or if a woman, her utensils. The shield and war bonnet of a warrior were given to his son; the flesher of a woman was given to her daughter. Everything else was given away, generally to nonrelatives, and the family lodge itself usually was burned. The survivors of an adult male lived with relatives until the widow remarried.[27]

Invocation of Maheo, the Sacred Persons, or the Sacred Powers
was achieved through prayer and smoking, but rituals supplicating
divine beings and invoking blessings or help were to a large degree
mechanical. They were those taught by Sweet Medicine and Erect
Horns, the great culture heroes and teachers of the Tsistsistas and
the Suhtai, or by their predecessors and successors. These rituals
were believed to work if performed properly. If supplicants failed
to perform them, or did so improperly, they would be without divine aid and disaster could result. Tribal priests or medicine men
were trained in the knowledge of the rituals and of the various
taboos that must be observed.[28]

The great ceremonies of the Cheyennes included the Renewal of
the Sacred Arrows, the Sun Dance, and the Animal Dance or Massaum. Of these the most important was and remains the Sacred
Arrow Renewal, a four-day long ceremony of renewal, purification,
and sanctification of the whole tribe. The four Sacred Arrows, or
Mahuts, were a gift to the Tsistsistas by Sweet Medicine, who had
received them from Maheo through a Maiyun who had taken human
form. Two of the arrows had red shafts and were called "buffalo
arrows," symbolizing the procurement of food. The remaining two
arrows had black shafts and were called "man arrows." They represented the power of the tribe in war. Properly venerated, the
Sacred Arrows protected the Cheyennes and assured them good life
and victory over enemies. The ceremony of renewal was not an
annual event. It was undertaken upon the pledge of a member of
the Council of Forty-four or of a warrior during difficult times, such
as when there was widespread sickness, or when a murder had
been committed within the tribe. This was the supreme act of wor-
ship for the Cheyennes; all kindreds and bands were present for it.
Loss of the Sacred Arrows (which occurred in 1830 when they were
captured by the Pawnees) presaged disaster, for the tribe then
found itself without their power and protection.[29]

Unlike the Renewal of the Sacred Arrows, which was a ritual
unique to the Cheyennes, the Sun Dance, or Medicine Lodge, was
common to many of the Plains tribes. It is said that the Sun Dance
was brought to the Cheyennes by the Suhtai, who had received it
from Erect Horns. The Sun Dance was usually held annually, in
late May or June, as the result of a pledge made by some tribal
member who had promised it to Maheo in return for divine aid or

intervention. Like the Renewal ceremony, it required the presence of the entire tribe and resulted in a renewal of the earth. It took eight days to complete and was centered around a special medicine lodge built in the middle and toward the front, or east side, of the camp circle. The lodge was formed by a large circle of upright posts and a center pole to which they were joined by smaller poles or stringers. Usually this roof arrangement was partially covered by buffalo robes. Within the lodge the altar was built and the most sacred part of the ceremony performed. Here also dancers performed the well-known acts of self-sacrifice: hanging on ropes that were attached to the center pole of the lodge and inserted through the skin of the breast by skewers, or pulling buffalo skulls attached by ropes that passed through the flesh of the dancer's shoulder blades.[30]

The Massaum, or Animal Dance, was a hunting ritual taught to the tribe by Sweet Medicine and intended to ensure success in the hunt and plenty of meat for all. Usually performed in years in which the Arrow Renewal ceremony was not pledged, it took five days and nights. In contrast to the Arrow Renewal and the Sun Dance, it was a joyful occasion.[31]

The pervasiveness of religious beliefs and practices heavily influenced the conduct of all tribal affairs, including war. Cheyenne warriors were brave to the extreme, but whether they fought, and when and where they fought, were matters dependent upon medicine made and taboos and signs read by medicine men. Living as they did in a vast area containing other nomadic tribal enemies, the Cheyennes emphasized military virtue beyond nearly all else. The need to take and hold hunting grounds having buffalo and other wildlife sufficient to sustain the tribe made the art of war as important as the art of the hunt. Tribal survival was at stake. But the emphasis on bravery, honor, and glory created a form of fighting not well suited to the warfare they soon would experience with whites and reservation Indians. A show of bravery became of greater importance to the warriors than the need to defeat the enemy. War thereby became a ritualized display of courage in which counting coups—striking or touching an enemy with weapons or bare hands—gave prestige but frequently denied them victory. Heroic deeds in battles were given like credit. A warrior's standing and regard in the tribe as a fighting man was the sum of the coups he had counted and his abilities as a leader of successful war or raiding parties.[32]

Cheyenne war parties included those organized by present or aspiring leaders and others in search of a reputation, those organized by a military society, and tribal war parties where the object was vengeance or punishment of tribal enemies. By far the most common were the first two. Usually the object was to take horses or to exact vengeance for the deaths of friends and relatives. Any such venture, however, required the blessing and instruction of a medicine man; the approval of the mission and offerings to Maheo, the Sacred Persons, and the Sacred Powers; and perhaps prayers or offerings to the tribal fetishes—the Sacred Arrows and the Sacred Buffalo Hat. Preparation for a war party or for battle required lengthy ceremonies—the consecration of shield, war bonnet, and weapons, sacrificial offerings, and the singing of war songs. The ceremonies assured participants that their medicine (divine protection and aid) would be strong and the undertaking successful. Failure to obtain the appropriate blessing or properly to purify oneself, failure to follow tribal taboos, or failure properly to treat or use shields or war bonnets would destroy a war party's medicine and invite defeat. The tribe was small and could not withstand many losses in battle; therefore the dictates of tribal custom and religion were usually carefully followed. So strong was this belief that even a warrior's war horse had to be prepared for battle by means of prayers, sacred songs, and paint.[33]

Although their methods of war were not suited to fighting disciplined bodies of troops armed with long-range rifles and other firearms, some factors favored the Cheyennes. Their bravery was legendary among even the Plains Indians, nearly all of whom held bravery in the highest esteem. They did not fear death, for they always entered battle with the firm conviction that Maheo was with them and that if death came to any warrior it would bring honor and glory to his name and to the tribe. He would then cross the great Hanging Bridge of the Milky Way to Se'han and the eternal company of Maheo. The Cheyennes were among the greatest horsemen of the plains and could perform incredible feats from the back, side, or underside of a galloping horse. They were highly trained and accurate with their weapons, whether bows and arrows, lances, or firearms. If it became necessary to leave a battle, both they and their war horses had toughness and endurance that enabled them to outdistance and outlast most pursuers. They were superlative scouts and knew their country as no intruders possibly could. It was warriors such as these who met the First Cavalry on Solomon's Fork.[34]

Appendix B

The First Cavalry

What premonition of the afterwhile
Could darken eyes that saw such glory pass
When, lilting in a muffled blare of brass
Off yonder near the sundering prairie rim,
The Girl I Left Behind Me floated dim
As from the unrecoverable years? (174)

The Birth of a Regiment

In 1855 the United States was in the throes of expansion. Following the annexation of Texas and the conquest of New Mexico and California (including present-day Arizona and parts of several other states), the country was more than one-third larger than it had been. Much of the new territory was relatively unexplored and unknown, except by a handful of fur trappers, hunters, and Indian traders. But settlements were now stretching westward and long wagon trains of immigrants were moving along the trails to California and Oregon. As they passed through the homelands of the Plains Indians—country the natives held sacred and believed no whites had the right to enter—they were highly vulnerable and in need of protection.

The Indians of the Great Plains were as fine a group of horsemen as the world had known, and mounted troops were the only effective means of combating them. In the early 1850s the United States Army was a small organization, consisting of only fifteen regiments, including eight regiments of infantry, four of artillery, two of dragoons, and one of mounted rifles. The mounted service had existed in one form or another since before the American Revolution, but it had been established on a permanent basis only on March 2, 1833, when Congress passed an act creating the United States Regiment of Dragoons. As a policy of Indian removal was adopted and the need for protection of white settlers grew, Congress added the Second Regiment of Dragoons, on May 23, 1836. This was followed on May 19, 1846, by creation of the Regiment of Mounted Riflemen.[1]

Dragoons were originally organized to act both as cavalry and as infantry,* but because of the great distances over which they had to move and the elusiveness of mounted Plains Indians, they performed their service in the West primarily as light cavalry, fighting from horseback. The Mounted Riflemen were originally intended as mobile light infantry, able to respond rapidly to need but fighting on foot. But the need to garrison posts along the Oregon Trail and to provide protection for immigrant trains and frontier settlements throughout the West soon required that they too serve as cavalry. While originally different, organization of the Mounted Rifles soon was altered and made identical to that of the Dragoons—ten companies to the regiment and seventy privates to the company. After April 25, 1849, the Dragoons were equipped with the U.S. Model 1847 smoothbore musketoon carbine, Model 1840 dragoon sabres, and Colt .44 caliber dragoon revolvers. The Mounted Rifles were armed with U.S. Model 1841 .54 caliber percussion rifles and Colt .44 caliber dragoon revolvers, but did not commonly carry sabres.[2]

By 1855 the requirements of protecting immigrants and patrolling such a vast expanse of territory had overwhelmed the army. Consequently, on March 3, 1855, Congress authorized the raising of an additional two regiments of infantry and two regiments of mounted troops. The two new mounted regiments, designated the First and Second Cavalry, were the first regular American military units to bear that name. The uniforms of the new units were much like those of the Dragoons, except that their shell jackets were trimmed with yellow braid (afterward the trademark of all United States cavalry). Cavalry soldiers, officers and enlisted alike, wore

---

*Dragoons took their name from the dragon crest, a device commonly worn on the helmet of mounted soldiers during the Middle Ages. See Albert G. Brackett, *History of the United States Cavalry*, 159.

a black felt hat looped up and fastened by a brass eagle on the right side and decorated with a worsted yellow cord, a black feather, and, for enlisted personnel, their company letter. They were armed with Model 1840 dragoon sabres, Colt Model 1851 .36 caliber navy revolvers, and, depending upon the company, U.S. Model 1854 .58 caliber rifled carbines (three squadrons); Merrill, Latrobe and Thomas .54 caliber breech-loading percussion carbines (Fifth Squadron); Sharp's Model 1852 percussion carbines (one company); or Model 1855 Springfield pistol-carbines (one company).* Otherwise they were organized in the much same manner as the Dragoons.[3]

The First Cavalry was recruited and organized in the spring of 1855 at Jefferson Barracks, St. Louis, Missouri, and in August was ordered to Fort Leavenworth. By September it had embarked on its first important assignment, an expedition against the Sioux that lasted until early November. There was a major engagement with the Sioux, but First Cavalry troops were not involved in the fighting. During 1856 the regiment divided its time between defending the frontier against Indian attack and trying to maintain peace between the pro-slavery and free-state factions among the new immigrants in Kansas Territory. It was thus employed when orders for the Cheyenne Expedition were formulated.[4]

Organization of the Regiment and Its Officers and Men

The two new regiments of cavalry were authorized in 1855 with the understanding that all field-grade officers (majors or above) and one-half of the company-grade officers (captains and lieutenants) would be selected from existing units within the army, with the remaining company-grade officers to be appointed from civilian life. Secretary of War Jefferson Davis and his staff exercised great care in making these selections, and the complement of officers of both regiments was filled with names destined to gain immortality during the War Between the States, then still six years away.[5]

Each of the new regiments had four field-grade officers, includ-

*The U.S. Model 1854 .58 caliber rifled carbines originally were manufactured as .54 caliber. In July 1855 the secretary of war approved adoption of the .58 caliber. Subsequent production was .58, and most of the 300 production models made between mid-1854 and mid-1855 were rebored to .58. See Louis A. Garavaglia and Charles G. Worman, *Firearms of the American West, 1803–1865*, 181.

ing a full colonel commanding, one lieutenant colonel as deputy commander, and two majors. At full strength each regiment was comprised of ten companies, and each company consisted of one captain, one first lieutenant, one second lieutenant, four sergeants (one first sergeant and three duty sergeants), four corporals, two buglers, one farrier and blacksmith, and eighty-four privates.[6]

For the First Cavalry the commanding officer selected was Lt. Col. Edwin Vose Sumner of the First Dragoons. A native of Massachusetts, Sumner had entered the army as a second lieutenant of the Second Infantry in March 1819 and had become a first lieutenant in 1823 and captain of the First Dragoons in March 1833. His distinguished service with the Dragoons during the Mexican War and thereafter in various posts in the West, particularly in Kansas and New Mexico, established him as a highly competent and professional leader. During this period he earned the sobriquet "Bull of the Woods," the result of his booming parade-ground voice.* He consistently shared the same rigors and hardships as his men and insisted that his officers do the same. Accordingly, he commanded both the admiration and the loyalty of his troops.[7]

Lieutenant colonel of the new First Regiment was Joseph Eccleston Johnston. A Virginian and an 1829 West Point graduate, he had been cited for gallantry in action in Florida and during the Mexican War, where he was twice wounded in action. With a background in the Topographical Engineers, after the Mexican War he was engaged in making roads and surveying routes across the plains of the Great Southwest. Majors for the regiment included William H. Emory of Maryland and John Sedgwick of Connecticut, both officers with outstanding records of service in the Mexican War and elsewhere.[8]

The ten companies of the First Cavalry were designated A, B, C, D, E, F, G, H, I, and K. By the fall of 1856, after several changes resulting from transfers, promotions, and resignations, Company A was commanded by Capt. William N. R. Beall, Company B by Capt. Delos B. Sackett, Company C by Capt. Thomas J.

---

*It is said that Colonel Sumner was given the nickname of "Bull" when a musket ball glanced off his skull during the Battle of Cerro Gordo in the Mexican War. This was subsequently expanded to "Bull of the Woods" by his men in recognition of his great voice. See Robert M. Peck, "Rough Riding on the Plains," *The National Tribune* (Washington, D.C.), Feb. 21, 1901, 7; Robert M. Utley, *Frontiersmen in Blue*, 121.

Wood, Company D by Capt. James McIntosh, Company E by Capt. Samuel D. Sturgis, Company F by Capt. William D. DeSaussure, Company G by Capt. William S. Walker, Company H by Capt. Edward W. B. Newby, Company I by Capt. George T. Anderson, and Company K by Capt. George H. Stewart. Regimental adjutant was 2d Lt. Albert V. Colburn.[9]

Horses were assigned to each company by colors. Company A had sorrels; B, grays; C, sorrels; D, bays; E, roans; F, sorrels; G, blacks; H, bays; I, sorrels; and, K, bays. Variations in color not only served to make each company distinctive and uniform, lending dramatic effect on parade or on the march, but also had the more practical purpose of helping troopers identify their own units in the thick of battle. Buglers, two to the company, were mounted on white horses, primarily to help the unit commander pick them out quickly to communicate a command to his men. The noise generated by a cavalry unit on the march usually was considerable: saddle leather creaking, weapons slapping against horse and rider, horses blowing, hooves striking rock or soil, human voices and coughs, and a variety of other sounds. Such noises—along with the great distance between the front and rear of a column—made it nearly impossible to control a unit in the field with even the strongest voice; hence the need for the bugle and its variety of calls, each signaling some desired response. The copper bugles used in that period gave a louder sound than the brass bugles of a later day.[10]

The government provided mounts, uniforms, and equipment for all enlisted personnel, but not for officers, who were required to purchase their own. For some obscure reason, officers were not limited in selecting the colors of their horses, and hence usually suited themselves based upon personal preference. Generally each had at least two horses, to ensure against the loss of one. Because other duties left little time to attend to grooming and caring for their animals, and because these activities were considered inappropriate for an officer, most of them required help with this task. Some used servants or slaves, but most hired troopers who preferred the care of horses to regular company duty, from which they were thereby excused. The imposition of menial service on a soldier was strictly forbidden by army regulations and by express orders of the army commander-in-chief. Even voluntary service was discouraged. But frontier conditions made procuring civilian servants impossible; therefore, volunteers were essential for this task. Fortunately, the number of enlisted men who preferred that work to company duty usually was sufficient, and it was never necessary to make it mandatory. Those who volunteered for such service were called "dog robbers" by both officers and enlisted men, and the term was so familiar it became a legitimate title that carried with it no reproach. [11]

To fill the ranks of the new regiment, recruiting was necessary. Each company sent out a lieutenant and a sergeant to scour cities and towns in the States for able-bodied men. They moved from city to city, enlisting men until they had brought their company to full strength, usually starting in the states located closest to the eastern boundary of the Indian country or the territories, then working farther east, until their quota was met. Most states had one or more recruiting offices in the largest cities, but enlistment at these could not guarantee which arm of the service the enlistee would be assigned to—infantry, artillery, or cavalry—nor any assurance as to where he might serve or what kind of duty he might be assigned. Enlistment directly into a unit of the mounted service promised the imagined adventure of frontier warfare, the glamour of the mounted forces, and the sure knowledge of the nature of the service. [12]

To entice men to enlist, the recruiting sergeant placed yellow recruiting posters in prominent locations within a town or city. These read:

WANTED

Ablebodied unmarried men between the ages of 18 and 45, to enlist as soldiers in the First Regiment, U. S. Cavalry, for active service against Indians on the frontier, to whom will be given good clothing, rations and medical attendance, and pay at the rate of $12.00 a month for privates, $14.00 for corporals, $17.00 for Duty Sergeants, and $22.00 for First Sergeants. Promotion open to all men of merit.

A recruiting sergeant was allowed a bonus of two dollars per head for each recruit he enlisted; thus it is easy to imagine that recruiters grossly exaggerated the glamour and rewards of the life, along with the likelihood of promotion. Although they acknowledged that the pay sounded small, they generally painted a glowing picture in which the government liberally supplied all wants, pay being necessary only as a monthly allowance of pocket change. By stressing that promotion was readily available for "all men of merit" and that a prospective enlistee obviously had exceptional soldierly qualities, a good recruiter had little difficulty in exciting the active imagination of younger prospects to such a pitch that they saw only a few months of experience in the field separating them from command of the unit.[13]

Once enlisted, new troopers were given cursory physical exams and, if they passed, were sent to the company's post, Fort Leavenworth, for rigorous training designed to make them proper horsemen and cavalrymen, "as hardy as a buffalo and tough as an Indian." Enlistees enrolled during the height of winter, when the Missouri River was frozen over, were detained and trained at Jefferson Barracks, St. Louis, Missouri, until the spring thaw permitted riverboats to transport them upriver to Fort Leavenworth. There were then no railroads west of St. Louis except a short branch to Jefferson City, the state capital, and river travel usually was discontinued sometime in December until the ice broke up enough to permit navigation, normally in mid-February.[14]

Once the enlistees had joined the regiment and passed a more rigorous physical exam, the process of equipping and training them began in earnest. They were marched to their company quarters, issued uniforms, and ordered to dispose of any civilian clothing in their possession. They were prohibited from possessing or wearing civilian clothes for the duration of the five-year enlistment. Such clothing usually was sold to secondhand clothing dealers, then generally located near each military post. The new uniforms included coarse (but comfortable and durable), light-blue woolen trousers, dark-blue jackets trimmed with bright yellow braid, fatigue caps of dark-blue cloth, the dress hat previously described, sturdy and comfortable sewn boots, woolen socks, cotton-flannel drawers, and woolen undershirts. In addition, each man was issued a good cape overcoat of the same light-blue cloth as the trousers, and one pair of gray blankets with the letters *US* imprinted in the center. One bed sack was issued for each two men, to be filled with straw or hay. Company tailors made certain that all outer garments fit well, ensuring a smart-looking outfit.[15]

Considerations of fitness, appearance, discipline, and the requirement of living in close proximity with others have always made the cleanliness and personal hygiene of its personnel a prime concern of any fighting force. While each man was responsible for cleaning and maintaining his own clothing, the army did make some remarkable provisions to ensure this was properly accomplished by those souls who harbored a dislike for such menial tasks. By regulation, four married men were allowed to each company, and their wives were provided with quarters and rations in exchange for doing the company washing and mending while they were in garrison. For that service they were entitled to charge the sum of ten cents per piece for washing and ironing. Officially designated company laundresses, these women were unofficially referred to by the troopers as "hay-bags." When in the field, each man was on his own and usually carried a little bag with needles, thread, thimble, and scissors.[16]

In addition to clothing, the army provided its men with mess kits consisting of camp kettles, mess pans and frying pans of sheet iron, Dutch ovens or skillets of cast iron, and a coffee mill, but nothing more. Each man provided his own plate, cup, knife, fork, and spoon, or reasonable substitutes, as best he could. Frequently a soldier had to eat with a sheath or Bowie knife, which he carried on his belt. In some companies personal utensils of the troopers and some foodstuffs, such as fresh vegetables, eggs, butter, and other luxury items, were provided by the "Company fund," money accumulated by the sale of government rations not consumed by the men.[17]

Government issue also included weapons kits consisting of a rifled carbine, sabre, sabre belt, and a cartridge box for each man. Enlisted men were required to polish all metal surfaces of their equipment, including buttons on their jackets, and to keep them shining. Belts and cartridge boxes were shined with shoe blacking and polished until they reflected like a mirror. Colt's navy pistols were not issued until a unit took the field.[18]

Each new trooper was provided a horse, assigned a stall at the company stable, and issued necessary equipment, including saddle, bridle, saddle blanket, currycomb, and brush. Except for the Fifth Squadron, which used Campbell saddles, the saddle issued to the enlisted men of the First Cavalry in 1856 and 1857 was the standard Grimsley dragoon saddle adopted by the army in 1847, along with its associated equipment. Many of the officers, who were required to supply their own, used the Hope, or "Texas," saddle, which they much preferred. With the equipment issued, the soldiers embarked on the long days of arduous training that would change them from green civilians into highly trained horsemen capable of traveling long distances under adverse conditions and entering combat, if the need arose, as a well-disciplined fighting force. Each day was a succession of training exercises and drills designed to improve the horsemanship and military skills of the men. These included target practice, manual of arms, marching, care and grooming of mounts, riding (with saddle or bareback), mounting and dismounting, jumping hurdles, care and cleaning of equipment, sabre exercises, and many other aspects of soldiering. By the spring of 1857, though not experienced in the field or in battle, the First Cavalry was at last a well-trained, disciplined unit of mounted troops.[19]

The Regiment in the Field

Because motion pictures and television have created the illusion of a cavalry unit galloping many miles across the plains with only the equipment and supplies that could be carried in saddlebags, it is important to consider the realities experienced during a field march or expedition by a large body of mounted troops. Logistics was a major problem. A march might last many days, weeks, or even months, and that meant providing for the needs of men and animals over a protracted period. Cavalry horses, in contrast to the tough, self-sufficient Indian horses, were heavy, grain-fed, and unaccustomed to the hardships of the plains. Grain and forage were therefore necessary to supplement grazing during the anticipated length of an extended march. Grazing itself was an unsure thing, dependent upon the season, extremes of temperature, rainfall, terrain, and available native vegetation. Wildfire and overgrazing by Indian horses, buffalo, and various wild animals were additional concerns in determining whether grazing would be sufficient along the route of march.[20]

Soldiers also had to be fed at least a minimally nutritious diet during the same period, which meant transporting beans, rice, and other vegetables (dried or fresh), flour for bread or biscuits, coffee, sugar, salt, bacon or salted pork, and fresh meat. Fresh meat generally was supplied from a herd of steers that was driven along in the rear of the column and slaughtered as need arose. Wild game often supplemented fresh beef, but its availability was uncertain and attempts to catch and kill it frequently unsuccessful.[21]

The marching cavalry unit required a good-sized wagon train to remain in the field for long periods of time. Such trains carried the needed food supplies, grain and forage, ammunition, spare weapons and parts, tents for sleeping and for hospital purposes, camp cooking equipment, spare leather and parts for saddle repair, horseshoes and equipment for the farrier-blacksmith, mess equipment, medical supplies and equipment, and numerous other items needed to keep the unit fed, housed, supplied, and mobile.[22]

During the course of a march, one of the buglers with the unit was detailed each day at guard mount as "orderly bugler." His job was to stay near the commanding officer, sounding regular calls at the prescribed times, and any other calls ordered by the commander or adjutant. On the march he rode just to the rear of the commanding officer. At night, in camp, after taps was sounded, he slept in the guard tent to be available to sound the alarm in the event of an attack, stampede, or other danger, and to sound first call for reveille the following morning at the time established by the commander.[23]

First call for reveille was usually sounded as soon as the sun's red glow began to appear on the eastern horizon. The troopers turned out, dressed hurriedly, then, as the bugler sounded assembly, fell in in front of the tents under arms, carbines at the "carry." They were brought to "order arms" by their company first sergeant and then to "parade-rest" while the bugler sounded reveille. At its last note, he brought them to attention and to "carry-arms," stepped to the front of the company, and called roll. With the roll called, he reported any absences to the company commander. The bugler then sounded "stable call," whereupon the men broke ranks, removed all arms and belts except waist belts, pistols, and knives, got their currycombs, brushes, and saddle blankets, and went to the forage wagon to draw their ration of shelled corn. The corn was poured into the saddle blanket and taken by each man to where his horse was picketed, then spread on the ground for the horse to eat while being groomed. Grooming was supervised by one of the company officers. When the horses had been fed and curried, the men were dismissed to report to the cook tent just as breakfast call was sounded.[24]

Breakfast generally consisted of a quart of coffee, a hunk of bread—sometimes hardtack and sometimes soft—and a ration of meat, alternating bacon or mess pork and fresh beef. After breakfast came sick call, when ailing soldiers presented themselves to the regimental doctor for whatever treatment was indicated and available, then returned to duty if able. Following this the bugler sounded "the general," the signal to strike camp. Tents were taken down, poles removed, canvas rolled up, and pins gathered; all was taken to the company wagon, in the rear of the company camping area, and packed away, along with the blankets and other baggage. Next came water call, when each man was required to bring his horse from the picket line and lead him to water. After water came "boots and saddles," at which time the horses were saddled and the troopers put on their belts and arms. At the call "to horse" horses were led into line and first sergeants gave the commands "count fours," "prepare to mount," "mount," and "form ranks." They were then ready to commence the day's march.[25]

Each company in turn took its day at the head of the column, a brief but welcome respite from "eating the dust" of those ahead. With the column properly mounted, the bugler sounded "advance" and each company, in its turn, marched out by fours. Then the wagon train began to string out behind the cavalry column, followed by the extra horses and mules, the beef herd, and finally by the rear guard.

Once under way a cavalry column moved at a walk, barring some emergency or specific need, and it did not stop for a noon meal, nor until it had found the next night's campground. Generally the only pauses in the march were those required to water the horses, usually once or twice daily, with a halt of about fifteen minutes each hour after the march began, during which the girth and saddle were tightened. A normal day's march was between fifteen and twenty miles, its length depending on the availability of good camping, distance to destination, march time allotted, and other factors. The essential requirements for a camping place were wood, water, and grass. On the plains the lack of wood often necessitated resorting to other forms of fuel or even doing without fire.[26]

When the commanding officer had selected a campsite, after consulting with the scouts, the troopers and their horses were formed in line, with a water supply (river, stream, or pond) to their rear. Then the bugler sounded the calls that successively directed them to dismount, unsaddle, water the horses, and picket them in front of the company line. Following a hard day's march, particularly during hot weather, when the saddles were removed, the saddle blankets were turned and left on the horses, strapped on by the surcingle, to prevent saddle boils. During cold weather, care was taken to see that the horses were well blanketed at night. That done, each man was required to gather an armful of wood for cooking; or if wood was not available, he was to fill a sack or saddle blanket with buffalo chips. When the company baggage wagon pulled up to its assigned place in the rear of the line, the men unpacked it and pitched the tents exactly in line on the ground on which they had halted. The cooks (company enlisted personnel assigned to the task on a rotating basis) then set about preparing the evening meal, a combination of dinner and supper, there being only two meals per day during the march.

The day's march probably lasted only six or seven hours, but it began early, to take advantage of the day's coolest temperatures and best light. Back in camp there was much to do, not only in establishing the new camp itself, but in tending to the needs of the animals and cooking the evening meal. The meal generally consisted of coffee, bread, meat, and soup, alternately made of beans, rice, or desiccated vegetables. Periodically the regimental doctor would order an extra issue of pickles, molasses, or other items as antiscorbutics for the prevention of scurvy. When available, fresh vegetables, purchased from a trading post with cash from the company fund, provided a welcome change.[27]

When the last wagon and animal had arrived in camp, the guard was established in position, with a tent in front of the center of the camp, just outside the area where the cavalry horses were picketed. With the onset of evening, guard mount, stable call, retreat, and tattoo closed out the duties of the day, and the camp was left in the care of the guard.[28]

The tents used by the First Cavalry in 1857 were conical Sibley tents (named after their designer, Maj. H. H. Sibley of the Second Dragoons), which were then undergoing field testing by various units. They accommodated twelve to fifteen men, closely spaced. Saddles were used for pillows, with a trooper's folded jacket thrown across to soften the headrest. Arms and belts were kept at the side in case of a night alarm. The men lay with their heads to the outside and feet to the center. Not luxury accommodations, to be sure, but at the end of each day most troopers were so tired that sleeping was seldom a problem.[29]

Care of horses included more than the feeding, watering, and

grooming provided by the troopers. Shoes were inspected frequently, and often required changing or replacing. This was the
job of the farrier-blacksmith found with each company of cavalry.
In addition to his portable smithy for heating and forming the
shoes, the farrier's equipment included shoeing tools—shoeing
knife, toe knife, shoeing hammer, clinching iron, clinch-cutter,
pair of pincers, and rasp. At the start of a march each horse had
two spare shoes that had been fitted so the farrier could simply nail
them on if any were lost during the march.[30]

Some marches, depending on the need for rapid movement, terrain, and the like, were made without a supply train. Food,
ammunition, farrier supplies, cooking gear, and other necessary
items were packed on mules or horses, which were then formed
into a pack train. This train was positioned close behind the cavalry column during the march, followed by the beef herd and the
extra mounts and pack animals. Tents were not taken during such
marches and the troopers had to sleep under the stars, in their
uniforms, and with weapons at their sides, prepared for action.
While traveling in inclement weather, they would roll up the bedding and put their oilcloths over it and their overcoats over that—
the best they could do to "sleep dry." Grain for mounts was
packed, but there was no way to transport forage. Limited to grain
and what grazing might be available, horses often suffered greatly
from lack of nourishment, thereby restricting the length of a march
and frequently increasing its duration.[31]

Thus was a cavalry march made in the sixth decade of the nineteenth century. Usually long and arduous, such marches required
that men and animals move under their own power for extended
periods over difficult and unknown terrain, in a climate of extremes, at great distances from any source of resupply, and with
the ever-present danger of attack by hostile Indians. This was the
kind of march the First Cavalry undertook in May of 1857.

Appendix C

Official Communications and Reports Pertaining to the Cheyenne Expedition

1. Extract, Wharton to Cooper, September 8, 1856

These Indians are now openly hostile, and there is no possible safety in traveling through this country, except with a large and well-armed force; all small parties will doubtless be sacrificed. There is a combination of the Cheyennes of the Arkansas with those of the Platte in this matter, and most certainly do they need summary punishment. They are emboldened by its delay. There is an urgent and immediate necessity for a large garrison on the Arkansas, near the old site of Fort Atkinson. The Cheyennes have been troublesome ever since the abandonment of that post. Beside being the location of several bands of this tribe, it is likewise the congregating ground of the Arapahoes, Comanches, and several other troublesome tribes. It is likewise absolutely necessary that this post should be garrisoned by a mounted force; at least three companies of cavalry are needed here, with one company of infantry, for the protection of the public property. Had it not been for the cavalry company now here, I should have been unable to punish the Indians for the recent attack upon the mail party.

(*KHC* 4:492–94)

2. Extract, Smith to Cooper, September 10, 1856

This tribe must be severely punished, and but that the troops most disposable are engaged here, I would instantly march with the whole garrisons of this post and Fort Riley to chastise them;

but no trifling or partial punishment will suffice, and as no one can be spared from this neighborhood, I will postpone extensive operations until spring. In the meantime, if necessary, I can send some of the force from the posts above this to strengthen Fort Kearny and render it secure for the winter, and, by throwing forward forage and provisions there, to prepare for an early movement in force on the springing of the first grass.   (*KHC* 4:489–90)

3. Jefferson Davis, Secretary of War, Endorsement of October 24, 1856

WAR DEPARTMENT, Oct. 24, 1856

The evils resulting from the hostility of the Cheyennes, as reported within, were anticipated by the Department, and, in accordance with the recommendations of General Harney, it was proposed to have sent out last spring the First Regiment of cavalry, with a view to chastise these Indians for past offenses, and otherwise to impress upon them the necessity of future good conduct. The demand for troops arising from the disturbed conditions of the Territory of Kansas, deprived the department of the power to execute its plans in relation to the Cheyenne Indians; and it now only remains, in accordance with the long-entertained design, to make a campaign, as soon as it is practicable, against those Indians, that they may be reduced to submission, and be compelled to release the captives held by them, restore the property taken, and deliver up the criminals by whom these offenses were committed.

The commander of the department will look to the needful arrangements for the execution of this purpose.

JEFF'N DAVIS, Secretary of War
(*KHC* 4:494)

4. Smith to Cooper, November 11, 1856

Being no longer occupied with the affairs in this Territory, which have caused so much uneasiness, undivided attention can be paid to preparations for punishing the Cheyenne Indians. In pursuing them in the spring, the great want will be forage and transportation for supplies; pasturing animals in rapid movements is impossible, nor can horses perform a regular day's work on grass; in short daily journeys grass is sufficient, for there is time to pasture and very little labor to undergo; additional appropriations will therefore be necessary to provide for the expedition, which must be chiefly of mounted men, and ought to be ready by the middle of April. The details of the force and the direction of the operations cannot now be determined, but a general appropriation of an additional sum, much less, however, than that given to the Sioux expedition, will be advisable.   (*KHC* 4:517–18)

5. Army General Order No. 5, April 4, 1857

General Order,)   Head-Quarters of the Army,
    No. 5.   )   New York, April 4, 1857.

The General-in-Chief, with the approbation of the War Department, directs the following movements, changes and preparations:

1. Brevet Brigadier General Harney, turning over the command in Florida to the next officer in rank, will repair without delay to Fort Leavenworth and assume the command of that post. Special instructions will be addressed to him, at that place, from the War Department.

2. Lieut. Col. Johnston, First Cavalry, will proceed to St. Louis, Mo., to make preparations for the survey of the southern boundary of Kansas, with which he has been charged by the War Department, and thence to Fort Leavenworth. On his arrival, the commanding officer there will place at the disposition of Lieut. Col. Johnston a column to be composed of two squadrons of the First Cavalry and two companies of the Sixth Infantry, now at that post—the companies to be designated by the respective regimental commanders.

This column will be independently commanded by Lieut. Col. Johnston, under special instructions from the War Department.

3. A column of two squadrons of the First Cavalry will be moved along the line of the Arkansas river, as soon as the season permits, equipped and supplied for distant service during the summer. The companies to compose it will be designated by the regimental commander.

4. The remaining squadron of the First Cavalry will move, in like manner, along the line of the Platte river, and will be joined by the squadron of the Second Dragoons, now at Fort Kearney, and by three of the companies of Sixth Infantry now at Fort Laramie, at such time and such manner as may be directed by the officer commanding the whole force described in this and the preceding paragraph.

A fourth company of the Sixth Infantry, to be designated by

the commanding officer of Fort Laramie, will remain to garrison that post.

5. Col. Sumner, First Cavalry, will exercise the general command of the two moving columns last designated above, and will march with either as he may elect. Special instructions for his guidance will be addressed to him from the head-quarters of the army.

6. One or more prairie howitzers may be taken from Fort Leavenworth with each of the three columns.

7. The Tenth Infantry will move by water from Fort Snelling to Fort Leavenworth, and there take post as early as practicable, leaving two companies, (to be designated by the regimental commander) one to remain in garrison at Fort Ridgely; the other, for the present, at Fort Ripley.

Fort Ripley will be abandoned as soon as the necessary measures can be taken for the disposition of the public property, when the company occupying it will take post at Fort Snelling.

8. The six companies of the Second Dragoons, now at Fort Riley, will proceed to take post at Fort Leavenworth.

9. A supply of forage, for some ten days or more, will be thrown out from Fort Leavenworth in advance of each of three marching columns above designated, and their movements will be commenced in anticipation of grazing.

10. Desiccated vegetables will be furnished to the troops to a sufficient extent to secure them against scurvy.

11. Provision will be made for wagons and packs to accompany the troops, and mules, not to exceed five hundred will be purchased for the march.

12. The proper departments of the staff will promptly make all necessary preparations for the equipment, supply and maintenance of the movements above ordered.

By command of Brevet Lieutenant General Scott.

I. THOMAS, Assistant Adjutant General.

(*Frank Leslie's Illustrated Newspaper*, April 25, 1857)

6. Sumner to Army Headquarters, May 31, 1857

HDQTRS 1ST CAVALRY   CAMP ON "LITTLE BLUE"
80 miles from Fort Kearny   May 31st, 1857

SIR: I wish to inform the General-in-chief, that the emigration to California this year, by this route, is much larger than anyone anticipated. They are driving across an immense number of cattle, and I feel obliged to time my movements in some measure, so as to cover the road up the Platte, until the most of these Emigrants have passed.

The revival of this route of travel to California, which will no doubt increase on the completion of the road, (for which the appropriations have been made) would seem to make the continuance of Forts Kearny and Laramie highly important. It is not too much to say, that if these posts are withdrawn, this whole road—from the "Big Blue" to the Rocky mountains—will be thrown open to Indian depredations.

E. V. SUMNER
Col I Cavly Comdg.

ASST. ADJT. GEN'L
Hd Qtrs Army.
(AGO, Letters Received, 1857, Book 33, 399 S, and S 85, NA)

7. Sumner to Army Headquarters, June 26, 1857

Hdqrs

Camp near Fort Laramie   June 26, 57

SIR: I have the honor to report that I shall march tomorrow morning for the Cheyenne country, with two companies of cavalry, and three of infantry, and I expect to meet my other column, under Major Sedgwick, on the south fork of the Platte, on the 4th of July—I leave the squadron of the 2d dragoons at this Post to await the orders of Gen. Harney—I intend to establish a large camp in the heart of the Cheyenne country, and have two columns, without baggage, constantly in motion after the Indians—I hope to accomplish the object of the expedition, but the country is very extensive, and some of it very difficult of access, owing to the want of water and grass.

Very respectfully, Your obt. Servt.

E. V. Sumner
Col. I Cavly Comdg.

To the Act G
Head Qrs Army
             (AGO Letters Received, 1857, 466 S, S 102, NA)

8. Lowe to Sumner, July 3, 1857

                                        Camp on Cache la Poudre,
                                        July 3 1857, 10 P.M.
To Colonel E. V. Sumner, Commanding Cheyenne Expedition,
Camp on Crow Creek:
Colonel:—On leaving you I traveled due west about twenty-five
miles over a fairly level country and arrived here at 7 o'clock.
Found the water from ten to twenty feet deep and storms in the
mountains indicate that it will continue so, rendering this route
impracticable for the train. I will meet you on the South Fork of
Platte tomorrow. I send Armijo with instructions to be in your camp
by sunrise.
                           I am, Colonel, very respectfully,
                           P. G. LOWE
         (Percival G. Lowe, *Five Years a Dragoon*, 197–98)

9. Cooper to Sumner, July 22, 1857
                           HEAD QUARTERS ARMY FOR UTAH
                           Fort Leavenworth, July 28th 1857
COL. E. V. SUMNER
1st Cav. Commanding Cheyenne Expd.
   COLONEL. The following telegraphic communications have been
received by General Harney from the Adjutant General, viz.-
(First Telegraph)
                           ADJUTANT GENERAL'S OFFICE
                           Washington, July 22nd, 1857
   Send the following by Express to Col. E. V. Sumner, First Cavalry, Commanding Cheyenne Expedition;—The Secretary of War
directs that you break up the Cheyenne Expedition and out of the
Six Companies of the First Cavalry subject to your orders make up
four full companies send them with Major Sedgwick and the two
companies of the 2nd Dragoons and the three companies of the
Sixth Infantry belonging to the Cheyenne Expedition to Fort Laramie, there to receive the orders of General Harney. With the two

remaining companies of your regiment you will return to Fort Leavenworth.

By order of the Secretary of War

(Signed) S. COOPER Adjutant General.

(Department of Utah, *Letters Sent*, 1857–61, 1:8–9, NA)

10. Colburn to Commanding Officer, Fort Kearny, Nebraska Territory

Headquarters Cheyenne Expedition,

Camp on Walnut Creek,

August 3, 1857.

SIR:—We had a fight with the Cheyennes on the 29th of last month, on Solomon's creek, in which we were entirely successful. About 300 warriors were drawn up in battle array to meet us.

The six companies of cavalry advanced upon them immediately. When near them two companies were detached to turn their flanks, and the whole then made a headlong charge, broke them, and pursued them 7 miles. A large number of warriors were killed and wounded; tho' it is impossible at this time to state how many. We lost two privates killed; Lieut. Stuart and several men were wounded, it is believed that they will all recover.—Lieut. Stuart is not dangerously wounded. A post was established, garrisoned by one company of infantry, to take charge of the wounded, and the command immediately started in pursuit.

After a march fourteen miles, we came to the principal town of the tribe, where we found 171 lodges standing, and nearly as many more which had been hastily taken down and most of the poles left on the ground. A large amount of dried meat, and other property of every description, was found in the town—the Indians evidently having taken nothing except what could be gathered up hastily in their flight.

The town and everything it contained was immediately burned to the ground.—The next morning we took the trail and are now upon it. It leads in the direction of the Arkansas, where we expect to be in a few days.

On the day of the fight the Indians had sent off all their families before we came up to them.

By order of Col. Sumner.

A. V. Colburne,

2d Lieut. and Adjt.

To the Commanding Officer
    Fort Kearny, N.T.

(Kansas Constitutionalist, October 7, 1857)

11. Sumner to Army Headquarters, August 9, 1857

HEADQUARTERS CHEYENNE EXPEDITION
Arkansas River, near the site of Fort Atkinson
August 9, 1857

SIR: I have the honor to report that, on the 29th ultimo, while pursuing the Cheyennes down Solomon's Fork of the Kansas, we suddenly came upon a large body of them, drawn up in battle array, with their left resting upon the stream and their right covered by a bluff. Their number has been variously estimated from two hundred and fifty to five hundred; I think there were about three hundred. The cavalry were about three miles in advance of the infantry, and the six companies were marching in three columns. I immediately brought them into line, and, without halting, detached the two flank companies at a gallop to turn their flanks, (a movement they were evidently preparing to make against our right,) and we continued to march steadily upon them. The Indians were all mounted and well armed, many of them had rifles and revolvers, and they stood, with remarkable boldness, until we charged and were nearly upon them, when they broke in all directions, and we pursued them seven miles. Their horses were fresh and very fleet, and it was impossible to overtake many of them. There were but nine men killed in the pursuit, but there must have been a great number wounded. I had two men killed, and Lieutenant J. E. B. Stuart, and eight men wounded; but it is believed they will all recover. All my officers and men behaved admirably. The next day I established a small fort near the battleground, and left my wounded there, in charge of a company of infantry with two pieces of artillery, with orders to proceed to the wagon train, at the lower crossing of the south fork of the Platte, on the 20th instant, if I did not return before that time.

On the 31st ultimo I started again in pursuit, and at fourteen miles I came upon their principal town. The people had all fled; there were one hundred and seventy-one lodges standing, and about as many more that had been hastily taken down, and there was a large amount of Indian property of all kinds of great value to them. I had everything destroyed, and continued the pursuit. I trailed them to within forty miles of this place, when they scattered in all directions. Believing they would reassemble on this river, (for there are no buffalo in their country this summer on which they can subsist,) I have come here hoping to intercept them and to protect this road. I was obliged to send my wagon train back to Laramie from near Fort St. Vrain, and to take pack-mules.

My supplies have been exhausted for some time, except fresh beef, and I have beef only for twenty-four days. I shall send an express to Fort Leavenworth to have supplies pushed out to me as soon as possible, for I do not think these Indians have been sufficiently punished for the barbarous outrages they have recently committed. The battalion of the 6th infantry, under Captain Ketchum, belonging to my command, has had a long and arduous march. It is matter of deep regret to them, as it is to myself, that I could not wait to bring them into the action. As I have no supplies with which I can send these troops back to Laramie, I must take them to Fort Leavenworth; and if they are to return to Laramie this fall, I would respectfully ask for authority to send them up in a light train.

I have the pleasure to report, what I know will give the lieutenant general commanding the army the highest satisfaction, that in these operations not a woman nor a child has been hurt.

I am, sir, very respectfully, your obedient servant.

E. V. SUMNER
Colonel 1st Cavalry, Commanding Expedition

To ASSISTANT ADJUTANT GENERAL,

Headquarters of the Army, New York, N.Y.

(AGO, Letters Received, 1857, S 514, NA; also *Report*, Secretary of War, House Ex. Doc. 2, 35 Cong., 1 Sess., 2:96–97 (Serial 943))

12. Sumner to Army Headquarters, August 9, 1857

HEAD QUARTERS CHEYENNE EXPEDITION
Arkansas river (near the site of Ft. Atkinson)
August 9, 1857

SIR   I have the honor to inclose herewith a return of the killed and wounded, in an action with the Cheyennes on the 29th of July

1857. A detailed report of the operations against the Cheyennes
has been forwarded to the Commanding General.

                    I Am Sir   Very Respectfully   Your Obt Servt,
                                                    E. V. SUMNER
                         Col I Cavlry   Commanding Expedition
ADJUTANT GENERAL, U.S.A.,
Washington D.C.

[Enclosure, with above]

RETURN OF KILLED AND WOUNDED IN AN ACTION WITH THE CHEY-
    ENNES ON SOLOMONS CREEK   July 29th 1857

KILLED

Martin Lynch.—Arrow wound in head & Pistol wound through
    chest.
George Cade.—Arrow wound entering at one side & passing out
    at the other.

WOUNDED

J. E. B., Stewart, 1st Lt.—Pistol wound in the chest, from pres-
    ent symptoms thought not dangerous.
George C. McEawen.—Rifle wound through arm and chest
    (Dangerous).
Henry B. Robinson.—Sabre wound of hand.
Franz Piot.—Arrow wound entirely through Chest (Dangerous).
Francis T. Freer.—Arrow wound deep in hip.
Alexander Wilkey.—Arrow wound in face, slight.
James M. Cooke.—Arrow wound in Abdomen (Dangerous).
Rollin Taylor.—Arrow wound in head. Pvt. Taylor killed the
    Indian who wounded him, with his sabre.
Thomas Wilson.—Arrow wound through arm.

                                                    E. V. SUMNER
                                          Col. I Cavlry Comdg
A. V. COLBURN
2d Lt Ast Adjt.

            (AGO, Letters Received, 1857, 506 S, NA)

13. Sumner to Army Headquarter, August 11, 1857.

                HEADQUARTERS CHEYENNE EXPEDITION
            Arkansas River, one march below Fort Atkinson
                                              Aug. 11, 1857

SIR: I have received authentic information from the mail party
today that the agent for the Cheyennes has gone up to Bent's Fort

with the yearly presents for that tribe, and that he has been informed by them that they would not come to receive their presents in the usual way, but that he should never carry the goods out of the country. Under these circumstances, I consider the agent and the public property in his charge in jeopardy. I have therefore decided to proceed at once to Bent's Fort with the elite of my cavalry, in the hope that I may find the Cheyennes collected in that vicinity, and, by another blow, force them to sue for peace; at all events, this movement will secure this agent and the public property. Another motive is, that by this march up the river I shall more effectually cover this road from Indian depredations this summer.

I have directed Captain Ketchum, with his battalion and a part of the cavalry, to proceed, by easy marches, to Walnut Creek, and there await my return.

I am, sir, very respectfully, your obedient servant,

E. V. SUMNER
Colonel 1st Cavalry, Commanding

ASSISTANT ADJUTANT GENERAL,
Headquarters of the Army, New York City.
(AGO, Letters Received, 1857, S 515; also *Report*, Secretary of War, House Ex. Doc. 2, 35 Cong., 1 Sess., 2:97–98 (Serial 514))

14. Sumner to Robert C. Miller, August 19, 1857.

HEAD QUARTERS CHEYENNE EXPDN
Bents Fort August 19th 1857

SIR: The object of the Cheyenne Expedition was to demand from that tribe the perpetrators of their late crimes against the whites and ample security for their future good conduct—failing in this, those Indians were to be chastized. As they showed no disposition to yield to the demands upon them, but on the contrary, met the troops in battle array, they have been whipped, and their principal town burnt to the ground. Under these circumstances I know it would not be the wish of the Govt that the Arms Ammunition and other goods sent into the country for those Indians should be left here a prey for them to seize, (which they would certainly do) as some indemnity for the chastisement they have received. I therefore feel it to be my duty to direct, that all the goods for the Cheyennes now at this place be disposed of as follows. As you have no means of transportation you will please turn over to Lieut. Wheaton, Act. Asst Comg, all the subsistence stores, to be paid for at costs and charges, or replaced at this point whenever required by your dept. The ammunition will be destroyed. The guns and as many of the goods as the Quartermaster can transport will be taken out of the country, the residue of the goods, you will please distribute as you may think proper to the friendly Indians as an advance on their next years annuity—This however, will of course be subject to the approval of your dept. As I am not authorized to leave troops here for your personal protection, and as you cannot of course, remain here without it, you will please accompany the Command when it leaves the Indian Country.

I Am Sir   Very respectfully   Your obt servt

(Signed) E. V. SUMNER

Col. 1st Cavalry Comdg Cheyenne Expn

Official A. V. COLBURN

2d Lieut.   Ast Ajt

MAJOR ROB. C. MILLER Agent for the Cheyennes

Walnut Creek   September 3d 1857

(AGO, Letters Received, 1857, 550 S, NA)

15. Sumner to Army Headquarters, September 3, 1857

HEAD QUARTERS CHEYENNE EXPEDITION

Walnut Creek, September 3d 1857

SIR I reached this yesterday on my return from Bents Fort and found the order breaking up the Cheyenne Expedition. I regret extremely after my success against these Indians, to leave this matter unfinished. They are now more hostile than they were before they were punished, and it will require another severe blow to bring them to sue for peace. I inclose my order to the Indian Agent disposing of the Cheyenne goods.

It certainly seems very strange that Arms and Ammunition should have been sent to these Indians at the same time that I was directed to punish them. I hope the Com. General will approve of my measures with regard to the Cheyenne presents, and if he does, I would respectfully ask him to put an indorsement to that effect upon my order to the Indian Agent.

I Am Sir   Very Respectfully

E. V. SUMNER

Col I Cavalry   Commanding

Cheyenne Expedition

ASST ADJT GENERAL

Head Quarters Army New York City, N.Y.

[On back of Document] INDIAN AFFAIRS. Colonel Sumner orders seem to have been judiciously adapted to the existing circumstances of the moment. Respectfully submitted to the Secretary of War

WINFIELD SCOTT

(AGO, Letters Received, 1857, 550 S, NA)

16. Pleasonton to Sedgwick, September 8, 1857

HEAD QUARTERS, ARMY FOR UTAH
Fort Leavenworth, September 8, 1857

MAJOR JOHN SEDGWICK

1st Cav. Comd 4 Companies En route for Utah, Fort Laramie

SIR: You are instructed by the General Commanding to repair with your Command to this Post.

I am, Sir, very respectfully, Your Obt. Servt

A. Pleasanton. Captain 2nd Dragoons A.A.A.G.

(Department of Utah, Letters Sent, 1857–61, 1:33, NA)

17. Sumner to Army Headquarters, September 20, 1857.

HEADQUARTERS FIRST CAVALRY,
Fort Leavenworth, K.T., September 20, 1857

SIR: I have the honor to submit a report of my operations during the past summer, or rather a brief recapitulation of the reports already forwarded. I detached Major Sedgwick, with four companies of cavalry, from this post on the 18th of May, to move by the Arkansas River, and to meet me on the south fork of the Platte on the 4th of July. I marched, with two companies of cavalry, on the 20th of May for Fort Kearney, where, in compliance with orders, I took up two companies of the 2d dragoons stationed at that post, and moved on towards Fort Laramie. When about eighty miles from the latter post, I received an order to leave the two companies of dragoons at Fort Kearney for General Harney's expedition to Utah. As they were then so near Fort Laramie, instead of sending them back to Fort Kearney, to march over the same ground three times, I took them to Fort Laramie, and left them there; which, I trust, was approved by the general commanding the army. On the 27th of June I moved south from Fort Laramie with two companies of cavalry and three companies of the sixth infantry.

On the 4th of July I reached the south fork of the Platte, and should have formed a junction with Major Sedgwick on that day, but the river was entirely impassable. On the next day I attempted to establish a ferry with the metallic wagon beds, but found them entirely useless, and was obliged to abandon it. The two commands then moved down the river until I found a ford, and I then brought Major Sedgwick's command over to my camp.

It was my intention to establish a larger camp somewhere in that vicinity, and form two columns for the pursuit of the Indians; but hearing they would be in force, and would resist, I determined to abandon my wagons, train, tents, and all other incumbrances, and proceed with my whole command in pursuit of the Indians. The train was sent back to Fort Laramie, with orders to meet me at the lower crossing of the south fork of the Platte in twenty days; but in pursuing the Indians, I was drawn across the country to the Arkansas River, and we had nothing but fresh beef to subsist upon for some time. I found the trail of the Indians on the 24th of July, and on the 29th came upon them, as already reported; which report narrates the battle, the destruction of the town, and the pursuit through to the Arkansas. On arriving there, I found the agent for the Cheyennes had taken to Bent's Fort the annual presents for that tribe, including arms and ammunition. I knew the government could never intend to send an expedition against a tribe of Indians, and at the same time give them arms and ammunition. I therefore determined to proceed at once to Bent's Fort to prevent the Indians from getting this property, especially as they had threatened that it would not be taken out of the country.

I had also a hope of finding the Indians collected again in that vicinity. I trust my reports in relation to this matter were satisfactory to the commanding general, and that he endorsed them to that effect, for without his approval the measures that I felt bound to take may involve me in difficulty with the Department of the Interior. On my arrival at Walnut Creek, I received the order to break up the expedition, and to detach four companies of cavalry and three of infantry for the expedition to Utah. I immediately put the detachment in as good order as possible, by stripping the two companies which were to return to this post, and directed Major Sedgwick to proceed across the country to Fort Kearney, on his route to

Utah. We had then marched sixteen hundred miles, and, although this order was entirely unexpected, and the men and horses were much worn down, not a man deserted, when they could easily have made their escape by taking the best of the horses. The conduct of my command throughout the summer has been all I could wish; the officers and men have not only shown bravery in action, but they have shown the higher quality of a manly and cheerful endurance of privations.

Six days after I detached Major Sedgwick, as I was returning to this post with the two remaining companies, I was very happy to receive the countermand of the order for Utah. I arrived at this post on the 16th instant, after marching over eighteen hundred and fifty miles.

I am, sir, very respectfully, your obedient servant,

E. V. SUMNER
Colonel 1st Cavalry, Commanding
Cheyenne Expedition

ASSISTANT ADJUTANT GENERAL,
Headquarters of the Army, New York City.
(AGO, Letters Received, 1857, S 589; also *Report*, Secretary of War, House Ex. Doc. 2, 35 Cong., 1 Sess., 2:98–99 (Serial 943))

18. Robert C. Miller to John Haverty, October 14, 1857

LEAVENWORTH CITY,
October 14, 1857

SIR: I present the following as my annual report for the year 1857:

The train containing the annunity goods for the Comanches, Kiowas, Apaches, Cheyennes, and Arapahoes, which I accompanied, left Westport, Missouri, June 20, and proceeded without any interruption or incident, save the usual reports against the Kiowas, as far as Walnut Creek, where it arrived on the 3d of July. From there I sent forward a "runner" to notify the Comanches, Kiowas, and Apaches, of my approach, and to gather them together, near Fort Atkinson, for the purpose of receiving their presents.

The morning after my arrival at Walnut creek, a band of Kiowas who had been out in search of the Pawnees, their natural enemies, came into Allison and Booth's ranche; they appeared to have been out for some time, and represented themselves as very poor and hungry. After being fed, and receiving some few presents from me, they left, apparently well pleased, for the purpose of joining their people whom they expected to find near Fort Atkinson. The train arrived at the village of the Comanches and Kiowas (the Apaches being encamped some distance above the fort) on the morning of the 8th of July. There being some of the principal bands of both tribes absent, I declined to make the distribution until they could be brought in, in consequence of which the Kiowas left the council very much exasperated, and returning in the evening with a large body of young men, who surrounded the wagons with their bows strung, demanding their goods immediately, and threatening to help themselves if their demands were not complied with. I remonstrated with them, and resisted as long as I could, using every argument to persuade them to wait until their "brothers" could come in; but I soon found that it was useless to contend with them, and that my words have no effect upon them, and, feeling at the same time it would be madness to resist so large a number, I was about to yield to their wishes, when the Comanches, always reasonable, and ever ready to show their friendship for the whites, stepped forward and offered their services to protect the train. The conduct of the Comanches on this occasion deserves all praise, manifesting, as it did, a sincerity in their profession of friendship, and exhibiting a real anxiety to maintain peace and amity with the government. . . .

On the morning of the 12th of July all bands having come in, and having all things ready, I called the chiefs of the two tribes together for the purpose of having a talk before making the distribution. The Comanches came forward as friends in a friendly manner; the Kiowas with sullen countenances, and with bows strung and their hands full of arrows, impatient for the least excuse to make an attack. I spoke to them as plainly as circumstances surrounding would permit, telling them their Great Father had heard of the wrongs they had committed on the road, and that he was angry, and if they persisted in their outrageous conduct he would certainly send his soldiers against them, who would destroy them as fire does the grass on the prairie. To which they replied, as might have been expected, in a taunting and contemptuous manner. They said they knew their Great Father sent them presents because he feared them; that he was no brave, or he would not talk so much, but would act; would send the soldiers, of whose coming they had been told of from year to year, but had never seen yet on the prairie.

There is no use of disguising the fact, that the sending of presents to these Indians from year to year, notwithstanding their continued and almost daily outrages on the Santa Fe trail, can have no other effect than to create a contempt in their minds for the government; and if persisted in, must inevitably result in an outbreak of all the other tribes in my agency. The head men of their tribes told me that it was with the greatest difficulty they are able to control their young men, who seeing the Kiowas have not only thus far escaped the punishment due them, but received their presents as if they had done no wrong, and this regularly every year.

I would, therefore, earnestly, but respectfully, urge that the punishment so richly deserved be no longer withheld, and that no more presents be sent to them until they have been brought to a proper sense of their obligations to the government. I subsequently learned at Bent's Fort, that on the very day I distributed to them a war party of Kiowas laid waste a ranche near Moro, New Mexico.

The several claims placed in my hands for damages against the Kiowas, for theft and other depredations upon certain citizens of Los Vegas, New Mexico, were, agreeably to the instructions of Colonel Cumming, laid before the chiefs in regular council. They acknowledged the justice of the claim of Franco Pinal, amounting to the sum of six hundred and forty-four dollars, but expressed a decided objection to its being deducted from their annuity goods. They preferred to take recompense themselves, and said they would return in *kind* what they had stolen.

The Rev. Mr. Pinal will have to exercise a wonderful degree of patience if his only dependence is upon the word of the Kiowa Indians. The other claims they protest against, claiming to be entirely innocent, charging the depredations upon the Cheyennes; but on an examination of the dates of the several claims it will be observed that these depredations were committed within a few days and miles of each other; so, if they were guilty in one instance, it is reasonable to suppose them guilty in the others. I am clearly of the opinion that these outrages are attributable to the Kiowas alone, as the Cheyennes, I subsequently learned, were not in New Mexico at the time.

After distributing to the Comanches and Kiowas, I proceeded

with the train towards Bent's Fort. On the evening of the 13th I came upon the camp of the Arapahoe Indians upon the Arkansas River, some ten miles above Fort Atkinson. They were driven to seek the buffalo country for want of food, and they were thus far on their way when I met them. They seemed very glad to meet me, stating that their people were in a starving condition, and expressed the hope that I would not compel them to return to Bent's Fort in order to receive their presents, but that I would give them to them there so they might proceed on their way without further interruption; to which I unhesitatingly consented.

They were assembled in much larger numbers than last year, numbering about three hundred lodges; consequently they got a large portion of presents. My interview with the chiefs of this tribe was very agreeable and pleasant. They expressed an earnest desire to maintain peace and friendship with the whites. The distribution was made without the least interruption or complaint on their part, they appearing to be perfectly satisfied.

In council the chiefs spoke of the conduct of their young men at Bent's Fort on the occasion of my previous visit among them, at which time they had demanded their goods immediately, declaring "they would not wait the coming of the Cheyennes," for I had sent over to the "Smoky Hill Fork" of the Kansas River, excusing themselves by saying "they had been waiting many days for their goods, and their women and children had become very faint and hungry," and "their young men would not be controlled," "but now their hearts were very glad, their Great Father had sent them many presents, and they would never be seen making war upon the whites like the Cheyennes, nor murdering and stealing like the Kiowas." Little Raven, the principal chief, expressed a wish for his people to learn to cultivate the soil and become farmers, as he felt the buffalo and other game were rapidly disappearing from the prairie, and in a few years would be entirely gone, when, unless they had some other resource, they must starve. He desired I would ask the Great Chief to send them hereafter farming instruments and white men to teach them their use.

It was my intention, if the state of affairs had permitted me to remain in the country, to have examined the district embraced within my agency, with a view of reporting to the department the points adapted to cultivation and susceptible of producing sufficient to sustain the several tribes, should it hereafter be deemed expedient to colonize them.

From Walnut Creek, along the Arkansas River, to within a short distance of Bent's Fort, there is not a foot of country fit for the plough; but immediately around the fort, and for a distance of one hundred miles above, about the regions of the "Boiling Springs," the bottoms are extensive, with deep, rich soil, susceptible of the highest degree of cultivation, and the uplands afford the finest grazing.

Arriving at Bent's Fort on the 19th of July, I applied to Captain Bent for permission to store the goods within the fort until I could communicate with Colonel Sumner, commanding the Cheyenne expedition, but he, without hestiation, refused; giving as the reason, that as soon as the Cheyennes learned that the goods were within the fort and would not be distributed until the soldiers came, an attack would be made which would result not only in the loss of the government property, but also of everything he possessed, and the massacre of every one within. I then turned to Mr. Childs, the contractor for the land transportation, and remarked that I would be compelled to detain his wagons until an express could go and return from Colonel Sumner's camp, which was said to be near old Fort St. Vrain, on the South Platte, but he utterly refused to remain. I then replied, I would not receive the goods of him, as I claimed the right to detain the wagons until I was prepared to make the distribution, and went immediately in search of some one to ride the express. After great difficulty, as the country was very dangerous to cross, there being small bands of Indians (very hostile) roving to and fro, I succeeded in inducing a Frenchman by the name of Dubray to undertake the trip, provided he could pursuade two Mexicans to accompany him, in which he was successful. He was to start on the following morning at daybreak. That night, about nine o'clock, Bent, fearful that if the goods remained even in the vicinity of the fort any length of time without being distributed he would suffer thereby, came to me, proposing to abandon the fort and deliver it up to me, for which rent and storage was to be paid; I accepted of his proposition, and entered into a written agreement with him, for the terms of which I refer you to the paper accompanying my letter to Colonel Cumming, then superintendent, of the 20th July. He accordingly, having packed up all his goods and transported them to his wagons, left on the morning of the 21st, with his family, cattle, and horses, for the States, leaving behind, however, according to agreement, wagons and teams sufficient to remove the government goods to the States, in case Colonel Sumner should deem it improper that they should fall into the hands of the Cheyennes.

After riding all night and day, the messenger I had despatched to Colonel Sumner returned on the 27th without finding him, or learning anything of his whereabouts. Having no further control over the wagons which Captain Bent had left behind, they left on the following morning for the States, leaving me with but four white men and one negro, I having control only over one man and the negro.

Notwithstanding my weak force, I believed the goods were safer behind stone walls than in the wagons on the road, as it was said to be infested with hostile Indians as far as the crossing of the Arkansas. It was well I did remain at the fort, as I have since learned that the day after the wagons left Fort Atkinson the whole of the Cheyennes, flying from Colonel Sumner after his battle with them, crossed the Arkansas forty miles above. If the wagons had been loaded they would have travelled slower, and would have been just in time to have met the Indians in their full flight, who, smarting from their recent defeat, would have wiped the train entirely out.

A few days after the departure of Bent's wagons, learning from two Apaches who came from the Cheyenne village, on the Smoky Hill fork, that a few of the principal chiefs and a number of young men of influence were anxious for peace, and were using their influence to bring it about, and believing that good might be the result of an interview, I procured the services of a Mexican and an Arapahoe Indian, and despatched them to their village to invite all the head men who were so disposed to come to the fort. They had proceeded several days on their way, when they were met by a party of straggling Cheyennes, who informed them that a great battle had been fought, in which six of their principal chiefs had been killed, and their village of near two hundred lodges had been destroyed—burnt to the ground. They said though their people had been defeated by the loss of many horses and their entire village, they were not subdued, "but had only gone over to Crooked Creek for the purpose of joining the Kiowas, who had promised to unite with them against the whites, and that so soon as they could recruit, they were coming to the fort to help themselves to the goods, and take the scalp of the agent and every one with him."

The report was repeated to me by every Indian who came to the fort. Various reports came to my ears of the treatment of the prisoners they had taken during the summer, the details of which are too disgusting and horrible for repetition here. Suffice it to say, that they were the most terrible that can be possible for even Indian iniquity in inventing modes of cruelty to conceive.

On the 5th of August, I despatched an express man to the crossing of the Arkansas, to meet the mail, with some official papers, who, after being absent a sufficient length of time, returned with a story trumped up, as it turned out afterwards, that he had arrived the proper point on the morning of the 9th, and remained there until the evening of the 12th, without meeting the mail, which should have passed on the 10th. He said that on his arrival at the spot he noticed the fresh tracks of seven animals, five mules and two horses, which indicated that they might have been moving in a very rapid manner, as if they were flying from danger; from the fact of the animals being shod, they must have belonged to the mail party, which doubtless had been attacked by Indians, and were able to make their escape with only that small number of animals, leaving their wagons behind to the mercy of the Indians. The state of the country and the hostilities of several tribes of Indians rendered his story very plausible. On the same day of his return to the fort, (the 15th of August,) an expressman arrived bearing me a letter from Colonel Sumner, stating that he was marching to my relief and would be with me by the 18th, having learned from a gentleman, by Santa Fe mail, that I was at Bent's Fort, unable to get away. He arrived accordingly on the 18th, and on the 19th addressed me the accompanying communication. Having no alternative but to comply with his directions, I proceeded to turn over to his quartermaster the sugar, rice, coffee, hard bread and flour. The powder and lead and flints were thrown into the Arkansas River. To the few Arapahoes who were present I distributed all the goods, excepting what could be transported in two wagons, which I intended for distribution to the Arapahoes I might meet on the road. Colonel Sumner with his command, which I accompanied, took up his line of march for the States on the morning of the 20th. On the third day after leaving the fort, the cattle, being very poor, and only seven yoke in number, gave out completely. The wagons having mired down to the axle-trees, there seemed to be no alternative but to abandon them on the prairie. Fortunately, a village of the Apaches was discovered on the opposite side of the river; I sent for the chiefs and delivered to them all the goods, (excepting the guns, which had been brought to Fort Leavenworth, and where they are now in store,) giving them to understand that these presents were given to them as a reward for their good behavior, and, as they were the goods designed for the Cheyennes, also, we show them that it was the determination of their Great Father to punish that tribe for the violation of the treaty with the government.

Colonel Sumner informed me that while at Bent's Fort, that he had learned from passengers by the inward-bound Santa Fe mail, which he had met at the "crossing," that a party of four or five Kiowa Indians came up with Colonel Johnson's command on the Cemmerone, and for several days followed it in an apparently very friendly manner, but on the first opportunity shot the driver of his private ambulance and cut his mules loose from the harness, with which they fled. The driver had fallen behind the command. I have been subsequently informed that they were Comanches and not Kiowas, but am not inclined to believe the Comanches would be guilty of such an outrage.

The Cheyennes, before they went into battle with the troops, under the direction of their "Great Medicine Man," had selected a spot on the Smoky Hill, near a small and beautiful lake, in which they had but to dip their hands, when the victory over the troops would be an easy one, so their medicine man told them, and that they had but to hold up their hands and the balls would roll from the muzzles of the soldiers' guns harmless to their feet. Acting under this delusion, when Colonel Sumner came upon them with his command, he found them drawn up in regular line of battle, well mounted, and moving forward to the music of their war song with as firm a tread as well disciplined troops, expecting no doubt to receive the harmless fire of the soldiers and achieve an easy victory. But the charm was broken when the command was given by Colonel Sumner to charge with sabres, for they broke and fled in the wildest confusion, being completely routed. They lost, killed upon the field, nine of their principal men, and many more must have died from the effects of their wounds, as the bodies of several were found on the route of their flight. Their village, which was about fourteen miles distant, was found to have been deserted in a most hasty manner, everything having been left behind, even their winter supply of buffalo meat, amounting to between fifteen and twenty thousand pounds. Colonel Sumner ordered everything to be destroyed either by fire or otherwise.

The loss of their winter supplies, and the destruction of their lodges, is a blow that they will not soon recover from; still they are not yet subdued, have not yet been brought to respect the government, and I trust the government will not be content with the punishment inflicted upon them by Colonel Sumner, but will continue to follow them up until they shall have been brought to subjection, and been taught that they cannot commit their depredations with impunity. This is necessary for the protection of the immense amount of travel passing over the various roads through their country.

Before closing, I would call the attention of the department to the immense number of small Mexican traders that are continually roving over the country, and to whom many of the difficulties with the Indians may be traced. They come into the country ostensably to trade provisions to the Indians, but in reality to introduce among them their miserable Mexican whiskey, using their influence, which is in many instances very great, to keep up the hostile feeling against the whites. There were several of these miscreants about Bent's Fort during my stay there, going in and out whenever they chose, they having been in the employ of Bent for some time. I had no reason to apprehend any harm from them; but I was informed by an Arapahoe Indian, on the day I left, that they were in league with the Cheyennes, and had determined to massacre every one within the fort, but the coming of Colonel Sumner prevented the carrying out of their plans.

I would, therefore, urge that some decisive measures be adopted to rid the country of these people. The agent can do nothing—he is utterly powerless, and only the presence of a strong military force will be able to keep them back.

ROBERT C. MILLER
Indian Agent

JOHN HAVERTY, ESQ.,
Superintendent of Indian Affairs, St. Louis.
(*Annual Report*, CIA, 1857, 141–48)

19. Agreement Between Robt C. Miller and William W. Bent,
July 20, 1857

Article of Agreement made and entered into at Bents Fort, Big
Timbers, K.T. this the 20th day of July 1857 between Robt C.
Miller, U.S. Indian Agent of the one part and William W. Bent of
Bents Fort of the other part.

This agreement witnesseth that the said Robt C. Miller, Indian
Agent on behalf of the United States and the said William W. Bent
have mutually covenanted and agreed and by these presents do
mutually agree to and with each other in the following to wit:

That the said William W. Bent shall furnish well sheltered storage for Certain Indian goods about twenty-eight thousand pounds
more or less belonging to the United States and the said William
W. Bent further agrees to furnish rooms in his Fort for Robt. C.
Miller, Indian Agent, and three other persons under Said Millers
employ. It being understood that the said Bent is under no circumstances to be held responsible for the goods nor is he obliged to
protect the same against any attempt to take them by hostile Indians or others.

The said William W. Bent further agrees to leave of the Fort,
Wagons and Teams sufficient to remove the goods in case it is
deemed necessary after communication can be had with the officers
Commanding the U.S. Troops said to be encamped near Bents Old
Fort on the South Platte.

2nd The said Robt. C. Miller, Indian Agent, on behalf of the
United States agrees to pay the said William W. Bent at the rate of
$25 per month for storage, $5 per day for the detention of his
Wagons and Teams in case the Goods are not removed from the
Fort, and at the rate of Three Dollars and Eighty-eight & a half
cents per Hundred pounds for the transportation of the Goods
to Walnut Creek or if deemed proper by the Said Miller to Westport, Mo.

(Files of the Bureau of Indian Affairs, RG 75, NA)

Appendix D

Schedule of Daily Marches of the Cheyenne Expedition

Sedgwick's March to the South Platte

Date	Departure Time	Time Back into Camp	Total Miles Marched	Location of Evening's Camp
Monday May 18, 1857	9:00 A.M.	4:00 P.M.	12 mi.	West bank Stranger Creek opposite Eastin
Tuesday May 19, 1857	7:00 A.M.	2:00 P.M.	23 mi.	West bank Grasshopper Creek opposite Ozawki
Wednesday May 20, 1857	6:30 A.M.		17 mi.	2 miles west of Indianola next to Fort Leavenworth-Fort Riley Trail
Thursday May 21, 1857	8:00 A.M.		9 mi.	8 miles from Kansas River below junction of trails from Smith's and Papan's ferries
Friday May 22, 1857	6:30 A.M.		18 mi.	West bank of Dragoon Creek off trail
Saturday May 23, 1857	6:45 A.M.		19 mi.	West bank of 142 Mile Creek off Santa Fe Trail
Sunday May 24, 1857	6:30 A.M.		20 mi.	West bank of Neosho River off Santa Fe Trail next to Council Grove
Monday May 25, 1857			In camp	West bank of Neosho River off Santa Fe Trail next to Council Grove
Tuesday May 26, 1857	6:30 A.M.		16 mi.	Diamond Springs

Date	Departure Time	Time Back into Camp	Total Miles Marched	Location of Evening's Camp
Wednesday May 27, 1857	6:30 A.M.	2:00 P.M.	26 mi.	Along headwaters of East Turkey Creek off Santa Fe Trail, 6 miles west of Lost Springs
Thursday May 28, 1857	6:30 A.M.		12 mi.	Along Santa Fe Trail 3 miles west of Cottonwood Crossing
Friday May 29, 1857	6:00 A.M.	12:30 P.M.	20 mi.	Next to Turkey Creek off Santa Fe Trail
Saturday May 30, 1857	6:25 A.M.		19 mi.	East bank of Little Arkansas River off Santa Fe Trail
Sunday May 31, 1857	6:25 A.M.		16 mi.	Little Cow Creek off Santa Fe Trail
Monday June 1, 1857	6:15 A.M.	1:00 P.M.	21 mi.	Great Bend of Arkansas River off Santa Fe Trail
Tuesday June 2, 1857	6:30 A.M.		15 mi.	Along Arkansas River, 1 mile off Santa Fe Trail
Wednesday June 3, 1857	6:30 A.M.		20 mi.	South bank of Pawnee Fork off Santa Fe Trail
Thursday June 4, 1857	6:44 A.M.		18 mi.	Along west bank of Arkansas off Santa Fe Trail
Friday June 5, 1857	6:30 A.M.	1:30 P.M.	21 mi.	Along west bank of Arkansas off Santa Fe Trail
Saturday June 6, 1857	6:40 A.M.	2:00 P.M.	25 mi.	Along Arkansas River near junction of Wet Route with Dry Route
Sunday June 7, 1857	7:30 A.M.	11:00 A.M.	11 mi.	Along Arkansas River off Santa Fe Trail, 3 miles west of Fort Atkinson
Monday June 8, 1857	7:15 A.M.	12:30 P.M.	18 mi.	Along Arkansas River, 3 miles west of Middle Crossing of Santa Fe Trail
Tuesday June 9, 1857	8:00 A.M.	12:00 P.M.	17 mi.	Along Arkansas River off Santa Fe Trail, 12 miles west of upper Middle Crossing and below upper Point of Rocks
Wednesday June 10, 1857			In camp	
Thursday June 11, 1857	6:55 A.M.	12:50 P.M.	21 mi.	Along north bank of Arkansas River, 12 miles east of Upper Crossing

Date	Departure Time	Time Back into Camp	Total Miles Marched	Location of Evening's Camp
Friday June 12, 1857	6:30 A.M.		17 mi.	Along north bank of Arkansas River, 5 miles west of Upper Crossing
Saturday June 13, 1857	6:30 A.M.		18 mi.	Along north bank of Arkansas River off Santa Fe Trail
Sunday June 14, 1857	6:30 A.M.		19 mi.	Along north bank of Arkansas River off Santa Fe Trail
Monday June 15, 1857	6:53 A.M.	12:30 P.M.	16½ mi.	Along north bank of Arkansas River at mouth of Buffalo Creek, off Santa Fe Trail in Big Timbers
Tuesday June 16, 1857	7:00 A.M.		23 mi.	Along north bank of Arkansas River, 2 miles east of Bent's New Fort
Wednesday June 17, 1857	6:30 A.M.		21½ mi.	Along north bank of Arkansas River
Thursday June 18, 1857	6:30 A.M.	12:00 noon	16 mi.	Along north bank of Arkansas River
Friday June 19, 1857			In camp	Along north bank of Arkansas River
Saturday June 20, 1857	6:30 A.M.	1:15 P.M.	20 mi.	Along north bank of Arkansas River off Santa Fe Trail, across from and a little below Patterson's Creek
Sunday June 21, 1857	6:00 A.M.	1:30 P.M.	20 mi.	Along north bank of Arkansas River off Santa Fe Trail
Monday June 22, 1857	8:00 A.M.	1:00 P.M.	18 mi.	Along north bank of Arkansas River off Santa Fe Trail
Tuesday June 23, 1857	6:50 A.M.	1:20 P.M.	20 mi.	Along east bank of Fountain Creek off Trapper's Trail
Wednesday June 24, 1857	6:30 A.M.	11:00 A.M.	13 mi.	Off Trapper's Trail at junction of Jimmy Camp Creek and Fountain Creek
Thursday June 25, 1857	6:30 A.M.	3:00 P.M.	24 mi.	Off Trapper's Trail, 1 mile beyond headwaters of Black Squirrel Creek

Date	Departure Time	Time Back into Camp	Total Miles Marched	Location of Evening's Camp
Friday June 26, 1857	6:30 A.M.	10:00 A.M.	10 mi.	Along east bank of East Cherry Creek off Trapper's Trail
Saturday June 27, 1857	7:10 A.M.	1:00 P.M.	16 mi.	Along east bank of Cherry Creek off Trapper's Trail
Sunday June 28, 1857	6:30 A.M.		14 mi.	Along east bank of Cherry Creek off Trapper's Trail
Monday June 29, 1857	6:30 A.M.		14 mi.	Along east bank of Cherry Creek, ¼ mile above junction with South Platte
Tuesday June 30, 1857			In camp	Along east bank of Cherry Creek, ¼ mile above junction with South Platte
Wednesday July 1, 1857	7:00 A.M.	12:00 noon	18 mi.	Along east bank of South Platte River off Trapper's Trail
Thursday July 2, 1857	6:30 A.M.		20 mi.	Along east bank of South Platte River, little below mouth of St. Vrain Creek
Friday July 3, 1857	8:00 A.M.		3 mi.	Along east bank of South Platte River, 2 miles below ruins of Fort St. Vrain
Saturday July 4, 1857			In camp	Along east bank of South Platte River, 2 miles below ruins of Fort St. Vrain
Sunday July 5, 1857	7:00 A.M.	12:00 noon	16 mi.	South bank of South Platte River, 1 mile below Powder River
Monday July 6, 1857	6:30 A.M.		18–20 mi.	South bank of South Platte River
Tuesday July 7, 1857	8:00 A.M.	10:30 A.M.	¾ mi.	North bank of South Platte River, "Camp Buchanan"

Sumner's March to the South Platte

Date	Departure Time	Time Back into Camp	Total Miles Marched	Location of Evening's Camp
Wednesday May 20, 1857	8:00 A.M.		18 mi.	North bank of Stranger Creek
Thursday May 21, 1857 TO	6:30 A.M.			
Sunday May 31, 1857				East bank of Little Blue River, 80 miles below Fort Kearny
TO				
Thursday June 4, 1857				Fort Kearny, N.T.
Friday June 5, 1857			In camp	Fort Kearny, N.T.
Saturday June 6, 1857 TO	6:30 A.M.			
Monday June 8, 1857				Off Oregon Trail next to Platte River at mouth of Plum Creek
TO				
Saturday June 13, 1857				Next to Platte River off Oregon Trail, 4 miles below Lower California Crossing
Sunday June 14, 1857			In camp	Next to Platte River off Oregon Trail, 4 miles below Lower California Crossing
Monday June 15, 1857	5:00 A.M.		11 mi.	Off Oregon Trail, 6 miles beyond California Crossing of South Platte
Tuesday June 16, 1857	6:30 A.M.		13 mi.	Off Oregon Trail by Ash Hollow Spring
Wednesday June 17, 1857 TO	6:30 A.M.			
Monday June 22, 1857				1½ miles above Fort Laramie on south side of Laramie River
TO				
Friday June 26, 1857				1½ miles above Fort Laramie on south side of Laramie River

Date	Departure Time	Time Back into Camp	Total Miles Marched	Location of Evening's Camp
Saturday June 27, 1857	8:00 A.M.		10 mi.	Off Trapper's Trail in-Goshen's Hole on south bank of Cherry Creek
Sunday June 28, 1857	6:00 A.M.	12:00 noon		Off Trapper's Trail in Goshen's Hole on banks of Box Elder Creek
Monday June 29, 1857	6:00 A.M.		17½ mi.	Off Trapper's Trail on south bank of North Bear Creek
Tuesday June 30, 1857	6:00 A.M.	4:00 P.M.	19 mi.	Off Trapper's Trail on Mud Creek
Wednesday July 1, 1857	6:00 A.M.		22 mi.	Off Trapper's Trail on Big Mud (Muddy) Creek
Thursday July 2, 1857	6:00 A.M.		20 mi.	Off Trapper's Trail on east bank of Crow Creek
Friday July 3, 1857	6:00 A.M.		20 mi.	Off Trapper's Trail on west bank of Crow Creek
Saturday July 4, 1857	6:00 A.M.		13 mi.	Along north bank of South Platte River
Sunday July 5, 1857			In camp	Along north bank of South Platte River
Monday July 6, 1857	6:30 A.M.		18–20 mi.	North bank of South Platte River, "Camp Buchanan"
Tuesday July 7, 1857			In camp	North bank of South Platte River, "Camp Buchanan"

Expedition's March from Camp Buchanan on South Platte

Wednesday July 8, 1857			In camp	"Camp Buchanan," north bank of South Platte River, 21 miles below Powder River
Thursday July 9, 1857			In camp	"Camp Buchanan," north bank of South Platte River, 21 miles below Powder River
Friday July 10, 1857			In camp	"Camp Buchanan," north bank of South Platte River, 21 miles below Powder River

Date	Departure Time	Time Back into Camp	Total Miles Marched	Location of Evening's Camp
Saturday July 11, 1857			In camp	"Camp Buchanan," north bank of South Platte River, 21 miles below Powder River
Sunday July 12, 1857			In camp	"Camp Buchanan," north bank of South Platte River, 21 miles below Powder River
Monday July 13, 1857	7:00 A.M.		9 mi.	South bank of South Platte River, 9 miles below Camp Buchanan
Tuesday July 14, 1857	7:30 A.M.	1:20 P.M.	18 mi.	South bank of South Platte, 5 miles below mouth of Bijou Creek
Wednesday July 15, 1857	7:00 A.M.		21 mi.	South-east bank of South Platte, 7 miles below mouth of Beaver Creek
Thursday July 16, 1857	7:30 A.M.	10:00 A.M.	7 mi.	South-east bank of South Platte, 14 miles below mouth of Beaver Creek
Friday July 17, 1857	7:00 A.M.	11:00 A.M.	10 mi.	On headwaters of "Parker's Creek" (Lt. Bryan)
Saturday July 18, 1857	6:30 A.M.	11:00 A.M.	12 mi.	On headwaters of "Dog Creek" (Lt. Bryan)
Sunday July 19, 1857	6:00 A.M.	12:00 midnight	35 mi.	On hill, 1½ miles from Chief Creek
Monday July 20, 1857	6:30 A.M.	7:00 A.M.	1½ mi.	On south bank of Chief Creek, 6 miles above Rock Creek
Tuesday July 21, 1857	7:00 A.M.		20 mi.	On Arickaree River at mouth of Willow Creek
Wednesday July 22, 1857	6:30 A.M.	2:00 P.M.	18 mi.	On south fork of Republican River at Mouth of Hackberry Creek
Thursday July 23, 1857	7:00 A.M.	11:00 A.M.	10 mi.	On top of hill, 7 miles east of South Fork of Republican
Friday July 24, 1857	6:00 A.M.	3:00 P.M.	23 mi.	On banks of Beaver Creek
Saturday July 25, 1857	6:30 A.M.	1:30 P.M.	15 mi.	On south bank of Beaver Creek at mouth of Little Beaver Creek

Date	Departure Time	Time Back into Camp	Total Miles Marched	Location of Evening's Camp
Sunday July 26, 1857	7:00 A.M.	1:00 P.M.	17 mi.	On south fork of Sappa Creek
Monday July 27, 1857	6:30 A.M.	2:00 P.M.	17 mi.	On north bank of North Fork of Solomon River
Tuesday July 28, 1857	6:30 A.M.	2:00 P.M.	20 mi.	On south bank of Bow Creek
Wednesday July 29, 1857	6:30 A.M.	4:00 P.M.	32 mi. (including charge and pursuit)	On south bank of South Fork of Solomon River across from site of charge
Thursday July 30, 1857			In camp	On south bank of South Fork of Solomon River across from site of charge
Friday July 31, 1857	6:30 A.M.		15 mi.	On north bank of Saline River
Saturday August 1, 1857	6:30 A.M.	3:00 P.M.	20 mi.	On banks of Downer's Creek
Sunday August 2, 1857	7:00 A.M.	3:30 P.M.	22 mi.	On banks of Wild Horse Creek
Monday August 3, 1857			In camp	On banks of Wild Horse Creek
Tuesday August 4, 1857	6:00 A.M.	1:00 P.M.	20 mi.	On banks of Guzzler's Gulch
Wednesday August 5, 1857	6:00 A.M.	10:00 A.M.	10 mi.	Heth's Branch (north fork) of Pawnee Fork
Thursday August 6, 1857	6:30 A.M.		15 mi.	Buckner's Branch (middle) of Pawnee Fork
Friday August 7, 1857	6:30 A.M.		15 mi.	Shaff's Branch (south branch or Saw-Log Creek) of Pawnee Fork
Saturday August 8, 1857	7:00 A.M.		17 mi.	On north bank of Arkansas River, 3 miles above Fort Atkinson
Sunday August 9, 1857			In camp	On north bank of Arkansas River, 3 miles above Fort Atkinson
Monday August 10, 1857				On north bank of Arkansas, 3 miles west of Fort Atkinson
Tuesday August 11, 1857	7:00 A.M.		9 mi.	On north bank of Arkansas, 6 miles east of Fort Atkinson
Wednesday August 12, 1857	6:00 A.M.	3:00 P.M.	20 mi.	On north bank of Arkansas, 2 miles east of lower Middle Crossing

Date	Departure Time	Time Back into Camp	Total Miles Marched	Location of Evening's Camp
Thursday August 13, 1857	6:00 A.M.	3:00 P.M.	24 mi.	On north bank of Arkansas, 6 miles west of upper Point of Rocks
Friday August 14, 1857	6:00 A.M.	2:00 P.M.	19 mi.	On north bank of Arkansas off Santa Fe Trail
Saturday August 15, 1857	7:00 A.M.	3:00 P.M.	20 mi.	On north bank of Arkansas just west of Indian Mound and Chouteau's Island
Sunday August 16, 1857	7:00 A.M.	2:30 P.M.	22 mi.	On north bank of Arkansas off Bent's Fort Trail
Monday August 17, 1857	(Sumner) 7:00 A.M.		30 mi.	On north bank of Arkansas, 25 miles east of Bent's New Fort
Monday August 17, 1857	(Sedgwick)		In camp	On north bank of Arkansas off Bent's Fort Trail
Tuesday August 18, 1857	(Sumner) 7:00 A.M.	4:00 P.M.	25 mi.	On north bank of Arkansas just east of Bent's New Fort
Tuesday August 18, 1857	(Sedgwick)		Few hundred yards west	On north bank of Arkansas off Bent's Fort Trail
Wednesday August 19, 1857	(Sumner)		In camp	On north bank of Arkansas just east of Bent's New Fort
Wednesday August 19, 1857	(Sedgwick)		In camp	On north bank of Arkansas off Bent's Fort Trail
Thursday August 20, 1857	(Sumner) 7:00 A.M.		Approx. 20 mi.	On north bank of Arkansas off Bent's Fort Trail
Thursday August 20, 1857	(Sedgwick)		In camp	On north bank of Arkansas off Bent's Fort Trail
Friday August 21, 1857	(Sumner) 7:00 A.M.		Approx. 20 mi.	On north bank of Arkansas off Bent's Fort Trail
Friday August 21, 1857	(Sedgwick) 7:00 A.M.		1½ mi. east	On north bank of Arkansas off Bent's Fort Trail
Saturday August 22, 1857	(Sumner) 7:00 A.M.	12:00 noon	Approx. 15 mi.	On north bank of Arkansas (with Sedgwick)
Saturday August 22, 1857	(Sedgwick) 10:30 A.M.	11:00 A.M.	Few hundred yards	On north bank of Arkansas (with Sumner)
Sunday August 23, 1857	7:00 A.M.		14 mi.	On north bank of Arkansas off Bent's Fort Trail
Monday August 24, 1857			17 mi.	On north Bank of Arkansas off Santa Fe Trail
Tuesday August 25, 1857			20 mi.	On north Bank of Arkansas off Santa Fe Trail

Date	Departure Time	Time Back into Camp	Total Miles Marched	Location of Evening's Camp
Wednesday August 26, 1857			17 mi.	On north Bank of Arkansas off Santa Fe Trail, just below upper Point of Rocks
Thursday August 27, 1857			20 mi.	On north bank of Arkansas off Santa Fe Trail, 3 miles east of lower Middle Crossing
Friday August 28, 1857			20 mi.	On north bank of Arkansas off Santa Fe Trail, 8 miles below Fort Atkinson
Saturday August 29, 1857			16 mi.	On north bank of Arkansas, 1½ miles off Santa Fe Trail
Sunday August 30, 1857			17 mi.	On bank of Arkansas, 1½ miles off Santa Fe Trail
Monday August 31, 1857			17 mi.	On bank of Arkansas at mouth of Cow Creek
Tuesday Sept. 1, 1857			23 mi.	On bank of Arkansas near Pawnee Rock
Wednesday Sept. 2, 1857			17 mi.	On bank of Arkansas, 1 mile below Walnut Creek
Thursday Sept. 3, 1857			In camp	On bank of Arkansas, 1 mile below Walnut Creek
Friday Sept. 4, 1857			1 mi.	On bank of Arkansas, 2 miles below Walnut Creek
Saturday Sept. 5, 1857			In camp	On bank of Arkansas, 2 miles below Walnut Creek
Sunday Sept. 6, 1857	(Sumner) 7:30 A.M.		25 mi.	Adjacent to Cow Creek crossing of Santa Fe Trail
Sunday Sept. 6, 1857	(Sedgwick)* 7:30 A.M.		14 mi.	On banks of Cow Creek
Monday Sept. 7, 1857	(Sumner) 7:00 A.M.		20 mi.	On east bank of Little Arkansas, ½ mile south of Santa Fe Trail
Tuesday Sept. 8, 1857	(Sumner) 6:30 A.M.		22 mi.	On banks of branch of Turkey Creek, 3 miles east of Big Turkey Creek on Santa Fe Trail
Wednesday Sept. 9, 1857	(Sumner) 6:30 A.M.		25 mi.	On banks of Cottonwood Creek next to crossing off Santa Fe Trail

Date	Departure Time	Time Back into Camp	Total Miles Marched	Location of Evening's Camp
Thursday Sept. 10, 1857	(Sumner) 6:30 A.M.		23 mi.	On banks of Six Mile Creek west of Diamond Springs off Santa Fe Trail
Friday Sept. 11, 1857	6:30 A.M.		23 mi.	Big John Springs and creek, 2 miles east of Council Grove
Saturday Sept. 12, 1857	6:30 A.M.		24 mi.	Prairie Chicken Creek crossing of Santa Fe Trail
Sunday Sept. 13, 1857	6:30 A.M.		18 mi.	On bands of Wakarusa River next to Brownsville (Auburn)
Monday Sept. 14, 1857	6:30 A.M.		21 mi.	Indian Creek, 3 miles east of Indianola
Tuesday Sept. 15, 1857	6:30 A.M.		35 mi.	Stranger Creek off Fort Leavenworth-Fort Riley Trail
Wednesday Sept. 16, 1857	6:30 A.M.		12 mi.	Fort Leavenworth

*The march of Sedgwick's column is not shown beyond September 6, 1857.

Notes

List of Abbreviations Used

AGO   Adjutant General's Office
CIA   Commissioner of Indian Affairs
KHC   *Kansas Historical Collections*
KHQ   *Kansas Historical Quarterly*
KHS   Kansas Historical Society
NA   National Archives
OIA   Office of Indian Affairs

Chapter 1. The Seeds of Conflict

1. Robert M. Utley, *The Indian Frontier of the American West 1846–1890*, 33–47.
2. Utley, *The Indian Frontier*, 37.
3. Ibid., 37.
4. H. Craig Miner and William E. Unrau, *The End of Indian Kansas*, 1–5; Utley, *The Indian Frontier*, 36–37.
5. T. R. Fehrenbach, *Comanches*, 139–49; Ernest Wallace and E. Adamson Hoebel, *The Comanches: Lords of the South Plains*, 3–32.
6. Mildred P. Mayhall, *The Kiowas*, 3–17; John Upton Terrell, *The Plains Apache*, 15–23, 194–217.
7. Utley, *The Indian Frontier*, 31–63.
8. House Ex. Doc. No. 79, 18 Cong., 2 Sess., 6; "The Journals of Captain Thomas William Becknell from Boone's Lick to Santa Fe and From Santa Cruz to Green River," *Missouri Historical Review* 4 (Jan., 1910): 76–79, also in *Missouri Historical Society Collections* (St. Louis), 2:57–75; Louise Barry, *Beginning of the West*, 97; R. L. Duffus, *The Santa Fe Trail*, 67–68; Kate L. Gregg, *The Road to Santa Fe*, 23–48; Leo E. Oliva, *Soldiers on the Santa Fe Trail*, 7–12; Hobart E. Stocking, *The Road to Santa Fe*, 10–11.

9. Sen. Ex. Doc. No. 46, 21 Cong., 1 Sess., 2; Fred S. Perrine, "Military Escorts on the Santa Fe Trail," *New Mexico Historical Review* 3 (July, 1928): 178—92; Macomb to Eaton, Nov., 1829, *American State Papers: Military Affairs* 4:155—56; Duffus, 118—23; Oliva, 25—33.

10. General Order No. 1, Headquarters Department of the West, April 15, 1833, AGO, NA; Henry Dodge, "A Frontier Officer's Military Order Book," Iowa State Historical Society Library, Iowa City, Iowa, 29—30; Capt. Clifton Wharton's Report of the 1834 Escort, July 21, 1834, in Fred S. Perrine, "Military Escorts on the Santa Fe Trail," *New Mexico Historical Review* 2, (July, 1927): 269—70; Philip St. George Cooke, "Journal of the Santa Fe Escort, May 27 to July 21, 1843," in "A Journal of the Santa Fe Trail," *Mississippi Valley Historical Review* 12 (June and Sept., 1925): 72—98, 227—55; Oliva, 35—36, 41—52.

11. Donald J. Berthrong, *The Southern Cheyennes*, 10—26, 76—80, 90—99; George Bird Grinnell, "Bent's Old Fort and its Builders," *KHC* 15:28—91; George E. Hyde, *Life of George Bent*, 59—68; David Lavender, *Bent's Fort*, 101—44; Nolie Mumey, *Old Forts and Trading Posts of the West, Bent's Old Fort and New Fort*, 9—20; Colorado Historical Society, *Bent's Old Fort*, 7—27.

12. Abraham Robinson Johnston, Marcellus Ball Edwards, and Philip Gooch Ferguson, *Marching With the Army of the West*, 73; Oliva, 55—76; Stocking, 229—54.

13. Barry, *Beginning of the West*, 669—71, 682—84, 688, 690, 695, 701, 702, 705, 706, 720—22, 724, 727—28, 731—33, 739—40, 750—51, 754—55, 758—61, 764—67, 778; Lewis H. Gerrard, *Wah-to-yah and the Taos Trail*, 325—359; LeRoy R. Hafen, *Broken Hand*, 247, 258—59; Thomas L. Karnes, *William Gilpin, Western Nationalist*, 194—95, 200—208; Oliva, 80—92.

14. Barry, *Beginning of the West*, 802—803, 854, 856, 860, 873, 961, 965—68, 991, 997, 1004, 1008, 1012—13, 1040, 1048, 1073, 1105—1106, 1108, 1112—14, 1117, 1121, 1145, 1153, 1170, 1174—75, 1216—17; Hafen, *Broken Hand*, 245, 280, 281; Hyde, *Life of George Bent*, 98; Lavender, *Bent's Fort*, 323—24; Percival G. Lowe, *Five Years a Dragoon*, 58, 106—108; Percival G. Lowe, "Kansas, as Seen in the Indian Territory," *KHC* 4:363—66; Remi Nadeau, *Fort Laramie and the Sioux*, 68; Oliva, 95—103; Peter J. Powell, *People of the Sacred Mountain*, 1:101—102; Annual Report, CIA (1851), House Ex. Doc. No. 2, 32 Cong., 1 Sess., 332—35; Henry Heth to Capt. Irwin J. McDowell, April 14, 1853, Upper Platte Agency, Letters Received; C. C. Isely to Kirk Mechem, August 12, 1947, Archives of the Kansas State Historical Society; James P. McCollom, "Statement and Sketch Map dated February 6, 1956," Archives, KHS; Merritt L. Beeson to George A. Root, Letter and sketch map dated April 24, 1935, Archives KHS; "Kansas History in the Press," *KHQ* 15:329—30.

15. Barry, *Beginning of the West*, 1162, 1164—70, 1187; Lowe, *Five Years a Dragoon*, 101—102, 108; Oliva, 101—102; C. C. Isely to Kirk Mechem, August 12, 1947, Archives, KHS; James P. McCollom, Statement and Map dated February 6, 1956, Archives, KHS; "Kansas History in the Press," *KHQ* 15:329—30; James Schiel, *The Land Between*, 46—48.

16. Ray Allen Billington, *Westward to the Pacific*, 49—50; LeRoy R. Hafen and Francis Marion Young, *Fort Laramie and the Pageant of the West*, 95—99; Merrill J. Mattes, *The Great Platte River Road*, 11—13; Nadeau, 43—49.

17. Billington, 50–51, 62–66; Hafen and Young, 99–111, 123–34; Mattes, *The Great Platte River Road*, 7–9, 13–14; Nadeau, 50–61.

18. Gregory M. Franzwa, *Maps of the Oregon Trail*, 2–7; Gregory M. Franzwa, *The Oregon Trail Revisited*, 56–58; Aubrey L. Haines, *Historic Sites Along the Oregon Trail*, 11–17; Mattes, *The Great Platte River Road*, 7–11, 103–21, 136–66, 238–310, 339–500.

19. Berthrong, 20–26, 76–99; George Bird Grinnell, *The Cheyenne Indians*, 40–46; Hafen, *Broken Hand*, 244–245; Hafen and Young, 53–64; George E. Hyde, *Spotted Tail's Folk*, 3–39, 71–73; George E. Hyde, *Red Cloud's Folk*, 3–98 Mattes, *The Great Platte River Road*, 14–16, 167–91, 480–500; Nadeau, 137–41.

20. Mattes, *The Great Platte River Road*, 167–69, 172–97, 202–203, 208–13; D. Ray Wilson, *Fort Kearny on the Platte*, 19–20, 23–37, 56–58, 67–70.

21. Hafen, *Broken Hand*, 244–245; Hafen and Young, 95–104, 137–43; David Lavender, *Fort Laramie and the Changing Frontier*, 7–11, 47–48, 52–57; Mattes, *The Great Platte River Road*, 483–500; Merrill J. Mattes, *Fort Laramie Park History, 1834–1977*, 9–10, 12–15; Nadeau, 43–49, 61–64.

22. Barry, *Beginning of the West*, 991, 997, 1012–13, 1029–34, 1037; Hafen, *Broken Hand*, 269–301; Hafen and Young, 177–96; Lavender, *Fort Laramie*, 68–73; Lowe, *Five Years a Dragoon*, 58, 60–71; Lowe, "Kansas," *KHC* 4:363–64; Mattes, *Fort Laramie*, 20–21; Mattes, *The Great Platte River Road*, 516–17; Nadeau, 66–83; Oliva, 98; Annual Report, CIA (1853), House Ex. Doc. No. 1, 33 Cong., 1 Sess., 1:366.

23. Duffus, 224–225; Margaret Long, *The Smoky Hill Trail*, 125–50; Mattes, *The Great Platte River Road*, 5; Oliva, 21.

24. Hafen and Young, 31–33; LeRoy R. Hafen, *Fort Vasquez*, 1, 6–9; Lavender, *Fort Laramie*, 27–40; Mattes, *The Great Platte River Road*, 481–82; Mattes, *Fort Laramie*, 5–6; Nadeau, 29–35; Guy L. Peterson, *Four Forts on the South Platte*, 4–12, 38–40, 50–51, 64–68.

25. Hafen and Young, 67–68; Hafen, *Fort Vasquez*, 8–10; Lavender, *Fort Laramie*, 40; Peterson, 12–13, 39–42, 54–55, 69–70.

Chapter 2. The Cheyenne Troubles

1. Hyde, Life of George Bent, 95; Lavender, Bent's Fort, 324; Eli Long, "Journal of the Cheyenne Expedition of 1857," June 17, 1857; Mumey, 126–28; Peck, "Rough Riding on the Plains," March 14, 1901, 1.

2. Annual Report, CIA (1853), House Ex. Doc. No. 1, 33 Cong., 1 Sess., 1:368; "Report of Explorations and Surveys," Sen. Ex. Doc. No. 78, 33 Cong., 2 Sess., 2: 16, 19, 25, 28; George L. Albright, *Official Explorations for Pacific Railroads, 1853–1855*, 119–32; Barry, *Beginning of the West*, 1167–69; William H. Goetzmann, *Army Exploration of the American West, 1803–1863*, 283–86; Lewis H. Haney, *A Congressional History of Railroads in the United States, 1850–1887*, 54; Lavender, Bent's *Fort*, 326–27; Allen Nevins, *Fremont, The West's Greatest Adventurer*, 2:461–62.

3. Heth to McDowell, April 10, 1853, Departmental Commands, AGO, NA; Fort Atkinson Post Returns, September 1852 to April 1853, NA; Barry, *Begin-*

ning of the West, 1162–63, 1169–70; Hafen, Broken *Hand*, 309–12; Oliva, 101–102.

4. Eugene Bandel, *Frontier Life in the Army, 1854–1861*, 23–24; Hafen and Young, 209–210; Nadeau, 86–88.

5. Missouri *Republican*, May 27, 1854; *Liberty Weekly Tribune*, June 2, 1854, and February 2, 1855; *Weekly Missouri Statesman*, May 5, 1854; Barry, *Beginning of the West*, 1215.

6. Annual Report, CIA (1854), Senate Ex. Doc. No. 1, 33 Cong., 2 Sess., 90; House Misc. Doc. No. 47, 33 Cong., 1 Sess.; Barry, *Beginning of the West*, 1217; Grinnell, *Fighting Cheyennes*, 102–103.

7. Office of Indian Affairs, Letters Received from Pottawatomie Agency, 1853–1854, NA, (M234-Roll 679); *St. Joseph Gazette*, April 24, 1854; Barry, *Beginning of the West*, 1201; Hafen, *Broken Hand*, 318.

8. *Statutes at Large*, 33 Cong., 1 Sess., 1854; "The Kansas Territorial Centennial," *KHQ* 21:1–7; Barry, *Beginning of the West*, 1218.

9. "The Kansas Territorial Centennial," *KHQ* 21:1; Barry, *Beginning of the West*, 1218.

10. Nadeau, 90.

11. Annual Report, CIA (1854), 89–98; Hafen and Young, 221–22; Nadeau, 91.

12. Grinnell, *Fighting Cheyennes*, 106; Nadeau, 90.

13. Annual Report, CIA (1854), 93; Latter Day Saints Journal History for August 19, 1854; House Ex. Doc. No. 63, 33 Cong., 2 Sess., 22; Grinnell, *Fighting Cheyennes*, 106; Hafen and Young, 222–23; Nadeau, 91.

14. House Ex. Doc. No. 63, 33 Cong., 2 Sess., 2; Grinnell, *Fighting Cheyennes*, 107; Hafen and Young, 222–223; Nadeau, 91–92.

15. House Ex. Doc. No. 63, 33 Cong., 2 Sess., 5; Grinnell, *Fighting Cheyennes*, 107; Hafen and Young, 223–24; Nadeau, 92.

16. House Ex. Doc. No. 63, 33 Cong., 2 Sess., 16, 18, 19, 21, 22 and 25; Grinnell, *Fighting Cheyennes*, 107–108; Hafen and Young, 224–29; Nadeau, 92–101.

17. House Ex. Doc. No. 63, 33 Cong., 2 Sess., 5, 21–22; Grinnell, *Fighting Cheyennes*, 108; Hafen and Young, 229; Nadeau, 101–104.

18. Grinnell, *Fighting Cheyennes*, 108; Hafen and Young, 231–33; Nadeau, 104–109.

19. Capt. John B. S. Todd, "The Harney Expedition Against the Sioux," Nebraska *History*, 43, No. 2: 91–92; Hafen and Young, 236–37; Mattes, *The Great Platte River Road*, 312–13; Nadeau, 114–15.

20. Annual Report, CIA (1854), 94–96; Hafen and Young, 232–233; Nadeau, 111.

21. House Ex. Doc. No. 36, 33 Cong., 2 Sess., 5; Bandel, *Frontier Life*, 28; Hafen and Young, 234–239; Nadeau, 111.

22. Twiss to Cumming, August 13, 1855, OIA, General Files, Upper Platte Agency, C 1590/1855; Hafen and Young, 239; Alden W. Hoopes, "Thomas S. Twiss, Indian Agent of the Upper Platte, 1855–1861," *Mississippi Valley Historical Review* 20, No. 3 (Dec.,1933): 355; Nadeau, 115–16.

23. Twiss to Robert McClelland, August 20, 1855, House Ex. Doc. No. 1, 34 Cong., 1 Sess., 398–400; Hafen and Young, 239–40; Nadeau, 116.

24. Nadeau, 116–17.

25. "Report of Gen. Harney, Commander of the Sioux Expedition," Sen. Ex. Doc. No. 1, 34 Cong., 1 Sess., 49–51; Bandel, *Frontier Life*, 34; Hafen and Young, 240; Mattes, *The Great Platte River Road*, 317–20; Nadeau, 117–18.

26. Bandel, *Frontier Life*, 34; Grinnell, Fighting *Cheyennes*, 108–109; Hafen and Young, 240–41; Mattes, *The Great Platte River Road*, 319–21; Nadeau, 119–21.

27. Grinnell, Fighting *Cheyennes*, 109; Hafen and Young, 241–42; Mattes, *The Great Platte River Road*, 321–24; Nadeau, 121–23.

28. Grinnell, The Fighting *Cheyennes*, 110; Hafen and Young, 243–45; Mattes, *The Great Platte River Road*, 328–29; Nadeau, 123–31.

29. Hoffman to A. Pleasonton, March 31, 1856, Fort Laramie, Letters Sent, United States Army Commands, NA.

30. J. W. Whitfield to G. W. Manypenny, September 4, 1855, Annual Report, CIA (1855), 435–36.

31. "Report of the Chief Topographical Engineer, Nov. 22, 1856," House Ex. Doc. No. 1, 34 Cong., 3 Sess., 2: 370; Goetzmann, 368–69; W. Turrentine Jackson, "The Army Engineers as Road Surveyors and Builders in Kansas and Nebraska, 1854–1858," *KHQ* 17:40–44; W. Turrentine Jackson, *Wagon Roads West*, 124–25.

32. Annual Report, Secretary of War (1857), 455–81; Goetzmann, 369–70; Jackson, "Army Engineers," *KHQ* 17:40–44; Jackson, *Wagon Roads West*, 125–30.

33. W. Hoffman to H. Heth, May 24, 1856, Fort Laramie, Letters Sent; Annual Report, Secretary of Interior (1856), House Ex. Doc. No. 1, 34 Cong., 3 Sess., 1: 638; Annual Report, CIA (1856), 87, 100; Grinnell, *Fighting Cheyennes*, 111–12; Hafen and Young, 277; Powell, *People of the Sacred Mountain*, 1:202–203.

34. W. Hoffman to H. Heth, May 24, 1856, Fort Laramie, Letters Sent; Annual Report, Secretary of Interior (1856), House Ex. Doc. No. 1, 34 Cong., 3 Sess., 1:638; Annual Report, CIA (1856), 87, 100; Grinnell, *Fighting Cheyennes*, 111–12; Hafen and Young, 277; Powell, *People of the Sacred Mountain*, 1:202–203.

35. *New York Tribune*, May 21, 1857; Hafen and Young, 277.

36. W. Hoffman to H. Heth, May 24, 1856, Fort Laramie, Letters Sent; Annual Report, Secretary of Interior (1856), House Ex. Doc. No. 1, 34 Cong., 3 Sess., 1:638; Annual Report, CIA (1856), 87, 100; Grinnell, *Fighting Cheyennes*, 111–12; Hafen and Young, 277; Powell, *People of the Sacred Mountain*, 1:202–203.

37. W. Hoffman to H. Heth, May 24, 1856, Fort Laramie, Letters Sent; Annual Report, Secretary of Interior (1856), House Ex. Doc. No. 1, 34 Cong., 3 Sess., 1:638; Annual Report, CIA (1856), 87, 100; Grinnell, *Fighting Cheyennes*, 111–12; Hafen and Young, 277; Powell, *People of the Sacred Mountain*, 1:202–203.

38. W. Hoffman to A. Pleasonton, June 18, 1856, Fort Laramie, Letters Sent.

39. H. W. Wharton to A. Pleasonton, June 7, 1856, AGO, Old Files Section, 322 H/1856, Enclosure 1.

40. Twiss to Commissioner of Indian Affairs, June 15, 1856, Upper Arkansas

Agency, Letters Received; H. W. Wharton to A. Pleasonton, June 7, 1856, AGO, Old Files Section, 322 H/1856, Enclosure 1; H. W. Wharton to E. V. Sumner, June 11, 1856, AGO, Letters Received; W. Hoffman to A. Pleasonton, June 20, 21, 28, 1856, Fort Laramie, Letters Sent; Grinnell, *Fighting Cheyennes*, 114–15; Powell, *People of the Sacred Mountain*, 1:205–206.

41. Twiss to Commissioner of Indian Affairs, June 15, 1856, Upper Arkansas Agency, Letters Received; H. W. Wharton to A. Pleasonton, June 7, 1856, AGO, Old Files Section, 322 H/1856, Enclosure 1; H. W. Wharton to E. V. Sumner, June 11, 1856, AGO, Letters Received; W. Hoffman to A. Pleasonton, June 20, 21, 28, 1856, Fort Laramie, Letters Sent; Grinnell, *Fighting Cheyennes*, 115–16; Powell, *People of the Sacred Mountain*, 1:206.

42. Grinnell, *Fighting Cheyennes*, 116; Powell, *People of the Sacred Mountain*, 1:206.

43. Grinnell, *Fighting Cheyennes*, 116; Powell, *People of the Sacred Mountain*, 1:206.

44. Grinnell, *Fighting Cheyennes*, 116; Powell, *People of the Sacred Mountain*, 1:206.

45. H. W. Wharton to A. Pleasonton, June 10, 1856, AGO, Old Files Section, 322 H/1856, Enclosure 2.

46. Berthrong, 32; Richard I. Dodge, *Our Wild Indians*, 287–90; Grinnell, *Cheyenne Indians*, 226–27, 262; Hoebel, *The Cheyennes*, 6–7, 58–64.

47. Grinnell, *Fighting Cheyennes*, 112; Powell, *People of the Sacred Mountain*, 1:203–204.

48. Annual Report, CIA (1856), 99; Annual Report, Secretary of Interior, 1856, House Ex. Doc. No. 1, 34 Cong., 3 Sess., 1:650–51; H. W. Wharton to S. Cooper, September 8, 1856, *KHC* 4:492–94; J. H. Dickerson to J. J. Abert, December 15, 1856, House Ex. Doc. No. 2, 35 Cong., 1 Sess., 2:530–31; Grinnell, *Fighting Cheyennes*, 112; Hafen and Young, 277–78; LeRoy R. Hafen and Ann W. Hafen, *Relations with the Indians of the Plains*, 16; Powell, *People of the Sacred Mountain*, 1:204.

49. Annual Report, CIA (1856), 99; Annual Report, Secretary of Interior, 1856, House Ex. Doc. No. 1, 34 Cong., 3 Sess., 1:650; Grinnell, *Fighting Cheyennes*, 112–13; Hafen and Hafen, 16; Powell, *People of the Sacred Mountain*, 1:204.

50. G. W. Stewart to H. W. Wharton, August 27, 1856, *KHC* 4:491–92; H. W. Wharton to S. Cooper, September 8, 1856, *KHC* 4:492.

51. G. W. Stewart to H. W. Wharton, August 27, 1856, *KHC* 4:491–92; H. W. Wharton to S. Cooper, September 8, 1856, *KHC* 4:492.

52. Grinnell, *Fighting Cheyennes*, 113; Powell, *People of the Sacred Mountain*, 1:204–205.

53. G. H. Stewart to H. W. Wharton, September 1, 1856, *KHC* 4:490–91; H. W. Wharton to S. Cooper, September 8, 1856, *KHC* 4:492–93; H. W. Wharton to A. Cumming, Sept. 17, 1856, OIA, General Files, Upper Platte Agency, C 535/1856; Twiss to A. Cumming, September 25, 1856, Annual Report, Secretary of Interior (1856), 650; Grinnell, *Fighting Cheyennes*, 113; Hafen and Young, 278; Hafen and Hafen, 17; Powell, *People of the Sacred Mountain*, 1:205.

54. H. W. Wharton to S. Cooper, Sept. 8, 1856, *KHC* 4:493–94; Twiss to A. Cumming, September 25, 1856, Annual Report, CIA (1856), 99–101, Annual

Report, Secretary of Interior (1856), 651; W. Hoffman to E. V. Sumner, July 10, 1857, Fort Laramie, Letters Sent; Grinnell, *Fighting Cheyennes*, 113; Hafen and Young, 278; Hafen and Hafen, 17; Powell, *People of the Sacred Mountain*, 1:205.

55. H. W. Wharton to G. Deas, September 27, 1856, *KHC* 4:494–95; Twiss to A. Cumming, September 25, 1856, Annual Report, Secretary of Interior (1856), 651; Hafen and Young, 278; Hafen and Hafen, 17; Powell, *People of the Sacred Mountain*, 1:205.

56. Grinnell, *Fighting Cheyennes*, 116; Hafen and Young, 278.

57. "Report of Lt. Francis T. Bryan dated February 19, 1857," Annual Report, Secretary of War (1857), 471; Annual Report, CIA (1856), 100.

58. Grinnell, *Fighting Cheyennes*, 116; Twiss to A. Cumming, September 25, 1856, Annual Report, Secretary of Interior (1856), 651.

59. Twiss to A. Cumming, September 25, 1856, Annual Report, Secretary of Interior (1856), 651; Hafen and Young, 279; Hafen and Hafen, 18; Powell, *People of the Sacred Mountain*, 1:206–207.

60. Twiss to A. Cumming, September 25, 1856, Annual Report, Secretary of Interior (1856), 651; Twiss to Manypenny, October 13, 1856, Annual Report, Secretary of Interior (1856), 652–54; Annual Report, CIA (1856), 99–103; Hafen and Young, 279; Hafen and Hafen, 18; Powell, *People of the Sacred Mountain*, 1:207.

61. Twiss to Manypenny, October 13, 1856, Annual Report, Secretary of Interior (1856), 652–54.

Chapter 3. The Cheyennes and the Path to Solomon

1. Powell, *People of the Sacred Mountain*, 1:175; Wayne C. Lee and Howard C. Raynesford, *Trails of the Smoky Hill*, 69.

2. Grinnell, *The Cheyenne Indians*, 1:72.

3. George Bird Grinnell, *By Cheyenne Campfires*, 59; Powell, *People of the Sacred Mountain*, 1:207.

4. Annual Report, Secretary of Interior (1856), 651–52; Annual Report, Secretary of Interior (1857), 140–41; Grinnell, "Bent's Old Fort and Its Builders," *KHC* 15:86–87.

5. Annual Report, CIA (1857), 144; Powell, *People of the Sacred Mountain*, 1:175.

6. Grinnell, *Fighting Cheyennes*, 117; Hyde, *Life of George Bent*, 102; Powell, *People of the Sacred Mountain*, 1:208.

7. Susan Bettelyoun Manuscript, Archives of the Nebraska State Historical Society.

8. George Bent to George E. Hyde, November 14, 1910, Bent Letters, William Robertson Coe Collection, Yale University Library.

9. Grinnell, *The Cheyenne Indians*, 1:51.

10. Hoebel, *The Cheyennes*, 7.

11. Grinnell, *The Cheyenne Indians*, 2:215; Hoebel, *The Cheyennes*, 7.

12. Hoebel, *The Cheyennes*, 11; Powell, *Sweet Medicine*, 2:443, 614.

13. Hoebel, *The Cheyennes*, 12–13.

14. Grinnell, *The Cheyenne Indians*, 2:214.

15. Grinnell, *The Cheyenne Indians*, 2:220.

16. Eli Long, "Journal," July 25, 1857.

17. Eli Long, "Journal," July 23, 1857.

18. Hoebel, *The Cheyennes*, 14; Powell, *Sweet Medicine*, 2:646.

19. Grinnell, "The Cheyenne Medicine Lodge," 248; Powell, *Sweet Medicine*, 2:614–15.

20. Grinnell, *Fighting Cheyennes*, 117.

21. Powell, *Sweet Medicine*, 2:777; Eli Long, "Journal," July 26, 1857.

22. David A. Dary, *The Buffalo Book*, 25–181; Mari Sandoz, *The Buffalo Hunters*, 6.

23. Eli Long, "Journal," July 27, 1857.

24. Whitfield to Cumming, August 15, 1857, Upper Arkansas Agency, OIA, Letters Received (M234-R878); Twiss to Cumming, November 14, 1855, Upper Platte Agency, Letters Received (M234-R889).

25. Grinnell, *Fighting Cheyennes*, 117; Hyde, *The Life of George Bent*, 102.

26. Lowe, *Five Years a Dragoon*, 198–202; Eli Long, "Journal," July 4, 1857; Peck, "Rough Riding on the Plains," March 14, 1901, 5.

27. Grinnell, *Fighting Cheyennes*, 117–18; Hyde, *The Life of George Bent*, 102; Powell, *People of the Sacred Mountain*, 1:211.

28. Grinnell, *Fighting Cheyennes*, 117–18; Hyde, *The Life of George Bent*, 102; Powell, *People of the Sacred Mountain*, 1:211–12.

29. *Kansas Weekly Herald*, May 2, 1857; *Kansas City Enterprise*, May 2, 1857.

30. "Report of Col. E. V. Sumner, August 9, 1857," Annual Report, Secretary of War (1857), House Ex. Doc. 2, 35 Cong., 1 Sess., 2:96–97; "Report of Major Sedgwick, August 11, 1860," Annual Report, Secretary of War (1860), Sen. Ex. Doc. 1, 36 Cong., 2 Sess., 2:18; Hafen and Hafen, 213; Eli Long, "Journal," July 31, 1857; Peck, "Rough Riding on the Plains," March 28, 1901, 1.

31. Peck, "Rough Riding on the Plains," March 28, 1901, 1.

32. Eli Long, "Journal," July 31, 1857.

33. David S. Stanley, *Personal Memoirs*, 47.

Chapter 4. An Expedition Against the Cheyennes

1. J. W. Whitfield to G. W. Manypenny, September 4, 1855, Annual Report, CIA (1855), 435–36.

2. "Report of General Harney, Commander of the Sioux Expedition," Sen Ex. Doc. No. 1, 34 Cong., 1 Sess., 1:49–51; "Council with the Sioux Indians at Fort Pierre," House Ex. Doc. No. 130, 34 Cong., 1 Sess., 12:1–39; A. Pleasonton to W. Hoffman, March 5, 1856, AGO, Letters Received.

3. W. Hoffman to A. Pleasonton, March 31, 1856, Fort Laramie, Letters Sent.

4. H. W. Wharton to A. Pleasonton, June 10, 1856, AGO, Old Files Section, 322 H/1856, enclosure 2.

5. H. W. Wharton to S. Cooper, September 8, 1856, *KHC* 4:492–94.

6. P. F. Smith to S. Cooper, September 10, 1856, *KHC* 4:489–90.

7. Hafen and Young, Fort *Laramie*, 279.

8. Jeff'n Davis endorsement, October 24, 1856, *KHC* 4:494.

9. P. F. Smith to S. Cooper, November 11, 1856, *KHC* 4:517–18.

10. Army General Order No. 5, April 4, 1857, from *Frank Leslie's Illustrated Newspaper*, April 25, 1857.

11. J. B. Floyd to J. Thompson, April 10, 1857, OIA, General Files, Upper Platte Agency, I501/1857.

12. Albert G. Brackett, History of the United *States Cavalry*, 168; Gregory J. W. Urwin, *The United States Cavalry*, 96; Theo. F. Rodenbough and Wm. L. Haskins, eds., *The Army of the United States*, 211–12; Theo. F. Rodenbough, *From Everglade to Canon With the Second Dragoons*, 204–208; P. F. Smith to S. Cooper, November 11, 1856, *KHC* 4:517–18.

13. Samuel J. Bayard, *The Life of George Dashiell Bayard*, 97.

14. Peck, "Rough Riding on the Plains," February 14, 1901, 2.

15. Rodenbough, 204–205.

16. Bayard, 113.

17. Bayard, 116; Peck, "Rough Riding on the Plains," February 28, 1901, 1; Eli Long, "Journal," May 18, 1857; AGO, Post Returns, Fort Leavenworth, K.T., May, 1857, NA, (M 617-Roll 611).

18. Bayard, 120; Peck, "Rough Riding on the Plains," February 28, 1901, 1; Eli Long, "Journal," May 18, 1857; Lowe, Five Years a *Dragoon*, 186–91.

19. Nyle H. Miller, "Surveying the Southern Boundary Line of Kansas," *KHQ*, 1:108; Peck, "Rough Riding on the Plains," February 28, 1901, 1; Army General Order No. 5, April 4, 1857, from *Frank Leslie's Illustrated Newspaper*, April 25, 1857; AGO, Post Returns, Fort Leavenworth, Kansas Territory, May, 1857, NA, (M 617-Roll 611).

20. Peck, "Rough Riding on the Plains," February 28, 1901, 1; Bayard, 124–25; Eli Long, "Journal," May 18, 1857; Army General Order No. 5, April 4, 1857, from *Frank Leslie's Illustrated Newspaper*, April 25, 1857.

21. Peck, "Rough Riding on the Plains," February 28, 1901, 1; Bayard, 121.

22. Peck, "Rough Riding on the Plains," February 28, 1901, 1; "Report of Col. E. V. Sumner, September 20, 1857," Annual Report, Secretary of War (1857), House Ex. Doc. No. 2, 35 Cong., 1 Sess., Vol 2, 98–99; Army General Order No. 5, April 4, 1857, from *Frank Leslie's Illustrated Newspaper*, April 25, 1857.

23. Peck, "Rough Riding on the Plains," February 28, 1901, 1; Bayard, 117.

24. Bayard, 118.

25. Peck, "Rough Riding on the Plains," February 28, 1901, 1.

26. *Kansas Weekly Herald*, May 2, 1857; *Kansas City Enterprise*, May 2, 1857.

27. Bayard, 118.

Chapter 5. The March of Sedgwick's Column

1. AGO, Post Returns, Fort Leavenworth, Kansas Territory, May 18, 1857, NA, (M617-Roll 611); Eli Long, "Journal," February 18, 1857; Peck, "Rough Riding on the Plains," February 28, 1901, 1.

2. Bayard, 114, 118–19; Eli Long, "Journal," May 18, 1857; Lowe, *Five Years a Dragoon*, 185; Peck, "Rough Riding on the Plains," February 28, 1901, 1.

3. William H. Mackey, Sr., "Looking Backwards," *KHC* 10:645–48; Eli Long, "Journal," May 18, 1857; Peck, "Rough Riding on the Plains," February 28, 1901, 1.

4. Eli Long, "Journal," May 19, 1857; Peck, "Rough Riding on the Plains," February 28, 1901, 1.

5. Charles W. Smith, "Battle of Hickory Point," *KHC* 7:534–36; Dr. Albert Morrall, "Brief Autobiography," *KHC* 14:134–35; Eli Long, "Journal," May 19, 1857; Peck, "Recollections," *KHC* 8:487.

6. Eli Long, "Journal," May 20, 1857; Peck, "Recollections," *KHC* 8:487.

7. Peck, "Recollections," *KHC* 8:487; George A. Root, "Ferries in Kansas—Part II—Kansas River," *KHQ* 2:363–76; Root, *KHQ* 3:15–17.

8. Eli Long, "Journal," May 21, 1857; Peck, "Recollections," *KHC* 8:487; Rodenbough, 206; Root, *KHQ* 2:363–76; Root, *KHQ* 3:15–17.

9. Eli Long, "Journal," May 21, 1857; Root, *KHQ* 3:15–17.

10. Alfred T. Andreas, *A History of Kansas*, 1:595; Eli Long, "Journal," May 22 and 23, 1857; Stocking, 79; Morris F. Taylor, *First Mail West*, 35, 42.

11. Rex Buchanan, *Kansas Geology*, 19–20; Daniel F. Merriam, *The Geologic History of Kansas*, 161, 164–65; Stephen Jackson Spear, "Reminiscences of the Early Settlement of Dragoon Creek, Wabaunsee County," *KHC* 13:350.

12. Eli Long, "Journal," May 23 and 24, 1857; Mamie Stine Sharp, "Homecoming Centennial at Council Grove," *KHC* 16:557–58; Alice Strieby Smith, "Through the Eyes of My Father," *KHC* 17:709–10.

13. Bayard, 120–22; Eli Long, "Journal," May 24, 1857; Peck, "Rough Riding on the Plains," February 28, 1901, 1.

14. Bayard, 120–22; Eli Long, "Journal," February 24 and 25, 1857; Peck, "Rough Riding on the Plains," February 28, 1901, 1.

15. Eli Long, "Journal," May 26, 1857.

16. Gregg, 46, 60; Eli Long, "Journal," May 26, 27, and 28, 1857; George Pierson Morehouse, "Diamond Springs," *KHC* 14:794–97; Peck, "Rough Riding on the Plains," February 28, 1901, 1.; Peck, "Recollections," *KHC* 8:487; Taylor, 28–35.

17. Eli Long, "Journal," May 28, and 29, 1857; Peck, "Rough Riding on the Plains," February 28, 1901, 1.

18. Gregg, 59, 62; Eli Long, "Journal," May 24, 1857, May 30 and 31, 1857.

19. Eli Long, "Journal," May 30 and 31, 1857; Peck, "Rough Riding on the Plains," February 28, 1901, 1.

20. Eli Long, "Journal," May 31 and June 1, 1857.

21. Eli Long, "Journal," June 1, 1857; Peck, "Rough Riding on the Plains," March 7, 1901, 1; Peck, "Recollections," *KHC* 8:488–89.

22. Eli Long, "Journal," June 2, 1857.

23. Bayard, 123; Eli Long, "Journal," June 2, 1857; Peck, "Rough Riding on the Plains," March 7, 1901, 1; Peck, "Recollections," *KHC* 8:489; Louise Barry, "The Ranch at Walnut Creek Crossing," *KHQ* 37:121–47.

24. Bayard, 122; Eli Long, "Journal," June 2, 1857; Peck, "Rough Riding on the Plains," February 28, 1901, 1.

25. Jones to Gilpin, July 23, 1848, House Ex. Doc. 1, 30 Cong., 2 Sess., 1:138; James H. Birch, "The Battle of Coon Creek," *KHC* 10:409–13; Eli Long, "Journal," June 3 and 4, 1857; Oliva, 86–89.

26. Eli Long, "Journal," June 4, 1857; Peck, "Rough Riding on the Plains," March 7, 1901, 1.

27. Eli Long, "Journal," June 5, 6, and 7, 1857; Peck, "Rough Riding on the Plains," March 14, 1901, 1; Peck, "Recollections," *KHC* 8:489–90.

28. Eli Long, "Journal," June 7, 1857; Peck, "Rough Riding on the Plains," March 14, 1901, 1; Peck, "Recollections," *KHC* 8:489–90.

29. Eli Long, "Journal," June 8 and 9, 1857; Peck, "Rough Riding on the Plains," March 14, 1901, 1; Peck, "Recollections," *KHC* 8:490; Stocking, 140–41, 146; Louise Barry, "The Ranch at Cimarron Crossing," *KHQ* 39:345–50.

30. Eli Long, "Journal," June 10, 1857; Barry, "Ranch at Cimarron Crossing," *KHQ*, Vol. 39, map of AT&SF Railroad preceding 353.

31. Eli Long, "Journal," June 11 and 12, 1857; Peck, "Rough Riding on the Plains," March 14, 1901, 1; Peck, Recollections," *KHC* 8:490.

32. Barry, *Beginning of the West*, 76, 151–52, 160–63, 202–203; Louise Barry, "Kansas Before 1854," *KHQ* 27:378–79; Grinnell, "Bent's Old Fort," *KHC* 15:91; Eli Long, "Journal," June 13, 14, and 15, 1857; Dale L. Morgan, *Jedediah Smith*, 329–30; Stocking, 148–62.

33. Grinnell, "Bent's Old Fort," *KHC* 15:91.

34. Bayard, 123; Eli Long, "Journal," June 16, 1857; Peck, "Rough Riding on the Plains," March 14, 1901, 1.

35. Eli Long, "Journal," June 17, 1857; Mumey, 126–28; Peck, "Rough Riding on the Plains," March 14, 1901, 1; Peck, "Recollections," *KHC* 8:491.

36. Bayard, 123; Eli Long, "Journal," June 17, 1857; Peck, "Recollections," *KHC* 8:491.

37. Grinnell, "Bent's Old Fort," *KHC* 15:91; Eli Long, "Journal," June 17, 1857; Stanley, *Personal Memoirs*, original manuscript, 147.

38. John and Halka Chronic, *Prairie, Peak, and Plateau*, 16–18; Eli Long, "Journal," June 17, 1857; Peck, "Rough Riding on the Plains," March 14, 1901, 1; Peck, "Recollections," *KHC* 8:491.

39. Bayard, 124; Eli Long, "Journal," June 18, 1857.

40. Eli Long, "Journal," June 18, 19, and 20, 1857; Mumey, 103–14; State Historical Society of Colorado, *Bent's Old Fort*, 31–38.

41. Grinnell, "Bent's Old Fort," *KHC* 15:89–90; Eli Long, "Journal," June 20, 1857.

42. Eli Long, "Journal," June 21 and 22, 1857.

43. Eli Long, "Journal," June 21 and 22, 1857.

44. Eli Long, "Journal," June 22, 1857.

45. Eli Long, "Journal," June 22, 1857.

46. Janet Lecompte, *Pueblo, Hardscrabble, Greenhorn*, 234–35, 252; Eli Long, "Journal," June 22, 1857.

47. Eli Long, "Journal," June 22, 1857.

48. Eli Long, "Journal," June 23, 1857.

49. Edward Broadhead, *Fort Pueblo*, 27; Lecompte, 35, 45, 252; Eli Long, "Journal," June 23, 1857.

50. Eli Long, "Journal," June 23, 1857; Peck, "Rough Riding on the Plains," March 14, 1901, 1.

51. Eli Long, "Journal," June 24, 1857; Stanley, *Personal Memoirs*, original manuscript, 147.

52. Lecompte, 281; Eli Long, "Journal," June 25, 1857; Margaret Long, *The Smokey Hill Trail*, 161.

53. Eli Long, "Journal," June 26, 1857; Peck, "Rough Riding on the Plains," March 14, 1901, 5; Peck, "Recollections," *KHC* 8:492.

54. Eli Long, "Journal," June 27, 1857.

55. Eli Long, "Journal," June 27, 1857; Peck, "Rough Riding on the Plains," March 14, 1901, 1, 5; Peck, "Recollections," *KHC* 8:492.

56. Eli Long, "Journal," June 27 and 28, 1857.

57. Eli Long, "Journal," June 29 and 30, 1857; Peck, "Rough Riding on the Plains," March 14, 1901, 5; Peck, "Recollections," *KHC* 8:492–93.

58. Hafen, *Fort Vasquez*, 12–13; Eli Long, "Journal," July 1 and 2, 1857; Peck, "Rough Riding on the Plains," March 14, 1901, 5; Peck, "Recollections," *KHC* 8:492–93; Peterson, 29, 68.

59. Eli Long, "Journal," July 2, 1857.

60. Eli Long, "Journal," July 3, 1857; Peck, "Rough Riding on the Plains," March 14, 1901, 5; Peck, "Recollections," *KHC* 8:493; Peterson, 39.

61. Eli Long, "Journal," July 3, 1857.

Chapter 6. The March of Sumner's Column

1. AGO, Post Returns, Fort Leavenworth, K.T., May 1857, NA, (M617-R611); Lowe, *Five Years a Dragoon*, 139–86, 191.

2. Post Returns, Fort Leavenworth, K.T., May 1857, NA, (M617-R611); Lowe, *Five Years a Dragoon*, 185–86.

3. Post Returns, Fort Leavenworth, K.T., May 1857.

4. Lowe, *Five Years a Dragoon*, 186.

5. Lowe, *Five Years a Dragoon*, 186.

6. "Origin of City Names," *KHC* 7:481; Dr. A. Morrall, "Brief Autobiography," *KHC* 14:135; William E. Connelly, "Wild Bill—James Butler Hickok," *KHC* 17:9–11; *Marysville Advocate*, October 15, 1965.

7. Mattes, *The Great Platte River Road*, 147–48.

8. AGO, Letters Received, 1857, Book 33, 399S and S85, NA; Mattes, *The Great Platte River Road*, 150–53

9. Franzwa, *The Oregon Trail Revisited*, 175–76; Haines, 52–53; Mattes, *The Great Platte River Road*, 161.

10. Mattes, *The Great Platte River Road*, 161–66.

11. Lowe, *Five Years a Dragoon*, 186; Mattes, *The Great Platte River Road*, 209–13.

12. Lowe, *Five Years a Dragoon*, 186.

13. Lowe, *Five Years a Dragoon*, 186.

14. Lowe, *Five Years a Dragoon*, 186; Mattes, *The Great Platte River Road*, 240–44.

15. Haines, 60–84; Lowe, *Five Years a Dragoon*, 191; Mattes, *The Great Platte River Road*, 263–64.

16. Lowe, *Five Years a Dragoon*, 186–87; Mattes, *The Great Platte River Road*, 264.

17. Lowe, *Five Years a Dragoon*, 187.

18. Lowe, *Five Years a Dragoon*, 187.

19. Lowe, *Five Years a Dragoon*, 188.

20. Lowe, *Five Years a Dragoon*, 188.

21. Lowe, *Five Years a Dragoon*, 188–89.

22. Lowe, *Five Years a Dragoon*, 189.

23. Haines, 78–79; Lowe, *Five Years a Dragoon*, 189–90; Mattes, *The Great Platte River Road*, 266.

24. Haines, 79–87; Lowe, *Five Years a Dragoon*, 190; Mattes, *The Great Platte River Road*, 280–83.

25. Mattes, *The Great Platte River Road*, 311–38.

26. Franzwa, *The Oregon Trail Revisited*, 206–208; Haines, 92–95; Mattes, *The Great Platte River Road*, 339–77.

27. Annual Report, Secretary of War (1857), House Ex. Doc. No. 2, 35 Cong, 2 Sess., 2:98–99; AGO, Letters Received, 1857, S589; Franzwa, *Maps of the Oregon Trail*, 99; Mattes, *The Great Platte River Road*, 413–14.

28. Haines, 95–107; Mattes, *The Great Platte River Road*, 421–79.

29. Fort Laramie Post Returns, June 1857, NA, (M617-R595); Franzwa, *Maps of the Oregon Trail*, 105–107; Haines, 107–35; Lowe, *Five Years a Dragoon*, 190–91.

30. Mattes, *Fort Laramie*, 42–48.

31. Lowe, *Five Years a Dragoon*, 191.

32. Fort Laramie Post Returns, June, 1857; Sixth Infantry Regimental Returns, July 1857; Lowe, *Five Years a Dragoon*, 191.

33. Lowe, *Five Years a Dragoon*, 191–92.

34. Lowe, *Five Years a Dragoon*, 192.

35. Lowe, *Five Years a Dragoon*, 192.

36. Lowe, *Five Years a Dragoon*, 192–93.

37. Lowe, *Five Years a Dragoon*, 194.

38. Lowe, *Five Years a Dragoon*, 194.

39. Lowe, *Five Years a Dragoon*, 194.

40. Lowe, *Five Years a Dragoon*, 194–95.

41. Lowe, *Five Years a Dragoon*, 195–96.

42. Lowe, *Five Years a Dragoon*, 196–98.

43. Lowe, *Five Years a Dragoon*, 198–99.

Chapter 7. On the South Platte

1. Eli Long, "Journal," July 4, 1857; Lowe, *Five Years a Dragoon*, 199; Peck, "Rough Riding on the Plains," March 14, 1901, 5; Peck, "Recollections," *KHC* 8:493.

2. Eli Long, "Journal," July 4, 1857; Lowe, *Five Years a Dragoon*, 199; Peck, "Rough Riding on the Plains," March 14, 1901, 5; Peck, "Recollections," *KHC* 8:493.

3. Eli Long, "Journal," July 4, 1857; Lowe, *Five Years a Dragoon*, 199; Peck, "Rough Riding on the Plains," March 14, 1901, 5.

4. Annual Report, Secretary of War (1857), House Ex. Doc. No. 2, 35 Cong, 1 Sess., 2:98–99; AGO, Letters Received, 1857, S.589; Eli Long, "Journal," July 5, 1857.

5. Eli Long, "Journal," July 5, 1857; Lowe, *Five Years a Dragoon*, 199–200.

6. Eli Long, "Journal," July 6 and 7, 1857; Lowe, *Five Years a Dragoon*, 200–201.

7. Eli Long, "Journal," July 7, 1857; Lowe, *Five Years a Dragoon*, 201.

8. Eli Long, "Journal," July 7, 1857; Lowe, *Five Years a Dragoon*, 201; Peck, "Rough Riding on the Plains," March 14, 1901, 5.

9. Eli Long, "Journal," July 8, 1857; Lowe, *Five Years a Dragoon*, 201.

10. Nick Eggenhofer, *Wagons, Mules, and Men*, 18–21; Eli Long, "Journal," July 9, 1857; Lowe, *Five Years a Dragoon*, 201–202.

11. Eli Long, "Journal," July 9, 1857; Lowe, *Five Years a Dragoon*, 201.

12. Eli Long, "Journal," July 9 and 10, 1857.

13. Eggenhofer, 17–18; Eli Long, "Journal," July 11 and 12, 1857; Lowe, *Five Years a Dragoon*, 202–203.

14. Eli Long, "Journal," July 25, 1857; Lowe, *Five Years a Dragoon*, 202.

Chapter 8. Across the Plains in Search of the Cheyennes

1. Eli Long, "Journal," July 13, 1857; Lowe, *Five Years a Dragoon*, 202–203.

2. Eggenhofer, 17; Eli Long, "Journal," July 13, 1857.

3. Annual Report, Secretary of War (1857), House Ex. Doc. No. 2, 35 Cong., 1 Sess., 2:468; Eli Long, "Journal," July 13, 1857; Peck, "Rough Riding on the Plains," March 14, 1901, 5; Peck, "Recollections," *KHC* 8:494.

4. Annual Report, Secretary of War (1857), 2:468–69; Eli Long, "Journal," July 14, 1857.

5. Annual Report, Secretary of War (1857), 2:469; Eli Long, "Journal," July 15 and 16, 1857.

6. Annual Report, Secretary of War (1857), 2:469; Eli Long, "Journal," July 15 and 16, 1857.

7. Annual Report, Secretary of War (1857), 2:469; Eli Long, "Journal," July 17, 1857; Peck, "Rough Riding on the Plains," March 14, 1901, 1; Peck, "Recollections," *KHC* 8:494.

8. Eli Long, "Journal," July 17, 1857.

9. Annual Report, Secretary of War (1857), 2:469–70; Eli Long, "Journal," July 18, 1857.

10. Annual Report, Secretary of War (1857), 2:470; Eli Long, "Journal," July 19, 1857.

11. Annual Report, Secretary of War (1857), 2:470; Eli Long, "Journal," July 19, 1857.

12. Eli Long, "Journal," July 19, 1857.

13. Eli Long, "Journal," July 20, 1857.

14. Annual Report, Secretary of War (1857), 2:470; Eli Long, "Journal," July 21, 1857; Diary of 1st Lt. J. E. B. Stuart for July 22 and 23, 1857, Collections of the Virginia Historical Society.

15. Eli Long, "Journal," July 21, 1857.

16. Eli Long, "Journal," July 22, 1857.

Chapter 9. The Wagon Train Moves to the South Platte

1. Eli Long, "Journal," July 13, 1857; Lowe, *Five Years a Dragoon*, 202; Peck, "Rough Riding on the Plains," March 14, 1901, 5.

2. Lowe, *Five Years a Dragoon*, 202; "Report of Col. E. V. Sumner, September 20, 1857," Annual Report, Secretary of War (1857), House Ex. Doc. No. 2, 35 Cong., 1 Sess., 2:98–99; AGO, Letters Received, 1857, S589, NA.

3. Lowe, *Five Years a Dragoon*, 202–203.

4. Lowe, *Five Years a Dragoon*, 203–204.

5. Lowe, *Five Years a Dragoon*, 204; "Report of Col. E. V. Sumner, September 20, 1857," Annual Report, Secretary of War (1857), 2:98–99; AGO, Letters Received, 1857, S589.

6. Lowe, *Five Years a Dragoon*, 205.

Chapter 10. On the Trail of the Cheyennes

1. Eli Long, "Journal," July 23, 1857; Stuart, "Diary," July 23, 1857.

2. Peck, "Rough Riding on the Plains," March 14, 1901, 1.

3. Eli Long, "Journal," July 23, 1857; Stuart, "Diary," July 23, 1857; Peck, "Rough Riding on the Plains," March 14, 1901, 1.

4. Eli Long, "Journal," July 23, 1857; Stuart, "Diary," July 23, 1857; Peck, "Rough Riding on the Plains," March 14, 1901, 1.

5. Eli Long, "Journal," July 24, 1857; Stuart, "Diary," July 24, 1857; Peck, "Rough Riding on the Plains," March 21, 1901, 1.

6. Eli Long, "Journal," July 25, 1857; Stuart, "Diary," July 25, 1857.

7. Eli Long, "Journal," July 25, 1857; Stuart, "Diary," July 25, 1857.

8. Eli Long, "Journal," July 26, 1857; Stuart, "Diary," July 26, 1857.

9. Eli Long, "Journal," July 26, 1857; Stanley, *Personal Memoirs*, 43 (original manuscript, 149–50); Stuart, "Diary," July 26, 1857.

10. Eli Long, "Journal," July 27, 1857; Stuart, "Diary," July 27, 1857.

11. Eli Long, "Journal," July 28, 1857; Peck, "Rough Riding on the Plains," March 21, 1901, 1; Stuart, "Diary," July 28, 1857.

12. Eli Long, "Journal," July 29, 1857; Peck, "Rough Riding on the Plains," March 21, 1901, 1; Peck, "Recollections," *KHC* 8:494; Stuart, "Diary," July 29, 1857.

13. Eli Long, "Journal," July 29, 1857; Peck, "Rough Riding on the Plains," March 21, 1901, 1; Peck, "Recollections," *KHC* 8:494; Stuart, "Diary," July 29, 1857.

Chapter 11. The Cheyennes Move to Solomon's Fork

1. "Report of Agent Robert C. Miller, October 14, 1857," Annual Report, CIA (1857), 141–48; Grinnell, *Fighting Cheyennes*, 117–123; Powell, *People of the Sacred Mountain*, 1:212.

2. Grinnell, *Fighting Cheyennes*, 117–23; Hyde, *Life of George Bent*, 102; Eli Long, "Journal," July 29, 1857; Powell, *People of the Sacred Mountain*, 1:212; Stanley, *Personal Memoirs*, 44–45; Stuart letter to wife, Flora, July 30, 1857, Archives of the Virginia Historical Society.

3. "Report of Agent Robert C. Miller, October 14, 1857," Annual Report, CIA (1857), 141–48; Grinnell, *Fighting Cheyennes*, 117–23.

4. "Report of Agent Robert C. Miller, October 14, 1857," Annual Report, CIA

(1857), 141–48; Grinnell, *Fighting Cheyennes*, 117–23; Powell, *People of the Sacred Mountian*, 1:212.

5. Bayard, 124–25; Grinnell, *Fighting Cheyennes*, 117–23; Eli Long, "Journal," July 31, 1857; Peck, "Rough Riding on the Plains," March 28, 1901, 1; Peck, "Recollections," *KHC* 8:496; Powell, *People of the Sacred Mountain*, 1:212–13; Stanley, *Personal Memoirs*, 44 (original manuscript, 150); Stuart letter to wife, Flora, July 30, 1857.

Chapter 12. The Battle

1. Peck, "Rough Riding on the Plains," March 21, 1901, 1.
2. Peck, "Rough Riding on the Plains," March 21, 1901, 1.
3. Bayard, 124–25; Eli Long, "Journal," July 29, 1857; Peck, "Rough Riding on the Plains," March 21, 1901, 1.; Peck, "Recollections," *KHC* 8:495; Stuart, "Diary," July 29, 1857; "Report of Col. E. V. Sumner, August 9, 1857," Annual Report, Secretary of War (1857), House Ex. Doc. No. 2, 35 Cong., 1 Sess., 2:96–97.
4. Eli Long, "Journal," July 29, 1857; Peck, "Rough Riding on the Plains," March 21, 1901, 1.; Stanley, *Personal Memoirs*, 43–44 (original manuscript, 150).
5. Peck, "Rough Riding on the Plains," March 21, 1901, 1.; Peck, "Recollections," *KHC* 8:495–96.
6. Peck, "Rough Riding on the Plains," March 21, 1901, 1.; Peck, "Recollections," *KHC* 8:496.
7. Eli Long, "Journal," July 29, 1857; Peck, "Rough Riding on the Plains," March 21, 1901, 1.; Peck, "Recollections," *KHC* 8:496.
8. Philip St. George Cooke, *U.S. Army Cavalry Tactics*, 10–11, 174–75, 177; Eli Long, "Journal," July 29, 1857; Peck, "Rough Riding on the Plains," March 21, 1901, 1.; Peck, "Recollections," *KHC* 8:496; Stuart, "Diary," July 29, 1857, contained in letter written to his wife, Flora, July 30, 1857.
9. Eli Long, "Journal," July 29, 1857; Peck, "Rough Riding on the Plains," March 21, 1901, 1.; Peck, "Recollections," *KHC* 8:496; Stuart, "Diary," July 29, 1857.
10. Bayard, 124; Eli Long, "Journal," July 29, 1857; Peck, "Rough Riding on the Plains," March 21, 1901, 1; Peck, "Recollections," *KHC* 8:496; Stanley, *Personal Memoirs*, 43–44 (original manuscript, 150); Stuart, "Diary," July 29, 1857.
11. Eli Long, "Journal," July 29, 1857; Peck, "Rough Riding on the Plains," March 21, 1901, 1; Peck, "Recollections," *KHC* 8:497; Stuart, "Diary," July 29, 1857; "Report of Col. E. V. Sumner, August 9, 1857," Annual Report, Secretary of War (1857), House Ex. Doc. No. 2, 35 Cong., 1 Sess., 2:96–97.
12. Peck, "Rough Riding on the Plains," March 21, 1901, 1.; Peck, "Recollections," *KHC* 8:496.
13. Peck, "Rough Riding on the Plains," March 21, 1901, 1.; Peck, "Recollections," *KHC* 8:496–97; S. L. Seabrook, "Expedition of Col. E. V. Sumner Against the Cheyenne Indians, 1857," *KHC* 16:311; Stuart, "Diary," July 29, 1857.
14. Eli Long, "Journal," July 29, 1857; Peck, "Rough Riding on the Plains,"

March 21, 1901, 1.; Peck, "Recollections," *KHC* 8:497; Stanley, *Personal Memoirs*, 44 (original manuscript, 150); Stuart, "Diary," July 29, 1857.

15. Peck, "Rough Riding on the Plains," March 21, 1901, 1.; Peck, "Recollections," *KHC* 8:497.

16. Eli Long, "Journal," July 29, 1857; "Report of Col. E. V. Sumner, August 9, 1857," Annual Report, Secretary of War (1857), House Ex. Doc. No. 2, 35 Cong., 1 Sess., 2:96–97.

17. Cooke, *Cavalry Tactics*, 201–208; Eli Long, "Journal," July 29, 1857; Peck, "Rough Riding on the Plains," March 21, 1901, 1.; Peck, "Recollections," *KHC* 8:497–98; Stanley, *Personal Memoirs*, 44 (original manuscript, 150–51); Stuart, "Diary," July 29, 1857.

18. Peck, "Rough Riding on the Plains," March 21, 1901, 1.; Peck, "Recollections," *KHC* 8:497–98; Stanley, *Personal Memoirs*, 44 (original manuscript, 150).

19. Peck, "Rough Riding on the Plains," March 21, 1901, 1.; Peck, "Recollections," *KHC* 8:498; Stanley, *Personal Memoirs*, 44 (original manuscript, 150); Stuart, "Diary," July 29, 1857.

20. Eli Long, "Journal," July 29, 1857.

21. Peck, "Rough Riding on the Plains," March 28, 1901, 1.

22. Peck, "Rough Riding on the Plains," March 28, 1901, 1.

23. Peck, "Rough Riding on the Plains," March 28, 1901, 1.

24. Eli Long, "Journal," July 29, 1857; Stanley, *Personal Memoirs*, 44–45 (original manuscript, 151); Stuart, "Diary," July 29, 1857.

25. Peck, "Rough Riding on the Plains," March 21, 1901, 1, 7; Peck, "Recollections," *KHC* 8:498–99; "Report of the Killed and Wounded," Annual Report, Secretary of War (1857), House Ex. Doc. No. 2, 35 Cong., 1 Sess., 2:57; AGO, Letters Received, 1857, 506S, NA.

26. Eli Long, "Journal," July 29, 1857; Peck, "Rough Riding on the Plains," March 21, 1901, 1; Peck, "Recollections," *KHC* 8:478; Stuart, "Diary," July 29, 1857.

27. Eli Long, "Journal," July 29, 1857; Peck, "Rough Riding on the Plains," March 21, 1901, 1; Peck, "Recollections," *KHC* 8:498.

28. Peck, "Rough Riding on the Plains," March 21, 1901, 1; Peck, "Recollections," *KHC* 8:498.

29. Peck, "Rough Riding on the Plains," March 21, 1901, 1; Peck, "Recollections," *KHC* 8:499.

30. Peck, "Rough Riding on the Plains," March 21, 1901, 1; Peck, "Recollections," *KHC* 8:499; "Report of the Killed and Wounded," Annual Report, Secretary of War (1857), House Ex. Doc. No. 2, 35 Cong., 1 Sess., 2:57; AGO, Letters Received, 1857, 506S, NA.

31. Peck, "Rough Riding on the Plains," March 21, 1901, 7; Stuart, "Diary," July 29, 1857.

32. Eli Long, "Journal," July 29, 1857; "Report of Col. E. V. Sumner, August 9, 1857," Annual Report, Secretary of War (1857), House Ex. Doc. No. 2, 35 Cong., 1 Sess., 2:96–97.

33. Bayard, 124; Eli Long, "Journal," July 29, 1857; Peck, "Rough Riding on the Plains," March 21, 1901, 7; Peck, "Recollections," *KHC* 8:498; Stuart, "Diary," August 14, 1857.

34. Peck, "Rough Riding on the Plains," March 21, 1901, 7; Peck, "Recollections," *KHC* 8:499.

35. Peck, "Rough Riding on the Plains," March 28, 1901, 1.

36. Eli Long, "Journal," July 30, 1857; Peck, "Rough Riding on the Plains," March 81, 1901, 1; "Report of Col. E. V. Sumner, August 9, 1857," Annual Report, Secretary of War (1857), House Ex. Doc. No. 2, 35 Cong., 1 Sess., 2:96–97.

37. Peck, "Rough Riding on the Plains," March 28, 1901, 1.

38. Eli Long, "Journal," July 30, 1857; Peck, "Rough Riding on the Plains," March 28, 1901, 1; Affidavit of Carl Kobler dated January 6, 1858, Library of Fort Hays State University, Hays, Kansas.

39. Bayard, 125; Peck, "Rough Riding on the Plains," March 28, 1901, 1.

40. Eli Long, "Journal," July 30, 1857.

Chapter 13. The Flight of the Cheyennes

1. Eli Long, "Journal," July 31, 1857; Peck, "Rough Riding on the Plains," March 28, 1901, 1; Stanley, *Personal Memoirs*, 47 (original manuscript, 152).

2. "Report of Col. E. V. Sumner, August 9, 1857," Annual Report, Secretary of War (1857), House Ex. Doc. No. 2, 35 Cong., 1 Sess., 2:96–97; "Report of Agent Robert C. Miller, October 14, 1857," Annual Report, CIA (1857), 141–48; Grinnell, *Fighting Cheyennes*, 120–21; Hyde, *Life of George Bent*, 104; Eli Long, "Journal," July 31, 1857, August 1, 1857; Peck, "Rough Riding on the Plains," March 28, 1901, 1; Powell, *People of the Sacred Mountain*, 1:213; Stanley, *Personal Memoirs*, 47–48 (original manuscript, 152).

3. Eli Long, "Journal," July 31, 1857, August 1, 1857.

4. "Report of Agent Robert C. Miller, October 14, 1857," Annual Report, CIA (1857), 141–48.

5. "Report of Col. E. V. Sumner, August 9, 1857," Annual Report, Secretary of War (1857), 2:96–97; "Report of Agent Robert C. Miller, October 14, 1857," Annual Report, CIA (1857), 141–48; Grinnell, *Fighting Cheyennes*, 120–21; Hyde, *Life of George Bent*, 104; Eli Long, "Journal," July 31, 1857, August 1–8, 1857; Peck, "Rough Riding on the Plains," March 28, 1901, 1; Powell, *People of the Sacred Mountain*, 1:213; Stanley, *Personal Memoirs*, 47–48 (original manuscript, 152).

6. "Report of Agent Robert C. Miller, October 14, 1857," Annual Report, CIA (1857), 141–48; "Report of Col. E. V. Sumner, August 9, 1857," Annual Report, Secretary of War (1857), 2:96–97; Grinnell, *Fighting Cheyennes*, 120–21; Hyde, *Life of George Bent*, 104; Eli Long, "Journal," August 13, 1857.

7. Grinnell, *The Cheyenne Indians*, 1:226; Grinnell, *Fighting Cheyennes*, 120–21; Powell, *People of the Sacred Mountain*, 1:213.

8. Grinnell, *Fighting Cheyennes*, 120–21; Hyde, *Life of George Bent*, 104; Powell, *People of the Sacred Mountain*, 1:213.

9. E. G. Marshall to S. Cooper, August 2, 1857, AGO, Letters Received, 1857, 489 M; E. G. Marshall to S. Cooper, August 4, 1857, AGO, Letters Received, 1857, 500 M; W. E. Connelley, "Personal Recollections of Charles R. Morehead," *Doniphan's Expedition and the Conquest of New Mexico and California*, 603–605.

10. Eli Long, "Journal," August 3, 1857; Stuart, "Diary," August 3–5, 1857, contained in letter written to wife, Flora, August 19, 1857.

11. E. G. Marshall to S. Cooper, September 12, 1857, AGO, Letters Received, 1857, 613 M; E. G. Marshall to Adj. Gen., V.S.A., September 15, 1857, AGO, Letters Received, 1857, 625 M.

12. Lowe, *Five Years a Dragoon*, 212–13; Powell, *People of the Sacred Mountain*, 1:213.

13. Lowe, *Five Years a Dragoon*, 212–14.

14. Lowe, *Five Years a Dragoon*, 206–14.

15. Lowe, *Five Years a Dragoon*, 213.

Chapter 14. The Trail to the Arkansas

1. Bayard, 125; Eli Long, "Journal," July 31, 1857; Peck, "Rough Riding on the Plains," March 28, 1901, 1; Stuart letter to wife, Flora, July 31, 1857.

2. Eli Long, "Journal," July 31, 1857; Peck, "Rough Riding on the Plains," March 28, 1901, 1; Peck, "Recollections," *KHC* 8:500–501.

3. Eli Long, "Journal," July 31, 1857; Stanley, *Personal Memoirs* (original manuscript), 151–52; "Report of Col. E. V. Sumner, August 9, 1857," Annual Report, Secretary of War (1857), House Ex. Doc. No. 2, 35 Cong., 1 Sess., 2:96–97.

4. Eli Long, "Journal," July 31, 1857; Peck, "Rough Riding on the Plains," March 28, 1901, 1; Peck, "Recollections," *KHC* 8:501; Stanley, *Personal Memoirs*, 45 (original manuscript, 152); "Report of Col. E. V. Sumner, August 9, 1857," Annual Report, Secretary of War (1857), House Ex. Doc. No. 2, 35 Cong., 1 Sess., 2:96–97.

5. Eli Long, "Journal," July 31, 1857; "Report of Agent Robert C. Miller, October 14, 1857," Annual Report, CIA (1857), 141–48; Stanley, *Personal Memoirs*, 45 (original manuscript, 152).

6. Eli Long, "Journal," July 31, 1857; Peck, "Rough Riding on the Plains," March 28, 1901, 1; Peck, "Recollections," *KHC* 8:501; Stanley, *Personal Memoirs*, 45 (original manuscript, 152); "Report of Col. E. V. Sumner, August 9, 1857," Annual Report, Secretary of War (1857), House Ex. Doc. No. 2, 35 Cong., 1 Sess., 2:96–97.

7. Eli Long, "Journal," August 1, 1857; Peck, "Rough Riding on the Plains," March 28, 1901, 1.

8. Bayard, 125.

9. Eli Long, "Journal," August 2, 1857.

10. Eli Long, "Journal," August 2–3, 1857.

11. *Kansas Constitutionalist*, October 7, 1857.

12. Eli Long, "Journal," August 3, 1857; Stuart, "Diary," August 5, 1857.

13. Eli Long, "Journal," August 4, 1857.

14. Eli Long, "Journal," August 5, 1857.

15. Eli Long, "Journal," August 5, 1857; "Report of Col. E. V. Sumner, August 9, 1857," Annual Report, Secretary of War (1857), House Ex. Doc. No. 2, 35 Cong., 1 Sess., 2:96–97.

16. Eli Long, "Journal," August 6, 1857; Peck, "Rough Riding on the Plains," March 28, 1901, 1.

17. Eli Long, "Journal," August 7, 1857; Peck, "Rough Riding on the Plains," March 28, 1901, 1.

18. Eli Long, "Journal," August 8, 1857.

19. Eli Long, "Journal," August 9, 1857.

20. Eli Long, "Journal," August 10, 1857.

Chapter 15. The Wagon Train's Encounter on the South Platte

1. Lowe, *Five Years a Dragoon*, 205–12.

2. Lowe, *Five Years a Dragoon*, 212–14.

Chapter 16. Sumner's March to Bent's New Fort

1. Annual Report, CIA (1857), 141–48.

2. Annual Report, CIA (1857), 141–48.

3. Annual Report, CIA (1857), 141–48.

4. Annual Report, CIA (1857), 141–48.

5. Annual Report, CIA (1857), 141–48; Mumey, 138–46.

6. Annual Report, CIA (1857), 141–48.

7. Annual Report, CIA (1857), 141–48; Mumey, 138–46.

8. Annual Report, CIA (1857), 141–48; Eli Long, "Journal," August 13, 1857.

9. Annual Report, CIA (1857), 141–48.

10. Annual Report, CIA (1857), 141–48.

11. Eli Long, "Journal," August 8, 1857.

12. "Report of Col. E. V. Sumner, August 9, 1857," Annual Report, Secretary of War (1857), House Ex. Doc. No. 2, 35 Cong., 1 Sess., 2;96–97; AGO, Letters Received 1857, S514.

13. Eli Long, "Journal," August 9, 10, 11, 1857; "Report of Agent Robert C. Miller, October 14, 1857," Annual Report, CIA (1857), 141–48; "Report of Col. E. V. Sumner, August 11, 1857," Annual Report, Secretary of War (1857), House Ex. Doc. No. 2, 35 Cong., 1 Sess., 2:97–98; AGO, Letters Received 1857, S589; "Report of Col. E. V. Sumner, September 20, 1857," Annual Report, Secretary of War (1857), House Ex. Doc. No. 2, 35 Cong., 1 Sess., 2:98–99; AGO, Letters Received, 1857, S589.

14. Eli Long, "Journal," August 11, 1857 and September 2, 1857; Stanley, Personal *Memoirs* (original manuscript), 152–53; "Report of Col. E. V. Sumner, August 11, 1857," Annual Report, Secretary of War (1857), House Ex. Doc. No. 2, 35 Cong., 1 Sess., 2:97–98; AGO, Letters Received 1857, S589.

15. Peck, "Recollections," *KHC* 8:503.

16. Eli Long, "Journal," August 12 and 13, 1857; "Report of Agent Robert C. Miller, October 14, 1857," Annual Report, CIA (1857), 147; Peck, "Recollections," *KHC* 8:500; Peck, "Rough Riding on the Plains," April 4, 1901, 1.

17. Eli Long, "Journal," August 13, 1857.

18. Eli Long, "Journal," August 14, 1857.

19. Eli Long, "Journal," August 15, 1857.

20. Eli Long, "Journal," August 16, 1857.

21. Eli Long, "Journal," August 17 and 18, 1857.

22. "Order of Col. E. V. Sumner to Indian Agent Robert C. Miller, August 19, 1857," AGO, Letters Received, 1857, S550.

23. "Report of Agent Robert C. Miller, October 14, 1857," Annual Report, CIA (1857), 146.

24. Eli Long, "Journal," August 17, 18, 19, and 20, 1857.

25. Eli Long, "Journal," August 21, 1857; Peck, "Rough Riding on the Plains," April 4, 1901, 1.

26. Eli Long, "Journal," August 21, 1857; Peck, "Rough Riding on the Plains," April 4, 1901, 1.

27. "Report of Agent Robert C. Miller, October 14, 1857," Annual Report, CIA (1857), 146–47.

28. Eli Long, "Journal," August 22, 1857.

29. Eli Long, "Journal," August 24, 25, 26, and 27, 1857.

30. Eli Long, "Journal," August 27, 28, 29, and 30, 1857.

31. Eli Long, "Journal," August 31, 1857 and September 1 and 2, 1857.

Chapter 17. The Wagon Train's Return

1. Lowe, *Five Years a Dragoon*, 215–21.

2. Lowe, *Five Years a Dragoon*, 221–23.

Chapter 18. The Expedition Ends

1. Department of Utah, Letters Sent, 1857–61, 1:8–9, AGO, Letters Received, NA.

2. Eli Long, "Journal," September 2 and 5, 1857; "Report of Col. E. V. Sumner, September 20, 1857," Annual Report, Secretary of War (1857), House Ex. Doc. No. 2, 35 Cong., 1 Sess., 2:98–99; AGO, Letters Received, 1857, S589.

3. Eli Long, "Journal," September 2, 3, 4, and 5, 1857; Peck, "Rough Riding on the Plains," April 4, 1901, 1.

4. Eli Long, "Journal," September 4, 1857; Peck, "Rough Riding on the Plains," April 4, 1901, 1.

5. Eli Long, "Journal," September 3, 1857; Col. E. V. Sumner, letter dated September 3, 1857, AGO, Letters Received, 1857, S550.

6. Eli Long, "Journal," September 4 and 5, 1857.

7. Eli Long, "Journal," September 6, 1857; Peck, "Recollections," KHC 8:503.

8. Bayard, 126.

9. Bayard, 126.

10. Bayard, 126; Lowe, *Five Years a Dragoon*, 223.

11. Department of Utah, Letters Sent, 1857–61, 1:33; Lowe, *Five Years a Dragoon*, 224–25.

12. Lowe, *Five Years a Dragoon*, 224–25.

13. Lowe, *Five Years a Dragoon*, 225; Rodenbough, 186.

14. Lowe, *Five Years a Dragoon*, 226.

15. Bayard, 126–27; Lowe, *Five Years a Dragoon*, 226–27.

16. Bayard, 127–28.

17. Eli Long, "Journal," September 6, 7, and 8, 1857.

18. Barry, "The Ranch at Walnut Creek Crossing," *KHQ* 37:126; Eli Long, "Journal," September 9, 1857.

19. Eli Long, "Journal," September 10, 11, 12, and 13, 1857.

20. Eli Long, "Journal," September 14, 1857.

21. "Report of Col. E. V. Sumner, September 20, 1857," Annual Report, Secretary of War (1857), House Ex. Doc. No. 2, 35 Cong., 1 Sess., 2:98-99; AGO, Letters Received, 1857, S514.

Chapter 19. The First Cavalry's Wounded

1. Return of the Sixth Regiment of Infantry, July, 1857, NA (M665 Roll 68); Peck, "Rough Riding on the Plains," March 28, 1901, 1.

2. "Report of Col. E. V. Sumner, August 9, 1857," Annual Report, Secretary of War (1857), House Ex. Doc. No. 2, 35 Cong., 1 Sess., 2:96-97; AGO, Letters Received, 1857, S514; Peck, "Rough Riding on the Plains," March 28, 1901, 1.

3. Eli Long, "Journal," July 30, 1857; Peck, "Rough Riding on the Plains," March 28, 1901, 1; Affidavit of Carl Kobler, dated January 6, 1958, Library of Fort Hays State University, Hays, Kansas.

4. Stuart, "Diary," August 1, 1857.

5. Stuart, "Diary," August 2 and 3, 1857.

6. Stuart, "Diary," August 4, 1857.

7. Stuart, "Diary," August 5, 1857.

8. Stuart, "Diary," August 5 and 6, 1857.

9. Peck, "Rough Riding on the Plains," April 11, 1901, 1; Stuart, "Diary," August 7, 1857.

10. Stuart, "Diary," August 8, 1857.

11. Stuart, "Diary," August 8, 1857.

12. Stuart, "Diary," August 9 and 10, 1857.

13. Stuart, "Diary," August 11, 12, and 13, 1857.

14. Return of Capt. Rensselaer W. Foote's Co. "C," Sixth Infantry, August 1857, Fort Laramie, Nebraska Territory, NA (M617-Roll 595); Stuart, "Diary," August 14, 1857.

15. Stuart, "Diary," August 14 and 15, 1857.

16. Stuart, "Diary," August 15, 1857.

17. Stuart, "Diary," August 17, 1857.

18. Stuart, "Diary," August 17, 1857.

19. Stuart, "Diary," August 17, 1857.

20. Stuart, "Diary," August 17 and 18, 1857.

21. Return of Capt. Rensselaer W. Foote's Co. "C," Sixth Infantry, August 1857, Fort Laramie, Nebraska Territory, NA (M617-Roll 595); Post Returns, Fort Kearny, Nebraska Territory, August 1857, NA (M617-Roll 564); Peck, "Rough Riding on the Plains," April 11, 1901, 1; Peck, "Recollections," *KHC* 8:506 and 515.

22. Return of Capt. Rensselaer W. Foote's Co. "C;" Post Returns, Fort Kearny, Nebraska Territory, August 1857.

23. Post Returns, Fort Kearny, Nebraska Territory, August 1857; Post Re-

turns, Fort Leavenworth, Kansas Territory, October 1857, NA (M617-Roll 611); Burke Davis, *J. E. B. Stuart, The Last Cavalier*, 42.

Epilogue

1. Ely Moore, "The Lecompton Party Which Located Denver," *KHC* 7:451; Peck, "Recollections," *KHC* 8:492.
2. "Report of Agent Robert C. Miller, August 17, 1858," Annual Report, CIA (1858), 96–100; "Report of Col. E. V. Sumner, October 5, 1858," AGO, Letters Received, 1858, s 404; Berthrong, 143–44; Grinnell, *Fighting Cheyennes*, 124; Powell, *People of the Sacred Mountain*, 1:223–25.
3. "Report of Agent Robert C. Miller, August 17, 1858," Annual Report, CIA (1858), 96–100; Oliva, 113–20.
4. Louise Barry, "With the First Cavalry in Indian Country, 1859–1861," *KHQ* 24:402–412; Brackett, 204–205; Philip Katcher, *U. S. Cavalry on the Plains 1850–90*, 6; Mumey, 173–78; Oliva, 123–29; Powell, *People of the Sacred Mountain*, 1:233–34.
5. Grinnell, *Fighting Cheyennes*, 123; Powell, *People of the Sacred Mountain*, 1:214–28.
6. Berthrong, 143–44; Grinnell, *Fighting Cheyennes*, 124–25; Powell, *People of the Sacred Mountain*, 1:223–25.
7. Berthrong, 143–48; Grinnell, *Fighting Cheyennes*, 125–26; Powell, *People of the Sacred Mountain*, 1:223, 231–34.
8. Berthrong, 148–51; Grinnell, *Fighting Cheyennes*, 126; Powell, *People of the Sacred Mountain*, 1:234–37.
9. "Statement of Col. William Bent," Report, Joint Committee on the Conduct of the War, Massacre of the Cheyenne Indians, Sen. Ex. Doc. No. 142, 38 Cong., 2 Sess, 4, 1865, Appendix 95; John M. Carroll, *The Sand Creek Massacre*, 184.
10. S. S. Seabrook, "Expedition of Col. E. V. Sumner Against the Cheyenne Indians, 1857," *KHC* 16:314–15.
11. Carl Kobler, Statement dated January 6, 1958; John W. Metcalf, letter to W. Y. Chalfant, September 23, 1977.
12. John W. Metcalf, letter to W. Y. Chalfant, September 23, 1977.
13. John W. Metcalf, letter to W. Y. Chalfant, September 23, 1977.
14. John W. Metcalf, letter to W. Y. Chalfant, September 23, 1977.

Appendix A. The Cheyennes

1. Berthrong, *The Southern Cheyennes*, 3–4; Grinnell, *The Cheyenne Indians* 1:1; Grinnell, *The Fighting Cheyennes*, 3; Hoebel, *The Cheyennes*, 1; Hyde, *Life of George Bent*, 3; Powell, *People of the Sacred Mountain*, 1:xvii; Powell, *Sweet Medicine*, 1:18–22; Tom Weist, *A History of the Cheyenne People*, 9.
2. Berthrong, 27; Grinnell, *The Cheyenne Indians*, 1:2–3; Grinnell, *Fighting Cheyennes*, 3–4; Hoebel, 1; Hyde, 3; Powell, *People of the Sacred Mountain*, 1:xxxix; Powell, *Sweet Medicine*, 1:24; Weist, 9.
3. Berthrong, 4–6; Grinnell, *The Cheyenne Indians*, 1:4–8; Hoebel, 1; Hyde, 4–12; Powell, 1:19–22; Weist, 9–18.

4. Berthrong, 7–13; Grinnell, *The Cheyenne Indians*, 1:7–13; Grinnell, *Fighting Cheyennes*, 7–11; Hoebel, 1; Hyde, 11–16; Powell, *People of the Sacred Mountain*, 1:22–23; Weist, 18–21.

5. Berthrong, 9–10,27; Grinnell, *The Cheyenne Indians*, 1:8–15; Hoebel, 1; Hyde, 14–17; Powell, *People of the Sacred Mountain*, 1:23–27; Weist, 21–24.

6. Berthrong, 10–19; Grinnell, *The Cheyenne Indians*, 1:8–31; Hyde, 15–21; Powell, *People of the Sacred Mountain*, 1:23–28; Weist, 25–29.

7. Berthrong, 10–19,27–30; Grinnell, *The Cheyenne Indians*, 1:8–33; Hyde, 16–22; Powell, *People of the Sacred Mountain*, 1:23–30; Weist, 25–28.

8. Berthrong, 15–20,27–31; Grinnell, *The Cheyenne Indians*, 1:28–41; Hyde, 21–32; Weist, 27–30.

9. Berthrong, 18–20; Harlin M. Fuller and LeRoy R. Hafen, *The Journal of Captain John R. Bell*, 190–203, 210–13; Grinnell, *The Cheyenne Indians*, 1:38–41; Hyde, 31–33; Weist, 29–32.

10. Berthrong, 20–26; Grinnell, *The Cheyenne Indians*, 1:39–46; Hyde, 31–40; Powell, *People of the Sacred Mountain*, 1:175; Weist, 29–32; Kansas Historical Society, Sixth Bienniel Report, *KHC* 4:361.

11. Berthrong, 81; Grinnell, *The Cheyenne Indians*, 1:38–46; Grinnell, *Fighting Cheyennes*, 35–37; Hyde, 20–21,31–40; Mayhall, 78; Powell, *People of the Sacred Mountain*, 1:27–28; Weist, 29–30.

12. Berthrong, 81–84; Fehrenbach, 250–51; Grinnell, *The Cheyenne Indians*, 1:46; Grinnell, *Fighting Cheyennes*, 37–43, 72–82; Hyde, 37–46; Mayhall, 12–15, 78–81; Powell, *People of the Sacred Mountain*, 1:38–46, 51–73; Wallace and Hoebel, 277; Weist, 30,42.

13. Berthrong, 58–59,80–81; Grinnell, *Fighting Cheyennes*, 70–74; George E. Hyde, *The Pawnee Indians*, 180–181; Powell, *People of the Sacred Mountain*, 1:3–15.

14. Hoebel, 69; Hyde, *Life of George Bent*, 89.

15. Berthrong, 80–81, 94, 121–128; Grinnell, *Fighting Cheyennes*, 75–78, 84–96, 101–104; Hyde, *Life of George Bent*, 89–92; Powell, *People of the Sacred Mountain*, 1:77–79, 160–62, 173–74.

16. Berthrong, 10–26, 76–80, 90–99; Grinnell, "Bent's Old Fort and its Builders," *KHC* 15:28–91; Hyde, *Life of George Bent*, 59–68; Lavender, *Bent's Fort*, 101–44; Mumey, 9–20; Colorado Historical Society, *Bent's Old Fort*, 7–27.

17. Berthrong, 27–49; Grinnell, *The Cheyenne Indians*, 1:127–157; Hoebel, 20–22; Weist, 32–37.

18. Berthrong, 45–46; Grinnell, *The Cheyenne Indians*, 1:86–101; Hoebel, 22–30; Weist, 37–38.

19. Berthrong, 73–75; Grinnell, *The Cheyenne Indians*, 1:88–101; Hoebel, 31–32; Weist, 37–38.

20. Grinnell, *The Cheyenne Indians*, 1:88–101; Hoebel, 31–32; Powell, *Sweet Medicine*, 1:175; Weist, 38.

21. Berthrong, 31–32,62,74; Hoebel, 31,58–59; Weist, 37–38.

22. Berthrong, 67–69; Grinnell, *The Cheyenne Indians*, 1:48–79; Hoebel, 33–36; Weist, 38–39.

23. Berthrong, 70–72; Grinnell, *The Cheyenne Indians*, 1:336–58; Hoebel, 37–48; Weist, 38.

24. Grinnell, *The Cheyenne Indians*, 1:88–91; Hoebel, 86; Powell, *Sweet Medicine*, 2:433–37, 863–65.

25. Hoebel, 86; Powell, *Sweet Medicine*, 2:437–439.

26. Berthrong, 51; Grinnell, *The Cheyenne Indians*, 2:91–94; Hoebel, 86–87; Powell, *Sweet Medicine*, 2:441.

27. Grinnell, *The Cheyenne Indians*, 2:167–65; Hoebel, 87–88.

28. Grinnell, *The Cheyenne Indians*, 2:87–88; Hoebel, 82–85; Powell, *Sweet Medicine*, 2:442–44.

29. Berthrong, 52–53, 56–67; Grinnell, *The Cheyenne Indians*, 2:211,285; Hoebel, 6–17; Powell, *Sweet Medicine*, 2:442–471.

30. Berthrong, 62–67; Grinnell, *The Cheyenne Indians*, 2:211–284; Hoebel, 11–16; Powell, *Sweet Medicine*, 2:442–59, 467–71.

31. Berthrong, 61–62; Grinnell, *The Cheyenne Indians*, 2:285–336; Hoebel, 16–17.

32. Berthrong, 42–43, 55; Grinnell, *The Cheyenne Indians*, 2:1–38; Hoebel, 69–71, 75–76.

33. Grinnell, *The Cheyenne Indians*, 2:7–29; Hoebel, 70–76.

34. Berthrong, 42–43; Grinnell, *The Cheyenne Indians*, 2:1–7; Grinnell, *Fighting Cheyennes*, 12–13; Hoebel, 69–74.

Appendix B. The First Cavalry

1. Albert G. Brackett, *History of the United States Cavalry*, 140–41; Francis B. Heitman, *Historical Register and Dictionary of the United States Army, 1789–1903*, 2:594–95; Randy Steffen, *The Horse Soldier, 1776–1943*, 2:34; Gregory J. Urwin, *The United States Cavalry: An Illustrated History*, 9–54, 65, 89.

2. Brackett, 158–60; Steffen, 2:20–21; Urwin, 89–90, 97; Robert M. Utley, *Frontiersmen in Blue*, 20–23.

3. Brackett, 140, 160–61; Heitman, 2:596–97; Steffen, 2:34–35, 45–53; Urwin, 96; Utley, *Frontiersmen in Blue*, 22–28.

4. Brackett, 152, 168; Peck, "Rough Riding on the Plains," Feb. 14, 1901, 1, 6; Peck, "Recollections," *KHC* 8:484–486; Theophilus F. Rodenbough and Wm. L. Haskins, *The Army of the United States*, 211–12; Urwin, 96.

5. Brackett, 141, 160; Rodenbough and Haskins, 211; Urwin, 96; Utley, *Frontiersmen in Blue*, 22, 34.

6. Heitman, 2:596–97; Peck, "Rough Riding on the Plains," Feb. 14, 1901, 6, and Feb. 21, 1901, 7; Peck, "Recollections," 8:485–86; Rodenbough and Haskins, 211; Utley, *Frontiersmen in Blue*, 22.

7. Brackett, 141; Heitman, 1:70; Peck, "Rough Riding on the Plains," Feb. 21, 1901, 7; Peck, "Recollections," 8:485; Rodenbough and Haskins, 211; F. Stanley, *E. V. Sumner*, 90–235; Urwin, 56, 58, 74, 89; Utley, *Frontiersmen in Blue*, 121.

8. Brackett, 141–42; Heitman, 1:70; Peck, "Rough Riding on the Plains," Feb. 21, 1901, 7; Peck, "Recollections," 8:485; Rodenbough and Haskins, 211; Urwin, 96.

9. 2d Lt. Eli Long, "Journal of the Cheyenne Expedition," May 18, 1857; Heitman, 1:70; Fort Leavenworth, Kansas Territory, Post Returns for Nov. 1856 and April 1857, NA (M617-Roll 611).

10. Peck, "Rough Riding on the Plains," Feb. 21, 1901, 1 and April 11, 1901, 1; Heitman, 2:596–597.

11. Peck, "Rough Riding on the Plains," Feb. 21, 1901, 1.

12. Peck, "Rough Riding on the Plains," Feb. 14, 1901, 1.

13. Peck, "Rough Riding on the Plains," Feb. 14, 1901, 1.

14. Peck, "Rough Riding on the Plains," Feb. 14, 1901, 1, 2.

15. Peck, "Rough Riding on the Plains," Feb. 14, 1901, 2.

16. Peck, "Rough Riding on the Plains," Feb. 21, 1901, 1.

17. Peck, "Rough Riding on the Plains," Feb. 14, 1901, 2.

18. Peck, "Rough Riding on the Plains," Feb. 14, 1901, 2.

19. Peck, "Rough Riding on the Plains," Feb. 14, 1901, 2, and Feb. 21, 1901, 1; Randy Steffen, *United States Military Saddles, 1812–1943*, 38–62.

20. 1st Lt. John J. Boniface, *The Cavalry Horse and His Pack*, 220–32, 400–27; Robert A. Murry, "Wagons on the Plains," *The Army Moves West*, 1.

21. Peck, "Rough Riding on the Plains," Feb. 28, 1901, 1.

22. Bayard, 121; Peck, "Rough Riding on the Plains," Feb. 28, 1901, 1.

23. Peck, "Rough Riding on the Plains," Feb. 28, 1901, 1.

24. Peck, "Rough Riding on the Plains," Feb. 28, 1901, 1.

25. Peck, "Rough Riding on the Plains," Feb. 28, 1901, 1.

26. Bayard, 121; Boniface, 223–25; Brackett, 164–65; Peck, "Rough Riding on the Plains," Feb. 28, 1901, 1.

27. Boniface, 223–25; Brackett, 164–65; Peck, "Rough Riding on the Plains," Feb. 28, 1901, 1.

28. Peck, "Rough Riding on the Plains," Feb. 28, 1901, 1.

29. Peck, "Rough Riding on the Plains," Feb. 28, 1901, 1; Steffen, *The Horse Soldier*, 2:48–50.

30. Brackett, 165–66; Peck, "Rough Riding on the Plains," Feb. 28, 1901, 1.

31. Boniface, 428–79; Robert A. Murry, "I'd Like to Be a Packer," *The Army Moves West*, 1–8.

Bibliography

I. U.S. GOVERNMENT DOCUMENTS
A. Executive Departments
1. Interior Department
Annual Report of the Secretary of the Interior, 1856, 1857. In U.S. Serials as:
  1856: House Ex. Doc. No. 1, 34 Cong., 3 Sess., Vol. 1, (Serial 893).
  1857: House Ex. Doc. No. 11, 35 Cong., 1 Sess., Vol. 2, Pt. 1 (Serial 919).
Office of Indian Affairs
  Annual Report of the Commissioner of Indian Affairs, 1851, 1853–1858. In
    U.S. Serials as:
    1851: House Ex. Doc. No. 2, 32 Cong., 1 Sess., Vol. 2 (Serial 633).
    1853: House Ex. Doc. No. 1, 33 Cong., 1 Sess., Vol. 1 (Serial 710).
    1854: Senate Ex. Doc. No. 1, 33 Cong., 2 Sess., Vol. 1 (Serial 746).
    1855: Senate Ex. Doc. No. 1, 34 Cong., 1 Sess., Vol. 1 (Serial 810).
    1856: Senate Ex. Doc. No. 5, 34 Cong., 3 Sess., Vol. 2 (Serial 875).
    1857: Senate Ex. Doc. No. 11, 35 Cong., 1 Sess., Vol. 2 (Serial 919).
    1858: Senate Ex. Doc. No. 1, 35 Cong., 1 Sess., Vol. 1 (Serial 974).
  Letters Received. Pottawatomie Agency. Upper Arkansas Agency. Upper Platte
    Agency.
2. War Department
Annual Report of the Secretary of War, 1857. In U.S. Serials as:
  House Ex. Doc. No. 2, 35 Cong., 2 Sess., Vol. 2, 1858 (Serial 997).
  Senate Ex. Doc. No. 11, 35 Cong., 1 Sess., Vol. 3, 1857 (Serial 920).
Office of the Adjutant General, Letters Received, U.S. Army Commands.
  Department of Utah, Letters Sent.
  Department of the West. Fort Atkinson, K.T., Letters Sent. Fort Atkinson,
    K.T., Post Returns. Fort Kearny, N.T., Post Returns. Fort Laramie, N.T.,
    Letters Sent. Fort Laramie, N.T., Post Returns. Fort Leavenworth, K.T.,
    Post Returns. Sixth Regiment of Infantry, Regimental Returns.

B. Congress
1. Senate
"Statement of Col. William Bent," Report to Joint Committee on the Conduct
of the War, Massacre of the Cheyenne Indians, Senate Ex. Doc. No. 142,
38 Cong., 2 Sess., Vol. 4, 1865 (Serial 1214).
"Report of Explorations and Surveys," Senate Ex. Doc. No. 78, 33 Cong., 2
Sess., Vol. 2, 1855, (Serial 759).
"Report of General Harney, Commander of the Sioux Expedition," Senate
Ex. Doc. No. 1, 34 Cong., 1 Sess., Vol. 1, 1855 (Serial 810).
"Report of Major Sedgwick, August 11, 1860," Senate Ex. Doc. No. 1, 36
Cong., 2 Sess., Vol. 2, 1860 (Serial 1079).
2. House of Representatives
House Ex. Doc. No. 79, 18 Cong., 2 Sess., Vol. 4, 1825 (Serial 116).
House Ex. Doc. No. 1, 30 Cong., 2 Sess., Vol. 1, 1848 (Serial 537).
House Ex. Doc. No. 36, 33 Cong., 2 Sess., Vol. 5, 1855 (Serial 783).
House Ex. Doc. No. 63, 33 Cong., 2 Sess., Vol. 8, 1855 (Serial 788).
House Ex. Doc. No. 1, 34 Cong., 1 Sess., Vol. 1, 1856 (Serial 841).
House Ex. Doc. No. 130, 34 Cong., 1 Sess., Vol. 12, 1856 (Serial 859).
House Ex. Doc. No. 1, 34 Cong., 3 Sess., Vol. 1, Pt. 2, 1856 (Serial 894).
House Ex. Doc. No. 2, 35 Cong., 1 Sess., Vol. 2, 1858 (Serial 943).
House Misc. Doc. No. 47, 33 Cong., 1 Sess., 1854 (Serial 741).

II. Newspapers and Periodicals
Frank Leslie's Illustrated Newspaper (New York, N.Y.), April 25, 1857.
Kansas City Enterprise (Kansas City, Mo.), May 2, 1857.
Kansas Constitutionalist (Doniphan, K.T.), October 7, 1857.
Kansas Weekly Herald (Leavenworth, K.T.), May 2, 1857.
Liberty Weekly Tribune (Liberty, Mo.), June 2, 1854, and February 2, 1855.
Marysville Advocate (Marysville, Kans.), October 15, 1965.
Missouri Republican (St. Louis, Mo.), May 27, 1854.
New York Tribune (New York, N.Y.), May 21, 1857.
St. Joseph Gazette (St. Joseph, Mo.), April 24, 1854.
Weekly Missouri Statesman (Columbia, Mo.), May 5, 1854.

III. Books
Albright, George L. *Offical Explorations for Pacific Railroads, 1853–1855.* Ed-
ited by Herbert E. Bolton. University of California Publications in His-
tory, no. 7. Berkeley: University of California Press, 1921.
Andreas, Alfred T. *A History of Kansas.* Vol. 1. Chicago: 1883; Topeka: Kansas
State Historical Society, 1976.
Bandel, Eugene. *Frontier Life in the Army, 1854–1861.* Edited by R. P. Bieber.
Southwest Historical Series, no. 2. Glendale, Calif.: Arthur H. Clark
Company, 1942; Philadelphia: Porcupine Press, Inc., 1974.
Barry, Louise. *The Beginning of the West.* Topeka: Kansas State Historical So-
ciety, 1972.
Bayard, Samuel J. *The Life of George Dashiell Bayard.* New York: G. P. Putnam's
Sons, 1874.

Bell, Captain John R. *The Journal of Captain John R. Bell.* Edited by Harlin M. Fuller and LeRoy R. Hafen. Glendale, Calif.: Arthur H. Clark Company, 1973.

Berthrong, Donald J. *The Southern Cheyennes.* Norman: University of Oklahoma Press, 1963.

Billington, Ray Allen. *Westward to the Pacific.* St. Louis, Mo.: Jefferson National Expansion Historical Association, 1979.

Boniface, 1st Lt. John J. *The Calvary Horse and His Pack.* Kansas City, Mo.: Hudson-Kimberly Publishing Company, 1903; Minneapolis, Minn.: C & K Publishing Company, 1977.

Brackett, Albert G. *History of the United States Calvary.* New York: Harper Brothers, 1865; Greenwood Press, 1968.

Broadhead, Edward. *Fort Pueblo.* Pueblo, Colo.: Pueblo County Historical Society, 1981.

Brown, John. *Mediumistic Experiences of John Brown, the Medium of the Rockies.* Edited by J. S. Loveland. San Francisco: 1897.

Brown, Lauren. *Grasslands.* New York: Alfred A. Knopf, Inc., 1985.

Buchanan, Rex, ed. *Kansas Geology.* Lawrence: University of Kansas Press, 1984.

Carroll, John M. *The Sand Creek Massacre, A Documentary History.* New York: Sol Lewis, 1973.

Carter, William H. *Horses, Saddles and Bridles.* Santa Monica, Calif.: Quail Ranch Books, 1982.

Chronic, John and Halka. *Prairie, Peak and Plateau.* Colorado Geological Survey Bulletin no. 32. Denver: Colorado Geological Survey, 1972.

Connelley, W. E. *Doniphan's Expedition and the Conquest of New Mexico and California.* Topeka, Kans.: Privately published by the author, 1907.

Cooke, Philip St. George. *U.S. Army Cavalry Tactics,* Vol. 1. Philadelphia: J. B. Lippincott and Co., 1862.

Dary, David A. *The Buffalo Book.* Athens, Ohio: Swallow Press, 1974.

Davis, Burke. *J. E. B. Stuart, the Last Cavalier.* New York: Holt Rinehart and Winston, 1957.

Dodge, Richard I. *Our Wild Indians.* New York: Archer House, 1959.

Duffus, R. L. *The Santa Fe Trail.* New York, 1930; Albuquerque: University of New Mexico Press, 1975.

Eggenhofer, Nick. *Wagons, Mules and Men.* New York: Hastings House Publishers, 1961.

Fehrenbach, T. R. *Comanches.* New York: Alfred A. Knopf, 1974.

Franzwa, Gregory M. *Maps of the Oregon Trail.* Gerald, Mo.: Patrice Press, 1982.

———. *The Oregon Trail Revisited.* Gerald, Mo.: Patrice Press, 1983.

Garavaglia, Louis A., and Charles G. Worman. *Firearms of the American West, 1803–1865.* Albuquerque: University of New Mexico Press, 1984.

Gerrard, Lewis H. *Wah-to-yah and the Taos Trail.* Norman: University of Oklahoma Press, 1979.

Goetzmann, William H. *Army Exploration of the American West, 1803–1863.* New Haven, Conn.: Yale Universary Press, 1959; Lincoln: University of Nebraska Press, 1979.

Gregg, Kate L. *The Road to Santa Fe*. Reprint, Albuquerque: University of New Mexico Press, 1968.

Grinnell, George Bird. *By Cheyenne Campfires*. New Haven, Conn.: Yale University Press, 1926, 1962.

———. *The Cheyenne Indians: Their History and Way of Life*. Vols. 1 and 2. New York: Cooper Square Publishers, 1962.

———. *The Fighting Cheyennes*. Norman: University of Oklahoma Press, 1956.

Hafen, LeRoy R. *Broken Hand*. Denver, Colo.: Old West Publishing Company, 1931; Lincoln: University of Nebraska Press, 1981.

———. *Fort Vasquez*. Denver: State Historical Society of Colorado, 1964.

———, and Ann W. Hafen, *Relations with the Indians of the Plains*. Farwest and Rockies Series, no. 9. Glendale, Calif.: Arthur H. Clark Company, 1959.

———, and Francis Marion Young. *Fort Laramie and the Pageant of the West*. Glendale, Calif.: Arthur H. Clark Company, 1938; Fort Laramie Historical Association edition, Lincoln: University of Nebraska Press, 1984.

Haines, Aubrey L. *Historic Sites Along the Oregon Trail*. Gerald, Mo.: Patrice Press, 1983.

Haney, Lewis H. *A Congressional History of Railroads in the United States, 1850–1887*. Madison: University of Wisconsin Press, 1908.

Heitman, Francis B. *Historical Register and Dictionary of the United States Army 1789–1903*, Vols. 1 and 2. Washington, D.C.: U.S. Government Printing Office, 1903; Urbana: University of Illinois Press, 1965.

Hoebel, E. Adamson. *The Cheyennes*. New York: Holt Rinehart and Winston, 1960.

Hyde, George E. *Life of George Bent*. Edited by Savoie Lottinville. Norman: University of Oklahoma Press, 1968.

———. *The Pawnee Indians*. Norman: University of Oklahoma Press, 1974.

———. *Red Cloud's Folk*. Norman: University of Oklahoma Press, 1967.

———. *Spotted Tail's Folk*. Norman: University of Oklahoma Press, 1961.

Inman, Henry. *The Old Santa Fe Trail*. New York: Macmillan Publishing Co., 1898.

Innis, Ben. *How T' Talk Trooper*. Williston, N.Dak.: Sitting Bull Trading Post, 1984.

Johnston, Abraham Robinson, Marcellus Ball Edwards, and Philip Gooch Ferguson. *Marching with the Army of the West*. Edited by Ralph P. Bieber. Southwest Historical Series, no. 4. Glendale, Calif.: Arthur H. Clark Company, 1942; Philadelphia: Porcupine Press, 1974.

Karnes, Thomas L. *William Gilpin, Western Nationalist*. Austin: University of Texas Press, 1970.

Katcher, Philip. *U. S. Cavalry on the Plains 1859–90*. London: Osprey Publishing, 1985.

Kraenzel, Carl Frederick. *The Great Plains in Transition*. Norman: University of Oklahoma Press, 1955.

Lavender, David. *Bent's Fort*. Garden City, N.Y.: Doubleday & Company, 1954.

———. *Fort Laramie and the Changing Frontier*. Washington, D.C.: National Park Service, U.S. Department of Interior, 1983.

Lecompte, Janet. *Pueblo, Hardscarbble, Greenhorn*. Norman: University of Oklahoma Press, 1978.

Leckie, William H. *The Military Conquest of the Southern Plains*. Norman: University of Oklahoma Press, 1963.

Lee, Wayne C., and Howard C. Raynesford. *Trails of the Smoky Hill*. Caldwell, Idaho: Caxton Printers, 1980.

Long, Margaret. *The Smoky Hill Trail*. Denver, Colo.: W. H. Kistler Company, 1943.

Lowe, Percival G. *Five Years A Dragoon*. Norman: University of Oklahoma Press, 1965.

Mattes, Merrill J. *Fort Laramie Park History*. Denver, Colo.: National Park Service, U.S. Department of Interior, 1980.

————. *The Great Platte River Road*. Lincoln: Nebraska State Historical Society, 1969.

Mayhall, Mildred P. *The Kiowas*. Norman: University of Oklahoma Press, 1962.

McClellan, H. B. *I Rode with Jeb Stuart: The Life and Campaigns of Major General J. E. B. Stuart*. Bloomington: Indiana University Press, 1958.

Merriam, Daniel F. *The Geologic History of Kansas*. State Geological Survey of Kansas Bulletin no. 162. Lawrence: University of Kansas Publications, 1975.

Miner, H. Craig, and William E. Unrau. *The End of Indian Kansas*. Lawrence: The Regents Press of Kansas, 1978.

Morgan, Dale L. *Jedediah Smith*. New York: Bobbs-Merrill Company, 1953.

Mumey, Nolie. *Old Forts and Trading Posts of the West, Bent's Old Fort and New Fort*, Vol. 1. Denver, Colo.: Artcraft Press, 1956.

Murry, Robert A. *The Army Moves West*. Fort Collins, Colo.: Old Army Press, 1981.

Nadeau, Remi. *Fort Laramie and the Sioux*. Englewood Cliffs, N.J.: Prentice-Hall, 1967; Lincoln: University of Nebraska Press, 1982.

Neihardt, John G. *The Song of the Indian Wars*. New York: Macmillan Co., 1925.

Nevins, Allen. *Fremont, the West's Greatest Adventurer*. Vol. 2. New York: Harper and Row, 1928.

Oliva, Leo E. *Soldiers on the Santa Fe Trail*. Norman: University of Oklahoma Press, 1967.

Peterson, Guy L. *Four Forts on the South Platte*. Fort Myer, Va.: Council on America's Military Past, 1982.

Powell, Peter J. *People of the Sacred Mountain*, Vols. 1 and 2. San Francisco: Harper and Row, 1981.

————. *Sweet Medicine*, Vols. 1 and 2. Norman: University of Oklahoma Press, 1969.

Pride, W. F. *The History of Fort Riley*. Fort Riley, Kans.: privately printed, 1926.

Rodenbough, Theophilus F. *From Everglade to Canon with the Second Dragoons*. New York: D. Van Nostrand, 1895.

————, and Wm. L. Haskins, eds. *The Army of the United States*. New York: 1896.

Rydjord, John. *Indian Place Names*. Norman: University of Oklahoma Press, 1968.

————. *Kansas Place Names*. Norman: University of Oklahoma Press, 1972.

Sage, Rufus. *Scenes in the Rocky Mountains*. 1846. Reprinted in *Rufus B. Sage: His Letters and Papers, 1836–1847*, edited by LeRoy R. Hafen and Ann W. Hafen. The Far West and Rockies Historical Series, no. 4. Glendale, Calif.: Arthur H. Clark Company, 1957.

Sandoz, Mari. *The Buffalo Hunters*. New York: Hastings House Publishers, 1954; Lincoln: University of Nebraska Press, 1978.

Schiel, James. *The Land Between*. Edited and translated by Frederick W. Bachmann and William Swilling Wallace. Great West and Indian Series, no. 4. Los Angeles: Westernlore Press, 1957.

Stanley, Major General David S. *Personal Memoirs*. Cambridge, Mass.: Harvard University Press, 1917. Original manuscript in the collections of the U.S. Army Military History Institute, Carlisle Barracks, Penn.

Stanley, F. *E. V. Sumner*. Borger, Texas: privately printed, 1969.

Steffen, Randy. *The Horse Soldier, 1776–1943*, Vol. 2. Norman: University of Oklahoma Press, 1978.

———. *United States Military Saddles, 1812–1943*. Norman: University of Oklahoma Press, 1973.

Stocking, Hobart E. *The Road to Santa Fe*. New York: Hastings House Publishers, 1971.

Taylor, Morris F. *First Mail West*. Albuquerque: University of New Mexico Press, 1971.

Terrell, John Upton. *The Plains Apache*. New York: Thomas Y. Crowell Company, 1975.

The State Historical Society of Colorado. *Bent's Old Fort*. Denver, 1979.

Unrau, William E. *The Kansa Indians*. Norman: University of Oklahoma Press, 1971.

Urwin, Gregory J. *The United States Calvary, an Illustrated History*. Poole, Dorset, U.K.: Blandford Books, 1983.

Utley, Robert M. *Frontiersmen in Blue, The United States Army and the Indians, 1848–1865*. New York: Macmillan Publishing Co., 1967.

———. *The Indian Frontier of the American West, 1846–1890*. Albuquerque: University of New Mexico Press, 1984.

Wallace, Douglass W., and Roy D. Bird. *Witness of the Times, a History of Shawnee County, Kansas*. Topeka, Kans.: Shawnee County Historical Society, 1976.

Wallace, Ernest, and E. Adamson Hoebel. *The Comanches, Lords of the South Plains*. Norman: University of Oklahoma Press, 1952.

Walton, George. *Sentinel of the Plains: Fort Leavenworth and the American West*. Englewood Cliffs, N.J.: Prentice-Hall, 1973.

Warner, Robert Combs. *The Fort Laramie of Alfred Jacob Miller*. Laramie: University of Wyoming, 1979.

Weist, Tom. *A History of the Cheyenne People*. Billings: Montana Council for Indian Education, 1977.

Wilson, D. Ray. *Fort Kearny on the Platte*. Dundee, Ill.: Crossroads Communications, 1980.

Worster, Donald. *Dustbowl: The Southern Plains in the 1930s*. New York: Oxford University Press, 1979.

Wright, Robert M. *Dodge City, The Cowboy Capital.* Wichita, Kans.: Wichita Eagle Press, 1913.

IV. ARTICLES, LETTERS, AFFIDAVITS, AND MANUSCRIPTS

Barr, Thomas P. "The Pottawatomie Baptist Manual Labor Training School." *Kansas Historical Quarterly* 43 (No. 4, 1977): 377–431.

Barry, Louise. "With the First U.S. Cavalry in Indian Country, 1859–1861." *Kansas Historical Quarterly* 24 (No. 4, 1958): 399–425.

Barry, Louise. "Kansas Before 1854: A Revised Annals. Part Three: 1804–1818." *Kansas Historical Quarterly* 27 (No. 3, 1961): 353–82.

Barry, Louise. "The Ranch at Cimmaron Crossing." *Kansas Historical Quarterly* 39 (No. 3, 1973): 345–66.

Barry, Louise. "The Ranch at Walnut Creek Crossing." *Kansas Historical Quarterly* 37 (No. 2, 1971): 121–47.

Becknell, Thomas William. "The Journals of Captain Thomas William Becknell from Boone's Lick to Santa Fe and from Santa Cruz to Green River." *Missouri Historical Review* 4 (Jan., 1910); *Missouri Historical Society Collections* (St. Louis) 2.

Beeson, Merritt L. Letter and sketch map, dated April 24, 1935. Archives of The Kansas State Historical Society, Topeka.

Letter from George Bent to George E. Hyde, November 14, 1910. George Bent Letters, William Robertson Coe Collection, Yale University Library, New Haven, Conn.

Bettelyoun, Susan. "Susan Bettelyoun Manuscript," First draft. MS Collections of the Nebraska State Historical Society, Lincoln.

Birch, James H. "The Battle of Coon Creek." *Kansas Historical Collections* 10(1907–1908): 409–13.

Campbell, Stanley. "The Cheyenne Tipi." *American Anthropologist*, n.s. 17 (No. 4, Oct.–Dec., 1915): 685–94.

Connelly, William E. "Wild Bill—James Butler Hickok." *Kansas Historical Collections* 17 (1926–1928): 1–27.

Cooke, Philip St. George. "Journal of the Santa Fe Escort." Published in "A Journal of the Santa Fe Trail." *Mississippi Valley Historical Review* 12 (June and Sept., 1925).

"A Frontier Officer's Military Order Book." MS Collections, Iowa State Historical Society Library, Iowa City.

Grinnell, George Bird. "Bent's Old Fort and Its Builders." *Kansas Historical Collections* 15(1919–1922): 28–91.

———. "The Cheyenne Medicine Lodge." American Anthropologist, n.s., 16 (No. 2, April–June, 1914): 245–56.

———. "Cheyenne Stream Names." *American Anthropologist*, n.s., 8 (No. 1, Jan.–March, 1906): 15–22.

"Homecoming Sentinel Celebration at Council Grove, June 27 to June 2, 1921." *Kansas Historical Collections* 16(1923–1925): 528–69.

Hoopes, Alden W. "Thomas S. Twiss, Indian Agent of the Upper Platte, 1855–1861." *Mississippi Valley Historical Review* 20 (No. 3, Dec. 1933): 353–64.

Isely, C. C. Letter dated Aug. 12, 1947. Archives of The Kansas State Historical
    Society, Topeka.
Jackson, W. Turrentine. "The Army Engineers as Road Surveyors and Builders
    in Kansas and Nebraska, 1854–1858." *Kansas Historical Quarterly* 17
    (No. 1, 1949): 40–44.
Kansas Historical Society, Sixth Bienniel Report. *Kansas Historical Collections* 4.
"The Kansas Historical Centennial." *Kansas Historical Quarterly* 21 (No. 1,
    1954–1955): 1–7.
"Kansas History as Published in the Press." *Kansas Historical Quarterly* 15 (No.
    3, 1947): 328–30.
Kobler, Carl. Statement dated Jan. 6, 1958. Library of Fort Hays State University,
    Hays, Kans.
Latter-Day Saints Journal History for August 19, 1854. LDS Church Archives,
    Salt Lake City, Utah.
Long, 2d Lt. Eli. "Journal of the Cheyenne Expedition of 1857, Monday, May 18,
    1857 through Monday, Sept. 14, 1857." MS Collections of the United
    States Army Military History Institute, Carlisle Barracks, Penn.
Lowe, Percival G. "Kansas, as Seen in the Indian Territory." *Kansas Historical
    Collections* 4 (1895–1896): 360–66.
Mackey, William H., Sr. "Looking Backwards." *Kansas Historical Collections* 10
    (1907–1908): 642–51.
McCollom, James P. Statement and sketch map, dated Feb. 6, 1956. Archives of
    the Kansas State Historical Society, Topeka.
Metcalf, John W. Letter to W. Y. Chalfant, September 23, 1977.
Miller, Nyle H. "Surveying the Southern Boundary Line of Kansas." *Kansas His-
    torical Quarterly* 1 (No. 2, 1931–1932): 104–39.
Montgomery, Mrs. Frank C. "Fort Wallace and Its Relation to the Frontier." *Kan-
    sas Historical Collections* 17(1926–1928): 189–283.
Moore, Ely. "The Lecompton Party Which Located Denver." *Kansas Historical
    Collections* 7(1901–1902): 446–52.
Morehouse, George Pierson. "Diamond Springs, 'The Diamond of the Plain.'"
    Kansas Historical Collections 14(1915–1918): 794–804.
Morrall, Dr. A. "Brief Autobiography of Dr. A. Morrall." *Kansas Historical Col-
    lections* 14(1915–1918): 130–42.
"Origin of City Names." *Kansas Historical Collections* 7(1901–1902): 475–86.
Peck, Robert M. "Recollections of Early Times in Kansas Territory." *Kansas
    Historical Collections* 8(1903–1904): 484–507.
Peck, Robert M. "Rough Riding on the Plains." Serialized in *The National Trib-
    une* (Washington D.C.), February 14, 21, and 28, March 7, 14, 21, and
    28, April 4 and 11, 1901.
Perrine, Fred S. "Military Escorts on the Santa Fe Trail." *New Mexico Historical
    Review* 2 (1927) and 3 (July 1928).
Root, George A. "Ferries in Kansas—Part II—Kansas River." *Kansas Historical
    Quarterly* 2 (No. 4, 1933): 343–76 and 3 (No. 1, 1934): 15–42.
Seabrook, S. L. "Expedition of Col. E. V. Sumner Against the Cheyenne Indians,
    1857." *Kansas Historical Collections* 16(1923–1925): 306–315.
Sharp, Mamie Stine. "Homecoming Centennial at Council Grove." *Kansas His-
    torical Collections* 16(1923–1925): 528–69.

Simons, W. C. "Old Settlers Association." *Kansas Historical Collections* 16 (1923–1925): 515–23.

Smith, Alice Strieby. "Through the Eyes of My Father." *Kansas Historical Collections* 17(1926–1928): 708–18.

Smith, Charles W. "Battle of Hickory Point." *Kansas Historical Collections* 7 (1901–1902): 534–36.

"Some of the Lost Towns of Kansas." *Kansas Historical Collections* 12 (1911–1912): 426–71.

Spear, Stephen Jackson. "Reminiscences of the Early Settlement of Dragoon Creek, Wabaunsee County." *Kansas Historical Collections* 13 (1913–1914): 345–63.

Stuart, James E. B. "Diary and Letters Sent During the Cheyenne Expedition of 1857." July 22–31, incl., and August 1–15, 17–18, 1857. Archives of the Virginia Historical Society, Richmond.

Todd, Capt. John B. S. "The Harney Expedition Against the Sioux." Journal edited Ray H. Mattison. *Nebraska History* 43(No. 2, June 1962): 89–130.

V. MAPS

Bryan, Francis T. "Reconnaissance of a Road from Fort Riley to Bridger's Pass, June 1856–Mar. 1857." NA, RG 77, Rds., 144.

Bryan, Francis T. "Reconnaissance of a Road from Fort Riley to the Big Timbers, July–Sept. 1855." NA, RG 77, Rds., 139.

Cooke, Philip St. George. "Map of the Santa Fe Trace from Independence to the Crossing of the Arkansas (with part of the Military Road from Fort Leavenworth, West Missouri), 1843." NA, RG 77, Q17.

Fick, Charles. "Sketch of the Country Lying Between the Post of Fort Leavenworth, Blue River, and Council Grove." No date. NA, RG 77, Civil Works Map File, US-168, No. 1.

Freyhold, E. "Map Exhibiting the Lines of March Passed Over by the Troops of the United States during the year ending June 30, 1858. Nov. 1858." NA, RG 77, Civil Works Map File, US-481.

Jackson, Henry. "Map of Indian Territory, with parts of neighboring states and territories, Sept. 1869." NA, RG 77, Q 148.

Merrill, William E. "Map of Kansas, with parts of neighboring states and territories, Sept. 1869." NA, RG 77, Q 140.

U.S. Army. "Map of New Military Road From Fort Leavenworth to Head of Vermillion River Laid Out by Maj. Ogden, Assistant Quartermaster." No date. NA, RG 77, Civil Works Map File, US-168, No. 2.

U.S. Office of Indian Affairs. "Map of Nebraska and Northern Kansas." No date. NA, RG 75, Map 396.

Woodruff, I. C. "Map of the Reconnaissance From Fort Leavenworth to the Arkansas River via the Route of the Republican Fork of the Kansas River and for the Selection of a Site for a Depot Common to the Santa Fe and Oregon Roads and for the Location of the Military Post on the Arkansas River." 1852. NA, RG 77, U.S. 187.

Index